Bristol Studies in International Theory series

Series Editors: **Felix Berenskötter**, SOAS, University of London, UK, **Neta C. Crawford**, Boston University, USA and **Stefano Guzzini**, Uppsala University, Sweden, PUC-Rio de Janeiro, Brazil

This series provides a platform for theoretically innovative scholarship that advances our understanding of the world and formulates new visions of, and solutions for, world politics.

Guided by an open mind about what innovation entails, and against the backdrop of various intellectual turns, interrogations of established paradigms, and a world facing complex political challenges, books in the series aim to provoke and deepen theoretical conversations in the field of International Relations and demonstrate their relevance.

D1724079

Also available

What in the World?
Understanding Global Social Change

Edited by **Mathias Albert** and **Tobias Werron**

Find out more at

bristoluniversitypress.co.uk/
bristol-studies-in-international-theory

Bristol Studies in International Theory series

Series Editors: **Felix Berenskötter**, SOAS, University of London, UK, **Neta C. Crawford**, Boston University, USA and **Stefano Guzzini**, Uppsala University, Sweden, PUC-Rio de Janeiro, Brazil

---

Find out more at
bristoluniversitypress.co.uk/
bristol-studies-in-international-theory

THE IDEA OF CIVILIZATION AND THE MAKING OF THE GLOBAL ORDER

Andrew Linklater

BRISTOL
UNIVERSITY
PRESS

First published in Great Britain in 2021 by

Bristol University Press
1-9 Old Park Hill
Bristol
BS2 8BB
UK
t: +44 (0)117 954 5940
e: bup-info@bristol.ac.uk

Details of international sales and distribution partners are available at bristoluniversitypress.co.uk

British Library Cataloguing in Publication Data
A catalogue record for this book is available from the British Library

ISBN 978-1-5292-1387-4 hardback
ISBN 978-1-5292-1391-1 paperback
ISBN 978-1-5292-1389-8 ePdf
ISBN 978-1-5292-1388-1 ePub

Cover design by blu inc, Bristol
Cover image credit: photo © Château de Versailles,
Dist. RMN-Grand Palais/Christophe Fouin

Printed and bound in Great Britain by CMP, Poole

Bristol University Press uses environmentally responsible
print partners

Contents

Preface and Acknowledgements

The central objective of this work is to explain the impact of the discourse of civilization on the global order by drawing on and extending the Eliasian or process-sociological analysis of the European civilizing process. In his classic investigation of that process – which first appeared in German in the late 1930s – sociologist Norbert Elias (1897–1990) argued that the idea of civilization came to prominence in French court society in the last quarter of the 18th century. It entered the political vocabulary of ruling establishments in neighbouring European societies in the following decades. With the spread of elite discourse to the lower social strata, it became part of everyday language and a core element of prevalent orientations to the social world. During the 19th century, the concept of civilization defined European self-images that revolved around feelings of cultural superiority in two interwoven respects. Confidence in intellectual and material progress beyond earlier eras such as the barbaric medieval period was linked with collective pride in the presumed cultural and technological superiority of European peoples over outlying societies. The supposed right to initiate civilizing missions to bring progress to humanity as a whole which emerged in that context had a profound effect on the formation of global order in the heyday of Western imperialism. Related standards of civilization have not exactly disappeared in the recent period, but their contestation and condemnation are distinctive features of the post-European society of states. Large questions now exist about whether the global order will become increasingly uncoupled from a foundation in agreed standards of civilization, such as those that existed in the age of European dominance, and about whether – or how far – it may become anchored in new conceptions of civilized existence which are shared by its constituent parts.

In his analysis of civilized self-images that have shaped the social and political world for the best part of two centuries Elias highlighted the development of the conviction that Europeans had succeeded in reducing levels of inter-personal violence and in eliminating cruelty within their societies. For example, critics of the public execution of criminals in the 19th century and opponents of the death penalty and other cruel methods of punishment in the 20th century concurred that the practices had no place in a civilized society. As part of that trend, many 'civilized' groups in the contemporary period continue to regard the public execution of criminals in other societies (in Saudi Arabia, for example) as a symbol of 'barbarism'. Similarly, Western societies have repeatedly expressed disgust or outrage at jihadi terrorist acts of violence that clash with their images of civilized societies and a civilized world order.

For Elias, changing social attitudes to what is permissible and forbidden in the relations within European societies did not spring from purely cognitive or intellectual transformations – from novel ideas about moral and immoral behaviour. Such changes were connected with the process of European state-formation and, more specifically, with an overall trend towards increasing social interdependencies in highly pacified societies and with marked changes in the balance of power between internal and external controls on behaviour. With the reduction of levels of interpersonal violence, encountering the use of force in the public domain tended to produce shock and revulsion. Of course, such violence did not exactly vanish from self-defining civilized societies even while it continued to produce emotive responses of outrage and repugnance. Moreover, states continued to use force to suppress social and political unrest or civil conflict. Crucially for Elias, who was unusual amongst sociologists of his generation in decrying the dominant tendency to separate intra- and inter-societal relations, civilized peoples had not broken with the ancient practice of believing that forms of violence that had been largely eliminated within their respective societies were entirely permissible and, at times, absolutely essential in struggles with external adversaries. Elias described that state of affairs as evidence of a deep 'split within civilization'. That was not to suppose that the influence of conceptions of civilized existence was confined entirely to the governance of intra-societal relations. Elaborating the point, Elias referred to the 'duality of nation-state normative codes' – to the reality that 'nationalist-Machiavellian' perspectives, which emphasize the supremacy of the interests of the state, co-exist and often clash with universal-egalitarian moral standpoints for which individual human rights are paramount. Here it is worth noting that, from the middle of the 19th century, leading proponents of the humanitarian laws of war argued that their embodiment in the society of states was demanded by the premise that Western peoples belonged to uniquely civilized ways of life.

In Eliasian terms, those international legal innovations were expressions of the changing conceptions of the permissible and the forbidden that were intrinsic parts of the European civilizing process. They can be regarded as primary examples of the radical project to embed universal-egalitarian principles in a European-dominated world order – alternatively, to enlarge civilization by promoting a global civilizing process. Elias did not use those terms to construct his analysis of the duality of nation-state moral codes or to reflect on the connections between the civilizing process and European imperial expansion. He observed that the new discourse of civilization had been explicit about the right to colonize or control less civilized or uncivilized peoples. There was an implicit recognition in his writings that theological standpoints that had extolled the right of the Spanish and the Portuguese to ensure the religious conversion of infidels in Central and South America had been overtaken by a predominantly secular defence of colonial rights to refashion social inferiors in non-European societies in accordance with new standards of civilization. Elias was well aware that 19th-century European imperial expansion had been instrumental in promoting the globalization of the discourse of civilization, but colonization occupied a surprisingly marginal place in his inquiry.

As the Introduction will show, the practice of translating the idea of civilization into numerous non-European languages in the second half of the 19th century was an intriguing dimension of the struggles by endangered regimes to re-orient themselves to rapidly changing global conditions – to attune themselves to the realities of radical shifts in the international distribution of power. Many ruling elites embraced the discourse of progress and initiated 'civilizing offensives' in their societies in an attempt to remake their systems of governments in the light of European models. They sought to emulate the European colonial powers in the hope of winning their approval, to improve their prospects of eventual admission into the international society of states and, not least, to compete with the global imperial establishment on more favourable terms. Most did succeed in gaining entry to the society of states on ostensibly equal terms with the original European sovereign members. Many played a central part in globalizing the civilizing process by adopting core features of the modern state and by subscribing not only to the dominant European ideas of progress but also to the firmly held belief that their own colonial projects could civilize native groups in regions under their control. Elias's analysis of the European civilizing process is an essential point of departure for understanding that phase in the development of the modern global order. But it is important to recall the postcolonial claim that members of the classical sociological tradition – and Elias must be included among them – regarded the study of colonialism as ancillary to an investigation of intra-European patterns of change that were being replicated across the non-European world.

The discussion will turn in a moment to the significance of the English School of International Relations for understanding major developments in the society of states in the recent period, including the role of the anticolonial revolution in the globalization of that form of world political organization in the second half of the 20th century. The influence of the anticolonial movement on the configuration of the modern world order illustrates the importance of Elias's far-reaching exploration over more than five decades of the main directions of change in relations between 'established' groups and 'outsiders' in civilized societies. Elias stressed how the dominant social strata in civilized societies – and indeed in all human groups – invariably looked down on inferiors and cajoled them to incorporate external perceptions of their backwardness in the collective consciousness. The established social strata promoted a broader acceptance of elite standards of civilization through 'civilizing missions' or offensives. Elias observed that ruling groups have considerable success when power relations are highly uneven, but he added that the prospects of securing change generally decline when established and outsiders have more equal power resources. In that condition, outsiders express resentment at and actively resist the condescending attitudes towards them that have been displayed by the established groups. They contest, among other things, the claim of the established to possess a monopoly of truth about civilized behaviour.

Such dynamics have been strikingly evident in the global order over approximately the last seven decades. In his 1939 study of the civilizing process, Elias (2012 [1939]: 426) observed that the globalization of European orientations to society and politics is the 'most recent wave of the continuous civilizing movement that we are able to observe'. That statement emphasized the reality that European societies formed a global establishment or 'upper class' that many non-European elite groups sought to emulate (Elias 2012 [1939]: 425). The comment existed alongside recognition of the centrality of discourses of civilization for European certitude about the right to rule 'savage' or 'barbaric' peoples. The observation stressed how far the dissemination of civilized values depended upon particular power relations that could change with obvious consequences for the stability and survival of seemingly over-extended polities such as the British Empire. But, as already noted, Elias was curiously silent in his later writings about the effects of the anticolonial revolt on the global political order – and no more forthcoming on the ensuing political challenges, namely whether the traditionally dominant Western peoples can make the requisite modifications to long-standing ethnocentric assumptions about innate cultural and racial superiority that are necessary in order to interact with other societies as equals in the quest to construct global arrangements that command the consent of the former establishment and long-standing outsiders.

For the best part of four decades, the initiative regarding those questions has rested not with process sociology but with other modes of investigation. For example, members of the English School of International Relations have explicitly discussed the prospects for global order and much attention has been paid to the origins, development and fate of the European 'standard of civilization'. Analyses of the civilizational dimensions of world politics through the 1990s and in the early 2000s were largely a response to Huntington's controversial thesis on an impending 'clash of civilizations' (see Hall and Jackson 2007; Katzenstein 2009). Novel debates and deliberations occurred at the time, but there was no serious engagement with the Eliasian analysis of the process in which Europeans came to believe that they alone were especially civilized and entitled to reshape non-European societies. The reasons for the neglect of Elias's writings are numerous. It is partly explained by his marginal influence in the academy. Like many other Jewish academics of his generation, Elias left Germany initially for France and then for England in the early 1930s. He was not appointed to a permanent position in sociology until 1954, when – at the age of 57 – he joined the thriving Department of Sociology at Leicester University (Mennell 1998: ch 1). Especially over the last twenty years, his impact has increased as a result of major publications by former colleagues and students in, among other places, Britain, Germany, the Netherlands and Ireland. Unsurprisingly, detailed reflections on Elias's writings in the study of international relations have been slow to develop.

Only recently – over approximately the past decade – have there been more concerted efforts to assess the significance of the analysis of the civilizing process for the study of global order. Few have explored Elias's claim that civilization should be understood as a process rather than as a condition, a contention that has parallels in critiques of Huntington's essentialist or homogenizing conception of civilization that can be taken much further by considering Elias's detailed examination of the European civilizing process. Few have recognized the explanatory value of a sociological perspective that became much more than an investigation of European social and political development, namely an exploration of the main directions of change in human societies from the emergence of the very first groups. Common to both explorations was the objection to 'process-reducing concepts' in the social sciences – for example, to the practice of referring to civilization rather than a civilizing process, bureaucracy rather than bureaucratization, or democracy rather than democratization. Invaluable for understanding the formation of the modern global order is Elias's use of process concepts in long-term perspectives on the social and political world; these investigated the conditions in which discourses of civilization first developed, the relative power relations between social groups, the largely precarious hegemony of such discourses, their unfinished or unrealized features, and their susceptibility to contestation as power balances alter within and between societies.

The commitment to process sociology that runs through this volume is far from uncritical, for reasons already provided. The point is not just to apply Eliasian sociology to explain the shifting contours of the global political order but to explore ways of taking the perspective forward. An emphasis on the strengths of Elias's explanation of the construction of civilized self-images in modern Europe has to be balanced by the recognition of major shortcomings. More specifically, as will discussed in the Introduction, Elias's inquiry – though broad in focus by virtue of analyzing the relations between state-formation, increasing interdependencies and changing emotional attitudes to violence and suffering – did not explore the historical interconnections between the rise of modern states, their 'civilized' international society of sovereign associations, and overseas empires. It did not consider how the interdependencies between those phenomena propelled most of humanity in particular directions that reflected the power of European conceptions of civilization.

For that reason, the following discussion of how the appearance of European civilized self-images moulded the global era combines the achievements of process sociology with English School investigations of the evolution of the European society of states, the epoch of colonial expansion, and the anticolonial struggles that led to the first universal international society. As noted earlier, the two perspectives have much in common since both have investigated civilizational undercurrents in the social and political world. The English School has explored the contribution of shared civilizational perspectives to the emergence and survival of societies of states. Its proponents have, on occasion, referred to the civilizing effects of diplomacy, international law and the balance of power in the modern society of states, and in so doing they have focused on restraints on violence in ways that run parallel to Elias's investigations. Largely missing from English School analysis is a discussion of how such phenomena were connected with the larger process in which European peoples came to regard themselves as distinctively civilized and as uniquely endowed to bring progress and enlightenment to peoples who were supposedly trapped in ignorance and superstition. There has been no appreciation of the extent to which the society of states, its colonial outposts and specific doctrines (including the 19th-century idea of the 'standard of civilization'), used to justify imperialism, were part of the broader European 'civilizing process'. But, as has been stressed, for its part, Eliasian sociology has failed to trace the relationship between that process and central features of the European society of states, including its global expansion and reconfiguration in the post-European age.

Despite its limitations, process sociology provides unique resources for exploring how the closely interwoven domestic and international dimensions of the civilizing process have shaped the main directions of change in the global order over the last two centuries. Further details about its approach or method of inquiry will be discussed in the Introduction. The main point at this stage is not just that it advanced a distinctive explanation of the European civilizing process. Just as relevant for the present inquiry is the original inventory of concepts that Elias created in the quest to explain the principal directions of change not only in modern European societies but also across human history. Its concentration on the importance of established–outsider figurations has been highlighted. That emphasis will be employed at various points in the following discussion to explain the making of the global order, to analyze specific phenomena that have affected humanity as a whole, and to contribute to ongoing deliberations about the prospects for a global civilization in the post-European era.

This inquiry has its origins in a series of undergraduate lectures given at Aberystwyth University in 2015 and 2016. The aim has been to provide a process-sociological perspective on the civilizational dimensions of the global era which is accessible to students of international politics and of sociology. A primary objective has been to produce a study that is relevant to researchers in those two disciplines who are involved in, or sympathetic to, endeavours to forge connections between fields that have evolved along separate pathways. To that end, the book discusses the immense contribution that process sociology has made to understanding European conceptions of civilization. It explores its particular strengths in synthesizing achievements in different spheres of investigation, and it seeks to encourage further inquiries into the potential to contribute to other research areas. This work builds on two earlier attempts to develop linkages between process sociology and the English School (Linklater 2011, 2016). It is a freestanding book, however, that can be read without any familiarity with those studies. Research on its principal themes occurred alongside a new project on symbols and world politics which has been discussed in Linklater (2019). In the course of its development, this book has become a bridge between an earlier investigation of violence and civilization in the Western states-systems and that new study of symbols in world politics in long-term perspective which employs Eliasian sociology to shed light on largely neglected features of the relations between human societies over the millennia.

Several friends and colleagues provided invaluable comments on an earlier draft of this work. Numerous discussions with André Saramago influenced the inquiry, as did his detailed comments and suggestions on the first draft of the manuscript. Artur Bogner, Brett Bowden, Michael Dunning, the late Johan Goudsblom, Jason Hughes, Richard Kilminster and Cas Wouters clarified some of the more complex and elusive features of process sociology, and I thank them for it. I especially want to thank Stephen Mennell and John Hobson for their support for this phase of a larger endeavour to build bridges between process sociology and the study of international politics. John's constructive criticisms on the penultimate draft of this work were inspiring and invaluable. Finally, I thank Stephen Wenham at Bristol University Press for wise counsel and generous support, and Vaarunika Dharmapala and other members of the production team for invaluable guidance and assistance.

Earlier versions of parts of this work were developed in lectures delivered at the University of Birmingham in May 2015, at Keele University in October of that year, and at the conference to celebrate the work of Stephen Mennell at Newman House in Dublin in January 2016. Some sections of the book have drawn from presentations at the conference on *Understanding Democracy Promotion* held at Aberystwyth University in July 2015, at the March 2017 symposium at the University of Leicester in honour of Eric Dunning and, finally, at the conference in honour of Richard Kilminster held at the University of Leeds in April 2018. I am indebted to Jeff Bridoux, Barbara Górnicka, Jason Hughes, Katie Liston, Lorna Lloyd, Ryan Powell and Nick Wheeler for the opportunity to present parts of the following argument at those events, and I am grateful to the discussants and participants for comments and advice.

None of the following chapters has been published previously but I have revised material that has appeared in the following publications: 'Torture and Civilization', *International Relations* 2007, 21(1), 111–18; 'Process Sociology and International Relations', in N. Gabriel and S. Mennell (eds) *Norbert Elias and Figurational Research: Processual Thinking in Sociology*, *The Sociological Review*, 59 (supplement), 48–64; 'Intervention and Civilization', in D. Held and K. McNally (eds) 'Lessons from Intervention for the Twenty First Century', *Global Policy Journal*, 2014; "Norbert Elias and International Relations", in A. Ohira (ed) *Norbert Elias as Social Theorist: Figurational Sociology and its Applications*, DTP Publishing, Tokyo 2014; ' "Civilization", Self-Restraint and International Society', in K. Booth and T. Erskine (eds) *International Theory Today*, Cambridge: Polity Press, 2016; ' "The Standard of Civilization" in World Politics', *Human Figurations: Long-Term Perspectives on the Human Condition*, 5 (2), 2016; 'The International Society of "Civilized" States', in H. Suganami, M. Carr and A. Humphreys (eds) *The Anarchical Society at 40*, Oxford: Oxford University Press, 2017; 'Process Sociology, The English School and Postcolonialism: Understanding "Civilization" and World Politics – A Reply to the Critics', *Review of International Studies* 2017, 43 (4), 700–19; 'Process Sociology and Human Emancipation: Involvement and Detachment Reconsidered', *Human Figurations: Long-Term Perspectives on the Human Condition*, 8 (1), 2019; and 'Symbols and World Politics: Towards a Long-Term Perspective on Historical Term Trends and Contemporary Challenges', *European Journal of International Relations*, 25 (3), 931–54.

Introduction: A Process-Sociological Approach to Understanding Civilization

This Introduction begins by providing examples of the globalization of the idea of civilization – that is, its dissemination beyond Europe to other regions in the 19th century. The illustrations indicate the value of Elias's analysis of state-formation and conceptions of civilized relations. They reveal the validity of his thesis that the civilizing process did not simply transform European societies but secured global change as a result of their political and cultural dominance and the enormous pressures that were placed on non-European societies to replicate modern state structures and conceptions of civilized behaviour. Elias's explanation of the European civilizing process will be considered in Chapter 2. A prior task is to explain why engaging with Elias's writings is valuable and what it adds to better-known lines of inquiry. Promoting that objective requires a more detailed analysis of Elias's distinctive method (as opposed to his methodology). The aim is to explain process-sociological thinking to readers who may be unfamiliar with the perspective by concentrating on eight central themes in that approach to the social world. The discussion begins with comments on how the concept of civilization 'went global' and why Elias's writings are central to understanding how that process took place.

The global language of civilization

The point of departure of this investigation is that the idea of civilization is ubiquitous in the contemporary world. In the recent period, it has been especially prominent in official statements, media reports and academic reflections on terrorist acts of violence. But, as Elias observed, the concept has not always enjoyed that high profile or status. His explanation of its rise maintained that the discourse of civilization became especially prominent among a select circle of social reformers that belonged to the French ruling strata in the last quarter of the 18th century. It quickly spread to other European governing elites who admired and set about adopting the rituals and manners of French absolutist court society. During the 19th century, the ascendant middle classes employed the concept to express their antipathy to cruel and degrading forms of punishment that seemed to them to be barbaric and obsolescent in a progressive bourgeois era. Notions of civilization quickly became central to the personal and collective identities of the groups involved. They became pivotal to what Elias (and Bourdieu) called the social 'habitus', which included the rules governing everyday conduct and the associated emotions and forms of emotion management that bound people together in the same figuration (see Dunning and Hughes 2013: 188ff). Those self-representations were intertwined with and strengthened by a keen sense of distinction from the 'lower orders' that were deemed to lack polish and refinement and also from non-European societies that were similarly depicted as inferiors. In the language of process sociology, notions of the civilized life became fundamental to the ways in which Europeans orientated themselves to the social world. As later chapters will show, the central coordinates of civilization included basic manners and rules of etiquette as well as hostility to barbaric forms of punishment and repugnance towards the violent resolution of disputes within advanced societies. They also consisted of specific attitudes to space and time – to ideas about the superiority of the modern territorial sovereign state over all other forms of political organization and about the supremacy of linear images of history over the pre-modern myths and superstitions of backward peoples marooned in the past. The coordinates of a civilized condition were anchored in contrasts between 'the established and the outsiders' that provided the rationale for colonial expansion and imperial domination (Elias and Scotson 2008).

The relentless outward expansion of established groups created irresistible pressures on non-European ruling groups to import key attributes of European understandings of civilized arrangements. Major transformations that began in Europe were exported to other regions in that way. Developments in East Asia illustrate how European characterizations of the civilized order affected the dominant modes of orientation more or less everywhere. Towards the close of the 19th century, Japanese intellectuals coined new terms, or injected novel meanings into existing ones, to convey the essence of European civilization. The idea of *bunmei* was one such innovation, as was *bunmei-kaika* which represented the link between civilization and enlightenment. In the case of *bunmei*, the relevant conceptual innovators reworked a traditional Confucian concept, which referred to the refinement of the individual person and society through learning and morality, to capture Enlightenment ideals of progress towards civilized government and social interaction (Aydin 2007: 26; Duara 2001: 108ff).

Key Japanese intellectuals scrutinized major European texts in order to adapt traditional ways of thought to European forms of life and modes of reasoning. They were influenced by François Guizot's early 19th-century study of the history of civilization in Europe which confidently announced that 'the idea of progress, of development [is] the fundamental idea contained in the word, *civilization*'; at its heart, the concept expressed 'the idea of a people marching onward, not to change its place, but to change its condition' (Guizot 1899 [1829–32]: 8, italics in original). Revealingly, for understanding the multiple transmission belts through which the globalization of the 'civilizing process' took place, Japanese authors influenced members of the Chinese intelligentsia who converted the ancient term *wenming* which referred to brightness and prosperity into the idea of 'education through culture' (Messner 2015: 235ff). Through such inventiveness they encapsulated their understanding of the societies that had promoted the humiliating subjugation of their ways of life.

As in Japan, Chinese semantic ingenuity revealed how non-European societies endeavoured to re-orientate themselves to European encroachment. In China, there were affinities between the idea of *wenming* and the older Confucian concepts of *jiaohua* and *shu* which described the goal of moral improvement.[1] But the growing influence of the former concept on elite orientations to the outside world was a dramatic shift away from the orthodox supposition that China was divinely placed at the centre of a civilized world surrounded by barbarians to the troubled understanding that it was inferior to Western civilization. Fundamental to this shift was the belief that China had fallen behind Western technological accomplishments and the legal, political and cultural revolutions that had made them possible, most obviously and decisively with respect to powerful state structures and military organization (Hirono 2008: 24ff; Wang 1991).

Other conceptual innovations that reflected the project of re-orientating societies in response to European expansion occurred in India, South East Asia and the Middle East. From the 1870s onwards, the Hindi term *sabhyata* mirrored Western images of civilized relations while the concepts of *unnati* and *sudhar* signified related concepts of progress or improvement and the necessity of radical political reform (Singh 2015). Their virtues were proclaimed by leading Hindu intellectuals who praised the Europeans for awakening India from the 'death-like slumber of misrule and oppression' (Singh 2015: 188). The idea of *siwilai* performed a similar function in Siam in the 19th century, as did the notion of *munmyeong-gaewha* in Korea following several official delegations to Japan to witness the initiatives that had been launched during the Meiji Restoration (Park 2015: 271). Similar conceptual changes were still under way in the early part of the 20th century. For example, in Vietnam in the 1920s, the idea of *van minh* was coined to describe Western achievements which were thought to demonstrate the profound inadequacies of Confucian theory and practice (Bradley 2004). The Turkish terms, *batililasma* (Westernization) and *muasir medeniyet* (modern civilization) were introduced to promote the new ethos that a society that hoped to become civilized was obliged to follow the path of Western progress or *terakki* with its connotations of orderliness, discipline and self-restraint (Behnam 2002: 187; Wigen 2015). Significantly, the concept *medeniyet* was chosen because of the emotive link with the Arabic term for city; the antonyms *bedeviyet* and *vahşi*, which were comparable to European notions of savagery, described the unruliness and coarseness of Bedouin Arabs and nomadic Turks (Wigen 2015). Linked with that conceptual labour was the assurance that the self-appointed modernizing Ottoman political elite had about reforming backward peoples within the Empire (Aydin 2007: 23). Also noteworthy in the European hinterland was the introduction of the concept of *tsivilizatsia* in Russia in the 1880s, a term that Russophiles used to criticize sycophancy towards the West that was blamed for the decline of *kul'tura* or the traditional national culture (Volkov 2000; see p. 59 on the significance of the distinction between *Kultur* and civilization for Elias's explanation of late 18th-century French conceptions of a civilized order). The last example provides a reminder that European conceptions of civilization were contested and not smoothly incorporated into the habitus of all social strata in other societies. They were combined in many distinctive ways with pre-existing orientations to the social world. But that does not alter the reality that the modern European discourse of civilization was transported across the world through the active efforts and agency of imperilled 'modernizing' non-European regimes.

External pressures to re-orientate societies to alien principles and practices developed hand in hand with evolving global power relations. Governing elites that formed regional establishments were suddenly relegated to the position of outsiders who Europeans often viewed with pity or contempt. Elements of the dominant strata in those societies appear to have internalized feelings of backwardness that were encouraged by Europeans who had little compunction in declaring their superiority through the stigmatization of outsiders. Coining equivalent terms to civilization was a key part of top-down initiatives to overhaul the political order and to win the acceptance of the global establishment. By taking measures that were designed to alter domestic balances of power between 'traditionalists' and 'modernizers' (often creating social tensions and conflicts that have existed ever since) they aspired to share in the collective pride that Europeans felt about their assorted triumphs – to have, at the very least, the vicarious experience of participating in the 'group charisma' of established groups (Elias 2009). But, as stated previously, the dominant strata in those societies were not united by supine and uncritical attitudes to 'social superiors'. Internal debates arose over what to import from the civilized world and what to interweave with local traditions in struggles to meld existing beliefs and practices in efforts to improve the prospects of minimizing external domination. Several groups in China and Japan or in the Ottoman Empire refused to concede that the European powers – however advanced in the technological sphere – matched their spiritual achievements. In that domain, they claimed to have the moral and cultural edge.

Far from being straightforward and automatic, then, the globalization of the civilizing process was often resented and the cause of bitter internal divisions and power struggles that are far from finished. It is telling that the Russian term for civilization, *tsivilizatsia*, was coined not by the advocates but by the opponents of Europeanization. Russophiles emphatically rejected pressures to devalue their form of life and to accept their cultural and political inferiority. Moreover, when the first Europeans visited China it was perfectly obvious to them that members of the ruling Chinese elite believed themselves to be at the centre of a civilized world surrounded by barbarians. Those responses to European encroachment raise the question of how different Europeans with their images of a civilized condition were from the peoples of classical antiquity or from non-European societies that proclaimed their superiority over barbarians long before the concept of civilization was introduced into the global political lexicon.

There are two points to make in this context. First, as Elias (2012 [1939]: 445) stated, there was no 'zero-point' with respect to the European civilizing process – no watershed moment or radical break or rupture with the past. Classical Greek and Roman perceptions of their superiority over barbarian peoples clearly left their mark on the construction of discourses of civility and civilization in later periods. More recent writings have enlarged the discussion by analyzing the 'Eastern origins of Western civilization' and by challenging traditional assumptions that European civilization developed in a separate silo (Hobson 2004; see also Go 2017). Second, the broad similarities between modern European notions of civilizational superiority and equally ethnocentric non-European orientations to the wider world should not obscure the distinguishing characteristics of European 'civilized self-images', however much these owed to classical antiquity or to social practices in non-European regions. Their very different features were encapsulated for Elias (2012 [1939]: vol 1) in the Enlightenment belief in linear histories that traced the supposed progression of human societies from primitive times to the European summit. Crucially, those narratives underpinned the unique global political project of the 'secular upper classes' (encapsulating specifically its commitment which became stronger with major tilts in the balance of power between traditional aristocratic groups and the modernizing bourgeoisie) to refashion European societies and to shape the global order accordingly. At the heart of Elias's analysis of the civilizing process was the realization that those orientations to the social world were integral parts of unique social and political constellations.

Japanese and Chinese intelligentsia who imported the idea of civilization were all too aware of how perilous the autonomy of their societies had become as a result of those Western cultural and political developments. They recognized that their governing elites were powerless to prevent the traumatic incorporation within a Western-dominated international order consisting of sovereign nation-states which justified their outward expansion in terms of promoting human progress and enlarging the circles of compliance with supposedly universal moral and political principles that symbolized the superiority of civilized peoples. The internationalization of the expression 'civilization' occurred in tandem with forced absorption within a tumultuous international order in which traditional struggles for national power and prestige were conducted on a global scale. The urgency in reshaping state structures and reforming society reflected the ambition – as in Japan's case – to undertake extensive changes in order to compete as effectively as possible with adversaries with unprecedented military power and global reach. That those peoples constituted civilizations in their own right need not be contested. But the idea that humanity consisted of a plurality of civilizations only gained support in the West in the 1860s, some nine decades after the idea of civilization in the singular rose to prominence (see Thomas 2018: 266–7 on the how the notion of a world consisting of multiple civilizations was self-serving and linked with the conviction that Europeans were indisputably much more 'broad-minded' or less 'parochial' than other peoples who were imprisoned within narrow cultural horizons).

The emergence in the 1860s of technical conceptions of civilization that recognized the sophistication of ancient empires in the Middle East or the achievements of state-organized societies in the Far East did not alter European images of the progressive achievement of modern forms of social and political organization. Non-European societies had to respond quickly to the encroachment of the Western powers and to acquire an understanding of alien forms of social and political development and peculiar notions of civilization – a foreign concept that was translated and absorbed, as discussed earlier, into many local languages. Essential was the task of comprehending the relations between European state-building, empire and international society – the interwoven parts of the European civilizing process which will be considered in the following chapters.

It is necessary to pause here to consider an earlier point about the remarkable career of the concept of civilization. In a relatively short period – over approximately ten decades – it migrated from French court society to other elite circles in Western Europe and downwards to the middle social strata and later to working-class groups in those societies. Its global reach widened as a result of the initiatives of modernizing elites in non-European societies in the age of imperialism. In short, it became a core political concept with universal meaning and resonance. Its central place in public discourse and in the prevailing modes of orientation to the social and political world seems assured if recent government statements, media reports and everyday discourse are a reliable guide. Indeed, civilizational discourse has acquired renewed vigour not only in Western circles (see the discussion of the 'war on terror' and the torture debate in Chapter 1) but also in Russian and Chinese critiques of the liberal global order (Coker 2019). The resulting challenge is how to explain the appearance of a unique ensemble of concepts, emotions, social attitudes, behaviour patterns and political structures that have conjoined everyday discourse in different parts of the world with the unrivalled global realignments of approximately the last two centuries. That is precisely what Elias set out to accomplish in a pioneering analysis of the European civilizing process.

The importance of Elias on civilization

The idea of civilization has featured prominently in the sociological literature for many decades (see Durkheim and Mauss 1971 [1913]; Nelson 1973; Melko and Scott 1987; see also Braudel 1993; Smith 2018). The concept has been prominent in the study of international relations, especially in the wake of Huntington's deeply contested reflections on the coming 'clash of civilizations' (Huntington 1996). Rare is the study in either discipline which considers Elias's analysis of the European civilizing process. Such omissions have not gone unnoticed. Provocatively, in his analysis of violence, Stephen Pinker (2011: 59) described Elias as 'the most important thinker you have never heard of'. A more recent study of religion and civilization has observed that Elias's writings are barely discussed in the mainstream study of international relations (Cesari 2019: 25; see also Steele 2019, especially introduction and ch 1). The oversight is all the more surprising given that the explanation of the civilizing process placed considerable emphasis on how relations between societies over the last two centuries, and indeed over the millennia, have influenced, and been influenced by, fundamental reconfigurations of human society including lengthening and deepening webs of interconnectedness. But efforts to build bridges between historical sociology and the study of international relations rarely explore the Eliasian perspective.

There are many reasons for this neglect, including Elias's exile from Germany and appointment to a position in sociology relatively late in an extraordinary life. His work was largely unknown even in that discipline before the 1990s (Mennell 1998: ch 1). Elias's defence of long-term perspectives on society and politics was out of fashion for much of that period. Exponents of the dominant positions in that field were largely unsympathetic to investigations of long-term processes, suspecting they were throwbacks to the discredited commitments to teleology and progress that suffused 19th-century grand narratives. Elias was highly critical of what he called the 'retreat into the present' (Elias 2009a), or to 'presentism' as it has been called in the study of international relations (Buzan and Little 2000: 18–19). Elias agreed with the rejection of 19th-century progressivist grand narratives but lamented an increasing tendency for sociologists to concentrate on relatively short-term and somewhat arbitrary timelines. As a result of the 'retreat into the present', the 'baby has been thrown out with the bathwater' (Elias 2012 [1939]: 512). Only recently, with the 'return of the grand narrative' (Sherrat 1995) have trends moved Elias's way (Linklater 2011a).

Elias is reported to have believed that his processual approach had the 'right of way' over the leading standpoints in the social sciences (Kilminster 1987: 215). But his writings seldom discussed the contemporary literature. Nor was Elias disposed to locate his approach in the classical sociological tradition (see, however, the essays on Marx and Freud in Elias 2012a and Elias 2014). The reasons are complex (Mennell 1998: ch 1; see also Mennell 2006). The upshot, as one of the leading process sociologists astutely stated, is that many who encounter his writings for the first time may find it hard to figure out 'what Elias was on about' (Mennell 2017). It has fallen to others to provide a detailed introduction to Elias's approach (Mennell 1998), to explain the evolution of his distinctive sociological outlook (Kilminster 2007), and to compare his approach with the perspectives of thinkers such as Parsons, Foucault and Bauman (Smith 2001: chs 4–6).

The rest of this section adds to that literature in two ways. It explains how students of international relations with an interest in the configuration of the modern global order can profit from a critical engagement with Elias's writings. It also outlines what sociologists with an interest in his processual approach to civilization can gain from reflecting on the significance of his writings on relations between states for analyses of long-term global change. To that end, the discussion provides brief commentaries on the relationship between process sociology and the classical sociological tradition, on links with the English School perspective on international society, and on the salience of postcolonial challenges to mainstream sociology for Eliasian inquiry. It was argued above that Elias's conception of sociological investigation is invaluable for comprehending major directions of change in the global political order. But his explanation of the civilizing process can be enlarged by exploring the complex relations between state-building, colonial expansion and the European international society. That inquiry can be undertaken in support of one of Elias's defining ambitions, namely promoting higher levels of synthesis in the social sciences. That aspiration frames much of the following discussion.

The classical sociological tradition to which the writings of Norbert Elias belonged attempted to explain quintessential features of the modern era, including capitalist industrialization, democratization and expanding bureaucratic organization. Path-breaking analyses by, among others, Comte, Marx, Tocqueville and Weber investigated what they believed were the dominant courses of social and political change in European or Western societies. Elias's contribution was to focus on the process in which Western European ruling elites and then entire populations came to regard themselves as supremely civilized.

The central thesis was that conceptions of civilization were evident in different spheres of life including changes in everyday manners, attitudes to interpersonal violence, modes of punishment and modern state institutions as well as in colonial mentalities and the conduct of external relations more generally.

To explain developments in those domains Elias maintained that it was vital to examine the accelerating social tendencies over the best part of five centuries. Particular emphasis was placed on how state-formation came to dominate the modern era. Special attention was given to how conceptions of civil behaviour and civilized conduct emerged within absolutist court societies. Uncommonly for sociologists at the time, Elias rejected the sociological practice of separating domestic and international politics and concentrating on what were presumed to be largely or wholly internal or endogenous developments. Struggles for power, security and survival had a prominent place in Elias's line of investigation, but the whole tenor of his thought was opposed to isolating the international from broader social and political forces – to regarding international politics, in the language of Waltz (1979), as a 'domain apart'. In the 1930s, Elias had already rejected what he regarded as failed endeavours to divide the social world into supposedly discrete realms of human interaction.

Elias's reflections on relations between states were a key dimension of his objective of constructing a more comprehensive framework of analysis for the social sciences. Nowhere is that ambition more apparent than in the attempt to weave the study of human emotions into the study of long-term developments. If Elias's analysis of state-formation owed much to Weber's writings, his inquiry into emotions revealed the influence of Freud's pioneering examination of psychological impulses and drives. The result was an explanation of overall patterns of change that superseded the most influential sociological perspectives by tracing the configuration of such basic emotions as shame and embarrassment. His reflections predated the focus on collective emotions that is now firmly established in sociology and more conspicuous than ever before in the study of international relations (Hutchison 2016). Arguably, to anticipate a later part of this discussion, Elias gave shape and direction to the study of emotions and society by focusing on the formation of social standards of restraint in civilized groups and the extent to which they were anchored in the individual's 'conscience'. Especially apposite was the investigation of the ever-changing conceptions of what is permissible and what is forbidden in the relations between people. That was coupled with the study of the scope of emotional identification between different social strata and between societies as a whole. Elias's contribution to the classical sociological tradition is evident in the scale of his ambition and in the scope of his analysis which attempted to show how the emotional dimensions of everyday experience were connected with large-scale structural changes including state-formation and international relations. Elias did not provide a detailed explanation of that scholarly contribution. Perhaps he thought it would be obvious to other sociologists in the late 1930s. It is not so clear today. But his contribution to classical sociology can support more detailed investigations of global political change in recent decades and centuries (Linklater 2016).

This is an opportune moment to note Elias's comment (see Chapter 5 for further discussion) that state-formation and discourses of civilization had not only remade Europe; they had radical consequences for humanity as a whole. Through those developments, more and more people became more and more interconnected in more and more intricate ways. They were drawn into longer webs of interdependence which reflected particular power relations and inequalities, and triggered new struggles for power, autonomy and prestige. Resulting tensions between integrative and disintegrative forces, according to Elias (see Chapter 7, pp. 220ff), shaped the degree to which societies were able to agree on the standards of restraint that should govern their relations or instead diverged along antithetical paths. The long-term issue was how far increasingly interdependent societies would find common ground in a global civilizing process or become entangled in competing decivilizing processes in which constraints on action weakened and the scope of emotional identification between human groups declined.

Elias wrote extensively about relations between states but devoted little attention to the academic study of international politics. His main observations stressed power struggles in which collective emotions contributed to rivalries that often spiralled out of control and culminated in destructive violence. This analysis of emotional drives was a major contribution to his explanation of the geopolitical dimensions of international relations. But students of world politics will be quick to stress that his perspective was narrow by contemporary standards. For example, there was no discussion of the society of states or of global norms that have been central to English School writings (and to constructivist scholarship). That omission is unsurprising given that the study of international society appeared late in Elias's life – too late to be assessed in conjunction with the aim of promoting higher levels of synthesis in the social sciences and countering the trend towards greater specialization.[2]

The essential point of departure is that the English School analysis of international society took issue with the realist focus on the dominance of 'power politics' and therefore implicitly contested Elias's central image of inter-state relations. To explain the contrast, suffice it to note that students of international society have explored basic institutions and beliefs that have contributed to order between states. Core institutions have included diplomacy and international law as well as renowned international organizations that facilitate the resolution of major disputes and the codification of shared principles. Influential global beliefs and norms have included the traditional assumption that the society of states was the product of European civilization. Central works on international society have concentrated on the 'standard of civilization', the 19th-century legal principle that divided the world into civilized, semi-civilized, and barbaric societies. In short, English School writings have stressed the relationship between colonialism and international society. They have emphasized that the society of states developed in Europe which colonized much of the rest of the world. They have also provided an explanation of the 'expansion of international society' or the process in which its basic practices and principles (including the ideas of sovereignty and non-intervention) won the support of non-European peoples. Such was the classical account of the changing global order. More recent scholarship has questioned traditional assumptions. It has contested an essentially 'diffusionist' model in which Western beliefs and practices were taken up by non-Western societies in large part as a result of the passive emulation and voluntary acceptance of global norms (Dunne and Reus-Smit 2017; see also Go 2017: 633ff on 'diffusionism' in classical sociology; Hobson 2020). That model of change is accused of ignoring the political tensions and power struggles that accompanied their inclusion within international society. How far Elias was guilty of advancing a similarly diffusionist model will be evaluated in the introduction to Chapter 5.

English School works have highlighted two phenomena that were not part of Elias's investigation – the rise of international society and its interdependence with European colonial expansion as expressed in the classical 'standard of civilization'. What they have not provided is a detailed account of how conceptions of civilization influenced the development of the society of states. Elias's writings on the civilizing process complement and augment English School inquiries which in turn add further depth to Elias's explanation of that phenomenon.

Those observations have clear ramifications for Elias's goal of social-scientific investigation that achieves new levels of synthesis. They suggest that an explanation of the civilizing process needs to consider the interdependencies between state-formation, colonialism and international society.

English School reflections on world politics recognized not only the relationship between colonialism and international society but also the powerful impact of anticolonial struggles and the 'revolt against the West' on the global order in the postimperial era. But analyzing empire was far from central to the inquiry. Here it is necessary to consider postcolonial criticisms of mainstream sociology which have significance for a contemporary appraisal of Elias's perspective. It is also valuable to consider some ways in which the latter can contribute to postcolonial inquiry.

A vast literature is relevant to this discussion and it is essential to be highly selective. Go (2013) provides a lucid and insightful guide to the central issues. Regarding the definition of postcolonial investigations, he states that they reject accounts of developments within Europe that largely ignore Europe's relations with the wider world as well as non-European influences on European societies (Go 2013: 29). Parallels with neo-Marxist dependency theory and the world-systems approach are identified, but what is deemed to distinguish postcolonial perspectives from those approaches is the emphasis on the 'cultural, ideological, epistemic, or even psychological structures' that underpinned European colonialism. On that argument, investigating the privileged role of cultural forces such as conceptions of race and ethnicity in the 'modern imperial experience' is the key contribution of postcolonial thought that conventional sociologists can usefully mine in order to escape traditionally Eurocentric biases (Go 2013: 27, 29). Also salient here is the contention that the classical sociological tradition developed in the age of colonial domination and invariably reflected broader imperial assumptions about the immense gulf between 'advanced' and 'backward' peoples (Go 2009: 782ff).

Those observations underpin the objection that Elias's investigation of the civilizing process assumed that Europe was a continent apart and barely touched by the non-European world (Go 2017). A broader and more comprehensive approach that analyzed the relations between European and non-European societies would highlight the impact of the Haitian slave revolt on radical conceptions of human rights in revolutionary France (Go 2013: 46–7; see also Go 2017; Lawson 2017). An additional critique of Eurocentric social science, which is also directed at Foucault's writings, has relevance for an evaluation of Eliasian sociology. The thesis is that Foucault's description of the decline of the public spectacle of violent punishment in Western Europe failed to register the persistence of brutal punitive measures in colonial territories. The point can be applied to Elias's analysis of the demise of public executions in the course of the civilizing process. The neglect of violent punishment in the colonies 'arbitrarily cuts "Europe" off from its colonies – as if imperial and colonial history were not also part of Europe's history' (Go 2013: 29–30).

Those reflections stress the role of empire in shaping the lengthening interconnections that Elias emphasized in his account of the civilizing process. Tracking the *'processes and relations between diverse but connected spaces in the making and remaking of modernity'* would be the essential breakthrough to escape 'civilizational isolationism' (Go 2013: 41, italics in original; Go 2017: 613ff; see also Çapan 2017). In defence of Elias, it can be argued that his writings did not endeavour to explain 'modernity' or the rise of the West but the more specific phenomenon of European conceptions of a civilized condition and allied notions of human progress (Linklater 2017). Those civilized self-images were undoubtedly influenced by the waves of colonial conquest (and therefore it is correct to argue that Elias's study of global interconnections did not go far enough), but how far non-European beliefs and practices left their impression on specific notions of civilization is unclear. It is perhaps best to add that further research is needed to explain what may be hidden connections (see Hobson 2017: 598–9 on possible lines of research).

What can be argued with some confidence is that Elias's analysis of civilization has direct relevance for postcolonial sociology which considers the 'cultural logics' associated with empire including those that were 'embodied in everyday discourse, novels, works of art, scientific tracts, or ethnographies' (Go 2013: 29–30). Of course, postcolonial thinkers have not ignored the power of the idea of civilization in colonial discourse (Shilliam 2012). But postcolonial sociologists and students of international relations more generally have not discussed the importance of Elias's analysis of the civilizing process for understanding global political realignments. Especially significant is Elias's analysis of how the relationship between state-formation, court society, conceptions of civilization and the changing emotional dimensions of everyday behaviour governed the principal social trajectories in the most powerful European societies and in the wider world. Those are matters that will now be discussed in more detail, as will some affinities between postcolonial method and process-sociological explanation that are especially germane to this investigation of how the idea of civilization has influenced the global order.

Elias's method: eight themes

Explaining what Elias's substantive inquiry contributed to the classical sociological tradition and how it can be strengthened along the lines noted above needs to be supplemented by an overview of his working method or mode of analysis. In the preface to the study of the civilizing process, Elias (2012 [1939]: 7–8) claimed to have a method rather than a fixed methodology that could be applied in a formulaic manner to the analysis of different historical episodes or case studies (see also Dunning and Hughes 2013: 133, 147ff). But none of his writings explained his modus operandi in detail (Elias 2012 [1939]: 493ff is a partial exception). Again, it has fallen to others to provide detailed elaboration (Dunning and Hughes 2013). The notion of constructing a methodology in advance of – and so in isolation from – empirical research went against the grain of Elias's perspective. The idea of research theorizing captures Elias's mode of analysis which proceeded through constant interaction and interplay between concrete inquiry, conceptual innovation and theoretical synthesis (Dunning and Hughes 2013: 188ff; also Landini 2013). In Elias's writings, there is a stark contrast between a fluid, developmental method that guides empirical research and the straightjacket of a preordained methodology with static rather than processual qualities.

That distinction provides the link to comments on the first of eight themes in Elias's image of sociological inquiry which have particular relevance for the discussion of the impact of the idea of civilization on the modern global order. It is perhaps best introduced by noting a direct parallel between what have been described as substantialist and relational modes of investigation. Central to substantialist approaches is the presupposition that the basic social units are static entities such as systems with causal power. At the heart of relationism is the premise that such units do not exist independently of relations between people but are in fact constituted by them (see Dépeltau 2013 for a process-sociological interpretation of relationism). Elias's inquiry was similarly relational, decrying the twin predilections to regard systems or structures as key determinants of human behaviour and to convert the 'variable' into the 'invariable' with the 'associated notion of immutability' (Elias 2012 [1939]: 497ff). Elias's target was Parsonian sociology (Elias 2012 [1939]: 500–1), but the argument can be applied to, among others, neo-realist systems-theorizing in International Relations (Waltz 1979; Lacassagne 2012). In both cases, from an Eliasian standpoint, abstraction or reification in the social sciences obscures relations between people that are constantly changing, however slowly and imperceptibility to those involved. The counterposition was a human-centred inquiry into, for example, the complex emotional dimensions of evolving social interdependencies that systems-theorizing often ignores.

The second theme complemented relational with processual analysis – to put it another way, with explaining the processes through which specific social relations developed. Elias illustrated that comment with respect to the idea of civilization. 'In everyday usage', he stated, 'the concept of civil*ization* is often stripped of its original process character (as a development of the French equivalent of 'to civilize'" (Elias 2008: 3, italics in original). It had become associated with a permanent or unchanging condition. Those who used the concept in that way were guilty of reducing 'processes to states' (Elias 2012 [1939]: 500). The argument for relationism required then the further shift to modes of analysis that were liberated from a 'process-reducing attitude' (Elias 2012 [1939]: 501).

A third theme was that mistaking social processes for fixed conditions can expose societies to unexpected dangers. Elias argued that, in the main, European peoples in the 1920s and 1930s were unprepared for the violence and cruelty that occurred under National Socialism – for a collapse into forms of savagery that had supposedly been eradicated from Europe. The majority of people were blind to the possibility of the 'breakdown of civilization' and the 'reversion to barbarism' on their continent (Elias 2013: 223ff). Their failings were bound up with the unexamined assumption that 'civilization' was a natural condition or biological endowment rather than the fragile outcome of largely unplanned, long-term changes. Most had little understanding of the relationship between state-formation and the concepts of courtesy, civility and civilization. They were unaware that the establishment of relatively stable state-organized societies had not been inevitable. Monopoly control of the instruments of violence and taxation had long been susceptible to decay and reversal, but they were not in the foreground of popular understandings of the social world.

The implications for the social sciences were clear to Elias. It was vital to understand civilization in processual terms and to understand how patterns of change had become static conditions in the minds of millions of people. No less apposite was recognizing that developments such as the process of civilization in which stricter restraints on violence emerged and the scope of emotional identification between people expanded did not eliminate opposing or countervailing forces. Elias preferred to stress how balances of power changed in societies so that, in the case of Europe, civilizing thrusts gained the upper hand in highly uneven and non-linear ways over decivilizing propensities that weakened controls on violence and contracted the scope of identification (see Fletcher 1997: 82ff for further discussion; see also Mennell 1990). In short, relationism was integrated with process-thinking in Elias's approach to social inquiry, and process-thinking was employed to examine shifts in the balance of power between competing forces that dictated the overall course of social and political change.

A fourth theme exemplified by the 'reversion to barbarism' is that social processes are not only often unpredictable but also largely unplanned. The point was central to Elias's reflections on the destructiveness of relations between societies over the millennia (Elias 2010). States had invariably believed that acts of violence that are forbidden in relations *within* the same state-organized society are legitimate and praiseworthy in relations with enemies. For the most part, civilized peoples have been no different from their ancestors when they have been entangled in what they see as life-or-death struggles. The disposition to use force to resolve major political differences was one reason why societies often found themselves in uncontrollably violent struggles for security and survival. If the historical evidence was any guide, according to Elias, human societies might never succeed in taming inter-state power struggles or eliminating the use of force.

The last few observations should quash any lingering suspicion that Elias's analysis of the process of civilization was a late example of the 'Whig interpretation of history' – a curious hangover from the flawed 19th-century theories of linear progress in which Europe was portrayed as the zenith of human development (Bauman 1989). Moreover, and this is the fifth theme, Elias explicitly stated that civilization is a problem in need of solution. In the opening pages of his investigation of the civilizing process, he observed that the issues addressed in the study had 'their origin less in scholarly traditions' than in the experience of the 'crisis and transformation of Western civilization' in 'whose shadow we all live' (Elias 2012 [1939]: 8). As witness to rising levels of intra- and inter-state violence in the first part of the 20th century, Elias stated in the 'gloomy' tone of so many contemporaries that civilization was a 'problem in need of sociogenetic and psychogenetic investigations' – of synoptic examinations of the interrelatedness of the structural transformations of modern societies (including state-building and lengthening webs of interdependence) as well as movements at the level of human emotions (including fluctuations in the levels of emotional identification between people) (Goudsblom 1994: 13). As later comments will show, Elias argued that analyzing principal long-term developments rather than prescribing solutions to existing problems was the primary task facing social scientists.

The question inevitably arises of whether the concept of a global civilizing process in the sense of greater restraints on inter-state violence and increased identification with other peoples should have a privileged place in efforts to forge closer connections between process sociology and the study of international relations. More precisely, the issue is whether the focus on changing balances of power between civilizing and decivilizing processes can shed light on the changing directions of global politics. A related issue is whether the social sciences should be animated by the ambition of producing knowledge that improves the prospects for civilizing dynamics at the level of humanity as a whole.

Those observations lead to a sixth theme in process sociology which is best approached by considering the distinction between emic and etic conceptions of civilizing processes (Mennell 2015). The distinction is crucial given that the move between the two standpoints in Elias's writings has been a consistent source of regrettable confusion. The emic perspective sought to explain in a non-evaluative way how Europeans came to see themselves as civilized. The aim was to understand how the idea of civilization consciously informed their orientations to the world including shared beliefs about 'barbaric' practices such as the death penalty or collective pride in symbols of superiority such as unrivalled technological prowess.

Elias used the concept of a civilizing process in the second, etic sense when describing specific social and political conditions in different ways of life, whether European or non-European. The expression referred to the plain fact that all societies confront:

> the problem of how people can manage to satisfy their elementary animalic needs in their life together, without reciprocally destroying, frustrating, demeaning or in other ways harming each other time and time again in their search for this satisfaction – in other words, without fulfilment of the elementary needs of one person or group of people being achieved at the cost of those of another person or group. (Elias 2013: 35–6)

As the definition indicates, the notion of a process of civilization was used in a technical manner to describe basic realities in all societies, including the need for controls on violence.

On that basis, Elias argued that the idea of a civilizing process could be used to compare 'different stages of the same society' or 'different societies' without making moral judgements about whether any particular phase in the development of a human group or any form of life was superior to the others (Elias 2008a: 59). Referring to China, Elias argued that a civilizing process of 'taming the warriors' took place there long before equivalent trajectories in Europe. Its existence was testimony to the ascendancy of 'a peaceful and scholarly officialdom' that attributed little value to 'military activity and prowess' (Elias 2012 [1939]: 453n19, 589). A more recent investigation of the mutation of the samurai from 'a class of semi-autonomous warriors into domesticated bureaucrats' in 19th-century Japan also employed the idea of civilization in the etic sense (Ikegami 1995: 12).

Confusion has arisen when, for example, Elias observed that the 'multi-party parliamentary regime' depends on 'a higher degree of self-constraint than an autocratic–monarchical or dictatorial regime, and in this sense represents a higher level of civilization' (see pp. 200–1). Readers may assume that an ethical position underpinned the notion of 'higher levels'. But the opposite was the case. The terminology was used to describe social characteristics that were centred on the intensification of controls over violence and the increased influence of internal as opposed to external restraints on human conduct.[3] Those criteria facilitate the comparative inquiries mentioned in the previous paragraph (and the analysis of different modes of world political organization as well as distinctive phases in their respective histories). Elias appreciated that difficulties might arise by virtue of using the concept of civilization for those social-scientific purposes. Shortly before his death in 1990, he pondered the fact that:

> [I] could have looked around for less ideologically charged terms for long-term changes of behaviour standards, or tried to free the concept of civilization from its ideological burdens and transform it into an ideologically neutral term with the aid of appropriate documentation. I did cast about for other possible expressions but did not find any that were more appropriate. Finally I decided to develop the concept of civilization into an ideologically neutral, fact-based term in conjunction with abundant empirical documentation. At the same time I wanted to develop it into a key concept of a theory of civilizing processes. (Elias 2008b: 8–9; see also Goudsblom 2006)

But the resulting problem was that it was not always clear to readers that Elias was mobilizing the term in a non-evaluative way. It was all too easy to assume that Elias was clinging to the idea of progress that was at the heart of the disgraced 19th-century theories of history.[4]

Misunderstandings could have been avoided had Elias clearly signalled when his focus switched from emic to etic analysis. As one interpretation has claimed, 'the distinction between Elias's "emic" and "etic" use of the term "civilization" is always clear in context to the careful reader', but the risk of misinterpretation would have been diminished if he 'had *consistently* used quotation marks to denote the emic sense' of the term – that is, to ensure that he was not taken to be expressing moral support for those who assumed they were uniquely civilized (Liston and Mennell 2009: 55, italics in original). That is the practice followed here when the meaning may not be obvious from the context. In short, this discussion follows Elias's method of using the notions of civilizing or decivilizing process in the etic sense to describe trends and developments regarding degrees of control on violence, the balance between internal and external restraints on aggressive behaviour, and changes in the level of emotional identification between people.

Those observations lead to a seventh theme, which is how Elias used the concept of established–outsider relations to track directions of change in any human group or figuration.[5] A brief description of Elias's working method emphasizes the importance of analyzing shifting power balances in any figuration (or group of interdependent human beings) in order to uncover the dominant structured developments. The following passage in the leading study of Elias's writings captures core elements of the method of research theorizing which informs the discussion of the relationship between the idea of civilization and the changing global order in Chapters 4–6 of this investigation:

> In studying the relations between groups of people, look first for the ways in which they are interdependent with each other. That will lead directly to the central balance of power in the figuration the groups form together. In assessing how far power ratios are tilted towards one side or the other, how stable or fluctuating they are, look at what goals and objectives, what human requirements are actually being pursued by each side. Ask to what extent one side is able to monopolise something the other side needs in pursuing these requirements. Then, if the balance of power is very uneven, be alert for the operation of group charisma and group disgrace, the process of stigmatisation, the absorption of the established group's view of the world within the very conscience and we-image of the outsiders, producing a high measure of resignation even though the

tensions remain. Where the balance of power is becoming more equal, expect to find symptoms of rebellion, resistance, emancipation among the outsiders. In all this it will be relevant to look to the past, to how one group came to impinge on the other, to how the way they are bonded to each other makes them pursue the objectives and human requirements they actually do pursue. (Mennell 1998: 138; see Dunning and Hughes 2013 and van Krieken 1998: ch 3 for further discussion)

Several of those points have particular relevance for the later discussion. Observable in every social group, Elias argued, is the tendency for the dominant strata to control the standards of correct behaviour and, accordingly, to confer high status on themselves in their relations with less powerful groups. They have often regarded greater power as evidence of the natural superiority which is the basis of their 'group charisma'. They have often regarded the deficiencies of the lower strata as markers of natural inferiority and as the source of 'group disgrace'. Over and again, they have not only stigmatized others but have also encouraged them to incorporate feelings of lesser worth in the collective psyche. As Elias (2008c: 6–7) stated:

attaching the label of 'lower human value' to another human group is one of the weapons used in a power struggle by superior groups as a means of maintaining their social superiority. In that situation the social slur cast by a more powerful upon a less powerful group usually enters the self-image of the latter and, thus, weakens and disarms them. (Elias 2008c)

He added that 'unmitigated contempt and one-sided stigmatisation of outsiders without redress, such as the stigmatisation of the untouchables by the higher castes in India, of that of the African slaves or their descendants in America' were clear examples of the means by which established groups maintain asymmetrical power relations (Elias 2008c: 6–7).

But balances of power between social groups can change – with radical consequences. For example, 'the power to stigmatise' has often declined and gone into:

reverse gear when a group is no longer able to maintain its monopolisation of the principal resources of power available in a society and to exclude other interdependent groups – the former outsiders – from participation in these resources. As soon as the power disparities or, in other words, the unevenness of the balance of power, diminishes, the former outsider group, on their part, tend to retaliate. (Elias 2008c: 6–7)

Examples included the 'peoples formerly subject to European domination' (Elias 2008c: 6–7). Traditional forms of compliance with the established strata were often superseded by open rebellion and resistance among outsider groups when power gradients became less steep. Elias's method of investigation therefore brought together relational and processual analysis in order to identify interrelated civilizing and decivilizing movements in human figurations.

The eighth and final theme leads to some of the most complex issues regarding the interpretation of Elias's unique perspective on social-scientific practice that informs the following inquiry. Elias's commitment to non-evaluative explanation may suggest opposition or indifference to normatively engaged social science as exemplified by various forms of critical or emancipatory theory. It is certainly the case that Elias rejected partisan sociology on the grounds that moral and political involvement in the practical outcome of existing rivalries and tensions invariably impoverish sociological analysis. Marx was singled out as a theorist who had made immense breakthroughs in understanding conflict between different social strata, as well as struggles to monopolize economic power and resources, but who had also succumbed to the distorting effects of assuredness in the privileged historical role of proletarian class organizations in shaping the future of humanity (Elias 2012a). Elias (2007: 73, 169–70) was an uncompromising advocate of the 'detour via detachment' which liberated sociology from mythical or ideological orientations. That was not to suppose that total neutrality or complete objectivity was achievable in the social sciences. Nor did it discount the 'possibility' or reject the goal of 'influencing the course of political events through the results of sociological research'; indeed, the 'opposite is the case' (Elias 2012 [1939]: 512).

The key point, however, was that the 'usefulness of sociological research as a tool of social practice is increased if the researcher does not deceive himself by projecting what he desires, what he believes ought to be, into his investigation of what is and has been' (Elias 2012 [1939]: 512). What was vital to increase the practical utility of the social sciences was not the abandonment of involvement for the sake of total detachment (which was impossible in any case) but a radical alteration of the balance of power between two major features of all social groups and all investigators – emotional engagement in internal and external power struggles and degrees of detachment that had facilitated, among other things, major breakthroughs in scientific knowledge and in the human control of natural forces. Repeatedly, Elias stressed the backwardness of the social sciences relative to experimental natural-scientific modes of analysis. Because of remarkable advances in detachment, the natural sciences had taken great strides towards acquiring greater 'reality-congruent' knowledge – knowledge that seemed to correspond with external realities but which could not be presumed to be absolutely true or final (Elias 2007: Introduction). Only recently, with the ascendancy of scientific orientations to the world, had humans reached a deeper comprehension of the universe and their place within it – including, as in the case of the Copernican and Darwinian revolutions, much that many found profoundly emotionally unsettling and fiercely resisted because of painful clashes with highly involved beliefs in the privileged position of humans in God's creation. The socially divisive rupture with the geocentric conception of the universe was not down to 'new discoveries' and the sudden 'cumulative increase in knowledge'; what was decisive was the radical remaking of human self-images in the shape of an increased 'capacity for self-detachment' and the greater aptitude for greater emotional self-control that were expressed in world views that contradicted the certainties of established groups (Elias 2012 [1939]: 520–1). To make similar progress in acquiring reality-congruent knowledge of societies in long-term perspective, social scientists had to break with the practice of allowing involvement in actual social conflicts to smother or overpower detached avenues of investigation.

Arguably, the absence of explicit commitments to normatively driven inquiry is one reason for the negative reception of process sociology in 'critical' circles or for scepticism towards a perspective that does not appear to be on 'our side' (Brincat 2013; Dunne 2009; Kilminster 2011). But points of convergence between those perspectives are easily overlooked. It is essential to stress that detachment was not an end in itself for Elias but a method of confronting the ways in which human interdependencies repeatedly subject peoples to processes which they are unable to control and which are the root cause of great misery and unhappiness. Elias's image of the sociological vocation was anchored in the judgement that more detached inquiry had the potential 'to assist human beings to orientate themselves in the figurations they form together and to help them to control the unintended social entanglements that threaten to escalate into destructive sequences such as mass killings and wars' (Kilminster 2011: 96). Such formulations reveal the 'intense human commitment' that underpinned process sociology (Kilminster 2011: 96; Kilminster 2014; see also Elias 2008d). They may appear to substantiate the claim that Elias's method was committed to Enlightenment certainties that greater knowledge of the social world would result in higher levels of control over social processes. The reality was far more complicated.

To elaborate, it is valuable to consider postcolonial opposition to visions of sociology as a 'mode of knowledge that assumes that the social world is fully knowable, that reason alone can arrive at such knowledge, and that the subsequent knowledge is objective and universal and so can be used to control the world' (Go 2013: 33). Those totalizing objectives, which are said to permeate the classical sociological tradition, have been deemed to be 'complicit with Western imperialism' and 'incompatible with the postcolonial project' (see Go 2013: 33ff for further discussion). But those are not the aims that have animated process sociology. At its heart is the critique of orientations to the world that blind people to basic realities about themselves and their social interdependencies and that compound their subordination to processes that defy their will. A recurrent problem was the flawed conviction (which underpinned classical Marxist inquiry) that knowledge of the world would enable human beings to control natural and social processes and to plan future change with great accuracy. To rephrase the point, there are certain affinities between the critical-theoretical analysis of ideologically distorted ways of thinking and Elias's defence of the sociologist as 'the destroyer of myths' (Elias 2012b: ch 2). But Elias did not start with normative claims; nor did he think it was plausible to assume that societies will ever achieve 'universal' knowledge that will enable them to control the social world. What they could hope to attain, however, were levels of understanding that facilitated at least the reduction of uncontrolled forces – or, more specifically, a shift in the balance of power between unregulated and regulated processes.

The question of why Elias maintained that detached sociological inquiry should deal with issues of control cannot be answered by assuming that it grew out of a philosophical stance on the good society (Saramago 2015). The approach rested on the empirical claim that humans have no choice but to try to control aspects of their individual and collective lives if they are to live together amicably. Elias invented the term the 'triad of controls' to capture basic social realities in all eras (Elias 2012b: 151–2). The concept referred first to the fact that, from infancy, every person must acquire levels of governance of basic impulses in order to become a functioning member of the relevant social group. Second, it described the observable fact that, throughout their adult lives, humans are expected to tame violent, threatening and other forms of harmful behaviour in accordance with the prevailing social standards of restraint. Third, it conveyed the reality that societies have to exercise some measure of control over natural processes to satisfy basic physical needs and, increasingly in the modern era, more restraints on the exploitation of nature (Elias 2009c: 255–7). In an intriguing passage, Elias (2007: 140–1) stated that a civilization in which people obey social restraints because of the compulsions of conscience rather than because of the fear of punishment or social disapproval may seem naively utopian. He added that such a condition was, in principle, possible and worth striving for. But steps in that direction would not take place, he argued, without levels of knowledge of human groups that are currently unattainable (see the discussion of ecological civilizing processes on pp. 247–8).

More detached modes of sociological inquiry were defended on the supposition that well-meaning interventions to improve human conditions had often deepened unplanned social processes that cause human misery. Underpinning that claim was Elias's humanism, which he described in a lecture on the Frankfurt School critical theorist, Theodor Adorno, as taking 'the side of the less powerful, the oppressed, the outsider and the exploited' (Elias 2009d: 84).[6] As argued elsewhere, Elias's sociological perspective is compelling because it combined a highly original approach to analyzing the social world with powerful humanist commitments that are more usually associated with the emancipatory goals of Frankfurt School critical theory (Linklater 2019). But Elias rejected critical-theoretical investigations that placed ethical questions about how society should be organized at the heart of the inquiry. His contention was that humans still know very little about social processes or indeed about the most basic concepts and conceptual frameworks that can promote increases in the fund of knowledge that are necessary to alter the balance between failed and successful practical interventions. On that argument, the urgent need to understand more about human figurations demanded that 'ought questions' or 'ideological convictions' about social goals should be placed on the 'back burner' (Kilminster 2011: 111). Exponents of critical-theoretical standpoints may be unconvinced by the deferral of ethical deliberations. But, as previously noted, Elias believed that the devotees of highly involved sociological standpoints might be reluctant to confront unpalatable truths about human figurations (Kilminster 2007: 59). They might be no less willing to concede that there were serious defects and deficiencies in their respective positions, given their entanglements in competition for power and status in academic organizations (Kilminster 2011: 112–13). The danger was the perpetuation of low levels of collaboration to acquire greater reality-congruent knowledge in contrast with areas of the natural sciences where commitments to the gradual accumulation of knowledge through detached experimental techniques were firmly embedded in expert research cultures and communities (Kilminster 2013; Kilminster 2014).

Those concerns were reflected in Elias's rejection of the continuing influence of national perspectives in the social sciences in a period of rapidly increasing global interconnections. Elias proposed 'a research programme in the service of an ardent secular humanism' – 'in the service of all humankind' and free from ties to any 'single segment, class, or faction thereof' (Kilminster 2014: 97–8). Fundamental was the argument for greater detachment in the social sciences via a radical break with methodological nationalism and the movement from society-centred to humanity-centred modes of investigation. Elias pointed to parallels between highly emotive societal responses to the insecurities and suspicions that were prevalent in the global political order and the national parochialism of much putatively social-scientific analysis and commentary. It is essential to reiterate that Elias's argument was based not on ethical claims but on the empirical observation that high levels of emotional involvement in the outcomes of particular rivalries have meant that calls for collaborative measures to reduce the danger of violent conflict and to settle major differences peacefully through diplomatic means have often been dismissed out of hand as clashing with vital strategic interests. They have often been ridiculed as foolishly utopian aspirations. Uncontrolled rivalries and the risk of war had often been intensified by influential national myths that fused collective self-love with the demonization or stigmatization of adversaries. One of the challenges for sociologists as the 'destroyers of myths' was to expose the one-sided and destructive nature of collective belief systems which have often commanded widespread support in their respective societies. Elias's opposition to partisan sociology, his robust defence of the 'detour via detachment', and his case for humanity-centred analysis reflected the supposition that the social sciences had yet to understand the complexities of inter-state relations and global interdependencies.

For those reasons, Elias contended that normative commitments should be placed to one side where they are unable '*to shape research*' (Kilminster 2011: 112, italics in original). But he stressed that if the results of 'theoretical-empirical inquiry' advanced significantly beyond current levels then social scientists could *return to them in a new form* (Kilminster 2011: 111, italics in original). As a result of such breakthroughs, social scientists could shift towards 'secondary involvement' (which was contrasted with primary involvement and participation in social practices without the levels of detachment that were the hallmarks of sophisticated social-scientific inquiry). They could engage directly with the problems that are the result of specific interdependencies between people (Kilminster 2011: 111). Secondary involvement would be guided not by some vision of the 'good life' with the connotations of an 'absolute and final state' (about which 'one can argue interminably') but by conceptions of a 'better life' based on rigorous, empirically tested comparisons with an 'earlier phase' (Elias 2008a: 58–9). Equipped with more realistic understandings of human interdependencies, societies could then intervene with greater prospects of success to reduce their subjection to uncontrolled and unforeseen forces. As one study has argued, a successful detour via detachment could lead to circumstances in which more reality-congruent knowledge enables generations of political organizations with the requisite expertise to 'intervene in the social world' with a reduced danger of the 'unintended consequences' that have often compounded human difficulties (Dunning and Hughes 2013: 14). The related contention is that Elias and those who are inspired by his writings share with critical sociologists the aspiration to 'make a difference' in the social world and, crucially, to remonstrate against social relations that are 'shown to embody constraints greater than are necessary, or which are inherently exploitative, dehumanising, or in other ways unsatisfactory' (Dunning and Hughes 2013: 14).

Elias was disposed to argue that it was premature to move to secondary involvement. Recent developments in process sociology have supported the somewhat different strategy of 'involved-detachment' which provides critical analyses of public policies that have negative effects for vulnerable groups in society (Lever and Powell 2017; Linklater 2019). They point towards new avenues of research in which detachment is conjoined with greater involvement in debates surrounding government policy. They are highlighted here to draw attention to emergent perspectives that rest on and develop the distinctive method of Eliasian sociology, and to point to links with more familiar critical-theoretical lines of research. The following discussion is undertaken in the belief that more detached methods of analysis anchored in secular humanism can make a significant contribution to the future development of critical theories of society and politics in the study of international relations, sociology and cognate fields.

Conclusion

This Introduction has provided examples of the globalization of the language of civilization as many non-Western governments responded to Western colonial expansion. It has argued that Elias's analysis of the European civilizing process is the necessary starting point for understanding how a specific concept which gained prominence in European court societies in the late 18th century acquired global resonance. To explain the contribution of process sociology, this Introduction has briefly discussed links with the classical sociological tradition and its position in relation to English School inquiries into international society and postcolonial sociology. It has identified ways in which process sociology will be taken further in the present work. A core contention is that Elias's analysis can be enlarged by investigating how the interdependencies between state-formation, colonialism and the development of the European society of states left their mark on the civilizing process. Eight core themes that distinguished Elias's method of inquiry have been highlighted. They have particular salience for an analysis of the impact of the idea of civilization on the development of the modern global order.

The argument is developed over seven chapters. Chapter 1 considers the role of the language of civilization and barbarism in public discourse in the United States in the aftermath of '9/11'. It describes its place in the discourse on the 'war on terror' and in subsequent public debates about torture. The latter reflected what Elias described as the peculiar entanglements of civilized peoples. Understanding Elias's study of the civilizing process explains how the relevant moral challenges emerged in the course of long-term transformations in European societies. An overview of his inquiry is provided in Chapter 2, while Chapter 3 discusses principal ideas in Elias's analysis of relations between states which contained fresh insights into 'the duality of nation-state normative codes' – the tensions between nationalist-Machiavellian attitudes to foreign policy conduct and ethical perspectives that attach higher value to the equal rights of all human beings. Resulting entanglements were particularly evident in the 'torture debate'.

Chapter 3 ends by developing a fundamental theme in Elias's analysis of the relations between states, namely the existence of the deep 'split within civilization'. That expression described the belief that behaviour that is largely forbidden in the interactions between the members of civilized societies is deemed be entirely permissible in violent struggles with adversaries. The observation that the 'split within civilization' was especially stark in the relations between European colonial societies and supposed 'savages' and 'barbarians' provides the foundations for the following three chapters which explore how the linkages between state-formation, colonialism and the development of international society defined the global order.

Chapter 4 notes that Elias's inquiry contained few references to colonialism and ignored the place of various narratives of conquest and discovery in the formation of European civilized self-images. The discussion concurs with postcolonial contestations that members of the classical sociological tradition were guilty of neglecting the impact of imperialism on the development of modern societies. It draws on process-sociological reflections on 'civilizing offensives' to explain how the European idea of the 'standard of civilization' was used to justify colonial efforts to transform non-European societies. That legal principle illustrates better than any other how the interdependencies between state-formation, overseas conquest and the dominant practices of international society stamped a global order that was predicated upon European conceptions of civilized arrangements.

European governments were not the sole agents of the globalization of major features of the civilizing process. Chapter 5 discusses several non-European state-driven 'civilizing offensives' that were designed to win the respect of the imperial powers and to construct the case for admission into the society of states. In so doing, it draws on the earlier discussion of Elias's more general reflections on established–outsider figurations in which dominant groups press the lower strata to accept their inferiority. That is not to suggest that non-European powers were resigned to demands from above or to suppose that the entire process took place without major internal tensions and struggles in those societies. A key claim in Chapter 5 is that the globalization of the civilizing process was not simply the product of Western diffusionism but was affected by non-Western ruling elites with their own political objectives and images of how to combine 'nation' and 'civilization'. Moreover, as will be discussed in Chapter 6, changing balances of power between the traditional global colonial establishment and outsiders were accompanied by organized resistance against the classical standard of civilization – the resented international symbol of colonial oppression. The chapter ends by considering analyses of the post-Second World War global order which have shown that a revised version of the standard of civilization endures in the contemporary global era.

Chapters 4, 5 and 6 discuss a range of 'civilizing offensives' that were intended to promote a global civilization that embodied European or Western moral and political preferences and predilections. They show how the European civilizing process left its imprint on the world order through the 19th and 20th centuries. The focus is on the emic conception of civilization. These chapters raise complex questions about the prospects for a global civilizing process in its etic sense. Chapter 7 advances criteria for identifying the main directions of change at the level of humanity as a whole. It interprets Huntington's image of the coming clash of civilizations and English School deliberations on the prospects for a consensus on civilized global principles as attempts to understand shifting balances of power between global civilizing and decivilizing processes. The chapter concludes by considering two developments – the national-populist revolt and organized responses to climate change or the 'climate emergency' – which have immense ramifications for the current prospects for a global civilizing process that affects the totality of human societies. Those forces raise large questions about the extent to which that process can take place without powerful common symbols. The same is true of the current COVID-19 global health crisis which dominated public discussion as this book was completed. Only preliminary comments can be made about those phenomena here. The issues will be discussed in more detail in a future study of the symbolic dimensions of world politics.

1

The Return of Discourses of Civilization and Barbarism

Seldom does a terrorist attack on Western citizens pass without immediate government statements or media reports condemning the barbarous assault on civilized societies and cherished liberal-democratic principles. A few examples may suffice to support the point. In his inauguration speech on 20 January 2017, President Donald J. Trump announced his intention 'to unite the civilized world against radical Islamic terrorism, which we will eradicate completely from the face of the earth'.[1] Commenting on 15 November 2015 on both attacks in Paris that had taken place two days earlier and attacks in Ankara on 10 October, President Barack Obama maintained that 'the killing of innocent people, based on a twisted ideology, is an attack not just on France, not just on Turkey, but ... an attack on the civilized world'.[2] Referring in a statement on 13 September 2014 to 'IS' policies of abduction, enslavement, rape and forced marriage, the US Ambassador-at-Large for Global Women's Issues, Cathy Russell, proclaimed that 'viciousness against innocents exposes ISIL's blatant rejection of the most basic progress we have made as a community of nations and the universal values that bind civilization'.[3] Similar reactions to 'IS' followed the destruction of major cultural sites such as ancient temples in Palmyra. On 1 September 2015, the Director-General of UNESCO, Irina Bokova, declared that the destructive acts were an 'intolerable crime against civilization'.[4] That discourse is not confined to the US and Western societies more generally. The same terminology was employed by the Chinese President, Xi Jinping at the meeting of the 23rd Asia–Pacific Economic Cooperation (APEC) in Manila on 19 November 2015 when he described terrorism as 'the common enemy of human beings' and added that decisive action would be taken against those who committed a 'terrorist crime that challenges the bottom line of civilization'.[5] Finally, in an address to the United Nations General Assembly on 2 October 2015, the Israeli Prime Minister, Benjamin Netanyahu, portrayed Israel as 'civilization's frontline in the battle against barbarism' and the 'fanaticism' of 'IS'.[6] Drawing on familiar contrasts between the medieval world and the modern world, he warned of the danger that terrorist organizations with access to weapons of mass destruction would recreate the 'barbarism of the ninth century'.

Those comments repeated the language of civilization and savagery that was used by the Bush administration during the 'war on terror'. They are illustrations of the return of the long-standing discourse of civilization to the centre of official government statements and broader public discussions. The notion of 'return' refers to how notions of the 'West' and 'Western values', which were powerful ideas in the bipolar era of the 'Cold War', are rather less central today (O'Hagan 2002). They have been largely overtaken by an overlapping discourse that was dominant in the colonial era in which civilized peoples were distinguished from mere savages and barbarians. The idea of the 'clash of civilizations' was the most obvious example of the shifting emphasis in the light of what were held to be the new fault lines of the post-bipolar era. Following 9/11, an older colonial discourse of civilization and savagery was invoked to affect the outcome of public debates, to legitimate foreign policy measures, and to rally domestic and international support for a specific image of global order.

The first part of this chapter provides a brief overview of that discourse. It examines some key themes in academic analyses of the civilizational dimensions of world politics before setting out recent process-sociological interpretations of the 'war on terror'. The second section enlarges the discussion by portraying the 'torture debate' as an intriguing example of what Elias called the distinctive entanglements in which civilized peoples repeatedly find themselves (see p. 42). From that standpoint, the debate over torture and the broader discourse of civilization can only be understood by taking the long-term perspective – by analyzing the civilizing process which will be discussed further in Chapter 2. Suffice it to add that most analyses of the 'war on terror' and the torture debate have not understood their relationship with the civilizing process. They have not drawn on Elias's investigation of social and political developments that stretched over the best part of five centuries to explain recent or current events. His inquiry points the way beyond 'presentist' stances which are commonplace in studies of national foreign policy and global politics.

The 'war on terror'

References to the enemies of civilization and the struggle for civilization featured repeatedly in post-9/11 US presidential statements on the 'war against terrorism'. For example, on 12 September 2002, in a speech at the United Nations General Assembly, President George W. Bush stated that:

> above all, our principles and our security are challenged today by outlaw groups and regimes that accept no law of morality and have no limit to their violent ambitions. In the attacks on America ... we saw the destructive intentions of our enemies. This threat hides within many nations, including my own. In cells and camps, terrorists are plotting further destruction, and building new bases for their war against civilization.[7]

In a speech on 10 November 2001 to the United Nations (two months after the 9/11 attacks), Bush maintained that:

> few countries meet their exacting standards of brutality and oppression. Every other country is a potential target, and all the world faces the most horrifying prospect of all: these same terrorists are searching for weapons of mass destruction, the tools to turn their hatred into holocaust. They can be expected to use chemical, biological and nuclear weapons the moment they are capable of doing so. No hint of conscience would prevent it. This threat cannot be ignored. This threat cannot be appeased. Civilization, itself, the civilization we share, is threatened.[8]

Bush had struck a similar chord in his 20 October 2001 speech at the Asia-Pacific Economic Conference summit in Shanghai in which he stated that: 'By their cruelty, the terrorists have chosen to live on the hunted margin of mankind. By their hatred, they have divorced themselves from the values that define civilization.'[9] In the same speech, he defended the US-led 'war on terror' as a struggle to defeat ruthless 'enemies...who hate all civilization and culture and progress'. On 21 September 2001, President Bush proclaimed in an *Address to a Joint Session of Congress* that, 'this is not, however, just America's fight. This is civilization's fight. This is the fight of all who believe in progress and pluralism, tolerance and freedom.'[10] Fewer than six weeks later, in the

Address to the Nation delivered on 9 November 2001, he contended that, 'we wage a war to save civilization, itself'.[11] In a speech on the USS Enterprise on Pearl Harbor Day (7 December) 2001, he again contended that the 'great divide in our time' is not 'between religions or cultures' but 'between civilization and barbarism'.[12] Earlier, on 20 September 2001, he had portrayed the barbarous enemy as 'heir to all the murderous ideologies of the twentieth century', one that was akin to 'fascism, and Nazism, and totalitarianism' in 'sacrificing human life to serve their radical visions' and in 'abandoning every value except the will to power' – a foe so evil and demonic that 'civilization' could only protect itself, so it was argued from early 2002, by concluding that the traditional laws of war did not apply to members of the Taliban and al-Qaeda.[13] The latter were depicted as 'unlawful enemy combatants' who could legitimately be refused the protection of the Geneva Conventions or what have often been regarded as the civilized laws of warfare (McKeown 2009).

Four themes in the literature on civilization warrant consideration before turning to process-sociological reflections on terrorism and civilization. First, the incorporation of the discourse of civilization in US presidential speeches had, it has been suggested, a dramatic amplification effect, drawing on deeply held views about reprehensible violence to mobilize support for military action against barbaric enemies (Collet 2009). Alternatively, it served to articulate public outrage at terrorist attacks against innocent civilians in order to legitimate what the administration claimed was a 'war of necessity' rather than a 'war of choice' (Freedman 2017). The same theme was also captured by the idea of 'civilization rallying', or the practice in which 'populist politicians' exploit 'civilizational commonality' to rally domestic support or to persuade 'hesitant governments' to enter into alliances united in the commitment to using force to subdue adversaries (Huntington 1993: 35, 38).

Second, such references to 'civilizational commonality' reopened long-standing discussions about how to characterize civilizations. On one account, a 'civilization is … the highest cultural grouping of people and the broadest level of cultural identity people have. … It is defined both by common objective elements, such as … history, religion, customs, institutions, and by the subjective self-identification of people' (Huntington 1993: 24). That definition broadly concurs with a recurrent theme in the distinguished history of civilizational analysis which is that civilizations are intermediate spheres of social interaction and identification between loyalties to nation-states and humanity at large (Durkheim and Mauss 1971 [1913]; Nelson 1973; Braudel 1993;

Smith 2018). But the extent of that identification – its emotional depth – is far from straightforward. As one analyst of the civilizational dimensions of world politics argued, most 'people do not think of themselves in the course of a normal day's activities as belonging to a civilization' (Cox 2000: 217). Civilizational consciousness is typically 'far down on the scale of self-conscious identities' (Cox 2000: 217). What has to be explained are the processes in which groups came to regard civilizations and civilizational identifications as 'social facts' of real emotional significance (Bettiza 2014, 2015).

Third, it is indisputable that the idea of civilization has been implicated in personal and collective identity-formation in the modern era but, as those citations indicate, people do not in the main identify as strongly with others in the same civilization as with conationals or fellow citizens in the same separate state. They may well regard the presumption that such practices as the death penalty have no place in a civilized society as a common reference point. What is especially interesting is how images of the nation and ideas of civilization are often woven together in official discourses and in broader societal orientations to the world. The rhetoric that was harnessed by the US administration to justify military action in Afghanistan did not just appeal to narrow national security goals but invoked ethical commitments to uphold a global civilized ethos that had been attacked by barbarous elements. The 'imbrication of nationalist and civilizational thinking' was a striking feature of public narratives that merged the objectives of 'national policy' with global leadership claims that placed the defence of the interests of humanity at the centre of an idealized image of world order (Palumbo-Liu 2002).

But the unison of nation and civilization is an unstable one, as has been conveyed by the observation that, in 'the era of nation states', civilizational allusions must simultaneously 'transcend and serve the territorial nation' (Duara 2001: 107). There is a major difference with ancient civilizations where the dominant ideology was 'immanent' ('intensifying the cohesion, the confidence and, therefore, the power of an already-established social group') rather than 'transcendent' (possessing a 'powerful autonomous role' that was thought to stand above political 'authority structures' and to be a powerful weapon that could be turned against them) (Mann 1986: 22ff). By contrast, no modern state can acquire monopoly control over the meaning of civilization or eliminate rival interpretations to which political opponents can appeal as they contest national objectives. For governments, and not least for those with global leadership ambitions, the resulting issue is how to bend conceptions of civilized relations to the national cause or how to wrap the latter in moral principles with purported universal validity. National governments have invoked the language of civilization in attempts to ward off criticisms that their actions are entirely self-serving; however, they may find it hard to elude the charge that the discourse is used strategically to clothe self-interest in a 'veneer of large-mindedness' (Connolly 1998). The reality is that the 'transcendent' meaning of civilization can be harnessed not only to represent the political community as the custodian of human principles but also to promote the 'critique of the nation'; the result can be fierce internal clashes about ultimate loyalties or rancorous disputes about correct balances and combinations (Duara 2001: 107). As the following section will show, the main divisions are between those for whom the concept of civilization connotes unyielding commitments to moderation and restraint, and those for whom it provides a licence for waging just wars against savage adversaries, albeit one which is invariably conjoined with declarations of national support for international law.

Walter Benjamin's memorable statement that there is no 'document of civilization which is not at the same time a document of barbarism' anticipated a fourth theme in the language of the 'war on terror', namely the similarities between state declarations in recent times and earlier Western colonial discourses which announced that the laws of war that governed the relations between civilized states did not apply in conflicts with cruel savages (Benjamin 1999: 248). Recent examples of narratives that originated in the colonial era include the speech that President Bush gave in North Carolina on 28 June 2005 in which he condemned the 'savage acts of violence' of terrorist groups who had no compunction in 'behead[ing] civilian hostages and broadcast[ing] their atrocities for the world to see'.[14] Echoes of the discourse of colonial warfare that justified violence to defend civilization from wild, lawless savages can be found in many other US presidential statements. Notable are the similarities between President Bush's contention that 'there are no rules' in the 'war against terror' (see Hurrell 2002) and the statement made by General Arthur MacArthur on 20 December 1900 during the US conflict in the Philippines, in which he insisted that guerrilla warfare was contrary to 'the customs and usages of war' (cited in Welch 1974: 237). The implication was that those who engage in that mode of warfare 'divest themselves of the character of soldiers, and if captured are not entitled to the privileges of prisoners of war' (cited in Welch 1974: 237). A further illustration of colonial legacies was the 'Bush Doctrine', which affirmed the United States' right to override the territorial sovereignty of rogue states that were accused of committing the crime of providing safe havens for terrorist organizations. That foreign policy standpoint has been compared to late 18th-century imperial perspectives which maintained that public order underpinned by effective policing was the first step towards civilized governance in colonized territories (Neocleous 2011). Needless to say, the doctrine was condemned by societies where memories of colonial domination remain strong, and where external attempts to weaken the sovereignty principle are quickly and routinely condemned as manifestations of neocolonialism.

Recent process-sociological literature has augmented those discussions in three ways – by tracing the evolving relationship between the ideas of terror and civilization in the latter part of the 18th century, by analyzing the role of concepts such as civilization in state projects to determine the ways in which subjects or citizens orientate or attune themselves to the social world, and by explaining how discourses of civilization and barbarism/terrorism can trap societies in forces which they are unable to control – in what Elias described as perilous 'double-bind processes' (see p. 93ff).

Regarding the first theme, process-sociological inquiries into terrorism have explained that in the early phase of the French Revolution, the idea of 'terror' had positive connotations, as exemplified by the Jacobins' use of the term to celebrate the popular insurrection to end tyrannical government (Dunning, 2017). The negative connotations of the concept which prevail today, and which may seem entirely natural or timeless to 'civilized' people, appeared around 1794 – after Robespierre's rule had ceased – when established groups framed the new idea of 'terrorism' to characterize the despised revolutionary elite and its European allies as enemies of civilization. Edmund Burke portrayed the French revolutionaries as those 'Hell-hounds called Terrorists' who waged brutal warfare contrary to the traditional rules of military engagement in their frenzied destruction of the European political order (Dunning 2017, citing Burke 1999 [1795]: 359). As part of the same trend, members of the British ruling class began to use the idea of terror as the antithesis of civilization to demonize political opponents in Ireland (Dunning 2017).

From then on the concept of civilization has been a 'praise word' (Elias 2007a: 6ff) that has been employed by established groups to announce the achievements of their societies in controlling violence and also to differentiate themselves from outsiders such as terrorist movements that resort to 'excessive' force to promote 'illegitimate' objectives. Discourses of civilization have been a powerful means of creating, preserving or enhancing 'group charisma' through the 'collective denigration' of others (Elias 2009: 76). That there is often a short step from stigmatizing outsiders to using force against them indicates how the idea of civilization can serve as one of the 'releaser symbols' that justify lifting civilized restraints on violence in struggles with barbarians (Elias 2013: 172; see also Linklater 2019). With respect to the 'war on terror', the civilizational narrative was used to channel public anger and outrage after the events of 9/11 into domestic and international support for military action. But it is hard to use such a discourse to support the principle that 'anything goes' in conflicts with the ultimate outsider – the terrorist group. Self-defining civilized populations usually pride themselves in the level of self-restraint they display in conflicts with enemies, thereby proclaiming their incontrovertible superiority over outsiders who show contempt for such controls. The former may insist that the violence they employ in defending themselves from very real dangers is measured, proportionate and restrained, as demanded by their collective commitment to civilized principles. The moral and political ambiguities or internal contradictions of civilization (considered in more detail in the next section) come into being because the concept can pulled in two opposing ways – to justify using force against adversaries but also to hold national leaders accountable to transcendent ethical principles.

Those observations invite discussion of two other themes in process-sociological investigations of how establishments have responded to global terrorism. They are, first, the relationship between struggles to control the 'means of orientation' in society that have consequences for the relative power resources (or 'power chances') of competing groups and, second, the danger that civilized societies will unleash 'double bind processes' which they cannot control.[15] It may be useful to provide an illustration of the first point and then to consider its import for process-sociological explorations. The 2002 Report of the Defence of Civilization Fund – *Defending Civilization: How Our Universities Are Failing America and What Can Be Done about It* – expressed alarm at the supposed gulf between 'mainstream public reaction' to 9/11 and the muted response of 'intellectual elites' who declined to support the unconditional condemnation of the terrorist attacks on the grounds that US foreign policy interventions in the Middle East had contributed to the rise of Islamic terrorism. The authors contended that a poisonous cocktail of 'moral relativism' and 'political correctness' underpinned the supposition that 'Western civilization is the primary source of the world's ills – even though it gave us the ideals of democracy, human rights, individual liberty and mutual tolerance' (Martin and Neal 2002: 4–5). They expressed considerable frustration over the perceived irony that 'instead of ensuring that students understand the unique contributions of America and Western civilization – the civilization under attack – universities were rushing to add courses on Islamic and Asian cultures' (Martin and Neal 2002: 6–7; Palumbo-Liu 2002; see Guhin and Wyrtzen 2013 for postcolonial reflections on the broader historical context).

In process-sociological terms, the open denunciation of unpatriotic 'intellectual elites' was part of a larger power struggle in which groups competed to control the means of orientation to the social and political world and, in so doing, to alter the balance between the restraining and releaser dimensions of civilization. Addressing the question of why such controls matter, Elias (2009e: 135ff) observed that: 'groups of people who are able to monopolise the guardianship, transmission, and development of a society's means of orientation hold in their hands very considerable "power chances" that are not available to other members of society, especially if the monopoly is centrally organised'. Prior to the emergence of modern nation-states, he added, the pre-eminent expression of such power relations in Europe was the Catholic Church whose power and authority was anchored in an effective 'monopoly of the most basic means of orientation', namely the governance of 'revealed religion' across most of the continent (Elias 2009e: 135–6). The case demonstrated how established strata have attempted 'to maintain and, if possible, to increase the high dependence ratio of their outsider groups and thus the power differentials between these and themselves' (Elias 2009e: 138). That monopoly power and its associated dependencies were weakened as a result of overall shifts in the relative influence of theological and secularized, natural-scientific perspectives; states played a decisive role in these shifts as they fought to establish controls over the means of orientation (see Inglis 2010 for further discussion). Building on Weber's state theory, Elias maintained that struggles to monopolize control of the instruments of violence had clearly shaped the course of European social and political development. It was essential, he argued, to add the state's decisive acquisition of the monopoly power of taxation. No less significant were state attempts to consolidate their power through controls of the means of orientation particularly, it should be added, through the intermingled discourses of nationalism and civilization.

From the French Revolution onwards, 'people in power' have been able to 'count on a warm response of approval and often of affection or love from their compatriots whenever they praise or add to the glory of the [national] unit they all form with each other' (Elias 2007:8). Since then, state initiatives to construct national identities have fostered the requisite 'personality dispositions' so that people will fight and die for national interests and ideals (Elias 2013: 172). Both points were illustrated by developments in the aftermath of 9/11. Strong feelings of anger in the United States led to popular support for restoring national pride and for avenging the sense of national humiliation by waging war against the Afghan government and al-Qaeda. Narratives of civilization and barbarism had a reinforcing effect. Elevating national claims through linkages with the ideals of civilization ensured a 'warm response of approval' for the Bush administration which reaped the reward of increased power capabilities regarding the case for military action. It was hardly surprising that efforts to influence the means of orientation by harnessing the emotive power of 'civilization' were prominent in public discussions and debates. For the authors of *Defending Civilization* (Martin and Neal 2002), the concept was a 'praise word' that was used to affirm collective pride in the ideals of democracy, human rights and tolerance that were rejected by barbaric forces. The idea was used in power struggles to weaken the position of what were deemed to be unpatriotic 'intellectual elites' that found more to criticize than to celebrate in Western civilization and who opposed national policies that defended the noble ideals and interests of civilized peoples. The observation that the idea of civilization transcends but can also be mobilized to serve the nation-state can be usefully recalled at this point. In major power struggles, critics of government action can employ 'civilization' in defence of what they regard as wholly justified national strategies. Governments and their supporters can embrace the concept to discredit political opponents and to try to reduce their power resources. From a process-sociological standpoint, recent debates in the United States made explicit the import of 'civilization' for struggles to control the means of orientation, to shape attitudes to government action, and to influence the level of public tolerance for using force.

Process-sociological analyses of competition to govern the means of orientation have been closely linked with studies of the balance of power between involvement and detachment – between highly charged, emotive standpoints and less passionate, more restrained perspectives on social tensions and conflicts. The relevant investigations stress how the power balance between those standpoints can shift with extraordinary rapidity in the context of heightened fear and insecurity. Increasing emotional involvement in particular clashes, the argument runs, can seriously weaken the capacity for more detached views of their causes or origins, including the honest confrontation with the question of how far one's own society may have contributed to adversarial relations. With highly involved standpoints, emotive commitments to attributing blame to rivals tend to crowd out more impassionate deliberations about how antagonistic relations developed (van Benthem van den Bergh 1978). Especially valuable for present purposes is the emphasis in process sociology on how power inequalities in different figurations can blind established groups to outsider perceptions of their privileged positions (Mennell 2007: ch 12). So free are the dominant strata from dependence on others, it has been stated, that they face few external pressures or compulsions to think from their standpoint, to contemplate in more detached ways how the less powerful perceive them and their actions, and to reflect on outsiders' reasons for holding the established primarily responsible for their plight.

Debates in the United States in the late 1990s around the 'blowback thesis' illustrate how blockages to higher levels of detachment can develop among established groups. According to that controversial thesis, US foreign policy had helped to create the political conditions in which anti-US terrorist groups formed in East Africa where local affiliates of al-Qaeda attacked US embassies. Critics condemned what they regarded as the unpatriotic assertion that such violence was an instance of 'blowback' as opposed to unprovoked terrorism (Johnson 2000: 10–11; see also Johnson 2001). Similar disputes emerged after 9/11 when the Bush administration and its supporters contended that the attacks were the product of ingrained evil and savagery. Opponents repudiated the attempt to absolve the United States from any responsibility for creating the environment in which terrorist organizations flourished (Johnson 2000).

Whether or how far the blowback thesis was correct need not detain us here. It is timely to stress instead the earlier point about how terrorism acquired its contemporary meaning as a term used by established strata to condemn the violence of outsider groups. Just as civilization is a 'praise word', so terrorism is a 'blame word' frequently deployed in the stigmatization of opponents. Dominant groups who are assured of the rightness of their cause employ the concept to denigrate violent outsiders. Similarly motivated, outsiders respond with counter-stigmatizing strategies. In Elias's language, the upshot is that adversaries intensify and harden political differences by comparing 'the minority of the best' in their group with 'the minority of the worst' on the opposing side (Elias 2008c: 5; Elias and Scotson 2008: 133ff; see also Sutton and Vertigans 2005: 151ff). In the accompanying social tensions, established and outsider groups with self-images that have a high fantasy content can drive themselves and each other towards escalating levels of violence which are connected with unbreakable cycles of stigmatization and counter-stigmatization. They can find themselves trapped in 'double bind processes' that are difficult to disrupt and may prove to be uncontrollable (Sutton and Vertigans 2005: 129ff; Vertigans 2010; Dunning 2016, 2016a; Dunning 2017). Opposing forces are then caught in a web of 'decivilizing' or 'brutalization processes' that have unanticipated consequences for all parties. In the case of the United States, the relaxation of conventional moral and legal restraints on torture was one such outcome that precipitated intriguing debates for analysts of the civilizing process – disputes about what is permissible and what is forbidden in the reactions of 'civilized' societies to the violence of 'savage' enemies.

The torture debate and the peculiar entanglements of civilized peoples

The discussion has described what process sociology adds to existing interpretations of the resurgence of discourses of civilization since the 'war on terror'. Particular attention has been paid to the emergence of 'civilization' as a 'praise word' (further details are provided in Chapter 2) that was the antithesis of the 'terrorism' of outsider groups. The idea of civilization has been deployed by opposing groups which understand that 'power chances' depend not just on material resources but on success in maximizing controls over the means of orientation. The previous section considered the extent to which the efforts of national governments to align the nation with civilization do not go uncontested. The political tensions that ferment in such conditions require discussion of what Elias called the distinctive torments and 'entanglements' of civilized people (Elias 2012 [1939]: 8). The latter were evident to an unusual extent in the debate over torture. The main disputes raised large questions about the relationship between civilization, foreign policy and the ideal configuration of the global order; these questions seem likely to recur well into the future.

Of particular relevance for the following discussion is Elias's analysis of the tensions within civilized societies between two ethics – the 'Machiavellian' code in which the supreme value is the state or nation 'to which an individual belongs', and the 'humanist egalitarian' code in which the precept which overrides 'all others', including loyalties to the state, is the dignity of 'the individual human being' (Elias 2013: 169ff). Chapter 3 will consider that conflict in more detail. Noteworthy as far as the torture debate is concerned was Elias's empirical claim that the two moralities coexist for the most part in a relatively harmonious but precarious manner. In the main, clashes between competing principles do not arise; people do not feel torn between national interests and universal ethical principles or face the compulsion to choose between them. However, emergency conditions can expose the latent tensions in an inherently contradictory set of moral beliefs (Elias 2013: 172–3). Conflicts between the two moralities can become elements in 'struggles for dominance' between 'different sections of a state population' as well as 'in the struggles of … individuals with themselves' over ideal ethical standpoints (Elias 2013: 173). Peculiar entanglements emerge because the idea of civilization, though often in alignment with national purposes, can be directed against them. The resulting conflicts reveal that the members of civilized society can confront distinctive, if not unique, ethical choices. But there is more to it, as the torture debate revealed. The power capabilities of groups that compete for public support can depend in part on how far they can construct discourses of civilization that provide compelling accounts of the relationship between national security objectives, legitimate foreign policy measures, and a humane global order.

Prior to 9/11, global legal norms prohibiting torture were widely regarded as one of the pre-eminent manifestations of shared commitments to 'civilized' norms – as an unquestionably positive symbol of civilization. It has been argued that 'while the practice of torture [had] been widespread, until recently it had come to be understood that no representatives of the state could openly admit that they would use torture for fear of being removed from office and of having their state ostracized by "civilized" nations' (Foot 2006: 132). The broad consensus on the reprehensible nature of torture explains why few were prepared for the assault on international legal principles which occurred in the wake of 9/11.

From a processual standpoint, it is imperative to consider the 'torture norm' in long-term perspective – to locate it within the civilizing process to which it belongs. Shifting attitudes to judicial torture as a means of extracting confessions warrant attention. That long-standing practice was outlawed as part of the broader 'civilizing offensive' to abolish what was portrayed as the medieval legacy of 'cruel and unusual punishments'. It reflected the moving boundaries between permissible and impermissible harm which were integral to changing perceptions of violent punishment from the middle of the 18th century and which were perhaps best exemplified by Beccaria's 1764 treatise, *On Crimes and Punishments* (Foot 2006). Major changes in power balances in the post-Second World War era facilitated the globalization of the political project to end such forms of state coercion that violated the ethical tenets of liberal civilization (Clark 2007: ch 6). With the development of the universal human rights culture, the modern instruments of torture were condemned as repulsive and uncivilized, just as judicial torture had been opposed because of its barbarism. The principal monument was the United Nations *Convention against Torture and other Cruel, Inhuman or Degrading Treatment or Punishment*, adopted on 10 December 1984.

The torture norm reflected a major alteration of the relative influence of the two dimensions of nation-state moral codes that were discussed earlier, and it represented a permanent advance in the more optimistic liberal circles. Developments after 9/11 revealed how departures from civilized principles such as the established anti-torture norm can emerge in wholly unforeseen ways in democratic political systems; they testified to the fragility of the social taboo against torture. Efforts by the Bush administration to redefine torture occurred secretively, exemplifying Elias's empirical observation that – in the course of the European civilizing process – whatever aroused disgust or revulsion, including state-inflicted violent punishment, was gradually hidden behind the scenes (see p. 70).[16] The decision to overturn or redefine the torture norm confirmed Elias's comment about governing elites in such societies, namely that:

> civilised standards of conduct are often meaningful for powerful ruling formations only as long as they remain, whatever their other functions may be, symbols and instruments of their own power. Hence power elites, superior classes or nations often fight in the name of their superior values, their superior civilisation, by means which are diametrically opposed to the values for which they themselves claim to stand. With their backs to the wall, the upholders of civilisation tend to become the principal destroyers of civilisation. They tend to become barbarians. (Elias 2013: 284)

As Elias also observed, such regressions do not go unchallenged. Exemplifying the point, disputes about torture within both the US political class and the larger US community showed how members of a civilized society can occupy a variety of points on a spectrum of opinion extending from the unconditional moral condemnation of torture, to opposition based on anxieties about serious reputational damage and diminished global status, to the pragmatic acceptance of coercive techniques under conditions of 'necessity', through to strategically driven support for demonstrations of state power to intimidate and destroy adversaries (Barnes 2016). Attendant controversies exemplified the claim that the members of civilized societies often find themselves with curious torments and contortions from which other societies have been largely immune.

An examination of the language that was used in navigating those difficulties can usefully begin with the 'torture memo' – the *Memorandum for the Council of the President* (Memorandum for Alberto R. Gonzalez in Greenberg and Dratel 2005: 174ff) issued in August 2002 which defended the legality of methods of extracting information from detained terrorist suspects or 'unlawful enemy combatants'. Its authors acknowledged that it was not the first deliberation on such matters. The 2002 Memorandum cited the 1978 ruling of the European Court of Human Rights (Greenberg and Dratel 2005: 196–8) which overturned the decision by the European Commission of Human Rights in 1976 that the United Kingdom was guilty of torture with respect to the 'hooded men' – twelve individuals from Republican families who had been subjected to 'deep interrogation' techniques including hooding, prolonged stress positions, white noise, sleep deprivation, and the denial of access to food and drink (Gallagher 2015). The European Court of Human Rights overruled that judgement on the grounds that although the 'five techniques' were 'inhuman and degrading treatment', they fell short of the levels of mental and physical suffering that constitute torture (Gallagher 2015).

Prior to commenting on the 'torture memo' it is valuable to highlight core principles of the United Nations *Convention against Torture* (which the United States ratified in 1994) that were especially germane to the subsequent debates. Article 1 defined torture as 'any act by which severe pain or suffering, whether physical or mental, is intentionally inflicted on a person for such purposes as obtaining from him or a third person information or a confession', a stipulation that included 'intimidating' as well 'coercing' detainees.[17] According to Article 2(2), 'no exceptional circumstances' such as 'a state of war or a threat of war, internal political instability or any other public emergency may be invoked as a justification of torture' – nor according to Article 2(3) could 'an order from a superior officer or a public authority' justify departures from international law. The Convention also bound signatories in Article 16 to 'prevent ... other acts of cruel, inhuman or degrading treatment or punishment ... which do not amount to torture as defined in Article 1'. At the point of ratification, it has been argued, the US administration, then under President Bill Clinton, subscribed to a 'more state-protective' definition than the one affirmed in the Convention (Levinson 2004: 29). From that standpoint, the 2002 Memorandum mirrored earlier official positions that the international legal prohibition of torture could place unreasonable restraints on state institutions with the primary responsibility to protect the security of citizens. The suggestion is that there were major continuities between the 2002 Memorandum and the perspective that had previously enjoyed support in official circles, that is that the US administration would remain faithful to civilized principles as long as methods of interrogation did not normalize 'barbaric' techniques such as sleep deprivation in the course of discharging national obligations (Elshtain 2004).

Against that background, the 2002 Memorandum stated that methods of interrogation may cause severe pain and be 'inhuman and degrading' but fall short of the pain thresholds that are associated with torture and which amount to the flagrant transgression of civilized norms. On the specific issue of how to distinguish between torture and 'inhuman' or 'degrading' behaviour, the 2002 Memorandum maintained that the concept should be restricted to describing interrogation techniques that cause 'intense pain or suffering of the kind that is equivalent to the pain that would be associated with serious physical injury so severe that death, organ failure, or permanent damage resulting in a loss of significant body function will likely result' (Greenberg and Dratel 2005: 183). The proposition was that the idea of torture should be confined to denote 'extreme' acts such as mock executions as well as rape or sexual assault which were unreservedly condemned as barbaric (Greenberg and Dratel 2005: 193).

Methods of interrogation that could result in 'the development of mental disorder such as post-traumatic stress syndrome which can last months or even years' were also deemed to cross the moral boundary between coercive acts that are consistent with civilized standards and harmful techniques that fall squarely within the realm of barbarism (Greenberg and Dratel 2005: 177). Techniques that pushed detainees to the 'brink of suicide' were regarded as the cause of unacceptable personality 'disruption' (see Greenberg and Dratel 2005: 182). A degree of sensitivity to the cultural origins of detainees informed the statement that 'acts of self-mutilation' by persons from societies with 'strong taboos against suicide' would be proof of profound 'disruption of the personality' (Greenberg and Dratel 2005: 182). Interrogation techniques that did not inflict the 'necessary intensity' of physical pain or mental suffering were distinguished from the brutalities of torture (Greenberg and Dratel 2005: 173).

The 2002 Memorandum attempted to overcome the civilized entanglements that sprang from the tensions between universal moral principles and national security considerations in two other ways. First, it affirmed the 'right to self-defence' under conditions of 'necessity' (Greenberg and Dratel 2005: 211), adding that the injuries of interrogation techniques would 'pale to insignificance' compared to the harm caused by a terrorist attack that 'could take hundreds or thousands of lives' (Greenberg and Dratel 2005: 208–9; see also Luban 2005). Second, and here Article 2(3) of the United Nations Convention is the key reference, the 2002 Memorandum declared that officials who authorized the resort to emergency measures – from the President and other members of the Executive to those in direct command of interrogators – were immune from 'criminal liability' (Greenberg and Dratel 2005: 207). Those positions were reinforced by distinctions between civilization and savagery that were redolent of colonial doctrines which stated that civilized peoples could not be shackled by moral and legal restraints on force that conferred tangible political-military advantages on enemies that did not respect the rudimentary principles of reciprocity in warfare.

Echoing imperial discourse on the relations between established groups and outsiders, the US Attorney General and the National Security Adviser, Condoleezza Rice, responded to attempts in the Senate to place restrictions on interrogation techniques (and to compel the Executive to report to Congress on methods employed by intelligence officers) by stating that the Bush administration would not grant 'protection to people who are not entitled to it' (Foot 2006: 138). But, as the discussion has shown, the 2002 Memorandum did not abandon all civilized restraints on violence. Whatever one's moral stance on its content, the very fact that the document was prepared at all reflected official concerns about the legality of interrogation techniques that would distinguish the Bush administration from despotic regimes that institutionalize torture. A useful summation of the official position on reconciling torture, as defined in the United Nations Convention, with the precepts of civilization was the presidential statement that the decision to treat 'unlawful combatants' with humanity was 'a matter of policy' rather than the result of binding international legal obligations since the Geneva Conventions did not apply to al-Qaeda or Taliban detainees (Foot 2006: 138). Even under emergency conditions, President Bush stated in a separate presidential memorandum of 7 February 2002, basic civilized self-restraints had to be observed but in a manner that was 'appropriate and consistent with military necessity' (cited in Strasser 2004: 4).

Several public responses to the 'torture memo' also provided insights into how civilized peoples deal with the contortions that were mentioned earlier. Reflections on legal frameworks that could create judicial controls over methods of interrogation are worth detailing. They should be considered in conjunction with the section of the 2002 Memorandum which declared that efforts to invoke the United Nations *Convention against Torture* or existing United States law to prevent the President from acquiring the necessary intelligence to defeat the terrorist threat would represent 'an unconstitutional infringement of the President's Commander-in-Chief authority' (Greenberg and Dratel 2005: 207). Endeavours to reconcile that judgement with expectations of executive accountability to other branches of government and to the broader public included the contention that ex post facto public inquiries could rule on the legitimacy of interrogation techniques that had been employed by intelligence officers. Also revealing was the argument for the 'torture warrant', which stated that the relevant officials should gain prior 'judicial approval' for proposed instruments of interrogation (Dershowitz 2004; Gross 2004). Such mechanisms are considered here as images of how the practice of interrogation might be placed within a restraining constitutional framework that attempted to reconcile civilized mores and conventions with exceptional violence (Elshtain 2004; Linklater 2007). It is a moot point whether large sections of the US public would have been convinced by such deliberations about possible judicial controls on excessive violence, which would – at the very least – have added new layers of complexity to existing entanglements.

Many internal and external critics of the Bush administration's standpoint maintained that restricting the meaning of torture to supposedly 'extreme acts' compromised and corrupted civilized values (Greenberg and Dratel 2005: 183). The majority ruling of the Supreme Court on 29 June 2006 declared that relations with 'unlawful enemy combatants' should observe the guarantees that the Geneva Conventions deemed essential for civilized conduct (Birdsall 2010).[18] In the same spirit, the Supreme Court ruled on 12 June 2008 that the foreign detainees at Guantanamo Bay did indeed possess the right of habeas corpus.[19] The December 2014 *Report of the Senate Select Committee on Intelligence* which examined the Central Intelligence Agency's Detention and Interrogation Programme concluded that the methods employed had 'caused immeasurable damage ... to the United States' long-standing global leadership on human rights in general and the prevention of torture in particular' (Report of the Senate Committee on Intelligence 2014: xii, xxv). By implication, divisions between civilized regimes or peoples and the savage world had been dangerously blurred. As a result of those developments, the earlier initiative to redefine torture was overturned. The 2002 Memorandum was withdrawn in 2014 and superseded by the 30 December 2004 *Memorandum Opinion for the Deputy Attorney General: Definition of Torture under 118 U.S.C* which was 'written for public consumption and released to the general public', unlike its predecessor (Barnes 2016: 114). It condemned modes of interrogation that were permitted by the 2002 Memorandum as 'barbaric cruelty which lies at the top of the pyramid of human rights misconduct'.[20] Civilized attitudes to torture were reaffirmed as part of a further shift in the balance of power between the different elements of the moral code. Revealingly, President Trump's remark in a speech delivered on 26 January 2017 that waterboarding was an effective method of interrogation was quickly condemned by influential political figures in the United States and beyond.[21]

The peculiar torments that emerged in the wake of 9/11 may have been resolved or submerged for now, but it would be unwise to suggest that their suspension is permanent (Cox 2018). Nor can one rule out the possibility that other state policies will lead to similar entanglements to those that resulted from the decision to relax the norm prohibiting torture.[22] Efforts to align the political community and foreign policy with civilized universal principles will probably clash in future with the image of a 'transcendent' civilization that underpins the ethical 'critique of the nation'.

Conclusion

This chapter has advanced a process-sociological perspective on the discourse of civilization and barbarism that was revived by the Bush administration in the aftermath of 9/11. It has highlighted several concepts in process sociology that enlarge other analyses of the civilizational dimensions of the recent era – established–outsider figurations including struggles to control the dominant means of orientation, modes of stigmatization and counter-stigmatization, changing power balances between involvement and detachment under conditions of insecurity, double-bind processes, and civilizing and decivilizing crosscurrents. Those concepts are valuable resources for analyzing a dramatic episode in the recent history of the global order; they will be reintroduced at various intervals in the following discussion. The chapter also drew on Eliasian references to the peculiar entanglements of civilized societies. Tensions between nationalist and universalistic moral positions that surfaced in the course of the civilizing process were considered in this context. The discussion of post-9/11 political developments also stressed the contrasting functions of the idea of civilization. As the debate surrounding the relaxation of the torture norm indicated, governments have drawn on civilized self-images to justify the use of force against purported savages whereas opponents have employed its transcendent qualities to condemn state actions that are thought to clash with higher principles.

It is remarkable, and not always realized, that a concept that only became part of the discourse of French court society in the late 18th century has so thoroughly permeated everyday language and orientations to the social world across different strata within Europe and across the world at large. It is extraordinary that an idea that was initially confined to small elite circles became incorporated in the self-images of modern peoples and came to inform habitual attitudes to violence. If the discourse of civilization and savagery had the amplificatory effects that have been noted, that was because it resonated strongly with the dominant social perspectives on the forms of violence that are permissible or forbidden in the relations between people. The notion of civilization is a 'praise word' that links mainly national self-images with orientations to the use of force that range across many societies, but it is fallacious to think that 'civilization' represents close emotional identification with a social group in the intermediate zone between the nation-state and humanity. Shared attitudes to force are not the same as a strong sense of attachment to others in the same civilization. Rather, common civilized tenets are usually fused with powerful national loyalties in complex, shifting and, in certain periods, unpredictable combinations.

Following the method of process sociology, this chapter has stressed the need to examine the 'war on terror' and the 'torture debate' in long-term perspective. Various questions follow. Under what conditions did civilizational discourse move to the forefront of everyday perspectives on society and politics? How did the idea of civilization become incorporated in what Elias (2012) [1939]: 7) called the 'social habitus' of people – in the 'second nature' attitudes to violence and cruelty that are central parts of their emotional lives? How did it shape orientations to other peoples, to the conduct of foreign policy, and to visions of world order? Those are questions that have preoccupied exponents of process sociology which remains marginal in the social sciences and is infrequently encountered in studies of the global era or globalization in sociology and International Relations.

The discussion now turns to Elias's sociogenetic and psychogenetic inquiry into how European peoples acquired their distinctive civilized orientations to society and politics in the course of largely unplanned and far from inevitable processes which unfolded over approximately five centuries.

Elias's Explanation of the European Civilizing Process

The main purpose of Elias's magnum opus was to explain the emergence of European civilized self-representations as embodied in the changing 'threshold of repugnance' towards violent and non-violent harm as well as in new social expectations of propriety and self-restraint in everyday life (Elias 2012 [1939]). The study set out to understand large-scale shifts in social and political organization which were intertwined with greater revulsion to violent punishment and with attendant social expectations regarding table manners and levels of self-control with respect to elementary bodily functions. Elias maintained that higher levels of synthesis in the social sciences were essential in order to understand the interlocked reconstitution of public institutions and collective emotions over the last few centuries. He argued that fundamental changes within the leading European states gave rise to global established–outsider figurations that had transformed all human societies. Later chapters will supplement Elias's synthesis by providing a more detailed examination of the earlier comment in the Introduction about how the relationship between European state-formation, overseas colonial expansion and the development of international society has defined the global political order. The immediate task is to provide an overview of Elias's explanation of the European civilizing process.

The scale and originality of the Eliasian sociological endeavour are evident in the analysis of how civilized sensibilities and emotions emerged from the relations between the formation of state monopoly powers, competition between social classes, internal pacification, increased economic interdependence and the growing complexity of the social division of labour. Some brief comments about Elias's place in the classical sociological tradition were made in the Introduction. They are developed here by comparing his approach with Marx's historical-materialist analysis of monopolizing processes in capitalist industrial societies. The aim is to explain Elias's breakthrough to greater comprehensiveness in social-scientific inquiry. He argued that the Marxian examination of class struggles to gain monopoly control of the means of production provided new insights into how power struggles and social conflicts shaped both pre-capitalist and modern capitalist societies. Largely missing from the investigation, he added – reflecting the influence of Weber's definition of the state – was the examination of struggles between social groups for monopoly control of the instruments of violence. The related contention was that the logic of economic monopolization which was central to Marx's analysis of modern industrial capitalism was fundamentally dependent on stable monopolies of physical power and on the major pacification of state-organized societies. However, this was not to imply that the rise and consolidation of state power could be explained without analyzing ever-shifting balances of power and tensions between social classes such as those involving the aristocracy and the bourgeoisie in the leading European court societies of the 18th and 19th centuries (Elias 2012a).

Elias criticized Marx's writings not only for their neglect of struggles to control the instruments of force within modern societies but also because their investigation of capitalist monopolization had failed to appreciate related processes at the international level – more specifically, how a 'monopoly mechanism' occurred through 'elimination contests' that led to modern states and to the global reach of the dominant European powers. The internal and international dimensions of European state-formation were central to Elias's alternative to the Marxian perspective. They were pivotal to his investigation of the civilizational dimensions of European social and political development. His chief contention was that a more synoptic long-term sociological perspective had to explain the following phenomena: how European notions of civility and civilization emerged in the absolutist court societies, and how the dominant understandings of refined behaviour in those figurations percolated downwards to bourgeois groups as a result of the conscious imitation of 'social superiors'; how those beliefs were dispersed across society as a whole by later 'civilizing offensives' to improve the 'lower orders'; how specific rituals and modes of refinement were transported from French court society to other European governing elites through their own endeavours to emulate 'advanced' groups; and how, from the Napoleonic era onwards, Europeans justified colonial expansion by asserting a natural right to undertake civilizing missions to elevate non-European peoples.

In his analysis of central developments in German society and politics from the late 19th to the middle of the 20th century – indeed, in every phase of his inquiry into civilizing forces – Elias maintained that 'processes within and between states are indissolubly interwoven' (Elias 2013: 193).[1] Suffice it to add that the international or inter-state dimension was more central to Elias's analysis of the European civilizing process than to Marx's study of industrial capitalism.

The explanation of the European civilizing process surpassed both Marxian as well as many non-Marxian investigations of class-divided or state-organized societies by examining the interrelated emotional dimensions of major changes in the social bonds and networks between people. Elias overtook Marx and Weber's analysis of the development of European societies by drawing on Freud's writings, albeit while criticizing their methodological individualism. The conviction that the reconfiguration of social and political structures cannot be understood without considering the psychogenetic features of human interdependencies was a major achievement in the social sciences. They were as 'indissolubly interwoven' as the domestic and international political forces noted in the previous paragraph. That highly original conception of the inseparable or interlaced dimensions of social and political life was integral to Elias's approach to the European civilizing process. Elias was critical of the false dichotomy between the economic and the political that was central to Marx's reductionist interpretations of the state and also of parallel erroneous divisions between the individual and society, the material and the ideational, the rational and the emotional, and the domestic and the international in the social sciences more generally.

Those dichotomies had two consequences. First, several disciplines had grown up around the assumption that their respective objects of inquiry – the economic or the political or the psychological – corresponded with discrete areas of human existence. Second, those distinctions had driven the social sciences along the wrong path of engaging in spurious debates about the relative causal power of what were presumed to be separate but were, in reality, inseparable phenomena. The point was not to increase the number of variables in order to promote multicausal analysis.[2] The real task was to achieve higher levels of synthesis in the social sciences in order to examine interconnected social processes in long-term perspective. Those were fundamental features of Elias's investigation of the European civilizing process which this chapter will examine in more detail.

The organization of Elias's major work (Elias 2012 [1939]) is echoed in the structure of this chapter. Part one of that study discussed the emergence of the concept of civilization in France and the contrast with the German idea of *Kultur.* Part two compiled extracts from exemplary manners books to trace changes in conceptions of propriety regarding the control of bodily functions and table manners. Reflecting the influence of Freud's writings, the investigation provided examples of self-regulation and emotion control that disclosed the nature and underlying course of the emergent civilizing process. Moving beyond Freud's psychologism, part three advanced an intricate account of the relationship between state-formation and the metamorphosis of everyday life. The volume concluded with a discussion in part four of the changing balance of power between external and internal constraints on behaviour. It explained how social pressures to exercise greater all-round self-restraint became incorporated in the individual's psyche through such powerful driving emotions as shame and embarrassment. Changes in personality characteristics ensured high levels of individual compliance with civilized standards in complex state-organized societies. The latter were bound together in international struggles for power that became increasingly worldwide in scope. Running through Elias's inquiry was the contention that only through the commitment to very high levels of synthesis could social scientists hope to explain with any precision how those phenomena were bound together in one long civilizing process that has transformed humanity as a whole. It was claimed that the investigation took no more than the 'first steps' in that direction (Elias 2012 [1939]: 7). As noted above, it did so by building on and transcending the leading standpoints in the classical sociological tradition.

The following discussion begins by considering Elias's analysis of the origins of the idea of civilization and it provides illustrations of its ascent to prominence in political discourse in the late 18th and 19th centuries. It then summarizes the main ingredients of Elias's explanation of the civilizing process – the process of state-formation, changing conceptions of manners, and the realignment of collective and individual emotional responses to force which were integral to an overall, long-term decline in the level of interpersonal violence within civilized societies. The chapter ends with an overview of Elias's reflections on the weakness and reversibility of civilization. The theme was explored most fully in his investigation of the 'decivilizing process' that occurred in the Nazi era; this further indicates that the analysis of long-term change clearly rejected the idea of progress which had been fundamental and central to so many 18th- and 19th-century universal histories.

Origins of a concept

It is necessary to begin by recalling that Elias's investigation was not undertaken in the spirit of endorsement but aimed to provide a relatively detached analysis of a unique pattern of social and political development which included collective beliefs and delusions about European cultural superiority. Nor was it a calculated assault on a 'civilization' in decay in the 1920s and 1930s. In short, the method of inquiry was not 'guided ... by the idea that our civilized mode of behaviour is the most advanced of all humanly possible modes of behaviour, nor by the opinion that "civilization" is the worst form of life and one that is doomed' (Elias 2012 [1939]: 8). The primary goal was to comprehend the processes that European societies had undergone over roughly five centuries including the 'civilizational perils' and 'entanglements' of the modern period (Elias 2012 [1939]: 8). Those resulting traps and ordeals were largely 'unknown to less civilized peoples' who had often been plagued by 'difficulties and fears' – such as catastrophic natural disasters – which modern 'civilized' societies mostly escaped (Elias 2012 [1939]: 8). Here the eighth theme that was discussed in the Introduction deserves special emphasis. The exploration was not an exercise in taking sides in ethical controversies about how civilized peoples should deal with distinctive problems. The point was to 'understand why we actually torment ourselves in such ways' – to acquire greater knowledge of how 'processes of civilization' have taken place so that 'we shall one day succeed in making accessible to more conscious control ... processes ... which we confront as medieval people confronted the forces of nature' (Elias 2012 [1939]: 8).

One of Elias's aims was to explain the collective illusions and self-deceptions of civilized peoples. A pivotal theme was that modern peoples have been exposed to dangers and difficulties because of too little awareness of the process in which the preceding generations came to regard themselves as civilized. Many assumed that 'being civilized' was part of their nature. Their 'civilized' condition could be taken for granted; it was an unchangeable fact of life. The distorted or mythical elements of civilized orientations to social realities helped to explain the general lack of foresight regarding the possibility of regressions to barbarism of the kind that occurred under National Socialism. Few anticipated the genocidal atrocities that lay ahead. It was assumed that savagery on that scale had been eliminated permanently from the European continent. The supposition that such violence was the preserve of 'backward peoples' in non-European regions was shown to be a dangerous delusion. Fantasy-laden conceptions of progress had contributed to the misconceptions of civilized peoples who did not think that modern rational societies could organize slaughter on a level that greatly exceeded the supposedly frenzied killing of 'savages' (Mennell 1998: 248–9). Explaining those misunderstandings was one of the underlying purposes of the analysis of the relationship between state-formation and the emergence of civilized sensibilities.

Elias's inquiry explained how the emergence of stable state monopoly powers imposed external restraints on behaviour which were later supplemented, and replaced to a large degree, by internal restraints anchored in deep-seated psychological drives and dispositions to comply with civilized norms. In the process of 'taming the warriors' and in many other practices across the centuries, the apparatus of self-restraint and self-control became stronger relative to external constraints and the fear of violent punishment. Greater self-regulation in the harmonization of social relations became an increasingly necessary component of the social integration of individuals who performed more specialized tasks within an increasingly complex division of functions. Such controls came to be regarded as entirely natural or normal in routine interactions (Elias 2012 [1939]: 405ff).[3] A more detailed summation of the overall trend explained how 'the increasing webs of interdependence spun by state-formation, the division of labour, economic growth and other "structural" processes' exerted pressures to increase the apposite self-controls which became 'more automatic' (people became 'more deeply habituated to do certain things with less need for conscious reflection'), 'more even' (behaviour was less volatile and less subject to fluctuate rapidly between emotional extremes), and 'more all-round' (applying 'more uniformly to all aspects of life and to all those with whom one has to deal') (Liston and Mennell 2009: 60–1). But Elias (2013: chs 4–5) described in detail how tilts in the balance of power between external and internal restraints can occur under conditions of social and political turmoil. During the Nazi era, for example, inner compulsions proved to be incapable of preventing the 'breakdown of civilization' that was instigated by a regime that freed itself from what were, in any case, weak civilized constraints on the exercise of state monopolies of power. Against all expectation, the highly self-disciplined nature of civilized people turned out to be a political resource that a murderous elite could employ to plan and administer industrialized slaughter. Analyzing shifts in the balance of power between civilizing and decivilizing processes was not only valuable for explaining past events. It was also the key to understanding the delicacy of fragility of 'civilized' arrangements and the reality that such fractures and 'regressions' could erupt again.

Elias (2012 [1939]: 17ff) began his non-evaluative investigation of civilization by comparing the concept of civilization, as forged in the late 18th century, to the German idea of *Kultur* with its narrow preoccupation with constructing a distinctive national identity based in part on contempt or disdain for the superficial fineries of French court society. By contrast, the idea of civilization 'plays down ... national differences between peoples; it emphasises what is common to all human beings – or in the view of its bearers – should be' (Elias 2012 [1939]: 17). Gradually, the notion of being 'civilized' replaced the terms that the upper classes used to express unquestioned feelings of superiority over the lower orders. The notions of *courtoisie* and *civilité* had that function for earlier generations. The first concept had been popular in medieval court circles until it was steadily replaced by *civilité* in France during the 17th century and then largely superseded in turn from around the mid-1770s by 'civilization', a concept that had been employed around 20 years earlier in specialist reflections on the criminal law (Elias 2012 [1939]: 105ff; Bowden 2009: 26ff). The idea became a pivotal part of bourgeois reformist discourse in court society, including the reasoning of the physiocrats – forebears of specialist students of economic life – whose express aim was to persuade rulers of the wisdom of enlightened government in conformity with a doctrine of progress and social improvement which was integral to their vision of the identity of the nation (Elias 2012 [1939]: 52ff; Mazlish 2004: ch 1). The new ethos would come to combine an assured sense of natural superiority among ruling groups with the certitude which became prominent in bourgeois circles that civilization had to be brought to backward societies and the unrefined lower echelons. The nature of the metamorphosis that was taking place was evident in the contrast with earlier phases of European history where aristocratic elites had assiduously ensured that anything that reminded them of the 'vulgar' lower orders 'was kept at a distance' (Elias 2012 [1939]: 464). Its qualities were underlined by the contrast with the idea of *Kultur* which rejected any conception of a universal political project to improve the lot of humanity as a whole.

Early in the study, Elias reflected on the centrality of the idea of civilization in the collective self-consciousness of colonizing groups. In their minds, the concept was a world-orientating 'praise word'. Its ascent was striking given that, only a few decades earlier, the advocates of *Kultur* had treated it with contempt. Elias maintained that it:

> sums up everything in which Western society of the last two or three centuries believes itself superior to earlier societies or "more primitive" contemporary ones. By this term, Western society seeks to describe what constitutes its special character and what it is proud of: the level of *its* technology, the nature of *its* manners, the development of *its* scientific knowledge or view of the world, and much more. (Elias 2012 [1939]: 15, italics in original)

The concept expressed the self-confidence of imperialist societies and their 'continuously expansionist tendency' (Elias 2012 [1939]: 17). That statement deserves further investigation given recurrent misunderstandings of Elias's ambitions. A major objection is that his writings advanced 'a purely European genealogy of learning and culture' that ignored the extra-European impact on the main societal developments across the continent (Goody 2010: 4, 58) and which, in the language of more recent postcolonial standpoints, was wedded to the flawed discourse of 'civilizational isolationism' (Go 2017; Çapan 2017). The contention resonates with criticisms of Eurocentric interpretations of society and politics which stress, among other things, repeated failures to trace 'the Eastern origins of Western civilization' (Hobson 2004; see also Hobson 2012; Bowden 2007).

There are basic problems with that line of argumentation. The critique assumes that Elias's analysis of specific discourses of civilization was, in effect, an attempt to explain the rise of Europe or the West and its eventual global political and military dominance – an endeavour that would indeed have required detailed analysis of extra-European influences (Hobson 2010; Linklater 2017). But Elias set out to understand how Europeans acquired their conceptions of civilized arrangements (Mennell 1996). His main writings did not attempt to explain how Europeans acquired, among other things, scientific knowledge and technological applications that supposedly surpassed the accomplishments of non-European peoples. The objective was not to assess the extent to which Europeans had attained their technological prowess totally unaided, relying on native creativity and ingenuity, or to establish how far their accomplishments were instead the result of prolonged cultural borrowing and extensive learning from others. As noted earlier, the real aim was far more specific; it nevertheless requires further research on whether, or how far, conceptions of propriety in non-European societies contributed to European civilized self-images (see p. 14).

Notwithstanding that defence of Elias's standpoint, questions arise about the relationship between colonial encounters and the emergence of perceptions of civilizational superiority. Elias's inquiry was strangely silent on the impact of global interconnections, and his remarks on imperialism were largely confined to considering how European colonial expansion had transformed the traditional world views of many non-European governing elites. He emphasized the globalization of intra-societal European developmental patterns in which relatively weak groups internalized elite perceptions of their inferiority while established groups initiated offensives to reform the behaviour of the lower strata, or unintentionally promoted their changing orientations to the world (see Chapter 5). Elias did not set out to explain the rise of the West; even so, his investigation paid little attention to how civilized ideas were constructed in the context of overseas expansion and colonial domination. Postcolonial commentaries on the limitations of classical sociology are worth recalling at this point.

Elias (2012: [1939] 46ff) wrote that French thinkers – the *philosophes* such as Mirabeau – were the principal architects of the new discourse of civilization. The freshly minted concept had been used by Mirabeau in 1756 to refer to the replacement of military law by civil law and to equivalent changes with respect to virtue and the refinement of manners (Mazlish 2001). In a relatively short time frame, it became part of the lexicon of European political and intellectual elites and it entered the vocabulary of their non-European counterparts around a century later. It is important to give examples of interesting steps in its rapid incorporation within other Western European languages by considering specific conceptual shifts in British political thought. The idea of civilization appears to have been used by the Scottish Enlightenment thinker, Adam Ferguson, in 1767 and possibly several years earlier by other writers (Febvre 1973; Pagden 1988; Bowden 2009: 32; see also Thomas 2018: 5ff on its use in the late 17th and early 18th centuries). However, a particular incident in the life of Dr Johnson provides a vivid illustration of how the concept quickly found favour beyond French aristocratic court circles. James Boswell reported a conversation on 23 March 1772 with Johnson on whether 'civilization' should be included in the fourth edition of his *Dictionary*. Initially, Johnson was disposed to exclude the term and declared his preference for the established notion of 'civility'. Taking the opposing view, Boswell argued that 'civilization' ['from civilize'] was 'better – in the sense opposed to barbarity – than civility' (Boswell 1873 [1791]: 187). It was Boswell's view that prevailed.

Presumably, as a result of many other such deliberations about the respective merits of conventional and freshly coined terms, 'civilization' was absorbed into other European languages. The development occurred in a period when several new nouns ending in '-ation' were composed from existing French verbs that ended in '-iser'. Examples included centralisation, democratisation and fraternisation (see Starobinski 1993: 1–2, who adds that 'civilization' had been used as early as the 16th century to describe the colonial practice of bringing civility to the Mexicans; see also Yurdusev 2003: ch 4). Before long, in Britain and elsewhere, leading thinkers made appropriate modifications to standard forms of exposition. A comparison of two passages in the writings of Edmund Burke illuminates the transition that was under way. The concept of civility was the term of choice in a letter of 9 June 1777 to William Robertson in which Burke observed that, with European expansion, 'the Great Map of Mankind is unrolld at once'. The map, he added, revealed 'the very different Civility of Europe and of China' which Burke compared to the 'savage' conditions and 'barbarism' of other peoples (cited in Mansfield 1984: 102). In *Reflections on the French Revolution*, published in 1790, Burke referred not to 'civility' but to 'civilization' when railing against the revolutionaries who 'undermine our manners, our civilization, and all the good things which are connected with manners and civilization … in this European world of ours' (Burke 1889 [1790], vol 3: 335–6). In the 1791 *Letter to a Member of the National Assembly*, Burke lamented that French military policy had 'destroyed … all the other manners and principles which have hitherto civilized Europe'; as a result, 'the mode of civilized warfare will not be practised: nor are the French … entitled to expect it' (Burke 1889 [1791], vol 4: 34–5).

The final part of that citation was not the first such warning that those living outside the advanced world opened themselves to the danger of violence that civilized people widely condemned in their relations with each other. French writers used similar language in describing the 'barbarism' of the English during the Seven Years' War (1756–63) and again during the revolutionary military struggles of the 1790s (Bell 2001: ch 3). In both cases, French 'war atrocity' literature likened the English to barbarous peoples with the derogatory caveat that at no point had the latter identified with European civilization whereas England had wilfully seceded from 'civilized' humanity as symbolized by France, the 'schoolmaster to the rest of the world' (Bell 2001: ch 3). Variations on the theme run through 19th-century European political thought. Some examples have been selected in the light of the overall argument in this work on how the civilizing process was the outcome of the interrelations between state-formation, overseas expansion and the evolution of international society. An example was David Hume's pronouncement that 'were a civilized nation engaged with barbarians, who observed no rules even of war, the former must also suspend their observance of them, where they no longer serve to any purpose; and must render every action or encounter as bloody and pernicious as possible to the first aggressors' (Hume 1975 [1777]: 187–8). John Stuart Mill (2002 [1859]: 487) expressed similar ideas in his essay on non-intervention with its explicit defence of the 'civilizing' role of colonialism. He maintained that:

> To suppose the same rules of international morality can obtain between one civilized nation and another, and between civilized nations and barbarians is a grave error. … In the first place, the rules of ordinary morality imply reciprocity. But barbarians will not reciprocate. They cannot be depended upon for observing any rules. … In the next place, nations which are still barbarous have not got beyond the period during which it is likely to be for their benefit that they should be conquered and held in subjection by foreigners. (Mill 2002 [1859])[4]

Later parts of this work will consider the subsequent impact of such ideas on the constitution of the European-dominated global order.

What was already apparent in Burke's observations about the French revolutionaries was the transition from 'civility' to 'civilization' which provided the sharper contrast, as Boswell had argued, with 'barbarity'. The new vocabulary of politics had initially been employed by revolutionary groups in their war against the British ruling class. Utilized as a 'releaser symbol', the discourse served notice that the French revolutionary armies felt no obligation to observe conventional civilized prohibitions on force. In Burke's writings, the concept was turned into a weapon that established groups used in condemnation of the violent actions of demonized regicidal outsiders. It was harnessed to support the thesis that the enemies of civilization forfeited the entitlement to be treated in civilized ways. In Hume's writings, the narrative of civilization and savagery was applied to relations between the European colonial establishment and non-reciprocating barbarians. In the passage from Mill's writings cited earlier (2002 [1859]: 487), 'civilization' acquired an additional dimension which is that the 'barbarous' would profit from prolonged benign colonial rule. Through such statements, the idea of civilization became integral to new established–outsider relations within the European states-system and between European societies and the wider world.

In his analysis of the 'civilizing process', Elias traced that aspect of 'civilization' back to Napoleon's address to his troops before they departed in 1798 on the mission to colonize Egypt. They were, 'undertaking', Napoleon boasted, 'a conquest with incalculable consequences for civilization' (Elias 2012 [1939]: 57; see also Conklin 1997: ch 1 on the relationship with the *mission civilisatrice* that flourished later under the Third French Republic). More than any other concept, 'civilization' gave 'colonial conquerors' a ready-made 'justification of their rule' (Elias 2012 [1939]: 57). It became the 'watchword' of the whole 'colonizing movement' (Elias 2012 [1939]: 474). It was a symbol of the self-assigned superiority of the new global establishment just as civility had been for the older 'courtly-aristocratic upper class' (Elias 2012 [1939]: 57). From its inception, Elias 2012 [1939]: 52ff) added, the term contained an inbuilt ambiguity since it could refer to a condition or 'state' or to a 'process' – to purportedly unchanging social circumstances as well as to fluid lines of development. Napoleon's speech marked a tilt away from the argument of the philosophes that civilization was a complex historical process that could only be protected from decline through constant effort to the simplistic view that it described a natural condition that was testimony to the 'higher gifts' of European peoples. Elias (2012 [1939]: 52ff) noted how the concept of civilization was steadily stripped of its earlier ambiguities since:

> unlike the situation when the concept was formed, from now on nations came to consider the process of civilization as completed within their own societies; they came to see themselves as bearers of an existing or finished civilization to others, as standard-bearers of expanding civilization. Of the whole preceding process of civilization nothing remained in their consciousness except a vague residue. Its outcome was taken simply as an expression of their own higher gifts; the fact that, and the question of how, in the course of many centuries, civilized behaviour had been attained [was] of no interest.

Unwavering confidence in the civilized condition of the European world underpinned self-elevating descriptions of the purpose of

French colonial rule in Egypt. As Jean-Baptiste Fourier, who had been entrusted with compiling the reports that would form the *Description de l'Egypte* proclaimed,[5] the aim was 'to render the constitution of the inhabitants softer and to procure them all the advantages of a perfected civilization' (Godlewska 1995: 8). More or less identical ideas about the completed nature of civilization became commonplace in European perspectives on the relations between the civilized and the barbarous throughout the colonial era.

To elaborate on Elias's argument, the 'Napoleonic moment' signified a major alteration in the balance of power between European and non-European societies which resulted in, among other things, influential 'Orientalist' standpoints that devalued the achievements of East Asian and South Asian societies. Europe's unique accomplishments were assumed to be entirely internal or endogenous in origin. Earlier non-European influences on, for example, European technological development were largely swept aside in the interplay between the 'group charisma' of the colonial establishment and the imputation of 'group disgrace' to colonized outsiders (Hobson 2012). Previously admired societies were relegated to the position of social subordinates in the process. By way of illustration, positive assessments of China's stable government that had been advanced by Voltaire and other leading Enlightenment thinkers were superseded towards the end of the 18th century by overwhelmingly negative portraits of oriental despotism (Marshall 1993; Israel 2006). Demonstrations of repugnance towards indigenous practices such as *sati* in India were examples of the denigration of 'uncivilized' peoples that ran through colonial discourse, reinforcing the belief in the legitimacy of imperial rule. In the language of the British Government Circular sent to military officers on 10 November 1828, the custom was necessarily 'abhorrent' in the eyes of every 'rational and civilized being', a standpoint that created tensions between the official policy of non-interference with respect to indigenous religious and cultural practices and the high-minded sense of responsibility for the protection of innocent victims through beneficent colonial government (Tschurenev 2004).

Different parties almost certainly agreed that India lacked the indigenous state institutions that could perform that humane civilizing role. At the heart of European colonial discourse (and of more recent 'civilizing offensives') was the assuredness that modern, state-organized societies are the crucible of civilization – the sole context in which civilized life can emerge and flourish. Also influential was the assumption that the European multi-state system possessed a restlessness – a deep thirst for change and progress – that was lacking in the stagnant, lifeless empires of the Far East. The implication was that non-European peoples were passively waiting for the external impetus to undergo the process of civilization, for the kickstart that would bring the wonders of the 'empire of civilization' (Bowden 2009). All such orientations to the non-European world reworked the conceptions of refined existence that first appeared in the 18th-century aristocratic court societies. Self-defining civilized strata emancipated them from national limits and converted them into the core principles of colonial international society.

State-formation

Elias's account of the European civilizing process concentrated on the revolutionary impact of the origins of the modern state with its monopoly control of the instruments of violence, as stressed by Weber, to which Elias added the monopoly power of taxation. Social and political transformations over the centuries were central to his inquiry but they were not portrayed as a complete break with the past. There was no critical moment when the civilizing process suddenly began and 'barbarism' was left behind – no specific historical rupture that totally destroyed barbarian practices and which guaranteed they could not resurface in social and political life. Balances of power had altered as earlier trends accelerated.

Needless to say, major revisions to the investigation of the European civilizing process are necessary in the light of more recent scholarship on the Middle Ages and the Italian Renaissance (Linklater 2016: chs 3–4). Experts in medieval history have often found more to contest or reject than to endorse in what has been regarded as Elias's exaggerated description of the violent Middle Ages (Linklater 2016: ch 3). Taking the long perspective, however, Elias maintained that the regulating role of courtesy and politeness in medieval court societies played its part in the genesis of European notions of civilization. He did not overlook the long-term ramifications of the social and political movements that were already under way in the tumultuous late Middle Ages. Particular emphasis was placed on the life-or-death struggles between feudal polities that led to ever larger territorial monopolies of violence. Defeated groups were either annihilated or absorbed in new concentrations of power in the course of relentless 'elimination contests'. The 'monopoly mechanism' that led to centralized controls over the instruments of coercion also intensified a process that was evident in the medieval period, as rulers became ever more reliant on skilled officials to administer the elaborate business of princely courts.

The taming or 'courtization of the warriors' took place over several decades and centuries, as nobles with traditionally violent modes of existence were drawn into court societies where they came under the watchful eye of territorial lords (Elias 2012 [1939]: 428ff). They were required to exercise greater control of violent emotions or aggressive inclinations and to regulate speech, gestures and comportment in accordance with strict court protocols. They were expected to undertake in diplomatic ways the 'unwarlike administrative and clerical' responsibilities that were vital for effective government and for success in future elimination contests (Elias 2012 [1939]: 281; Elias 2006: 118). The explanation singled out the radical changes that occurred in the court of Louis XIV at Versailles. The elaborate rituals and refined conventions that were introduced in the leading-edge French court provided the social ideal that admiring ruling elites in other European societies enthusiastically copied. New codes of conduct and 'social standards of self-restraint' moved outwards from the French absolutist state to other European court figurations as part of an emergent sense of identification with the same civilization (see also Duindam 2003 on the influential Viennese court). The stepping stone was a sense of belonging to one supranational court society (Elias 2010a: 4).

Absolutist states with the coercive capabilities to impose external restraints on subject populations facilitated the revival of populous towns that had been decimated by the collapse of the Roman Empire. With the increasing pacification of society, human interconnections increased. People became ever more dependent on one another for the satisfaction of basic needs. Pressures and incentives to control violent and aggressive drives, to avoid giving offence to others, and to display greater consideration for the interests of other people intensified. In a growing trend, new social standards of self-restraint became 'second nature' for many of those involved. Such changes were often imperceptible to those who were living through slow-moving reconfigurations of society. In Elias's language, they were examples of shifts that develop in slow and unplanned ways. People urged themselves and each other along pathways that were not mapped out in advance. But, looking back, the analyst could see that what might at first appear to be 'a jumbled succession of events' belonged to a 'structured long-term process'; seemingly disparate phenomena shaped the main trajectories of social change in which shared conceptions of propriety governed interactions within the established strata (Elias 2009f: 87). Empirical evidence of the overall course of events included the increasing number of 'manners books' which were eagerly consulted by the members of the literate social strata who sought reliable guidance on how to behave in a civil manner. Uncertainties and anxieties about proper conduct and related concerns about avoiding the crippling emotions of embarrassment and shame were driving forces behind the civilizing process. Those concerns were connected with a generalized desire to emulate social superiors and to escape the scorn or contempt that would result from violating civilized codes in their presence. Not that, as previously noted, the aristocratic court society was disposed to initiate 'civilizing offensives' to improve the attitudes and behaviour of subordinates. It was, rather, strongly inclined to reinforce and entrench social distinctions through an endless refinement of rules of etiquette (see Elias 2012 [1939]: 472 on the interplay between the 'attraction' of the lower ranks to upper class conduct and the 'repulsion' of the dominant groups at their mimetic behaviour). Even so, over the decades, shared understandings of propriety and the larger behaviour codes spread across the social divides and across Western Europe as a whole. More and more people came to steer their conduct in similar ways by appealing to the common language of civilization. Explaining the interdependencies between those 'sociogenetic' and 'psychogenetic' forces was Elias's principal contribution to the classical sociological tradition.

Manners books

Manners books or guides to conduct provided detailed advice on forms of social interaction that are not, at first glance, of obvious relevance for the study of the relations between societies. Some connections will be considered later in order to explain their salience for understanding how established–outsider figurations structured the global order. The discussion will emphasize linkages between the civilization of manners, 'supranational' court society, and diplomatic protocols in the European society of states. It will focus on how those interdependencies were bound up with judgements about levels of civilization and barbarism in two outsider groups – peripheral states in the European international society and outlying non-European governments.

Influential instruction books which appeared between the 1300s and the 1700s advised on the proper management and control of basic bodily functions. They contained guides on such elementary physical necessities as urination and defecation as well as nose-blowing and spitting. They provided information on correct table manners or eating etiquette following the greater use of the fork and knife in elite circles. Manuals on proper conduct provided a window onto changes in everyday behaviour that were grounded in evolving fears of personal shame and embarrassment.[6] They were evidence of a decisive tilt towards increased 'individualization' in which people became more introspective and self-regulating – given to more intense reflections on how their actions appeared to, and would be judged, perhaps negatively, by others. With those changing personality dispositions, major shifts in the relative power of internal and external controls on conduct steadily took place (Elias 2012 [1939]: 522ff).

The exploration of the civilizing process provided numerous examples of the emergence of new protective barriers between people which were intertwined with disgust at the 'animalic' features of human existence. An example was the increasing use of the fork in 16th-century elite circles. Its diffusion from Italy first to France and then to England and Germany reflected a growing revulsion at 'the mere approach of something that has been in contact with the mouth or hands of someone else' (Elias 2012 [1939]: 77). A parallel development was the break with the medieval custom in which people used to take 'meat with their fingers from the same dish' or 'wine from the same goblet' or 'soup from the same pot' (Elias 2012 [1939]: 77; see also Thomas 2018: 50ff). Only much later, according to Elias (2012 [1939]: 148), would such everyday practices arouse disgust because of concerns about hygiene (see Goudsblom 1986 whose comments about the later emergence of particular forms of self-control including handwashing have particular salience in the current COVID-19 global health crisis).[7] Evolving behaviour patterns were linked with erecting new barriers between people that had the effect of 'repelling and separating' human bodies; later fears about unhygienic behaviour would further entrench this (Elias 2012 [1939]: 77). The same overall trend was evident in transformed attitudes to nudity among members of the refined social elites. Medieval people had not been ashamed to be seen naked. But, as part of the civilizing process, people began to feel embarrassed about nakedness especially if 'animalic' natural functions were inadvertently 'exposed to the gaze of others' (Elias 2012 [1939]: 129ff, 162). On Elias's interpretation of events, which has been contested in the recent literature (see Thomas 2018: 53), people in medieval times did not have the same expectations of personal privacy as the later civilized strata who were subject to increasing 'individualization'.

Related movements included new standards of propriety with respect to bodily functions such as nose-blowing and spitting. People in the Middles Ages had usually blown their noses into their hands. Spitting in public was commonplace. From the end of the 16th century, the handkerchief appeared as a symbol of elite sophistication. As with the use of the fork, the handkerchief was at first the preserve of the most powerful and affluent groups, but their refined social interactions were copied by aspiring social strata and later by society as a whole. The trend towards the concealment of features of human interaction that had earlier been exposed to the public gaze without shame or embarrassment included stricter taboos against speaking openly about sexuality. In the medieval period, Elias (2012 [1939]: 160ff) argued, children slept in their parents' beds and were no stranger to parental nudity. But, in the course of the civilizing process, parents became more reserved about discussing sexual matters with their offspring given the fear of embarrassment; this 'conspiracy of silence' also reflected new concerns about the need to avoid 'soiling ... the childish mind' (Elias 2012 [1939]: 172). The 'expanding threshold of repugnance' regarding the 'animal' side of the self was manifested by the protective walls that shielded people from practices that had come to be seen as especially bloody and gory. An example was the practice of removing 'distasteful' practices, such as the carving (and, by implication, the slaughter) of animals, *'behind the scenes of social life'* where they could not offend or disturb civilized sensibilities (Elias 2012 [1939]: 122, italics in original). Similar behavioural alterations would occur in many different spheres including the governance of death and dying which became increasingly obscured from view rather than routinely encountered by both adults and children as in medieval times (Elias 2010).

Guides to conduct emerged in the context of rising interdependencies and the related surge of pressures on people to regulate behaviour in novel ways. They were fundamental to Elias's task of revealing 'the *order* underlying historical *changes*' (Elias 2012 [1939]: 6, italics in original), but they are not just of historical interest. Several present-day discussions about the erosion of standards of self-restraint are only intelligible when considered in long-term perspective – when viewed in conjunction with the civilizing process of which they are part. Current reflections on the peculiar 'torments' created by the social media illustrate the point. To understand them, it is useful to recall the imperative in the course of the 20th century that people should not openly display feelings of superiority over others in the manner of earlier elites. The members of civilized societies were expected to exercise higher levels of self-restraint by refraining from acting in ways that would humiliate others or instil fear or anxiety. They were obliged to display greater consideration for others as social equals (Wouters 1998).

Elias's argument about the impact of the manners books was confined to an explanation of the civilizing of relations within the leading European societies. An intriguing question is whether the emergence of civilized manners had any relevance for the relations between societies. Recent discussions of how interactions on social media have contributed to a coarsening of sensibilities in the public sphere should allay any doubts about the deep connections between developments in what may, at first sight, appear to be separate domains. A useful starting point is the 'online disinhibition effect' that enables people to relax hard-won standards of self-restraint that are generally observed in face-to-face encounters (Suler 2004). Behind the scenes – in the knowledge that they have immunity from the pressures to feel shame or embarrassment that exist in traditional social encounters – they can give free rein to opinions that go against the civilizing trends of recent decades. Misogynist and homophobic sentiments are a clear example of a counter-trend to the state's punishment of hate crimes in civilized societies. They are manifestations of a weakening of civility in which seizing opportunities to abuse other people and to express contempt for them has grown to unforeseen levels.

There is clearly more to feelings of revulsion towards such behaviour than the plain fact that particular individuals and groups use new technologies to find pleasure in abusing or humiliating other people in contravention of hitherto ascendant views about the forms of self-restraint that are incumbent upon civilized people. The 'disinhibition effect' has been associated with aspects of national-populist discourses that are openly racist, hostile to migrants, and aggressively Islamophobic. It has been deemed responsible for a harshening of language and sensibilities in some contemporary reaffirmations of national identity, in reactions against the global liberal order, and in interwoven attempts to alter distributions of power at the national and international level. In process-sociological terms, recent established–outsider figurations have at least temporarily altered balances between civilizing and decivilizing processes.

Viewed in long-term perspective, current anxieties about the unforeseen and shocking relaxation of what may have seemed to be secure controls on behaviour have their origins in largely forgotten, standard-setting, manners books that influenced the cultivation of inner restraints on conduct in an earlier phase of an ongoing process in which more and people are brought together in unexpected ways. The relevant guides to conduct did not only shape codes of behaviour within civilized societies. They influenced the diplomatic protocols and rituals that governed relations between absolutist court societies in Europe. They left their mark on the ways in which the established groups in the global order portrayed outsiders. Fundamental was the belief among members of the European governing classes that those protocols and the society of states to which they belonged were symbols or emblems of a civilization from which peoples of lesser worth were rightly excluded.

The international lawyer, Henry Wheaton (1936 [1886]: 243, 251) expressed a long established prejudice when he argued that 'there is no circumstance which marks more distinctly the progress of modern civilization than the institutions of permanent diplomatic missions between different States'; 'the usage of civilized nations', he added, 'has established a certain etiquette' – belonging to 'the code of manners' rather than formal laws – that steered the behaviour of 'members of the diplomatic corps, resident at the same court'. Outsider groups such as Eastern European ruling elites were expected to modify their behaviour to comply with the relevant standards of propriety. Many responded to external pressures to observe aristocratic etiquette in the supranational court society by advising diplomats on the correct behaviour code. Royal instructions to Polish ambassadors in 1601 are a case in point. Official guidance regarding comportment stressed the need to behave in ways that were 'manly and solemn according to the occasion – not womanly, not childish, not fearful, not shameful, not irritable, not frivolous' (cited in Bogucka 1991: 201). Revelatory was the necessity to 'look at the person to whom you are sent, without any movement'; ambassadors were informed that 'hands should be quiet, without any trembling' and they were required to conduct themselves 'without looking sideways, without shaking the head', or 'tugging at the beard' (cited in Bogucka 1991: 201). Especially interesting in the light of the Western European manners books were instructions to 'abstain from coughing, spitting, blowing the nose, and scratching the head or other parts of the body' as well as the accompanying injunctions not to 'pick your nose or teeth or bite your lips' (cited in Bogucka 1991: 201; see Elias 2012 [1939]: 142ff). Such developments need to be understood in the broader context of established–outsider relations since four years earlier – on 25 July 1597 – Elizabeth I had chastised the Polish ambassador for insolence in the presence of a monarch and for a breach of diplomatic etiquette that constituted a grave failure to understand and respect the law of nature and nations (Green 2000). Most probably, Polish concerns about the correct observance of diplomatic protocol reflected the bitter experience of an earlier 'status degradation ceremony' in which an established group centred in the English court seems to have affirmed its superiority by openly castigating and humiliating outsiders (Garfinkel 1956; see also Adler-Nissen 2014 and Zarakol 2011: ch 2 on the broader phenomenon of stigmatization in world politics).

The 1601 instructions indicated how outlying groups on the margins of European international society endeavoured to improve their position in the status hierarchy by falling into line with the customs of established groups. A second and much later illustration shows how Europeans stigmatized the exiled Portuguese court in Rio de Janeiro in the late 19th century. Members of the court displayed medieval attitudes to the body that were part of the outlook of the Christian missionaries who visited Japan in the 16th century. They had been struck by the attention to physical cleanliness but, given the import of negative images of Roman attitudes towards cleaning the body, they were themselves disinclined to adopt the local custom of daily bathing (Boxer 1951: 83–4, 214).[8] Members of the exiled Portuguese court shocked visiting Austrian court aristocrats by insisting that 'not washing was a point of honour' (Wilcken 2004: 180–1). In a telling parallel, one German envoy described the court as the European equivalent of the 'semi-Asian court of Constantinople' and remonstrated that the Portuguese king kept unemptied chamber pots in an apartment that was supposedly set aside for meeting distinguished guests; moreover, the crown prince had shocked aristocratic women by swimming in the nude and he had disgusted European military officers by defecating in the presence of his troops (Wilcken 2004: 211ff).

As global connections increased, the international establishment was all too prepared to regard the practices of non-European elites as woefully inadequate by civilized standards (Zarakol 2011: ch 2). The impact of Wheaton's 'code of manners' (1936 [1866]) was evident in various European assessments of the lack of civilization in peripheral regions. In a section on manners in the journal in which he described the famous 1793–4 diplomatic mission to China, Lord Macartney (2004: 179) commented on the 'abominable' fact that the Chinese 'spit about the rooms without mercy' and 'blow their noses in their fingers and wipe them with their sleeves, or upon anything near them' since very few had 'recourse to pocket handkerchiefs'. Also notable in the light of the European 'civilization' of table manners were references to the Chinese practice of drinking from the same bowl, which is 'sometimes rinsed' but 'never washed or wiped clean' (Macartney 2004: 179). Instructive were his remarks about the absence of 'water closets' or 'places of proper retirement' that had the unsurprising result that certain physical 'necessaries are quite public and open' while waste removal 'occasions a stench in almost every place one approaches' (Macartney 2004: 180). Links with the changing sensibilities which Elias discerned in the manners books will be apparent.

Revealingly, almost a century later, Chinese envoys who were about to depart for the United States received official instructions on how to avoid the opprobrium of their diplomatic hosts and how to avoid unnecessary embarrassment. The 1881 handbook for emissaries which was compiled by the Chinese official, Cai Jun, who had lived in Washington for several months, contained detailed information about the rules of propriety that governed social interaction in US homes as well as in public settings. 'If you have to cough', the handbook stated, 'you must use a handkerchief to cover your mouth and you must not let your nose run all over or spit anywhere' (cited in Arkush and Lee 1989: 53ff).[9] The handbook advised on greeting rituals, including the etiquette of shaking hands, and it offered guidelines on how to deal with the novel experience of interacting with female guests at official as well as informal gatherings (Arkush and Lee 1989: 53ff).

Reactions to the 1871–73 Japanese Iwakura mission to the West are a final example of how civilized norms regarding propriety influenced established–outsider figurations. Delegates to the United States were left in no doubt that social acceptance demanded the replacement of the kimono with the Western-style attire worn by civilized peoples. After a meeting with President Grant, the mission resolved that it would be prudent not to wear traditional Japanese dress in future diplomatic gatherings (Gong 1984: 20, 179). As for the delegation to Britain in 1872, following a dinner in August which was hosted by Lord Glanville, the British Foreign Secretary, a member of the Swedish Embassy expressed surprise that the Japanese dignitaries displayed an 'unusually high level of culture' for 'Easterners' (Kayaoğlu 2010: 87–8). Members of the mission had previously created a favourable impression by deciding to wear European clothes. Western attitudes to the behaviour of visiting Japanese dignitaries had not always been as positive. The delegation that visited San Francisco in 1860 aroused indignation by bathing publicly in the nude. Subsequently, curtains were placed around bathing areas to uphold civilized views on the imperative of concealing nakedness (Miyoshi 1979: 78; Henning 2000: 23ff).

In that period, several Japanese delegates appear to have been astonished that sculptures and paintings of nudes were allowed in public places and also by the fact that the formal dress code permitted American women to bare their shoulders (Miyoshi 1979: ch 2; Beasley 1995: ch 4; Kunitake 2009: chs 13 and 29).[10] The meeting of different civilizing processes in the etic sense – the sixth theme in the introduction to this volume – is apparent in those encounters. Different parties did not meet as social equals. During the Meiji period in Japan, government policies introduced new standards of restraint with respect to basic manners that were designed to phase out behaviour that many Westerners regarded as symbols of backwardness. Legislation was passed to outlaw barbaric practices including public nakedness, mixed bathing and urinating in public that tarnished Japan's reputation (Benesch 2015: 255–6). In the early years of the Meiji Restoration, the Emperor symbolized the nature of the 'civilizing endeavour', setting new social standards in the process by wearing Western dress, eating Western food and sporting a Western hairstyle (Benesch 2015: 254). Offensives to modify everyday conduct reflected asymmetries of power between the Western political establishment and non-Western outsiders and the unstoppable global dominance of Western 'standards of civilization' that reflected the influence of long-forgotten manners books. Further examples will be provided in the discussion of the globalization of civilized behaviour in Chapter 5.

Many scholars have stated that controls over courtesy and etiquette are far from innocent or merely ornamental but are effective means of wielding power through assertions of superiority (Ranum 1980). They may not seem as important as controls over the instruments of force and taxation for understanding the process of state-formation, but their role in shaping the societal means of orientation should not be underestimated. Elias's mode of analysis of the relationship between manners, established–outsider relations, acts of stigmatization, and pressures to accept social inferiority captured those power relations in an original contribution to classical sociological analyses of changing directions in European societies. This section has shown that controls over manners and etiquette affected power ratios in the relations between the members of civilized states as well as attitudes to outsiders who did not belong to refined international society.

A final comment concerns the relationship between the sources of power within those figurations. In his analysis of the formation and consolidation of modern European state structures, Elias (2006: 151) observed that capabilities in one domain (for example, controls over etiquette and the ceremonial) depended on, but could also influence, levels of power and authority with respect to controls over monopolies of force and taxation. Efforts to govern the most basic ways in which people attune themselves to the social world should be interpreted accordingly – hence the immense investments that the rulers of absolutist court societies such as Louis XIV made in that domain. They did not confine their endeavours to the domestic sphere but attempted to influence the global order through the interplay between attempts to control the meaning of civilized behaviour and to increase economic and political–military power. The international politics of etiquette and manners should be considered in that context.

Violence

Manners books reflected and encouraged revised orientations towards the use of force in the relations between civilized people. They illuminated how 'society ... was beginning at this time more and more to limit the real dangers threatening people' (Elias 2012 [1939]: 124). Evolving attitudes towards the knife were illuminating. They were an instance of how seemingly 'trivial' or 'worthless' phenomena in contrast with the great affairs of state were part of larger-scale social and political realignments (Elias 2012 [1939]: 118ff). With 'the advancing internal pacification of society', the knife which had long been 'a weapon of attack' and 'a symbol of death and danger' turned into a mundane eating utensil (Elias 2012 [1939]: 123–4). In an era when they were still a 'menacing instrument' and a 'threatening symbol', guides to conduct urged readers not to keep knives to hand like 'village people'; they strongly warned of the dangers of pointing a knife at others given the still vivid 'memory of the warlike threat' and the entirely 'rational' fear of imminent attack (Elias 2012 [1939]: 123ff). New forms of self-restraint were deemed essential to avoid actions or gestures that could arouse fear or anger in transitional times when many were quick to resort to violence in response to perceived insults to honour. The behaviour codes that were commended by the relevant manners books were indicative of how people were learning to manage aggressive impulses, and not least through greater attentiveness to how their behaviour could be interpreted by others, and how it might unintentionally trigger acts of violence that the leading groups increasingly regarded as reprehensible.

As previously discussed, the analysis stressed the largely unplanned nature of such trajectories. But it was essential to recognize the impact of later ruling class initiatives to abolish traditional violent practices including aristocratic duelling (Elias 2012 [1939]: 439). From the outset, the relevant offensives provoked powerful resistance among noble groups for whom the use of force to protect honour was a sacred entitlement. In their eyes, duelling was an ancient symbol of aristocratic identity, a timeless emblem of superiority over the lower ranks. But traditional rights to force were first eroded and then suspended as the consolidation of state monopolies of power advanced hand-in-hand with the taming of the warriors (Elias 2012 [1939]: 222, 409ff; see also Elias 2013: ch 2).

With internal pacification, public acts of violence that had been prized elements of, for example, French regal ceremony came to be seen as cruel and barbaric. To illustrate the movement that was under way, Elias (2012 [1939]: 197–8) referred to the custom of cat burning in Paris in the 16th century, often in the presence of the king and queen. Repugnance towards such practices and the reduced tolerance of cruelty to animals in 'blood sports' from the Victorian era to present times typified the overall course of the civilizing process (Elias and Dunning 2008; see also Thomas 1984). Process-sociological investigations of those changes can be taken further by noting related shifts regarding the civilized display of animals evident in the extraordinary menagerie which Louis XIV constructed at Versailles in 1662. The exhibition of domesticated, wild animals did not just symbolize royal power over nature. Displaying non-predatory birds that were selected for their graceful movement in lavishly gilded cages was designed to mirror the dignified comportment and refined gestures of the court nobility. Replaced in the process was the old convention of staging bloody animal combats at Vincennes. Such spectacles of violence had become anathema to a court society that valued the 'theatre of ... civility' over the 'theatre of the wild' (Sahlins 2012: 250). The menagerie at Versailles was not designed just to represent courtly elegance for the education or entertainment of the French aristocratic elite. Its broader function was to communicate the power and grandeur of French court society to the lower strata as well as to visiting ambassadors and foreign dignitaries.

The reconstitution of punitive measures similarly revealed how forms of violence came to be seen as repulsive and as incongruous in civilized society. Without compunction, early modern states used agonizing punishments that included burning and beheading as well as blinding and amputation in order to torture and degrade criminals. Painful ordeals could be drawn out over several days. They were carefully choreographed public spectacles of suffering and demonstrations of state power that served the purpose of instilling fear in subjects. So was the public execution of criminals and political enemies. In that period, people regularly gathered in large numbers in town centres to witness the violent death of prisoners. Process-sociological investigations have shown how later transformations of prevailing attitudes towards 'brutalising public punishments' including the death penalty signalled the direction of the civilizing process (Pratt 2004). Many empirical studies that have referred to civilizing tendencies without adopting an Eliasian standpoint have shed light on the overall momentum. They have shown that during the 19th century increasingly powerful middle-class groups in Britain and elsewhere expressed revulsion at the callousness of the lower classes at 'carnivalesque' gatherings as well as disgust at their plain indifference to the traumatic experience of the victims. Reform organizations launched influential 'civilizing offensives' to move the execution of prisoners 'behind the scenes' (Gatrell 1994). Other studies have shown how the moral conviction that the death penalty is incompatible with civilization gained higher levels of public support from the middle of the 20th century (Taïeb 2014). Those inquiries broadly confirm Elias's discussion of how concerns about the suffering of the victim deepened with the civilizing process. They reinforce his argument that emotional identification between people tended to increase – but not in an even or unilinear way – with their incorporation in the complex webs of interdependence that were made possible by new forms of state-led social organization.

As a consequence of evolving attitudes to violence, public opposition to the death penalty and to other perceived forms of cruel, inhumane and degrading punishment became 'second nature' or part of the habitus of civilized peoples. Such shifts further substantiated the main argument of Elias's analysis of the civilizing process, as have the 'entanglements' that arose in the lives of the people involved. Those contortions appeared in connection with the death penalty and also with respect to the 'torture debate'. Disputes about whether capital punishment is consistent with civilized sentiments regarding unnecessary suffering have occurred repeatedly in the United States. Claims to humanize capital punishment by administering lethal injections that cause painless death have been said to contravene the 1791 Eighth Amendment to the American Constitution, which outlawed 'cruel and unusual punishments' (Gatrell 1994; Banner 2002). At the centre of specialist legal deliberations in the US legal system and in the wider public debate has been the issue of whether 'medicalized' killing inevitably causes unacceptable physical pain and mental anguish. As already noted in Chapter 1, similar controversies regarding efforts to calculate levels of pain surfaced in critical assessments of attempts by the Bush administration to restrict the meaning of torture to methods of interrogation that cause the most severe forms of pain and suffering. Rebutting the fundamental premise, the December 2004 Levin Memorandum stated that no 'precise, objective, scientific criteria for measuring pain' currently exist (see Greenberg and Dratel 2005: sections 2340–2340a). Contrasts with earlier periods where there were few constraints on state power reveal the distinctiveness of civilized sensibilities about violence and suffering.

Citations from the writings of Burke and Mill were used earlier to describe key features of the European civilizing process. One further quotation from the latter's works usefully summarized elements of civilized self-images. In his essay on civilization, Mill (1977 [1836]:130–1) referred to the 'callousness to human suffering' in antiquity and added that 'the pain which they inflicted ... did not appear to them as great an evil, as it appears, and as it really is, to us, nor did it in any way degrade their minds'. He observed that in the modern period the infliction of pain is 'kept more and more out of sight of those classes who enjoy the ... benefits of civilization'; indeed it had been 'delegated by common consent to peculiar and narrow classes: to the judge, the soldier, the surgeon, the butcher, and the executioner' (Mill 1977 [1836]: 130–1). He stated that 'a great part of refinement consists' in 'avoiding the presence not only of actual pain, but of whatever suggests offensive or disagreeable ideas' (Mill 1977 [1836]: 130–1).

The first part of the quotation exemplifies Elias's discussion of the 'advancing threshold of repugnance' regarding acts of violence – the increasing levels of shock or disgust at the 'irruption' of physical force in social interactions, all the more so given that modern peoples, unlike their medieval forbears, rarely witness violence in public domains (Elias 2012 [1939]: 90; Mennell 1998: 106). In short, the level of interpersonal violence declined overall, albeit unevenly, with the appearance of the state's monopoly control of the means of coercion and with changes in the balance of power between compliance with social standards that was motivated by the fear of external sanctions, and conformity that was anchored in self-control or conscience (see the extensive review of the literature which is relevant to this analysis of the civilizing process in Pinker 2011: ch 3). From that standpoint, it is scarcely surprising that civilized peoples have been horrified by the 'medieval barbarism' of organizations such as 'IS' – not just the practice of beheading captives but also the act of broadcasting such spectacles on the internet in the calculated attempt to horrify civilized peoples and to instil fear (Steele 2019: ch 5).

The second part of Mill's statement, which described the place of the soldier in civilized societies, reflects Elias's thesis that state-controlled instruments of force became confined to sequestered 'barracks' with the trend towards internal pacification; typically, they only emerged from that hidden 'storehouse' under emergency conditions of 'war or social upheaval' (Elias 2012 [1939]: 411). The larger point was that societies had become accustomed to delegating gory acts of violence to specialists such as butchers who practised their trade behind closed doors where they could not offend civilized sensibilities. Elias finessed the point by arguing that the wider population believed that state officials such as the police, or the executioner in Mill's example, should respect social rules governing force. They were expected to comply with established legal and moral norms prohibiting gratuitous violence and cruelty. Key features of the recent torture debate are worth recalling at this juncture. Public expectations that states will use coercive power in civilized ways explain why Western governments cannot openly admit to using torture or to contemplating its deployment 'for fear of being removed from office' or 'ostracized by "civilized" nations' (see p. 43). Revealingly, as noted previously, official deliberations about the meaning of torture were conducted behind the scenes, evading public controversy and close scrutiny. Relaxations of the use of force remained 'in the barracks'. Constraints on the recourse to deep interrogation techniques were circumvented by locating 'unlawful combatants' in Guantanamo Bay and by implementing the 'extraordinary renditions' programme in which terrorist suspects were despatched to hidden 'black sites' in allied countries (Barnes 2016a). Unsurprisingly, photographic images (released in 2004) of the painful and humiliating treatment of detainees at Abu Ghraib produced revulsion at violent behaviour that openly clashed with civilized self-understandings. They provided unwelcome reminders of how some civilized military personnel can descend rapidly to the brutality of savage enemies in wartime conditions, and not least because the discourses of civilization and barbarism were influential 'releaser symbols' (see p. 38). Here it is worth remembering Elias's emphasis on how civilizing and decivilizing processes always coexist in the same societies, and how civilizing restraints on violence can 'crumble very rapidly' under conditions of insecurity – more quickly than many citizens realize (Elias 2012 [1939]: 576).

The third part of Mill's remarks on civilization identified a theme that can make uncomfortable reading for civilized people; this is that, to a considerable degree, refinement consists' in avoiding the 'offensive' or 'disagreeable' – in concealing them 'behind the scenes' in Elias's language. Particularly salient is the evidence that large numbers of people seem prepared to condone limited transgressions of civilized norms when they fear for their security – and many will support more serious violations as long as they are kept out of view and so do not openly contradict professed ethical convictions. Suffice it to add that the effects of the civilizing process are often exhibited in national concerns about the reputational costs of violating civilized norms. It is revealing that photographic images of the treatment of detainees at Abu Ghraib resulted in the condemnation of an 'aberrant minority' of military personnel who had been 'delegated', in Mill's formulation, with the use of the instruments of coercion for the benefit of the wider society (Tucker and Triantafyllos 2008). The clear implication was that a 'minority of the best' in the United States armed forces had failed to honour the responsibilities of civilized peoples. Through such devices, regimes have endeavoured to protect the nation's reputation for respecting civilized practices, including the uncompromising condemnation of cruelty and excessive violence. Elias was all too aware of such potentials in civilized societies. Contrary to any assumptions that he advanced a rose-tinted image of civilization, his analysis recognized the tensions and contradictions that complicate the lives of civilized peoples.

To draw this part of the inquiry to a close, it may be useful to recall how the manners books were tied up with distinctions between the more and less civilized in European societies and with related contrasts between the established and the outsiders in the global order. Changing intra-societal attitudes to violence had similar effects. Two interwoven trajectories were integral to the greater individuation of people – to a gradual process of division or separation which Elias (2010c: part three) described as the overall reconfiguration of the 'we/I balance' (see also the discussion of human rights on p. 194ff). First, Elias's analysis of the emergence of civilized manners emphasized the erection of the barriers between people in the context of revised emotional attitudes to the body. What would come to be regarded as rights to privacy were later expressions of deepening individuation in the reconfigured we/I balance. Second, as part of the same process, claims to physical integrity – to controls over one's own body – were asserted against state authorities that regarded the wounding of subjects as a legitimate means of punishment and necessary symbolic demonstration of absolute power. Middle-class civilizing campaigns to abolish judicial torture and to bring an end to cruel and degrading forms of punishment were not confined within national borders. Endeavours to globalize the prohibition of torture and to achieve the worldwide abolition of capital punishment are further expressions of the phase of the European civilizing process in which universal-egalitarian moral principles became influential in configuring social and political organization (Schabas 1997; see also Manners 2002 and Hobson 2013). All of those developments must be viewed as part of the long-term trends which Elias (2012 [1939]: 89) summarized by citing a key passage in Caxton's *Book of Curtesye*, 1477, in which he declared that 'thingis somtyme alowed is now repreuid' ('things that were once permitted are now forbidden'). That observation crystallized the reality that many were aware that social standards were changing. It was a useful 'motto for the whole movement' – the civilizing process – that was to come (Elias

2012 [1939]: 89). But that was not a movement that was destined to continue indefinitely, either within state-organized societies or in their external relations.

Decivilizing processes, Eurocentrism and progress

It has been difficult for process sociologists to shake off a recurring assumption in the scholarly literature that Elias's analysis of the civilizing process recast the theory of progress in several 19th-century grand narratives. The contention that the Holocaust had falsified any notion that Europeans had undergone a 'civilizing process' is one example of lingering misunderstandings of the approach (Bauman 1989; see Dunning and Mennell 1998). However, in the preface to his major study (2012 [1939]), Elias could not have been clearer that one of his main objectives was to comprehend the social and political turmoil across Europe 'in whose shadow we all live' (see p. 17). Undertaken in that context, the study of the civilizing process set out to explain social and political processes in a period of escalating dangers. Only much later, in his study, *The Germans*, did Elias use concepts such as the 'breakdown of civilization' and the 'regression to barbarism' to reflect on how the Nazi genocides could have occurred in a highly civilized European society (Elias 2013 [1989]: 233ff).

The investigation concentrated on the interdependencies between the social and political forces and psychological changes that were at the heart of an endangered civilizing process – specifically, on relations between class rivalries and state-formation, the interplay between domestic and international politics, and the customary emotional attitudes to violence in the relations between internal political units as well as at the inter-state level. Particular attention was paid to the formation of state structures, given their part in imposing external restraints on conduct which were steadily converted into inner restraints, as discussed earlier. Their 'second nature' quality was not easily eroded when stable state institutions were the ultimate guarantor of public order. They were prone to collapse whenever people feared for their security because of the weakening of state power and authority – and especially so if stable state structures had not developed in the first place (Elias 2012 [1939]: 484–5, 576). Struggles to seize control of state institutions and to use the instruments of violence to defeat internal enemies could then rapidly escalate with the result that balances of power between civilizing and decivilizing processes shifted dramatically.

Elias's primary study of those propensities focused on Germany's social and political development. Only a brief summary of key themes is possible here. A central argument was that the aristocratic warrior tradition survived for longer in German society than in comparable societies such as Britain and France. There was no German equivalent to the directions of change in those societies in which the bourgeoisie gradually gained entry into, and acquired a greater share of power in, one centrally organized, standard-setting court society (Elias 2013: 54ff). Competition between different courts prior to the unification of Germany in 1871 under Bismarck had ensured the continued hegemony of the aristocracy over bourgeoisie groups that espoused universal and egalitarian principles but to little effect. The deeply held belief that force was inescapable to resolve internal disputes and to settle inter-state conflicts commanded strong support because of the distinctive balance of class forces and nature of German state-formation. The humanistic moral code had limited political power in Germany during and after unification before being crushed under National Socialism. Moreover, the wider realm of inter-state rivalries had made its mark on one of the distinctive features of German political development: the predominance of group attachments to the 'praise word', *Kultur*, over the French idea of a universal civilization (see p. 59). National Socialism had shown the exceptional vulnerability of civilized restraints on force in the context of interconnected domestic and international crises. It revealed how state monopoly powers could be used to organise bureaucratized mass slaughter even though, as subsequent process-sociological investigations and other inquiries have maintained, genocidal killing was compartmentalized and carefully placed 'behind the scenes' in wartime conditions (de Swaan 2001, 2015).

Elias's observation that European peoples were largely unprepared for the processes of decivilization that occurred under the Nazi regime was mentioned earlier. The predominant orientations to social and political arrangements blinded many to the possibility that such horrors could erupt on the European continent. Unsurprisingly, the inhabitants of civilized societies were deeply shocked by the first visual images of the death camps – by the realization that an advanced society could organize mass killing on such a scale. Those images clashed with tacit assumptions that civilized peoples were superior to their European ancestors and to non-Western savages. 'Almost world-wide revulsion' at the killings reflected the assumption that 'in the twentieth century such barbarities could no longer happen' in civilized societies (Elias 2008e: 124). Crucially, the Nazi genocides 'served as a kind of warning' that modern restraints on violence were not part of the '*nature*' of civilized societies but were features of a 'type of social development

[that] could be reversed' (Elias 2008e: 124–5: italics in original). Elias considered the distinctive features of a German variant on the civilizing process while advising that it would be unwise to conclude that Germany would forever represent the solitary counter-example to the main course of European development. The relationship between German state-formation and the decivilizing process should not block the realization that the 'regression to barbarism' was not exactly divorced from the unprecedented organizational capabilities of modern societies such as the capacity to harness bureaucratic modes of control to administer industrialized killing (Elias 2013: 225). No civilized society was guaranteed permanent immunity from tilts in the power balances between civilizing and decivilizing processes that could culminate in similar violence.

Elias believed that presumptions about the natural state of civilization contributed to the myth that genocide could not occur in the region, but he failed to develop the observation. To do so it would have been necessary to recognize how the colonization of non-European societies contributed to a shared confidence in the global superiority of their science, technology, manners and overall attunement to the world. What Elias described as the efforts by non-European governing elites to incorporate European beliefs and practices in their own moral codes in the current phase of the civilizing process almost certainly reinforced the myths of superiority and separateness – the belief that Europeans had arrived at an advanced condition by their endeavours alone and the corollary that the primary challenge was to export civilization to backward regions (Elias (2012 [1939]: 426). As discussed earlier, postcolonial critics of process sociology have remonstrated against what they see as its 'civilizational isolationism'. It is necessary to ask, however, whether Elias's perspective contributes to postcolonial sociology by explaining how the global power shifts that occurred in the colonial era led to the judgement that European civilization was a natural state of affairs that owed nothing of substance to the wider global interconnections that have been analyzed by postcolonial scholars. Elias's use of italics in a previously cited passage invites the question of whether the aim was to stress that Europeans came to think that they had always held the upper hand in different spheres of human endeavour. That passage described how the European world believed in the 'special character' of '*its* technology... *its* manners [and] the development of *its* scientific knowledge' as opposed to calling attention to *its* part in adopting and augmenting scientific, technological and other breakthroughs that had occurred previously in other regions (see p. 60). The reasons for italicization are unclear but the statement can be read as implying that, in the context of new power balances, European peoples constructed images of themselves as a global establishment that was not indebted to, among other things, the scientific and technological achievements of outsider societies. At the very least, the observation contains the outlines of an account of the development of narratives of 'civilizational isolationism' that contributed to dangerous self-delusions. In short, stark contrasts between highly rational European societies that had succeeded in taming violence and non-European tribal peoples who were prone to engage in frenzied killing may have contributed to the diffusion of tacit assumptions that genocidal slaughter could no longer occur in the civilized world.

Core concepts in process sociology can therefore be deployed to explain the appearance of civilizational superiority and isolationism in the age of imperialism. Even so, postcolonial critics can reasonably argue that Elias's sparse observations about the relationship between overseas expansion and the civilizing process led to a limited understanding of the Europeans' lack of preparedness for, and subsequent shock at, the Nazi genocides. Recent studies of the Holocaust have emphasized Hitler's image of an anticolonial struggle against the Jewish 'invasion' in order to show how imperial practices of stigmatizing racial 'inferiors' were integral to state-organized, industrial murder (Moses 2010). In their professed struggle for survival with the Bolsheviks and the Jews, the Nazi regime imported violent practices into Europe that the colonial powers had long employed in relations with non-European 'savages', thereby confirming the prediction made by Rosa Luxembourg and others that imperial violence would blow back into the European continent (Moses 2008). The inevitable question is whether the Europeans would have been better prepared for the 'breakdown of civilization' – and more adequately equipped to resist or prevent Nazi 'decivilizing' offensives – if the history of colonial genocide had been more firmly in their minds and if they had not largely discounted the possibility that a political movement within Europe could gain control of the state's monopoly of violence and harness colonial and racial imagery in an alleged war of survival. But that was not just a deficiency in public consciousness. The same lacuna ran through the classical sociological tradition of which Elias's writings were part.

Conclusion

This chapter has shown that the Eliasian analysis of the civilizing process attempted to explain the connections between state-formation, internal pacification, lengthening webs of interdependence, the development of a complex social division of labour, changing class relations and major shifts in the emotional lives of the people involved, as exemplified by increased repugnance towards acts of violence and new expressions of shame and embarrassment that reflected the evolving social standards contained in leading manners books. One of Elias's primary contentions was that the relative influence of internal as opposed to external restraints – the balance of power between them – altered in conjunction with the dominant understandings of what is permissible and forbidden in civilized societies. The investigation replaced the somewhat static idea of civilization – with its connotation of invariable properties – with the notion of fluid, ever-changing civilizing processes. As discussed in the introduction to this work, process concepts were employed to explain unfinished and reversible developments. The overall direction of change was not presumed to be permanent but was regarded as easily weakened, especially when fears for security arose. As part of a more synoptic examination of long-term processes, unusual emphasis was placed on the complex interdependencies between intra- and inter-societal dynamics. Those interconnections were, for Elias, the key to understanding how struggles between groups within civilized societies and conflicts between states could unravel the constraints on violence. Elias's detached examination of the process of civilization therefore confronted the more involved notions of a civilized condition which underpinned the collective pride of modern peoples and distracted them from the deficiencies and limitations of their forms of life.

As the last section of this chapter maintained, Elias's perspective was not a triumphalist interpretation of the rise of Europe but a non-evaluative account of the European civilizing process. Elias anticipated more recent analyses of state structures by examining the links between the domestic and international political struggles that had affected European state-formation, but this approach now seems dated by virtue of the scant attention paid to the relationship between state-formation, colonial domination and the emergence of discourses of civilization. The importance of 'civilization' for European colonial expansion was recognized, but there was no systematic examination of how the relations between the European global establishment and non-European outsiders coloured civilized self-images. To advance Elias's inquiry, it is therefore necessary to explain how the civilizing process was influenced by the interdependencies between state-formation, colonialism and international society in the imperial and post-imperial eras. Some preliminary steps will be taken in the next chapter which discusses Elias's analysis of the different standards of restraint that have applied in relations within and between civilized societies. Chapter 3 emphasises that the gulf between intra- and inter-state restraints on violence was even greater in Europe's relations with the colonized peoples. The following three chapters (4–6) broaden the discussion by considering what the European standard of civilization disclosed about the links between state-formation, empire and international society, how it shaped the dominant images of the global order from around the late 19th to the middle of the 20th century, and what its contestation in the more recent period reveals about the prospects for a global civilization or worldwide civilizing process.

3

The Nation-State, War and Human Equality

Elias's exploration of the course of the civilizing process was principally focused on explaining long-run developments within the leading European societies but, as this chapter explains, his inquiry also encompassed relations between states with their monopoly control of the instruments of violence. As noted in the Introduction, Elias was rare among sociologists of his generation in firmly rejecting any investigations of social processes that neglected inter-societal relations. Throughout his writings – and often in unexpected places, including works on modern attitudes to dying and death and on the sociology of knowledge – Elias returned to a discussion of the impact of relations between states on the formation and transformation of human societies (see Elias 2007, 2010). He argued that the analysis of the inseparability of intra- and inter-state 'lines of development' represented a major advance beyond the dominant iterations of the classical sociological tradition (see p. 262, note 2).

Why did Elias accord the international domain such prominence in the study of the civilizing process? The answer is that the modern European states which had been the crucible in which civilized practices developed were also one of the main threats to their survival. Elias (2010: 5) referred to the 'Janus-faced' nature of state-formation to describe the recurrent feature of human history in which 'internal pacification' has coexisted with 'outward threat' and with permanent readiness for war. The most recent centuries reflected that long-standing condition. Achievements in pacifying modern societies facilitated the creation of complex social interconnections and interwoven assumptions about the nature of civil or civilized relations. But the same states were entangled in competitive relations that often ended in devastating violence. They had repeatedly displayed the willingness to cause levels of human suffering in military conflicts that clashed with professed civilized standards of behaviour. Moreover, stable state-organized societies with high levels of domestic support and considerable fiscal reserves that were the result of the monopoly control of public taxation had accumulated military capabilities without precedent. Modern peoples could pride themselves in the relative freedom from the danger of violence in everyday public encounters in their respective societies. The paradox was high exposure to violence that was no longer confined to the distant battlefield but could be inflicted in densely populated urban centres. In the post-Second World War period, civilized people were accustomed to high levels of personal security within nation-states but they were conscious of the very real danger of mass incineration in nuclear war (Elias 2007: 137ff; Elias 2010: 125ff).

The upshot was that relations between states in the modern era were not fundamentally different from – or manifestly more civilized than – relations between societies in the age of 'primitive' warfare (Elias 2007a: 125ff). The reality was that 'a curious split runs through our civilization' in the form of a stark division between, on the one hand, the standards of civilized behaviour in 'intra-state affairs' where 'violence among people is tabooed and, when possible, punished' and in 'inter-state relations where another code holds good' and where those who use force against other states are 'extremely highly valued' (Elias 2013 [1989]: 190–1). A perennial feature of the relations between peoples – however 'savage' or 'civilized' – is that violent acts that are prohibited and sanctioned in one sphere are 'in many cases praised and rewarded' in the other (Elias 2013 [1989]: 191). Those comments further underline the error in thinking that Elias supported a modern version of the idea of progress.

Part one of this chapter provides a summation of Elias's position on the timeless contrasts between the two spheres of domestic and international politics. Part two turns to a seeming tension within the approach which was the starting point for an earlier work (Linklater 2016: introduction), namely the conflict between the contention that the relations between peoples have barely altered in crucial respects since the age of humanity's so-called barbarism and the observation that modern peoples are shocked by genocidal killing, as the standard attitudes to violence and civilization would lead students of the European civilizing process to expect (Linklater 2016: introduction). The issue is explored further by examining Elias's ingenious discussion of the 'duality of nation-state normative codes', an expression that described recurring conflicts between the advocates of Machiavellian statecraft and the proponents of the fundamental rights of individual persons. The concept reflected the empirical reality that civilized peoples have not only struggled with various ethical problems that grow out of the complex interdependencies in the same society; they have also wrestled with moral claims about the imperative of restraining the use of force in conflicts with other societies. Resulting tensions between Machiavellian conceptions of power politics and normative doctrines that urge controls of force are built into civilized societies and the global order which is largely their invention.

As discussed in Chapter 1, some of the distinctive 'torments' of civilized societies were apparent in the tensions between competing positions on the 'anti-torture norm'. The 'torture debate' indicated how disputes about the morality of force can erupt in civilized societies and how the power balances between the advocates of Machiavellian approaches and of humanistic moral codes can fluctuate in unexpected ways. The very existence of those debates is evidence of unique features of the foreign policy perspective of civilized states which coexist with the striking similarities of state behaviour across human history. The former modified the Janus-faced nature of state-organized societies by introducing unique ethical controversies and entanglements. How far the universal and egalitarian dimensions of nation-state moral codes introduced new possibilities for civilizing the global order is an intriguing question to discuss later.

The third part of this chapter, which resonates with postcolonial sensibilities, recognizes that the 'split within civilization' was even deeper in colonial encounters between the 'civilized' and the 'savage' than in relations between 'civilized' peoples. Discourses of civilization were used to justify colonial violence in a parallel with the Machiavellian argument for the relaxation of ethical restraints in relations between societies. But, reflecting the duality of moral codes, many critics of abuses of imperial power sought to bring colonial authorities into line with the universal and egalitarian principles that are integral to the civilizing process. Part four discusses the overlapping trend from the middle of the 19th century in which the idea of civilization was used to promote respect for new standards of restraint on violence in the interactions between the sovereign members of European international society. Reformist associations set out to move the balance of power between Machiavellian foreign policy and universalistic moral standpoints by attempting to embed new humanitarian laws of war in the global order. Their civilizing legacy includes post-Second World War initiatives to construct the universal human rights culture, international criminal legal innovations, and the more permissive attitudes to humanitarian intervention that made a fleeting appearance in the aftermath of the end of the bipolar era before counter-trends once again gained the upper hand. Elias's reflections on the relations between states provide a distinctive approach to the fluctuating balances between such forces in civilized societies.

The two logics of domestic and international politics

There are similarities between, on the one hand, Elias's observation that there is a high probability of competition and conflict between state-organized societies that depend – in the absence of a higher monopoly of power – on accumulating the instruments of violence for their security and survival and, on the other hand, classical state-centric realism in the study of international relations (Elias 2012 [1939]: 296–7). Common ground is the conviction that societies are trapped in a tragic condition which is not of their making and which is hard and may be impossible to escape. That bleak interpretation is embraced by Elias's contention that, in key respects, international politics in the modern era are little different from inter-group relations in the age of humanity's 'so-called "barbarism"' where there was also 'no monopoly of force on the international level' (Elias 2013 [1989]: 190). Equally dark images were conveyed by the statement that little appears to change in the history of relations between what Elias called survival units than the methods of killing and the number of people involved (Elias 2007: 175; Elias 2007a: 128–9). Relations between states in the modern period mirrored recurrent patterns in human history. The European state was the unplanned outcome of 'elimination contests' between warring nobles – of the 'monopoly mechanism' that resulted in novel territorial concentrations of power (Elias 2012 [1939]: 301ff). Violent competition was gradually suppressed with the establishment of stable territorial concentrations, but classical elimination contests and power monopolization did not cease at that point. They were driven upwards to the emerging international domain and gradually became worldwide in scope.

From that standpoint, international politics over the last few centuries are part of a long chain of events in which conflicts between different types of 'survival unit' (such as city-states, archaic states and ancient empires) resulted in larger territorial power constellations. Many imploded because of violent internal power struggles and/or because of warfare and the crippling economic and political costs of international competition. Nevertheless, an unmistakable overall trend towards ever larger 'survival units' had shaped human history over the millennia.

The dominant tendency might well continue until global political institutions emerged with monopoly control of the instruments of violence and the capacity to pacify humanity as a whole (Elias 2012 [1939]: 287). It was questionable, Elias (2007a: 141–2) argued, whether a worldwide civilizing process could develop otherwise. Whatever the future might hold, the sheer scale of inter-group violence had also increased in the course of successive elimination contests. For most of human history, most 'survival units' had been 'attack-and-defence' associations that dealt with localized perils and initiated small-scale military offensives when compared to the 20th-century globalization of industrial warfare (Elias 2012b: 133–4; Kaspersen and Gabriel 2008). The post-second World War era had witnessed the appearance of what Elias termed 'annihilation units' that could totally destroy each other – and much of humanity and the natural world in the process (Elias 2010c: 186ff). The open question was whether current dangers would have a taming or civilizing effect on superpower rivalries. The issue was whether external compulsions would result in collaborative efforts that avoided the hegemonic wars that resulted from past great power struggles (Elias 2010: 90ff, 119ff).

Elias's contention that the modern state was both the crucible of civilizing processes and the main threat to their survival was taken further in a detailed explanation of destructive forces; this has parallels with realist explanations in International Relations, but there are significant differences. The focus on material interests is very much at the centre of those approaches which have been criticized for ignoring the role of group emotions such as fear, anger and resentment in inter-state struggles (Bleiker and Hutchison 2014). No such accusation can be directed at Eliasian sociology where the inquiry provided a more comprehensive sociological investigation of the emotional aspects of struggles that trap states in uncontrolled violent processes.

Central to the mode of analysis was the idea of the 'double-bind process' which referred to how the 'low ability to control dangers' can promote high fantasy content world views that contribute to the escalation of tensions (Elias 2007: 116, 137). The concept captured the reality that 'the less amenable a particular sphere of events is to human control, the more emotional will be people's thinking about it'; moreover, 'the more emotional and fantasy-ridden their ideas, the less capable they will be of constructing more accurate models of these nexuses, and thus of gaining greater control over them' (Elias 2012b: 152). Inter-state struggles had long been governed by double-bind processes with those properties. In that domain, the principal adversaries have often regarded themselves as 'uniformly good, while rivals or enemies tend to have no merits at all' and are presumed to be 'bad all round' (Elias 2007: 9). Sharp contrasts between 'the minority of the best' within their respective societies and 'the minority of worst' in other groups have flourished in such circumstances (see p. 41; see also Elias 2007: 11, 160ff). Each adversary can then take the view that its deep fears and actions are self-evidently 'rational' and 'right'; each can hold the other or others totally responsible for its anxieties and insecurities; and each can become convinced that security can only be achieved by crushing or eliminating foes (Elias 2007: 171).

Moreover, with the tightening of a vice of mutually reinforcing fears and suspicions, rivals often found it increasingly difficult to look 'at themselves [and] at each other' along with 'the whole situation' in which they find themselves with 'a measure of detachment' or in a realistic manner (Elias 2007: 11). In circumstances where short-term orientations dominate, the images that 'people have of themselves and each other' can become 'astonishingly simplistic' (Elias 2007: 9). Different parties can then descend into the extremes of doctrinal rigidity coupled with patterns of 'reciprocal stigmatisation' that make their relations less calculable and less secure (Elias 2007: 159, 173). The analysis of double-bind spirals therefore summed up the interdependencies between fear, insecurity, and unplanned and unwanted chains of events that included deepening enmities and the heightened risk of war. Those processes were at the heart of Elias's perspective on the contrast between domestic and international politics and on the obstacles to a global counterpart to intra-societal civilizing advances that could reduce the age-old differences between those realms.

At this juncture, it is useful to return to the discussion of the working principles of process sociology, and specifically to the necessity of the 'detour via detachment' for the acquisition of 'reality-congruent' knowledge about unplanned social processes – the eighth theme considered in the Introduction. As the discussion has just shown, the question of detachment was not confined to specialist discussions about the purposes of sociological inquiry. The idea of the double-bind process was used to show how social groups can become so involved in attributing blame to their adversaries that they fail to comprehend how they are propelled in directions that no one foresaw or desired (van Benthem van den Bergh 1986; Elias 2012b: 161).

Elias's inquiry into the ascendancy of involvement over detachment in struggles between societies drew on two other themes discussed in the Introduction – the image of the sociologist as the 'destroyer of myths' (or fantasy-laden perspectives) and the thesis that sociologists had to free social inquiry from parochial nation-state attachments and promote the advancement of the ' "human" means of orientation' (van Benthem van den Bergh 1986). Linking those themes was the need for closer investigation of one of the 'roots of the dangers which human groups constitute for each other', namely the 'remarkable propensity' of individuals to project part of their 'self-love into specific social units' that offer powerful feelings of collective 'identity' and the considerable emotional rewards of 'belonging' (Elias 2007: 8). It was essential to discover more about how connections between individual self-esteem and group pride could expose political leaders or groups that made the case for a more detached analysis of the prospects for negotiation and conciliation to accusations of weakness, if not outright disloyalty. Such reactions entrenched the power of the 'split within civilization' on foreign policy conduct and on the configuration of the global order. The upshot was that international relations in different periods have been remarkably similar although, Elias added, nuanced ethical perspectives emerged in civilized societies with the development of dualistic nation-state moral codes.

Chapter 1 explored those themes with reference to the discourse of a war against the 'enemies of civilization' in United States government statements and in public responses to the national humiliation of the 9/11 attacks in 2001. The relaxation of the constraints on torture may seem to confirm Elias's thesis that the core dimensions of inter-societal rivalries do not encourage optimism about future directions. A key question is whether any countervailing tendencies may gain the upper hand in the longer term. More specifically, the issue is whether there is any immediate prospect of global shifts in the relations between internal and external constraints that echo the general course of the European civilizing process.

Here it is valuable to consider Elias's disagreement with van Benthem van den Bergh (Mennell 1998: 219–23). In the leading process-sociological investigation of nuclear weapons, the latter described the balance of terror as the 'functional equivalent of a monopoly of power' – as the source of levels of prudence, self-restraint, foresight and detachment that Elias regarded as improbable in the absence of the global monopolization of the instruments of violence (van Benthem van den Bergh 1992). As evidenced most famously by the 1962 Cuban missile crisis and the diplomatic aftermath, the destructiveness of nuclear warfare exerted a taming or civilizing effect that is rare in the history of struggles between the great powers. The analysis clashed with Elias's contention in the study of the civilizing process that although international tensions had become more risky and incentives had increased 'to resolve future interstate conflicts by less dangerous means', the deeper, long-term trend towards the 'formation of monopolies of physical force over larger areas of the earth' through violence might be unstoppable (Elias 2012 [1939]: 488–9).

Returning to those issues almost five decades later, Elias struck a slightly different chord. With the invention of nuclear weapons, he contended, the great powers could no longer embark on the 'hegemonic wars' that had occurred repeatedly in the relations between their predecessors. Any attempt to attain dominance by overpowering or eliminating principal adversaries risked a return to 'life in caves' (Elias 2010 [1985]: 78, 128). Pressures had mounted to dampen great power tensions by controlling the temptation to engage in mutual demonization and by promoting 'ideological disarmament' (Elias 2010 [1985]: 153ff). But Elias was far from sanguine about the future. Human societies faced a stark choice between returning to the cave and learning how to avert the dangers of nuclear warfare. But nothing was pre-ordained. It was unwise to assume that 'realistic knowledge of the unprecedented destructiveness of warfare in our age … is enough to break the impetus of the self-perpetuating tradition of war between survival groups', not least 'while the institutions and above all the collective feelings and attitudes of such groups retain their traditional character' (Elias 2007 [1987]: 10–11). To think otherwise was to show how 'wishful thinking' so often displaces the 'more detached view' or the 'long term diagnosis oriented towards facts, however unwelcome' (Elias 2007 [1987]: 10–11). Underpinning the argument was the supposition that the internalization of restraints on force is far too weak to prevent future eruptions of the downward spiral of double-bind forces. As a result, the diplomatic achievements in taming superpower rivalries as discussed by van Benthem van den Bergh (1992) might turn out to be short-lived rather than presaging an end to the long history of great power elimination contests. Standards of restraint were weak because they were not part of the close interweaving of peoples and because they were not accompanied by profound alterations in psychological traits such as the 'civilization' of attitudes to violence that occurred alongside state-formation and substantial internal pacification. Nothing had altered the reality that the majority of people continued to identify strongly with the 'survival unit' which they regarded as the indispensable guarantor of personal and collective security. The supposition that force could justifiably be used to resolve major inter-state conflicts remained firmly embedded in the social habitus and world views of civilized peoples.

As Chapter 7 will explain, that was not Elias's final position on world politics. A more nuanced argument stressed the ways in which increasing global social and economic interdependencies had introduced new pressures to create 'survival units' such as the European Union that complemented, and might one day even supplant, sovereign nation-states. But there was no warranty that post-national or post-sovereign associations and loyalties would emerge that removed the 'split within civilization'. The 'growing integration of humanity' in the recent period could be reversed by a 'powerful disintegration process' with powerful 'decivilizing' consequences (Elias 2010c: 202). Notwithstanding the attractions and benefits of closer international cooperation, there was no hard empirical evidence of pronounced or especially secure civilizing advances in world politics. There was therefore little reason to think that relations between states in the contemporary period were on course to break with the governing trends since the earliest times although, looking further ahead, such a trajectory was not impossible (Elias 2010c: 186–7).

The 'duality of nation-state normative codes'

Elias's analysis of the 'split within civilization' stated that restraints on the use of force within societies had made little impact on relations between societies over the millennia. Recurring double-bind spirals had shaped world politics. They were the key to explaining the 'immanent order of change' that had been the focus of thinkers such as Comte, Spencer and Marx – the structured rather than haphazard developments in which elimination contests produced larger territorial concentrations of power that conducted geopolitical struggles over greater areas with ever more violent means (Elias 2012b: 145). On one level, the European civilizing process did not break with traditional assumptions about the legitimacy of force in international power struggles and conflicts. But, on another level, civilized societies were distinctive because of contradictions between national ideals and universal and egalitarian principles that underpinned various projects to restrain or eradicate forms of violent action that clashed with 'civilization'. To illustrate the point, Elias observed that civilized peoples were shocked by the Nazi genocides and supported the universal human rights culture in the attempt to prevent the return of such atrocities. The whole ethos can be regarded as one of the most recent expressions of the process of civilization – as revealing how steps have been taken in globalizing civilized prohibitions of violence as a consequence of political endeavours to alter the power relations between the nationalist-Machiavellian and universal-egalitarian elements of nation-state normative codes. The upshot is tangible inroads into traditional perceptions of the unbridgeable gulf between domestic and international politics and ongoing institutionalized efforts to 'civilize' the global order.

A detailed examination of the 'duality of nation-state normative codes' was included in a rich discussion of orientations to foreign policy in Elias's study, *The Germans* (Elias 2013 [1989]: 169ff). The investigation began with the observation that 'people are generally brought up to believe [that] it is wrong to kill, maim or attack human beings. ...They are at the same time taught to believe that it is right to do all these things, and to sacrifice their own lives, if that is found necessary in the interests of the sovereign society they form with each other' (Elias 2013 [1989]: 175). There is a parallel with reflections on the morality of statecraft in political theory and international relations which have stressed the duty of national leaders to override the standards of behaviour that are expected of citizens in their private capacity – alternatively, to overrule the dictates of conscience where they reject the use of force or to stand aside from public office which demands 'sacrifices of value' or the readiness to acquire 'dirty hands' when vital national security interests are at stake (Wolfers 1965; Elshtain 2004). What Elias added to standard accounts was a unique sociological focus on 'the duality of nation-state normative codes' in civilized societies that pointed the way towards more specific empirical inquiries.

The idea of the dual nature of nation-state moralities conveyed the fact that national populations are committed to 'a two-fold code of norms' with 'inherently contradictory' demands (Elias 2013 [1989]: 169). One dimension is 'egalitarian in character' and expresses the conviction that 'the single human being, the individual, is the supreme value' (Elias 2013 [1989]: 169, 174–5). The other is 'nationalist' and is 'descended from the Machiavellian code of princes ... whose highest value is a collectivity – the state, the country, the nation' (Elias 2013 [1989]: 169). From the first standpoint, there are occasions when the human rights of individuals should take precedence over national security claims whereas, from the second perspective, 'the sovereign collectivity, the nation-state, is the supreme value to which all individual aims and interests – even the physical survival of individuals – are to be subordinated' (Elias 2013 [1989]: 175). Elias drew on the philosophical writings of Henri Bergson to argue that there are times when civilized people are faced with the challenging question of which society has the greater claim on their sense of the most fundamental moral obligations – is it 'humanity as a whole' or the smaller constituency of 'compatriots' or 'fellow citizens' who are 'members of the same state'? (Elias 2013 [1989]: 169).

Those reflections on the relative importance of obligations to fellow-citizens and duties to humanity are not unfamiliar to historians of international political thought and students of international political theory (Linklater 1990 [1982]). But Elias's sociological perspective stressed that rarely do modern citizens have to face the competing moral claims that are integral to their civilized ways of life. For the most part, the argument ran, the related ethical dilemmas do not feature prominently in public deliberations or intrude into everyday life to the extent that people are confronted with a stark choice between the competing elements of a 'contradictory code of norms' (Elias 2013 [1989]: 176). In general, 'the contradictions, conflicts and tensions' which are inherent in 'civilized' orientations to the state and humanity 'may come into the open and become very acute only in specific situations, above all in national emergencies such as wars' (Elias 2013 [1989]: 176). In those circumstances, people may feel torn between Machiavellianism which defends using all necessary force to defeat adversaries and the humanitarian ethos which privileges the obligation to respect the rights of individuals to be spared unnecessary suffering. Whole societies may be divided as groups gravitate towards opposite ends of the moral spectrum. Elaborating the argument, Elias (2013 [1989]: 172) maintained that compromising or violating either of the two moral codes can 'expose an individual ... to punishment not only from others, but also from himself or herself in the form of guilt feelings, of a "bad conscience"'. Inner tensions between supporting the interests of the collectivity and defending the rights of individual persons were usually connected with wider fault lines in society. In the competition to influence public opinion, some political groups may 'lay greater stress ... on the values of the nationalist creed ... without necessarily completely abandoning those of the humanist, egalitarian moral tradition. The stress of others is the reverse, in a great variety of combinations' (Elias 2013 [1989]: 175). In the context of such power struggles, people may choose to align themselves with groups that stand at 'one or other pole of the spectrum', but a 'common feature of all societies of this type' is that most people occupy moral positions 'somewhere between these two poles' as they endeavour to reconcile or harmonize national security interests and the considerations of humanity (Elias 2013 [1989]: 175).

There is no need to look further than the 'torture debate' for an illustration of how moral tensions that do not usually preoccupy the inhabitants of civilized societies can erupt suddenly into the open and confront them with difficult choices regarding the claims of Machiavellian and humanitarian principles. It revealed how civilized peoples wrestle with the contradictory demands of a moral code, how some gravitate towards one or other of the moral poles, or how they link national and universal ethical claims in many different 'combinations' including attempts to resolve antithetical principles by occupying a middle point on the moral spectrum (see, for example, the discussion of 'judicial approval' and the 'torture warrant' on p. 48). The purpose of Elias's inquiry was to provide a sociological explanation of the origins and significance of such tensions and debates in civilized societies. His approach emphasized that movements in balances of power between class forces and the related reorganizing of state structures in the 19th century pushed universalistic claims to the centre of modern political discourse. The main contention was that the emergence of a 'contradictory code of norm' is 'one of the common features of all countries that have undergone the transition from an aristocratic-dynastic into a more democratic national state' (Elias 2013 [1989]: 176). Those clashes were a product of changing internal power relations, and specifically the rise of bourgeois forces that used commitments to universal and egalitarian moral principles in the struggle against absolutist rule and in opposition to the traditional code of the nobility which privileged military over non-military pursuits and virtues. The ascending middle classes scorned the aristocratic warrior code and envisaged a global political order in which peoples were ever more closely bound together by the pacifying or civilizing effects of commercial interdependence. But moral aspirations and political realities quickly came into collision. On gaining control of state power, the political representatives of bourgeois groups often compromised their ethical commitments by conducting foreign policy in orthodox Machiavellian ways (Elias 2013 [1989]: 71ff). Even so, they did not exactly abandon the universalistic and egalitarian beliefs that were at the core of shared middle-class ideals and identifications.

To recall an earlier point about the prevalence of perspectives that lie in the mid-point of the normative spectrum, bourgeois groups often placed universal ethical commitments at the heart of rousing images of an enlightened national identity. Political developments in 19th-century Britain revealed how the middle classes tried to 'amalgamate' the two moral codes in liberal visions of the humanitarian nation (Elias 2013 [1989]: 176). As a result, 'the mass of the people' came to expect 'that even Britain's foreign policy would be conducted in accordance with ... the principles of justice, human rights and help for the oppressed' although the actions of leaders such as Gladstone embodied the tensions within the habitus of 'middle class men' who sought to reconcile 'unswerving righteousness in principle with expediency, opportunism and compromise in practice' (Elias 2013 [1989]: 179, 184). The nation represented an 'ideal "we"' that provided collective emotional gratification by upholding moral principles that citizens did not always observe in everyday life (Elias 2013 [1989]: 181). Several other articulations, it might be added, peppered British political life in that era. One of the most memorable was the campaign to abolish the Atlantic slave trade; this promoted national pride through support for individual freedoms which provided incontrovertible evidence, so it was asserted, of British superiority over despotic rivals such as neighbouring France (Linklater 2016: 258–9). Further confirmation of Elias's theme was Palmerston's statement of support for political refugees which explicitly invoked the discourse of civilization. In the despatch of 6 October 1849 to British officials at Vienna and St Petersburg, he maintained that:

> if there is one rule more than any other that has been observed in modern times by independent states, both great and small, of the civilized world, it is the rule not to deliver up political refugees unless the state is bound to do so by the positive obligations of a treaty. … The laws of hospitality, the dictates of humanity, the general feelings of mankind, forbid such surrenders; [and] any independent government which of its own free will were to make such a surrender would be universally and deservedly stigmatised as degraded and dishonoured. (Correspondence respecting refugees from Hungary within the Turkish dominions presented to Parliament on 28 February 1851, nos 19 and 20, cited in Schuster 2003: 95, note 66)

The proclamation showed how the ideas of nation, civilization and humanity were intertwined in bourgeois conceptions of the normative code which argued that conscience should govern the course of action and that the failure to comply with civilized principles in the absence of specific treaty obligations should result in national disgrace and international condemnation. 'Nation' and 'humanity' were integrated in liberal characterizations of a civilized global order.

During the 19th century, nation-states as well as social groups and individuals in their own right occupied very different points on the moral spectrum. A comparison between the positions that successive German and British governments adopted on the tensions between the interests of the nation and humanitarian principles exemplifies the point (Elias 2013 [1989]: 177ff). In the case of Germany, collective feelings of insecurity that were tied to the fear that the society was engulfed by hostile enemies fuelled the conviction that Machiavellian precepts were indispensable in foreign policy. Government standpoints on the necessity of force, which reflected the relatively unchallenged dominance of the aristocracy in German court society, were not shared in Britain where, as has been noted, changing power balances between social classes had weakened the aristocratic warrior code. British governments professed their dedication to defend not just national self-interest but higher moral principles. The dominant German standpoint – shaped by the complex interweaving of class relations, late political unification and distinctive international struggles – dismissed such pronouncements as cynical ploys to disguise the self-serving objectives of British foreign policy. All talk of representing humanity and civilization was dismissed as little more than 'a piece of deliberate deception – of hypocrisy' (Elias 2013 [1989]: 178). Such divisions about the principles that should govern national policy contributed to the acrimonious nature of great power differences.

Such antagonistic positions were evidence then that the 'representative self-images and self-ideals of the members of different nations' can embody very different positions on a spectrum of opinion regarding the correct response to the contradictory nature of nation-state normative codes (Elias 2013 [1989]: 173). But there was a larger issue in Elias's inquiry which has considerable relevance for contemporary intra- and inter-societal power struggles and which is pregnant with suggestions for further empirical analysis (see p. 120ff). A key insight was that clashes between states are often interlaced with competing standpoints on the appropriate balance between national considerations and humanist values. This comment underlined a principal dimension of world politics which had been exemplified by the ways in which 'the interdependent states of the European power balance figuration' had tried to draw one another towards their respective images of the ideal relationship between national and international obligations and responsibilities (Elias 2013 [1989]: 182). Elias further maintained that the underlying disagreements often led to major 'blockages of communication between members of different state-societies' and helped to inflame or 'aggravate inter-state tensions', as in the case of British-German relations (Elias 2013 [1989]: 173). One of the main consequences – evident in the contemporary era as well as in past epochs – is that states often disagree bitterly about the standards of restraint that should be observed in foreign policy (Elias 2012

[1939]: 453, note 19). By extension, the development of the global order in the coming decades and centuries does not depend just on the reconciliation of clashing interests but on a deeper alignment of normative frameworks – on a broad consensus about how societies should resolve the tensions within nation-state moral codes or on a general agreement on how obligations to fellow citizens and duties to humanity should be balanced. Suffice it to add that analyses of global order and assorted political challenges are rarely discussed in those terms, either in diplomatic circles or in academic inquiries.

Elias observed that the historical record did not encourage much faith in the prospects for radical breakthroughs in that sphere. The reality was that throughout the history of relations between societies, adversaries had invariably promoted vital objectives more or less as they pleased unless deterred by the 'fear of retaliation by supernatural agencies'; only exceptionally had they concluded that it was prudent or necessary to cooperate closely to devise 'certain common rules of conduct and … corresponding restraints upon themselves' (Elias 2013 [1989]: 150–1). Separate 'strategies determined by fear and suspicion of others, and not subject to an agreed and effectively maintained common code' had fuelled 'self-perpetuating' cycles of insecurity or the 'double-bind processes' discussed earlier (Elias 2013 [1989]: 170–1; see Yair and Akbari 2014 for a contemporary discussion). As a general rule, a largely uncontested 'belief in the rightness and inevitability of conduct in inter-state relations along Machiavellian lines' had given rise to highly emotive societal responses to major tensions that contributed to such unchanging realities (Elias 2013 [1989]: 170). But, as noted in this section, complex interdependencies between class rivalries and state structures had created significant civilized constraints on governments that sought to free nationalist-Machiavellian orientations from humanitarian commitments with significant consequences for the global order.

That state of affairs revealed that an ethos of 'moderation' that was integral to the European civilizing process did indeed 'radiate outwards' onto the seemingly static realm of international politics (Elias 2008f: 102). Inter-state wars had become less cruel than conflicts in the Late Middle Ages or early modern Europe where armies lived off the land and exploited and tormented civilian communities (Elias 2006a). Demands to control violent and aggressive impulses were weaker in that era and warriors were usually less restrained. With increasingly mechanized warfare, armies became more disciplined, and the collective lust for killing was suppressed to some degree. Compared with their predecessors, modern warriors were required to undergo rigorous training, including psychological preparation for the ordeals of military combat. The transition from peace to war was demanding for the inhabitants of largely pacified, civilized societies. The contrast was with warriors in earlier periods who owned and habitually used their own weapons and who were, in addition, accustomed and attuned to witnessing death and suffering not just on the battlefield but in everyday life (Elias 2007 [1984]: 145). Moreover, as part of the trend towards lowering 'the threshold of repugnance' towards violence, modern warriors may have become more susceptible to psychological disorders – as embodied in the idea of post-traumatic stress syndrome – by virtue of having witnessed or transgressed social taboos against killing or injuring innocent civilians such as defenceless women and children (Elias 2008e: 113–14). Among civilized peoples, violating such prohibitions (or doing so without feelings of guilt or shame) reflects the mentality of the savage warrior (see also the discussion on p. 117ff).

Such examples of the recasting of social attitudes to violence in civilized societies were accompanied by many developments that Elias did not examine in detail (see Chapter 7 for further discussion). They include several respects in which civilized societies have gravitated towards the mid-point of the spectrum of nation-state normative codes and have indeed come to share broadly similar standards of restraint. Those developments are present in 'security communities' where a high level of emotional identification or 'we feeling' is linked with 'common rules of conduct' and 'corresponding restraints' that are expressed in powerful commitments to the non-violent resolution of disputes (Deutsch 1970; Adler and Barnett 1998). The human rights culture and international criminal law are additional examples of swings in the balance of power between national loyalties and universal principles that occurred in the aftermath of the Second World War. They show what societies can achieve in the way of agreeing on basic standards of restraint.[1] As the final part of this chapter will argue, related advances are built into the expectations of particular groups that Western governments will not stand aside when the egregious abuse of human rights takes place in other societies (although the controversies regarding the principle of humanitarian intervention demonstrate limited agreement about the scope of national obligations and the extent of international responsibilities).

One of the great realist thinkers in International Relations stated that it would be remarkable if 'civilized' societies lacked powerful advocates for the judgement that 'no civilization can be satisfied with

... a dual morality' in which one morality applies to private persons in their relations with each other and a second less demanding and 'inferior' ethic applies to the relations between states (Morgenthau 1965: 179–80). But, as realists have stressed and as Elias recognized, transitions to a less 'contradictory' moral code are far from smooth given endemic inter-state rivalries and the continuing potency of highly emotive nationalist loyalties. Proclaiming support for universal and egalitarian principles does not automatically lead to any particular course of action. By way of example, European political elites were distinctly uneasy about signing the United Nations *Convention on the Prevention and Punishment of the Crime of Genocide* (9 December 1948) because they feared that a cocktail of humanitarian injunctions and public expectations would clash at times with national security objectives and geopolitical calculations. The decision to sign the Convention owed a great deal to reputational considerations, and especially to the concern that civilized governments would be widely criticized for failing to agree on strategies to prevent the recurrence of similar atrocities to those that had been committed under National Socialism (Smith 2010).

In the more recent period, Western governments have been vulnerable to the criticism that they often pay little more than lip service to the principle that 'the single human being, the individual, is the supreme value' when national interests are at stake and display something of the 'deceit' and 'hypocrisy' that was prominent in the German condemnation of British foreign policy. The relaxation of the 'torture norm' during the 'war on terror' did much to reinforce such perceptions of the highly conditional nature of Western commitments to civilized precepts and to a civilized global order when they collide with national security objectives. But, as maintained in Chapter 1, the debates surrounding coercive interrogation techniques showed how tensions within nation-state normative codes can erupt unexpectedly in civilized societies and also how the relative influence of nationalist-Machiavellian and humanitarian principles fluctuates over time. Understanding such shifts and their connections with domestic and international power struggles is crucial for determining how far civilized states at any juncture are likely to use the universal-egalitarian dimensions of national moral codes in the quest to reduce inter-state tensions as part of the 'civilization' of global politics.

Civilization and barbarism

As well as drawing on process sociology to analyze the making of the global order, this work attempts to take forward Elias's exploration of the relationship between the civilizing process and world politics. To that end, the discussion now turns to the relevance of the 'split within civilization' and the duality of nation-state normative codes for European colonial expansion and for the development of European international society. As noted earlier in this chapter, the idea of a profound conflict within civilization referred to the continuation of the assuredness that the taboos on violence in relations between members of the same society can be loosened in life-or-death struggles with external adversaries. What Elias did not consider was that the rupture was as deep – if not deeper – in Europe's relations with subjugated peoples where violence, humiliation, enslavement and genocide were endemic. As one critical reading of Elias's writings has argued, the European civilizing process was 'double-sided' since it combined 'internal pacification' with colonial cruelties that were justified in the language of civilization (Burkitt 1996). In short, civilized self-images authorized forms of violence and cruelty against colonized outsiders that were largely forbidden in civilized societies and, to a considerable degree, in the larger international society to which they belonged (Mégret 2006; Neocleous 2011). The most radical formulation was the 'realist' thesis that 'barbarians have no rights' – alternatively, that the customary restraints on force did not apply to relations along the colonial frontier (Wight 1977: 34–5). But one of the consequences of the duality of normative codes was that such justifications of colonial violence did not go unchallenged. The legitimacy of the imperial foundations of the 19th-century international order would become keenly contested within the 'civilized' world and, of course, across the wider world.

Postcolonial sociologists will rightly stress that civilized societies did not alter their images of colonialism through their labours alone (see p. 13ff). To understand fundamental shifts in European attitudes to colonialism, the argument runs, it is necessary to analyze the influence of struggles between colonial and anticolonial forces on European attitudes to imperialism. Eliasian analysis of the civilizing process may have devoted little attention to European colonization or to global interconnections that shaped the development of more enlightened standpoints on imperial rule. However, Elias's approach considered at length the larger phenomenon of which imperialism was part, namely the condition in which stark divisions between self-professed superior groups and designated inferiors – between the established and the outsiders – emerge in conjunction with widening power inequalities (Elias and Scotson 2008). The following comments may have particular relevance for a much-needed discussion (which cannot be undertaken here) of how process sociology can contribute to, as well as learn from, postcolonial sociology. It is acknowledged that the classical sociological tradition did not investigate the 'cultural logics attendant with empire' (Go 2013: 29). But it is maintained that the Eliasian perspective contributes to that inquiry by providing a distinctive analysis of the relations between established–outsider figurations and the civilizing process that is especially germane to understanding those 'logics'.

Elias's focus on recurring collective needs for a sense of superiority over other groups resembles Durkheim's observation about the virtual 'law' which dictates that, 'whenever two populations, two groups of people having unequal cultures, come into continuous contact with one another, certain feelings develop that prompt the more cultivated group – or that which deems itself such – to do violence' to those deemed to be 'inferior'; the former can quickly become intoxicated by collective 'megalomania' where 'nothing restrains [them]' (Durkheim [1925] (1973: 192–3). To return to the seventh theme in the overview of Elias's method in the introduction to this study, his writings also considered the ways in which powerful groups often develop conceptions of superiority that lead them to cast aside the usual controls on force. Elias added that the dominant groups might come to regard their hegemony as evidence of natural virtues or innate talents. A related theme was that the most powerful often encourage subject groups to assimilate the belief in their lesser worth and to regard their relative lack of cultural and political resources and limited potentials as essential group properties – as tantamount to natural deficiencies. What most distinguished Elias's variant on the virtual law that arises whenever two unequal groups come into regular contact was the emphasis on the low levels of mutual dependence. His inquiry concentrated on how groups that do not rely on others for the satisfaction of basic needs and interests are relatively free from the compulsion to consider their well-being or to think from standpoints which they may deem to be worthless. The relevance of those ideas for the analysis of the dichotomies between the 'civilized' and the 'savage' is best explained by recalling basic themes in the Eliasian explanation of the European civilizing process.

Elias identified an overall trend in European societies in which the growth of an increasingly complex social division of labour rendered the dominant strata ever more reliant on others for the promotion of their interests (Mennell 2007: 17). Because of 'functional democratisation' (the process in which valued social functions are no longer largely monopolized by specific groups but are dispersed across and undertaken by different social strata), traditionally dominant groups found it necessary to take account of the interests and perspectives of inferiors; the established strata faced pressures to treat outsiders in more considerate and restrained ways. Developing Elias's inquiry, more recent processual analysis has focused on the contrary trend in which new social elites with relatively low levels of dependence on other social strata emerged with the global dominance of neoliberalism. With expanding global inequalities and shifting power relations, the tangible uncoupling of such groups from the lower echelons took place. External pressures to understand and sympathize with less powerful groups declined; self-interested reasons for displaying concern for the welfare of the lower strata weakened (Mennell 2007: 311–14).

Those observations are pertinent to the analysis of European colonialism where the social processes that Elias investigated often occurred in reverse. It was frequently the case that the first colonial settlers were highly reliant on indigenous groups for the means of survival. With the growth of more populous colonial settlements and shifting power balances, earlier relations of dependence withered. The colonizers became freer to accentuate feelings of collective superiority; such feelings often developed alongside increasing tensions with colonized groups and the rise of colonial violence. Sharp distinctions between 'civilized' and 'savage' peoples emerged with increasing power asymmetries; the latter led to the erosion or contraction of emotional identification with indigenous peoples or to the 'cultural logic' of 'disidentification' (de Swaan 1997). The belief that there were no moral barriers to imperial expansion and no ethical constraints on colonial societies in struggles with subordinate peoples became a recurring feature of the social habitus of 'civilized' colonizers. A distinctive variant on the 'split with civilization' appeared in the course of processes of 'decivilization'. 'Civilized' norms demanded self-restraint in relations between the dominant groups, but they also provided the rationale for releasing constraints on violence in conflicts with savages.

Elias's sociological perspective provides insights into how discourses of civilization and barbarism displayed more general features of established–outsider relations between human groups at intra- and inter-societal levels. His description of established–outsider forces emphasized how uneven power relations often give rise to hegemonic narratives about the 'group charisma' of the ascendant groups and the debased existence of social subordinates who were pressed to feel proportionate 'group disgrace' (Elias 2009). The analysis has clear ramifications for efforts to understand the formation of civilized–savage dichotomies. The transformation of European images of Africa illustrates the point. Noteworthy is the contrast between European wonder at the splendour of Mansa Musa's empire in 14th-century Mali and the disparaging conceptions of African peoples which became prevalent in the 19th-century European philosophical histories (Bull 1984).[2] Worth recalling is an earlier point about the shift from positive to negative evaluations of Chinese civilization as global power balances changed in the age of European colonial expansion. In both cases, there was a clear movement from an initial phase of respect and admiration for specific non-European societies to contempt for and condescension towards savage or barbaric outsiders.

Over the centuries, a global establishment of hegemonic European societies created an extraordinarily diverse range of derogatory images of non-European outsider groups – a bewildering inventory of cultural stereotypes which were used to justify violence in dealings with savages. Numerous symbols of cultural 'backwardness' – including nakedness and sexual licentiousness, cannibalism, idolatry and skin colour, as well as supposedly unalterable racial and biological differences – were deployed in colonial variants on the split within European civilization. Depictions of the violence and ferocity of 'savages' were often wedded to an anthropology of pain which included what Elias (2007a: 125ff) described as the supposition that 'tribal peoples' had a tolerance for mental and physical agonies – such as the ordeals of prolonged torture – which was virtually non-existent in refined civilized societies. Typical of the colonial perspective was the assumption that imperial forces would be seriously disadvantaged if they observed the laws of war in struggles with non-reciprocating natives who did not comply with the civilized distinction between combatants and non-combatants and who did not flinch from cruelty towards the innocent in warfare. As the *British Manual of Military Law* (1914) declared, the:

> rules of International Law only apply to warfare between civilized nations where both parties understand them and are prepared to carry them out. They do not apply in wars with uncivilized States and tribes, where their place is taken by the discretion of the commander and such rules of justice and humanitarianism as recommend themselves in the particular circumstances of the particular case. (ch 14, para 7)

A parallel with the governing discourse during the 'war on terror' will be observed. Necessarily, the argument was, struggles with savages were more brutal than wars between the civilized members of international society. Other perspectives were unashamedly nationalist-Machiavellian and expressed what Durkheim described as megalomania in the form of the determination that nothing should restrain them. An example was open support for employing 'unmitigated terrorism and even cruelty' to suppress 'rebellious tribes' that would yield only to brute force (see the statement by General Lothar von Trotha, the German military commander in South West Africa, in 1904, cited in Crawford 2002: 229). That notorious statement did not stand alone. Three years earlier, during the US war in the Philippines, Brigadier-General Jacob H. Smith reportedly told his subordinate officer that, 'I want no prisoners ... The more you kill and burn, the better you will please me ... the interior of Samara must be made into a howling wilderness' (Mettreaux 2003: 139).[3]

Such ferocity was often decried by those who were troubled by the lack of restraint along the colonial frontier. Two statements by Theodore Roosevelt reveal how Western leaders 'resolved' the 'split within civilization' that ran through colonial theory and practice. He argued:

> The growth of peacefulness between nations has been confined strictly to those that are civilized. ... With a barbarous nation peace is the exceptional condition. On the border between civilization and barbarism war is generally normal [and] in the long run civilized man finds he can keep the peace only by subduing his barbarian neighbour. ... Every expansion of civilization makes for peace. (T. Roosevelt, cited in Hobson 2012: 113)

Elsewhere, Roosevelt repudiated the nationalist-Machiavellian ethos that nothing is forbidden in attempts to subdue 'natives'. 'All civilized mankind', ran his argument, is indebted to the 'fierce settler who drives the savage from the land' but, crucially, a people relinquished all rights to call itself 'civilized' when it acted 'as barbarously as its barbarous foes' (cited in Mennell 2007: 326–7). Roosevelt's comments echoed a more general trend in Western societies. Critical reflections on colonial violence and concerns about the fate and maltreatment of subject peoples often owed as much, if not more, to self- rather than other-regarding considerations. Several reactions to the violent suppression of the Boxer Rebellion in China exemplify the point. In a discussion about whether the law of nations applied in relations between the civilized world and the Chinese government with its 'haughty' attitudes towards the West and international law, the German international lawyer, Georg Jellinek (1901: 62), argued that 'humanity' should be exercised, 'not because China can demand it as a right, but because it keeps the nations, who feel themselves the upholders of civilization, from sullying themselves before the judgment of history'. Other commentators framed their concerns even more narrowly.[4] But, in all cases, it is clear that the analysis of the established–outsider relations that emerged in the course of the European civilizing process contributes towards explaining key 'cultural logics attendant with empire'.

More critical reflections on civilization surfaced in Enlightenment deliberations on whether the true barbarians were the civilized settlers along the colonial frontier who were free from the moral and legal constraints on violence that existed in the metropolitan societies. Later perspectives on the problem of civilization, which included the British denunciation of Belgian rule in the Congo, maintained that colonial violence was 'infinitely more dangerous and terrible than primitive barbarism' precisely because it was 'free from all passion' and administered in 'an atmosphere of cold and sinister calculation' (Grant 2005: vii). The idea of 'civilized savagery' captured the view that the Belgian authorities were as barbaric as the barbarians but in more technologically sophisticated ways (Grant 2005). Photographic images of imperial atrocities in the Congo were among the first to publicize cruelties that were thought to clash with the sympathies that civilized people were expected to possess and the restraints they were expected to observe; they influenced political strategies to civilize European colonial rule in line with the changing threshold of repugnance towards violence in the advanced societies (Grant 2005: ch 2). Critics of colonial violence did lament failures to observe civilized standards, but it is essential not to exaggerate the level of public support for the universal-egalitarian elements of nation-state normative codes (see Hall 2002). Compassion for the victims of the Atlantic slave trade and chattel slavery did not rest on firm beliefs in the equal standing of civilized and savage peoples; however, it did at least express the humanitarian sensibilities that were integral to the nation-state's normative code (Linklater 2016: ch 6).

This section has shown that the 'split within civilization' which Elias regarded as a fundamental part of European inter-state relations was more profound in the relations between the colonizing and the colonized peoples. The discussion has emphasized the ways in which the idea of civilization was used to authorize violence against Europe's outsiders. Its 'transcendent' features were also harnessed to promote criticisms of colonialism that are equivalent to the 'critique of the nation' that was discussed in Chapter 1 (see p. 36). The concept was used to condemn imperial cruelties and to promote rights to be free from suffering that would come to be regarded as the birthright of all people. Elias's claim that the competing ethics that make up nation-state normative codes can be assembled in diverse 'combinations' captures core features of civilized orientations to colonial violence, as does his comment about the overall direction of social change in which peoples gravitated towards the mid-point of the spectrum. As part of that trend, the humanitarian elements of national moral codes often had a moderating effect on the 'split within civilization' in the colonial international society that was at the heart of the global order until the collapse of the European empires in the post-Second World War era (for further discussion see p. 138ff).

Violence, civilization and international society

Imperial dichotomies between the civilized and the savage were enshrined in late 19th-century conceptions of the law of nations as evidenced by the assertion by a leading international legal authority that the basic principles were the unique 'product of the special civilization of modern Europe' which could not be 'understood or recognised by countries differently civilized' (Hall 1880: 34). The main assertion was that European international society was an exclusive club of sovereign 'civilized' peoples. In a formulation that had all the hallmarks of aristocratic snobbery, the international lawyer, John Westlake, compared that global arrangement to a 'society consisting of persons interested in maintaining the rules of good breeding' and wedded to 'shunning intercourse with those who do not observe them' (Oppenheim 1914: 6). The corollary was that inferior groups had to be barred from the society of states until their domestic political structures had been overhauled to comply with European standards of civilization (Horowitz 2004). Such juridical conceptions of fault lines between the established and the outsiders revealed how state-formation, imperial expansion and the emergence of international society were part of one overall, globalizing process of civilization.

The 19th-century 'standard of civilization' (discussed further in Chapter 4) was a key link between the civilizing process and colonial international society. Pioneering work on the standard within the English School tradition has not analyzed it in those terms – that is, as an offshoot of long-term patterns of development in European societies. For their part, process-sociological reflections on relations between states have not examined the connections between the process of civilization, international society and its core institutions such as diplomacy and international law. In Elias's writings, the observation that comes closest to the spirit of English School inquiry stated that European absolutist courts in the 17th and 18th centuries were bound together in a distinctive 'supra-national' figuration (Elias 2010a: 4–5; Elias 2012 [1939]: 217ff). Aristocratic elites were in no doubt that they 'had more in common with one another, in terms of personality structure and manners, than with the lower strata in their own countries' (Elias 2010a: 4). Indicative of commonalities were the close parallels between the protocols and etiquette that governed diplomatic behaviour in relations between courtiers within each court and in the relations within the supranational court society. War was a recurrent feature of that particular figuration but the 'fact that members of the European court society waged war on one another and confronted each other as enemies on the battlefield hardly affected the relative homogeneity of the European court civilization of the seventeenth and eighteenth centuries' (Elias 2010 [1987]: 4). The reality was that 'martial–military behaviour was an aspect of court society' but 'the sense of solidarity of people civilized into the courts … found expression in the rituals of their behaviour, whether they encountered one another in war or in peace' (Elias 2010a: 5). Wars and rivalries were moderated to a degree by the code of conduct which was shared by the aristocratic military elites and which set them apart, so they believed, from inferiors.

The 18th-century European diplomatic culture was embedded in the aristocratic-courtly and cosmopolitan web of social relations that radiated outwards from French court society (Scott 2007). That statement broadly supports Elias's remark that courtly manners and diplomatic refinements at the court of Louis XIV at Versailles (and which were part of longer trajectories reaching back to the Italian Renaissance and beyond) were transmitted to neighbouring court societies which were keen to follow its standard-setting behaviour (Elias 2010a: 4). The emergence of a professional cadre of ambassadors with its distinctive ethos and code of conduct was an expression of the special role of French court society in that phase of the civilizing process (Linklater 2016: 216ff). A process-sociological investigation of 'meeting regimes' and 'meeting behaviour' has shown that the aristocratic military elite which controlled the traditional war councils had to share power with lesser nobles with greater refinement in the sphere of diplomatic interaction (van Vree 1999). To the 'detriment of [their] more martial strategies' of settling conflicts, the aristocratic establishment had to accept the need for more regulated contacts between European governments so that tensions were managed by discussion and the quest for agreement (van Vree 1999: 192–3, 329 who states that the new 'meeting regimes' may have been influenced by upper class 'civilized' behaviour in the Dutch Republic). The upshot was a shift in the balance of power between the traditionally dominant 'nobility of the sword', with its dedication to military virtues, and the 'nobility of the robe'; the latter was the social stratum with expertise in undertaking the administrative tasks that were vital for the smooth functioning of a complex state-organized society as well as the necessary command of court etiquette to be capable of discharging diplomatic responsibilities with due sensitivity in the meeting regimes that were integral to the European inter-state order (Elias 2006: 288ff).

The aristocratic European diplomatic code shows how elements of 'society' can exist in the context of 'anarchy' – expressed differently, how global standards of restraint can emerge in the relations between peoples that are not governed by political institutions with monopoly control of the instruments of violence (Bull 2002). The attention paid to the salient inter-state forces is one of the main differences between English School investigations and Eliasian analysis where the commentary on the relationship between state-formation and civilizing processes resulted in an overly realist perspective on world politics which the 'international society perspective' transcends. The implication of the English School standpoint is that the schism within civilization is not quite as deep as Elias alleged. Shared understandings about what is permissible and forbidden in the society of states, it is argued, have often tamed inter-state struggles for power and security. There are similarities between the two positions: both stress the key role of the 'central power balance' for understanding structured relations between groups and the main directions of change. The English School emphasis on the relevance of the balance of military power for the very existence and survival of the society of states resonates with the Eliasian analysis of the potentially civilizing effects of relatively even power relations (Dunne 2003). Moreover, both approaches highlighted the ways in which great power competition for hegemony have weakened or destroyed precarious restraints on force. There is an additional parallel between Wight's reference to the evidence that earlier societies of states ended in a violent conflict between the great powers which resulted in empire and Eliasian reflections on how 'elimination contests' in earlier eras culminated in a final struggle to dominate the international system that was driven by 'unbridled' hegemonic 'intoxication' (Wight 1977: ch 1; Elias 2010b: 98ff).

Of particular value for the present inquiry are affinities between Eliasian sociology and passing English School considerations of the civilizing role of international institutions such as diplomacy and international law (Linklater and Suganami 2006: 122, note 9). Central to foundational texts in the analysis of international society was the contention that order and stability within the ancient Chinese, Hellenic and European societies of states rested on the sense of belonging to the same culture or civilization and the corollary which consisted of common beliefs in cultural superiority over outlying savage and barbarian groups (Wight 1977: ch 1).[5] The related thesis was that such orientations underpinned the shared assumption that actions that were forbidden in relations within the global establishment (comprising the sovereign members of international society) were permissible in dealings with outsider groups. More specifically, members of the European society of states believed that non-European governments could not be considered for membership until they complied, among other things, with civilized diplomatic practice – with the protocols that legal authorities such as Hall and Westlake regarded as symbols of the vastly superior civilized world. This crystallized the affiliated 'cultural logics' of empire and international society which the Eliasian analysis of the civilizing process and the principle of established–outsider relations does much to explain.

Absent from English School analysis was recognition of the processual nature of civilization and, in the European case, of the long-term patterns of change that were shaped by state-formation, the intricacies of absolutist court societies and established–outsider figurations. The upshot is that English School writings have examined central features of inter-state relations that have been largely unexplored in Eliasian sociology, but the latter provides the necessary processual investigation of civilization – one that explores the formation of civilized self-images and their implications for relations between social groups, one that provides an inventory of social-scientific concepts with which to incorporate the study of international societies within more synoptic forms of inquiry. To explore this point in more detail it is essential to consider the relevance of the 'duality of nation-state normative codes' for English School reflections on changes in the relative power of the pluralist and solidarist conceptions of international society in the last few decades.

According to the pluralist interpretation, states are the ultimate members of the society of states; order is a shared primary objective, and diplomacy is a valued instrument for resolving inter-state disputes, for exploring the prospects for collaboration, and for embedding binding agreements in international law. According to the solidarist interpretation, the individual is the fundamental member of international society; government support for human rights is mandatory, and intervention, whether peaceful or involving military force, may be essential to protect the rights of individuals (Bull 1966; Wheeler 2000). What Eliasian investigation contributes to the discussion is a sociological explanation of their respective places within one overall civilizing process which was reconfigured by shifts in the power capabilities of aristocratic and bourgeois class forces. From that angle, conceptions of diplomacy that were associated with pluralist orientations to international order were part of the legacy of the old supranational aristocratic court society, whereas support for individual rights was the product of the rise of bourgeois strata and the greater influence of the universal-egalitarian dimensions of nation-state normative codes on foreign policy conduct and on the organizing principles of the global order. A new phase in the history of the civilizing process was manifest in the evolution of the humanitarian laws of war in international society from the second half of the 19th century.

To advance a processual analysis of international society it is useful to note some examples of how the international law of civilized nations replaced the international law of Christendom in the period under discussion (Steiger 2001: 66ff).[6] Indicators of the 'internationalization of civilization' (Keene 2002: 126ff) included the 1868 St Petersburg Declaration which prohibited the use of explosive bullets on the grounds that needless suffering was 'contrary to the laws of humanity' and unacceptable in wars between 'civilized nations'. Such pain and suffering were incompatible with the 'progress of civilization' which demanded 'alleviating as much as possible the calamities of war' (Roberts and Guelff 2001: 53–5). Later, at the 1899 and 1907 Hague Conferences, national governments referred explicitly to the special solidarity that pertained to the society of 'civilized' nations. Similarly, the preamble to the Fourth Hague Convention (the 'Martens clause') declared that civilians and combatants 'remain under the protection and the rule of the principles of the law of nations, as they result from the usages established among civilized peoples, from the laws of humanity, and the dictates of the public conscience' (Roberts and Guelff: 2001: 70). Those innovations were the antecedents of recent international legal developments including the 1997 United Nations *Convention on the Prohibition of the Development, Production, Stockpiling and Use of Chemical Weapons and on Their Destruction* in which the discourse of civilization was employed to prohibit the use of poisonous weapons that were associated with human societies in the age of 'savagery' (Price 1997: 26ff, 35ff).[7]

Historical studies of how international law came to embody the liberal 'conscience' of civilized peoples in the late 19th and early 20th centuries can be usefully linked with the earlier discussion of the dual structure of national moral codes (Koskenniemi 2001: chs 1–2). Intriguingly, in the light of Elias's reflections on German antipathy to the French idea of civilization, governmental and non-governmental actors affirmed their support for humanitarian principles by condemning the dangerously archaic phenomenon of *Kultur* (Koskenniemi 2001: 71ff). French political leaders, the national press and public intellectuals echoed that development by representing the First World War as a conflict between the aggressive nationalism of *Kultur* and Western liberal civilization (Kramer 2007: ch 5; Robertson 2003: 119ff).[8] Through such methods, narratives of civilization were harnessed in defence of liberal-bourgeois conceptions of the ideal relationship between sovereign rights and moral obligations to humanity. An overall shift in the relative standing of the pluralist and solidarist conceptions of international society was set in motion. It was linked with one of the main features of the civilizing process in that era, namely the proliferation of inter-state 'meeting regimes' that mirrored intra-societal commitments to steering social and political arrangements in agreeable directions (van Vree 1999). The multiplication of inter-governmental and non-governmental organizations and related international conferences that provided support for the humanitarian laws of war greatly expanded the diplomatic meetings that had been part of the older supranational court figuration. The increased density of international governmental and non-governmental organizations testified to the 'accelerated development' and internationalization of 'meeting behaviour' that was designed to civilize the global order by reducing unnecessary suffering in warfare (van Vree 1999: 324ff).

Those developments were pushed forward in 20th-century innovations with respect to international criminal law. The notion of 'crimes against civilization and humanity' had pride of place in the joint declaration of 24 May 1915 in which the United Kingdom, France and Russia condemned any Ottoman officials who had directly assisted, or who had been complicit in, the massacre of the Armenians (Myles 2002). The heralded 'practices of civilized nations' were at the heart of the idea of an international tribunal to investigate war crimes committed during the First World War. Appeals to 'civilization' were prominent again at the end of the Second World War. The prosecution at the Nuremberg tribunals contended that Nazi leaders who had been accused of committing 'crimes against humanity' could not be charged with breaching positive international law, but they knew all along that the extermination of the Jews violated 'civilized' principles and they had to be punished accordingly. At the Tokyo war crimes tribunal that began proceedings in April 1946, the prosecution team employed the same rhetorical device to state that Japanese leaders who had been accused of war crimes had contradicted Japan's earlier claim to have assumed its 'place among the civilized communities of the world' by embracing international agreements to outlaw military aggression and 'to mitigate the horrors of war' (see Majority Judgement in Boister and Cryer 2008: 110).

The radical statement at the Nuremberg tribunals was that the 'general principles ... derived from the criminal law of all civilized nations' trumped traditional conceptions of state sovereignty which guaranteed national leaders immunity from prosecution (Marrus 1997: 57ff). The upshot was that a principal feature of the civilizing process – the expansion of the 'threshold of repugnance' towards violence – led to a decisive shift in the post-Second World War liberal international order in the relationship between the pluralist norm of sacrosanct state sovereignty and the solidarist commitment to inalienable individual rights. Advances in criminalizing cruelty to women and children within liberal societies were extended outwards in the form of a new doctrine of international legal responsibility that rejected the classical doctrine that disputes about the ways in which governments treat their citizens fell entirely within their sovereign jurisdiction. New 'meeting regimes', which added international criminal proceedings to the existing institutions of the society of states, were part of the long civilizing process that goes back to and continues the 'taming of the warriors' within court societies. That is the larger process of civilizing the international political order to which efforts to tame the sovereigns and the colonialists belonged.

It is scarcely surprising that, as part of the same pattern of development, civilized governments after the Second World War created human rights conventions that prohibited genocide, torture and apartheid, which is not to presume – to recall an earlier theme – that the process was smooth, uncontested and irreversible. Favourable global power relations enabled liberal regimes with similar positions on the spectrum of national normative codes to shape international society in line with civilized norms. Article 38 of the Statute of the International Court of Justice which was created by the United Nations in April 1946 affirmed the supremacy of liberal commitments of the established powers by stating that the Court would 'decide such disputes as are submitted to it' in accordance with 'the general principles of law recognised by civilized nations'.[9] But the tide was turning against those who used the discourse of civilization to support such visions of world order. Distinctions between the civilized and the barbaric which had been tarnished by the catastrophe of the First World War became even harder to sustain in the aftermath of the Nazi genocides and the atomic bomb attacks on Hiroshima and Nagasaki. Their dissolution was ensured by struggles in non-Western countries to end colonialism with its anchorage in European conceptions of civilizational and racial superiority.

To draw this chapter to an end, it is valuable to consider how military courts have embodied Western deliberations about the moral and legal responsibilities of civilized armed forces towards adversaries that do not share their standards of restraint regarding violence. There is no space here to analyze courts martial in different periods. The aim is to build on an earlier point about the utility of Elias's investigation of the duality of nation-state moral codes for specific case-study explorations. Courts martial illustrate Elias's observation about how the analysis of micro-structures or small-scale figurations can contribute to understanding macro-structures or large-scale figurations (Elias 2008c: 5). They further indicate how specific 'meeting regimes' shed light on larger social and political processes.

One illustration of what small-scale figurations reveal about the civilizing process consisted of the official United States inquiries during the 1899–1902 war in the Philippines into whether the treatment of prisoners complied with civilized standards. In a cycle of massacres committed by both sides, United States armed forces initiated retaliatory action in response to the conflict at Balangiga on 28 September 1901 in which 48 US troops were killed. The investigations revolved around what are now familiar questions about military necessity, about the morality of torture and the status of civilized norms more generally in conflicts with 'savages', and about duties to observe and rights to disobey superior orders. The opinion of the Judge-Advocate General who examined reports of abuses by US officers was unambiguous. An enemy's 'flagrant disregard of the rules of civilized war', he argued, did not permit the relaxation of international legal prohibitions of torture (Mettraux 2003: 145). In the words of one of the generals responsible for the inquiry, 'any other view looks to the methods of the savage and away from the reasonable demand of civilized nations that war shall be prosecuted with the least possible cruelty and injustice' (Mettraux 2003: 138). Government statements maintained that US military personnel had behaved honourably throughout the war, notwithstanding the actions of a small minority. In a revealing letter to the Chairman of the Senate Committee on the Philippines, the Secretary of War, Elihu Root, referred to the 'unjustifiable severities' that will occur as long as war survives, and added that any departures from the law of nations had not been officially sanctioned and did not alter the reality that the military campaign in the Philippines had been conducted with 'scrupulous regard for the rules of civilized warfare, with careful and genuine consideration for the prisoner and the non-combatant, with self-restraint, and with humanity' (Mettraux 2003: 150n58). Moreover, the emphasis on the absence of official sanction supported the 'bad apple' thesis that Elias emphasized in his analysis of double-bind processes – the contention, in short, that only a 'minority of the best' had violated the standards of restraint that civilized people usually observed.

Also instructive in the light of more recent public debates about violations of the laws of war was the trial in 1901 of Lieutenant Brown. He was found guilty of manslaughter for killing an escaping prisoner of war, dismissed from the army and sentenced to five years hard labour, but later released and allowed to resume military duties, an outcome that seems to confirm the interpretation that officials accepted the plea of extenuating circumstances (see Welch 1974 on the widespread assumption, interlaced with racism, that guerrilla forces had violated, and did not deserve, the protection of the laws of war). The case showed how the conscience of civilized people can be satisfied by punishing its deviant members, how assumptions about the moral integrity and essential decency of the larger society are reaffirmed, and how deeper questions about the contributory role of discourses of civilization and savagery to wartime atrocities are avoided rather than openly confronted.[10]

Recent investigations of alleged violations of the laws of war and subsequent media discussions demonstrate how the central themes of this chapter can be used to analyze debates about the rules of engagement in conflicts with non-Western insurgent groups. (Those themes include the split within civilization, the duality of nation-state moral codes, disputes over Western attitudes to colonial warfare, and the incorporation of 'solidarist' humanitarian laws of war in the modern society of states). The most discussed British example was the trial in 2013 of 'Marine A' (subsequently named as Sergeant Alexander Blackman) who was found guilty of murdering a wounded Taliban captive and sentenced to ten years' imprisonment.[11] The consensus in the print media was that Marine A was guilty as charged of violating the laws of war (as he had admitted in a helmet recording in which he stated that he had 'just broken the Geneva Convention'). In an intriguingly entitled newspaper article in the light of the 'civilizing process' ('How soldiers must keep emotions under control to maintain the high moral ground'), a leading defence correspondent stated that the failure to observe the requisite level of 'self control' was 'a stain on the reputation' of the British armed forces (Coughlin 2013). No doubt because of the value attached to compliance with the laws of war – if not for its own sake then because of reputational factors – no leading commentator made the case for the total exoneration of Sergeant Blackman. But influential arguments which reflected key features of the European civilizing process were advanced in the public campaign for a reduced sentence (and the sentence was indeed reduced to eight years' imprisonment following an appeal in 2014; moreover, in March 2017, the initial verdict was changed from murder to manslaughter and the sentence reduced to seven years on the grounds of 'diminished responsibility' caused by 'exceptional stressors').

One part of the case for reviewing the original sentence was that 'the urge for revenge' was understandable given the traumatizing 'brutality of the enemy' as exemplified by the gruesome display of 'the limbs of British soldiers injured by roadside bombs' (Coughlin 2013). In a similar vein, a senior British military official maintained that Marine A was guilty of 'callousness' and 'brutality' rather than 'barbarism', and added that killing a Taliban captive, though inexcusable, was not 'tantamount to killing someone on the streets' of a British city (a contrast that may have been influenced by the murder of Fusilier Lee Rigby in London on 22 May 2013).[12] The reference to the 'urge for revenge' was an indicator of the legacy of the 'split within civilization' in imperial societies in which it was permissible to depart from civilized restraints on violence in conflicts with savages, although the reference to inexcusable brutality and callousness conveyed the idea that 'civilization' demands high levels of self-restraint on the part of military personnel (Tucker and Triantafyllos 2008). Moreover, many of those who campaigned for a reduced sentence argued implicitly that a civilized society should sympathize with members of the armed forces who bear the psychological scars of prolonged military action in brutalizing, savage environments. They combined the critique of a failure to exercise the levels of 'self-control' that are expected of civilized people in peacetime and in war with a public appeal for a sentence that displayed understanding and leniency that was influenced by patriotic loyalties (see Sergeant Blackman's account of events in Blackman 2019).

Public discussions that surrounded the case of Marine A revealed how civilized people continue to wrestle with the conviction that 'it is wrong to kill, maim or attack human beings' while generally believing 'that it is right to do all these things ... if that is found necessary in the interests of the sovereign society they form with each other' (see p. 98). They further illustrated how tensions can arise between 'nationalist' suppositions about the interests of the state or nation (and about the well-being of military personnel) and an 'egalitarian' ethic which holds that 'the single human being, the individual, is the supreme value'. They indicated how the different elements of the duality of nation-state normative codes can exist in a 'great variety of combinations' (see p. 99).

One of the strengths of process sociology is its capacity to consider such episodes and events in long-term perspective, thereby illuminating features of contemporary social and political life that may otherwise be hidden from view. The approach invites detailed empirical analyses of how attitudes to particular incidents fit within patterns of change that stretch over many centuries.[13] By way of example, developments with respect to the humanitarian laws of war, discussed in this chapter, are distinctive elements of a larger civilizing process which is reflected in the reduced tolerance of violence not only within but also in relations between civilized societies. To understand them, it is necessary to consider their relationship with state-formation and internal pacification, with the court societies and the supranational figuration to which they belonged, as well as with the competition between classes that altered the balance of power between nationalist-Machiavellian rules of statecraft and the humanistic principles which have influenced modern states and the global political order since the middle of the 19th century.

A final point is that Elias's largely realist observations about relations between states can be refined by engaging with the English School's analysis of international society. But, as this chapter has attempted to show, English School reflections on the civilizational dimensions of those arrangements, as well as postcolonial accounts of the 'cultural logics' of empires, can be enriched by drawing on the conceptual resources and substantive empirical findings of process sociology.

Conclusion

The final section of the last chapter summarized Elias's investigation of fluctuating balances of power between civilizing and decivilizing processes in Germany's distinctive historical development. A core theme was the weakness of civilizing processes in the absence of stable state monopolies of control over the instruments of violence. How perilous are civilizing processes in relations between states that are free from subjection to monopolies of power that can enforce compliance with global norms or social rules? How fragile must they be when external restraints have not been converted into powerful self-restraints as occurred in the course of the European civilizing process? Elias's idea of the 'split within civilization' contained his answers to those questions. His examination of highly emotive entanglements in double-bind processes underpinned the more pessimistic elements of his standpoint on relations between states.

A more subtle perspective on the inter-state relations ran through Elias's reflections on supranational court society and the duality of nation-state normative codes. The civilizing process in the age of absolutism was not confined to intra-societal developments. It was expressed in the diplomatic protocols and rituals that bound court societies in the larger supranational figuration. Such restraints as were observed in relations between absolutist court societies were largely restricted to Europe. In general, discourses of civility and civilization had a moderating role within international society but had little impact on the dominant attitudes and behaviour towards 'savages'. The split or schism within civilized societies cut deeper into relations between the civilized and the barbaric where power balances were exceptionally uneven. In that condition, decivilizing processes often had the upper hand in relations between the European global establishment and non-European outsiders.

Elias did not comment on varying balances between civilizing and decivilizing processes along the colonial frontier. Nor did he examine the impact of the universal-egalitarian elements of nation-state normative codes on the relations between the European powers and colonized outsiders. The final section of this chapter developed his argument by discussing political measures to eliminate colonial cruelties and to reduce unnecessary suffering in inter-state wars. Those were two pillars of liberal projects to globalize the civilizing process or to promote the civilization of international society.

There is one additional phenomenon to consider in the endeavour to advance the process-sociological interpretation of the global order. No study of the relationship between the civilizing process and world politics would be complete without an investigation of the 'standard of civilization' which was an influential theme in late 19th-century European colonial discourse. The idea was at the hub of the interconnections between state-building, imperialism and international society. The following two chapters draw on the core concepts and method of process sociology to build on Elias's achievement in analyzing long-term patterns of change in European societies. A first step is to seek to advance Eliasian inquiry by considering how civilized self-images were shaped not only by state-formation and inter-state struggles but also by the discovery and conquest of purportedly savage or barbaric peoples.

4

The Classical European 'Standard of Civilization'

Elias's stance on the connection between the European civilizing process and imperial expansion was encapsulated in the previously cited claim that the idea of civilization gave 'expression to the continuously expansionist tendency of colonising groups' (Elias 2012 [1939]: 17); it provided the rationale for 'civilizing initiatives' to deliver 'progress' to backward societies. Those formulations may create the impression that Europeans elaborated their images of civilization before the waves of colonial expansion – that they first developed the discourses of civilization and only later gained control over non-European peoples, drawing freely on old narratives to justify imperial domination. References to crusader expansion in the study of the European civilizing process provide a somewhat more nuanced portrait of the interrelations between intra- and extra-European developments (Elias [1939] 2012: 246ff). But the absence of much discussion of colonization and the process of civilization left Elias's 1939 inquiry vulnerable to the criticism that it was wedded to 'a purely European genealogy of learning', since no account was taken of the ways in which relations with non-European peoples had influenced developments within Europe (see p. 60). The objection could have been averted by closer examination of the historical reality that Europeans did not define themselves as civilized in isolation from other groups and then, as they encountered other peoples for the first time, begin to wrestle with how to comprehend strange customs and how to conduct relations with societies that were, at first glance, savage by comparison. The critique could have been pre-empted by exploring how global interconnections shaped European conceptions of civilizational superiority.

As conveyed by the idea of the 'empire of civilization', the European civilizing process developed hand-in-hand with the phases of colonial expansion and related 'standards of civilization' (Bowden 2009). Civilized self-understandings that celebrated European achievements in becoming more peaceful and restrained, more refined and highly mannered emerged in tandem with narratives that stressed the licentiousness, impulsiveness and cruelty of peoples who seemed 'animalic' or childlike because of seemingly low levels of emotion management and because free rein was apparently given to basic impulses. The Eliasian analysis of the relationship between state-formation and conceptions of civilization was a major breakthrough in the social sciences, but it was a limited one because it was so silent on the subject of state-initiated imperial projects and 'civilizing' missions that did not post-date but attended the whole civilizing process.

One postcolonial commentary on influential recent sociological analyses of the state – such as Tilly (1992) – draws attention to a focus on nation-states and neglect of states-as-empires (Go 2013a: 16ff). The comment applies to Elias's investigation of state-formation. Elias emphasized that the 'crises and transformation of Western civilization' in 'whose shadow we all live' had provided the motivation for writing his 1939 work, an observation that clearly alluded to the turmoil in Europe (see p. 17). But the problem of civilization was of much greater magnitude if one broadens the account to consider the colonial experience of non-Western peoples. A parallel objection in process sociology to the postcolonial line of argument noted above captures the point by stating that:

> [with the exception of] a few passages in *The Civilizing Process*, we do not get a very clear sense … that at the very time that civilization was developing in Western Europe, it was busily spreading itself over the whole globe in the most violent of ways, so that it is not unfair to say that the ritualized civility of European court society was built on the blood of murdered 'primitives' and bought with the land, labour and raw materials, which marauding Europeans plundered from 'their' empires. (van Krieken 1999: 300)

Van Krieken's critique resonates with the thesis that the violent nature of 'civilization' is often most visible or most dramatically expressed in clashes in the 'periphery' (Pepperell 2016). But the fact remains that, throughout the Eliasian explanation of the state's monopolization of violence:

> there is little examination of what states actually *did* with that monopoly, in relation to both their own populations

and those of the parts of the world they set about colonizing. Elias himself, for example, spoke of the 'spread' of Western civilization, the 'transformation of Oriental or African peoples in the direction of Western standards', and the 'integration' of the rest of the world within European standards of behaviour as an essential element of the 'civilization of the colonized' in a way which glossed over exactly how violent a process that really was.' (van Krieken 1999: 300, italics in original)[1]

The argument continues by claiming that:

it is important to supplement, systematically, the concept of 'civilizing *processes*' with that of 'civilizing *offensives*', to take account of the active, conscious and deliberate civilizing projects of both various powerful groups within societies and whole societies in relation to other regions of the world. Only then we will be able to develop a sense of the particular directions that civilization has been *steered*, rather than seeing it as a deus ex machina process which simply unfolds in automatic association with other processes of social development. (van Krieken 1999: 303, italics added)

The interpretation emphasizes the 'automatism' of Elias's explanation as conveyed by repeated statements that the civilizing process mostly unfolded in unplanned ways 'behind the backs' of those involved. It has fallen to others to investigate the series of civilizing offensives that were instigated by missionary groups within European societies and in other regions with the express aim of elevating the lower social echelons and improving 'savage' societies (Roberts 2004; Twells 2009). The implication of those analyses is that Elias's focus on how people were drawn unwittingly into patterns of social interdependence from which conceptions of civilized forms of life emerged can, with suitable revision, explain the main directions of change within Europe, but it does not explain how ideas of civilization took root in other parts of the world. Useful to recall at this juncture is Elias's thesis that modern Europeans came to the deluded view that their civilization was a condition rather than a process – that it was part of their birthright rather than an unfinished and reversible development. Elias was fond of using the metaphor of ascending a spiral staircase to describe the process in which people came to view earlier stages of their journey in a more detached or distanced manner. In a variant on the theme, he referred to a narrative in which:

> a group of people ... climbed higher and higher in an unknown and very high tower. ... In the course of time their descendants attained the hundredth storey. Then the stairs gave way. The people established themselves on the hundredth storey. With the passage of time they forgot that their ancestors had ever lived on lower floors and how they had arrived at the hundredth storey. They saw the world and themselves from the perspective of the hundredth floor, without knowing how people had arrived there. They even regarded the ideas they formed from the perspective of their floor as universal human ideas. (Elias 2007a: 110)

The citation prompts the question of how far civilized peoples lost sight of the historical connections between civilization, overseas imperial expansion and colonial violence from the distorted perspective from the hundredth floor.

The criticism that Elias's writings did not discuss what European states did with their monopoly control of the instruments of force while expanding to other parts of the world makes a valuable point about the extent to which Elias's quest for a more detached understanding of civilization neglected inter-societal dynamics that were obvious to people when they occupied what might now seem to be a lower position on the spiral staircase. In short, the explanation of civilization as a condition rather than a process ignored the place of imperialism and colonial violence in the formation of European civilized self-images. The basic point has been captured by the postcolonial claim that, even today, there are very few systematic attempts to 'relate the discourse of civilization directly to the problem of Atlantic slavery' and, more broadly, to 'elucidate the colonial legacy of the concept of civilization' (Shilliam 2012: 101–3). As stated above, the broader issue was conveyed by the statement (Benjamin 1989: 248) that there is 'no document of civilization' which is not at the same time 'a document of barbarism' (see p. 36). By extension, an investigation of the civilizing process is incomplete unless it includes an account of those images of 'the barbarian' which were inextricably connected with the emergence of civilized orientations to the social and natural worlds.

Elias did not examine the intermingled documents of civilization and barbarism, but his mode of analysis and its key concepts are especially well suited for that task. It is necessary to recall at this point the earlier discussion of its central working principles (see pp. 20–1), and particularly the method of analyzing the relationship between unequal power relations, 'the operation of group charisma and group disgrace, the process of stigmatisation, the absorption of the established group's view of the world within the very conscience and we–image of the outsiders, producing a high measure of resignation even though the tensions remain' (Mennell 1998: 138). Those themes inform the discussion in this chapter and the one that follows. They invite empirical analyses of the ways in which the relations between 'group charisma' and 'group disgrace' in colonial contexts influenced and were influenced by civilized self-understandings. The violent subjugation and suppression of social inferiors was a major part of the interplay. But collective pride in the superiority of civilized peoples also found expression in paternalistic assumptions that civilized societies could be a 'force for good' by bringing progress and development to backward peoples. That vision of the purposes of colonialism was important, alongside colonial violence, in shaping conceptions of what it meant to be civilized. Many proponents of that standpoint were not averse to using force to pacify unruly natives while criticizing or condemning colonialists who asserted the right to exploit and/or exterminate any savage groups that blocked their way. The 'standard of civilization' marked a change in the balance of power between those opposing images of colonial domination.

This chapter provides a process-sociological interpretation of the 'standard of civilization' which is designed to complement pioneering English School analyses of that core principle of colonial international society (Gong 1984). The earlier summation of the central working principles of process sociology stressed the 'absorption of the established group's view of the world' (Mennell (1998: 138) within the standpoints of outsider groups. Attempts by ruling groups to monopolize what Elias called the 'means of orientation' – the ways in which people attune themselves to the world – will be discussed in this context. Efforts to monopolize the meaning of discourse and to press others to internalize that perspective have consequences for the power resources of different groups. Elias (2012 [1939]: 474) alluded to that theme when arguing, with explicit reference to colonialism, that ruling groups have often exercised power most effectively by determining the ways in which people ruled themselves. The first section of this chapter aims to shed light on the processes through which Europeans claimed a monopoly of knowledge about civilized arrangements. It does so by discussing assorted narratives of conquest and discovery. That inquiry is followed by an examination of the idea of 'civilizing offensives' which was coined in the attempt to improve Elias's explanation of European developments. The standard of civilization, which is considered in the third part of the chapter, was one such example of a civilizing offensive in which European colonial authorities sought to internationalize what they regarded as their monopoly of truth about civilized beliefs and practices. It was designed to disseminate civilized norms across the global order, a project that involved demeaning non-European world views, promoting the cultural incorporation of feelings of backwardness, and encouraging or supporting local civilizing offensives to emulate European ways of life. Some illustrations of endeavours to persuade the global establishment of the depth of the commitment to progressing towards 'civilization' are provided in Chapter 5. They reveal in more detail how established–outsider figurations helped to circulate civilized norms across the European-dominated world order.

Narratives of conquest and discovery

As discussed in Chapter 2, Elias drew extensively on manners books to illustrate and explain European social and political change over several centuries. But other literary genres could have been selected to defend the overall thesis, including those that showed how European civilized self-images developed in successive phases of colonial expansion through discourses of savagery, reinventing in the process the extant perspectives of classical antiquity. Relevant 'cultural logics' were 'embodied in everyday discourse, novels, works of art, scientific tracts, or ethnographies' (Go 2013: 29–30; see p. 14). Numerous narratives of conquest and discovery – of early encounters with non-European peoples – make it clear that Europeans did not acquire civilized identities simply as a result of intra-European developments. They were formed through a series of influential 'global contrasts' which were constructed in detailed accounts of the 'New World' (Delanty 1995; see also Harbsmeier 1985; Said 2003: 166ff; Smith 2006: chs 2 and 5). By way of illustration, the idea of 'filthy rites' identifies a key dimension of the process in which the gulf between the civilized and the barbaric was created in the early phases of European colonial expansion (Greenblatt 1982). Displays of revulsion towards the practices of simpler peoples – persistent features of 'ethnological' and 'geographical' reports – reveal how the undercurrents of 'group charisma and group disgrace', and the accompanying 'process of stigmatisation', operate particularly when 'the balance of power' between social groups is very 'uneven' (see the discussion in Hodgen 1964: 131ff).[2] Several

16th-century representations of the 'newly discovered', South American peoples regarded the absence of shame and embarrassment about nudity as evidence of savagery. Telling narratives regarding the body and the emotions focused on the contrasts between savage peoples and Europeans whose uncontrollable tendency to blush if discovered naked was a key 'index of civilization' (Cummings 1999; Górnicka 2016; see p. 60).

Traveller accounts highlighted the nakedness and lasciviousness of native peoples as well as the primitive preference for raw over cooked food and 'barbaric' eating habits. Other deficiencies were found in high tolerance levels of violence and in the cruelties of ritual physical mutilation and routine infanticide (Jordan 1969: ch 1; Leão 2014). Elias may have assumed – and may have been right to believe – that the manners books were the primary influences on the genesis of civilized controls on bodily functions and on threatening behaviour and violence. But the Europeans' fascination with lurid descriptions of indigenous practices strongly suggests that the manners books were not the only means by which civilized self-images were constructed; narratives of conquest and discovery may have been at least as, if not far more, influential in forging the dichotomies between the civilized and the uncivilized that circulated within and between court societies. Further research is needed to assess the impact of different genres. Suffice it to add that some works bridged the two spheres. An example was the treatise, *Omnium Gentium Mores*, written by the German author, Johann Boemus. First published in 1520, the volume has been described as one of the first 'Renaissance collections of customs and manners' that existed – or were presumed to exist – in non-European societies (Hodgen 1964: 131ff). Specialist investigations may identify other influential works with that dual role.

As discussed in Chapter 2, Elias singled out Erasmus's treatise on the civility of boys to explain how the secular upper classes were steered, and steered themselves, towards new standards of civility. But the volume by Boemus (1485–1535) – a contemporary of Erasmus (1466–1536) – also enjoyed considerable fame and influence if the fact that it was reissued more than 20 times and published in several European languages between the 1530s and the early 1600s is any guide. That work did not provide a purely descriptive inventory of exotic customs and manners. Readers were invited to contemplate the barbarism of other ways of life, as revealed by the author's assertion that the world views of the Saracens and Turks were the product of 'the brainsicke wickednesse of a countrefeicte prophet' (Hodgen 1964: 140). For that reason, the treatise is best understood in conjunction with the 'avalanche' of anti-Turkish pamphlets (*Türkenbüchlein*) that appeared in Germany between the early and mid-15th century as part of the campaign to publicize barbaric atrocities against persecuted Christians (Bohnstedt 1968; Cole 1972). The pamphlets belonged to the larger gallery of representations of 'the Turk' as 'Europe's Other' that fed into the European discourse of civilization (Neumann and Welsh 1991). Similar representations of the Turk in the period in which 'civilization' was an increasingly vogue term included Edmund Burke's speech to Parliament on 29 March 1791 in which the Turks were described as even 'worse than savages' (cited in Marshall and Williams 1982: 165, citing *Parliamentary History of England*, xxix: 77). Similar orientations towards the Ottoman Empire will be considered in Chapter 5.

Other genres that contributed to civilized identities included such richly illustrated images of savagery as Theodor de Bry's work, *Great Voyages* – one of the first, if not the first, major treatise to disseminate pictorial representations of the peoples of the New World. Published in several volumes between 1590 and 1634, the book appears to have been widely discussed by members of the European nobility (and by aristocrats in German court societies in particular). It contained illustrations of the cruelty of 'newly-discovered' groups as well as images of 'barbarous and bloody manners' including the ceremonial consumption of human flesh (Bucher 1981: 11, 46ff, 90, 166). Also influential was de Bry's 1590 publication of John White's drawings of the 'naked Brazilians' (Hulton 1984). Accompanying the illustrations were representations of ancient Picts, which underscored the parallels between the 'civilizing mission' that had occurred alongside 'internal colonialism' in earlier phases of state-building and domestic pacification, and the imperial civilizing offensives which were launched in the wake of the unexpected discovery of similarly 'wild' non-European peoples (Hulton 1984; van Krieken 2011).

Representations of the internal savage deserve further consideration. Stark distinctions between civil society and cruel and lawless peoples such as the Scots, Welsh and Irish appeared in various 12th-century texts in the initial phases of English state-formation (Linklater 2016: 235ff). Later, in Elizabethan England, visual representations of the distinctions between the refined ruling establishment and untamed outsiders were conjoined with images of the contrasts between civilized peoples and naked or semi-naked savages in the Americas (Hodgen 1964: 152–3). They were most effectively codified in narratives which maintained that natives lived in a warlike 'state of nature' – the powerful metaphor in 17th- and 18th-century social and political thought which influenced renowned perspectives on the relationship between state power and internal pacification, imperial objectives of taming subordinate peoples, and emergent conceptions of a sui generis society of states (Jahn 2000). 'State of nature' perspectives underpinned the 'split within civilization'. They were used to justify departures from controls in force in the relations with savages that were generally observed in the relations between peoples who had mitigated the wildness of the state of nature through their integration in a civilized, rule-governed international society.

One other genre – the scientific map – contributed to the gulf between the standards of self-restraint pertaining to civilized and savage peoples. Early-16th-century maps which were produced by geographers such as Ortelius and Mercator sought to re-orientate people to the sheer scale of the human world and its physical environment through graphic representations of savagery in non-European regions. Ortelius's *Theatrum Orbis Terrarum* – a work of 1570 that was translated into six languages by 1612 – was the first systematic attempt to depict the Earth as a whole (Cosgrove 2001: 2–3, 130ff). One of the 43 constituent maps contained images of a 'semi-naked Africa' and a 'nude America' carrying a severed European head – the gruesome symbol of native cruelty and barbarism. Other treatises, such as the six-volume *Civitates Orbis Terrarum* edited by Georg Braun and Franz Hogenberg and published between 1572 and 1617, contained illustrations of major cities to place Europe at the zenith of a civilized condition (Cosgrove 2001: 133). Later collections of maps, including the 1747 *Atlas Complet,* broke the Ortelian mould by adding the temporal dimension. The aim was to connect contrasts between different places with particular phases in humanity's great ascent from classical antiquity to the civilized era (Cosgrove 2001: 197–8).

Non-European maps, including those that existed in East and South East Asia, were considered crude and primitive when compared to the more scientifically calculated European examples (see Zarakol 2014: 319ff). Basic omissions and errors were the other side of a limited capacity to delineate space in the manner of effective sovereign states. Imprecise measurements and speculative calculations of distance were evidence of lower levels of human control over nature (Adas 2015: 259ff). Accurate modern maps expressed the spatial and temporal coordinates of civilization which were found only in advanced forms of life. Pride in scientific and technological prowess was closely connected with more detached inquiry and increasing confidence in attaining levels of reality-congruence that were thought to surpass the achievements of other civilizations (Carrillo 1999). A sense of indebtedness to other civilizations for earlier cultural and technological breakthroughs was lost or suppressed in the process (Hobson 2004; Nelson 1973). But Europeans did not think their accomplishments were merely cognitive. In their eyes, the cartographic revolution was a symbol of scientific and technological sophistication which was closely linked with the Europeans' capacity to project their greater military power across the oceans – in short, with colonialism. Reflecting a broader trend, the absence of the European sense of perspective in Asian art was regarded as a symptom of cultural backwardness that explained why many Asian kingdoms lagged behind the military and political power of Europe's expansionist sovereign states and were easily subjugated (Adas 2015: 259ff; see also Salter 2002: 42 ff). Such patterns of stigmatization were integral to the views of the global establishment about their rightful fate and place in the world.

The position of technological prowess in the index of civilization was allied with the quest for increasingly scientific or pseudoscientific explanations of the deficiencies of less civilized peoples that were used to justify colonial domination. The construction of racialized distinctions between the established and the outsiders is a case in point (see Mennell 1998: 129ff). As the number of black African slaves imported into Europe rose, and as the Atlantic slave trade expanded, the dominant conceptions of distinctions between the civilized and the savage became heavily laden with racial imagery. With increasing power asymmetries, established groups placed ever greater emphasis on the symbolic meaning of skin colour. Positive images of white civilization developed hand-in-hand with stigmatizing representations of blackness which was equated with low levels of self-restraint that typified the indolence, infantilism and natural impulsiveness of 'savages' (Cole 1972). The imagery, which had at least some of its origins in Christian and Judaic theology, was reworked in a period of growing technological sophistication as orientations to the social world and the physical environment became more secular. The new 'science' of racial and biological differences provided novel foundations for negative characterizations of outsiders in the machine age (Adas 2015: 292ff). Scientific racism was part of what has been described as the process of 'racialization' in which dominant groups attached immense moral and political significance to skin colour (Dalal 2002). Process sociology has not discussed that phenomenon in detail but has stressed Elias's position on how the powerful have repeatedly affirmed their natural superiority through modes of stigmatization that accentuate the physical differences of the lower echelons (Mennell 1998: 129ff). From that standpoint, Elias (2008c: 15) argued, 'what are called "race relations" … are simply established–outsider relations of a particular kind'.

The Eliasian analysis of the role of manners books in the process of civilization can be enlarged by taking account of the explosion of travel writing in the 18th century. Interestingly, given Elias's focus on the standard-setting role of the absolutist court of Louis XIV, fascination with that literary medium was especially high among members of the 'erudite community' in France that had close ties with 'polite' court society (Dew 2009). Later, the proliferation of guidebooks for aristocrats that embarked on the obligatory, educative 18th-century Grand Tour helped to forge a cosmopolitan, civilized consciousness that combined admiration for classical antiquity with the stigmatization of indolent and unruly lower class groups (Calaresu 1999). Travel writing refurbished the binaries between the civilized and the savage that had been created in the earlier phases of state-formation and overseas conquest. It was one of the transmission belts through which the emergent and the more explicitly formulated discourses of civilization and savagery were relayed to the present day.[3] At every stage, notions of civilization did not develop simply as a consequence of growing interdependencies between people within European societies. They were shaped by 'global contrasts' with non-European peoples that were articulated in genres other than the manners books that had pride of place in Elias's major treatise on the civilizing process.

The argument that Elias devoted little attention to how states used their monopoly control of the instruments of violence in areas that fell within their sovereign jurisdiction points to the need for a more extensive process-sociological analysis of discourses of civilization and savagery. The contention also raises a second point: the decision to place state-formation at the centre of the analysis did not take account of two interrelated developments – the subjugation of non-European peoples and the emergence of European colonial international society (see Bull and Watson 1984: 6–7). These were three sides of one overall direction of change – the 'civilizing process' – which was expressed in collective pride in 'the level of [Europe's] technology, the nature of its manners, the development of its scientific knowledge or view of the world, and much more' and in the attribution of 'group disgrace' to social inferiors in non-European regions (Elias 2012 [1939]: 15). Postcolonial critics have argued that the great weakness of an Eliasian approach is that the emphasis on what Europeans regarded as their unique achievements posited an 'abyssal' image of a civilization that was presumed to be not only superior to but also separate from all others. The result was an alleged 'elision' of global influences on European patterns of development (Çapan 2017). Problems with this interpretation were discussed earlier (see pp. 60–1). As stated previously,

Elias's objective was to explain how Europeans developed the idea of civilization which became central to the collective consciousness of 'continuously expansionist … colonising groups' and provided the rationale for 'civilizing initiatives' (Elias 2012 [1939]: 17). The explanation emphasized how the ethos of civilizational superiority arose within uneven global power relations. But Elias's comments on civilization and colonization, which at times have the qualities of an afterthought, expose his processual approach to the postcolonial objection that it is Eurocentric or at least too Europe-centred. The inquiry needs to be revised to give imperialism (along with slavery and racism) a prominent place in the explanation of the formation of discourses of civilization and their impact on the global order (see Linklater 2016: ch 6). In that spirit, the discussion below considers the 19th-century 'standard of civilization', a unique point of convergence between state-formation, colonization, racialization, and international society.

'Civilizing offensives' in the global order

The argument that Elias's explanation of the European civilizing process needs to be supplemented by the systematic investigation of 'civilizing offensives' was noted in the opening section of this chapter. Dutch process sociologists introduced the concept in the 1970s and 1980s to analyze public policies designed to improve the behaviour of the lower strata and to promote the internalization of social norms regarding desirable levels of individual responsibility, foresight and self-restraint (Powell 2013). The term provided a necessary corrective to Elias's argument that the main course of the civilizing process was largely unplanned and only occasionally pushed forward by civilizing offensives in which the established set out to alter the conduct and to transform the world views of outsiders. However the European civilizing process should be explained, colonial relations were clearly not unforeseen and unplanned. As discussed at the start of this chapter, it is essential to analyze orchestrated civilizing offensives in long-term perspective in order to understand how Europeans elites used their monopolies of force in the non-European world.

It is useful to consider the etic sense of a civilizing offensive before turning to its emic meaning. As with the notion of a civilizing process, the concept of a civilizing offensive can be used in the technical (etic) sense to describe both Western and non-Western measures to transform the beliefs and behaviour of outsiders that existed long before European narratives of civilization came into being. There is no shortage of examples. Imperial China's conduct towards barbarian outsiders and minority ethnic groups (Hirono 2008: ch 2) and Roman imperial projects to export a 'superior' way of life to subjugated areas were etic civilizing offensives. They exemplify Elias's thesis that what is 'strange to observe' in human history is the frequency with which societies have constructed 'a self-praising vocabulary and a corresponding derogatory vocabulary directed against other groups', invariably with the aim of convincing themselves, if not others, of the rightness of their ways and, in many cases, the natural entitlement to conquer and rule (Elias 2007: 8). What is remarkable is how often peoples have taken 'strange delight in asserting their superiority over others', especially when dominance was achieved through 'violent means' (Elias 2007: 7). Over and again, Elias (2007: 8–9) added, 'group self-love' has been purchased by 'the attribution of a lesser human value to those who are less powerful' under such asymmetries. Those comments apply to imperial civilizing offensives in different regions and eras.

Civilizing offensives in the etic sense are constant features of civilizations as 'zones of prestige' (Collins 2001) where the strongest groups deploy their monopolies of force to refashion what they regard as defective social arrangements. In those zones, imperial ideologies expressed the 'group charisma' of an establishment and corresponding attitudes to outsiders that displayed 'group contempt, group ostracism, group disgrace and group abuse' (Elias 2009: 74). Outsider groups faced pressures to concur with perceptions of inferiority and to modify traditional world views and behaviour accordingly. Elias (2012 [1939]: 474–5) noted the same trend in the modern European empires which were based not only on the brutal labour exploitation of the plantation system but also on measures to wield power in non-coercive ways through the ' "civilization" of the colonised'. What distinguished European civilizing offensives in the emic sense was faith in a linear view of human progress – alternatively, the belief that societies should be assessed according to their fluid position in the movement of history rather than with respect to their fixed locations in a hierarchy of human types or immutable 'Great Chain of Being'. The 'standard of civilization' should be viewed in that light. It represented an attempt to control the means of orientation across the world by claiming a monopoly of truth not just about the nature of civilized existence but also about how lesser societies could profit from, and in some cases contribute to, the greater progress of humanity.

The above discussion has stressed the differences between etic and emic civilizing offensives but the two cannot be separated in a hard and fast way. Elias's claim that there is no 'zero point' with respect to the European civilizing process should be recalled here (see p. 5). The emergent emic sense of civilization was influenced by earlier etic civilizing processes. The same can be said about emic civilizing offensives. Many ruling groups in early modern Europe regarded the Roman Empire as the model that their particular imperial projects and civilizing missions should follow. Elizabethan elites believed that the campaign to bring civility to the wild Irish was comparable to ancient Roman efforts to civilize their native Briton ancestors. Such conceptions of the civilizing offensive in Ireland were transported to the Americas where they framed colonial projects to tame wild native populations. Colonial strategies that were shaped by celebratory images of the Roman Empire revealed how the chains that linked European peoples across the centuries contributed to the forging of uniquely modern colonial civilizing offensives in the emic sense of the term.

The migration of emic conceptions of European civilization and civilizing offensives to regions that had undergone their own civilizing processes in the etic sense will be discussed in Chapter 5. But it is worth pausing to consider one example of how a non-European society with its own etic sense of civilization looked outwards to Europe as it initiated its local civilizing offensive, just as European empire-builders had turned to the Roman Empire for inspiration. In the middle of the 19th century, Tsarist Russia embarked on an expansionist drive to bring 'civilization' to Central Asian peoples. The ruling elite hoped to raise Russia's standing in international society by persuading the European great power establishment that Russia was a civilized and civilizing force. External points of reference were invaluable. British imperial rule in India served as a model for the Russian civilizing offensive which, it is worth adding, did succeed in winning the approval of elements of the British governing class which welcomed its civilizing role in standing against the 'fanaticism and ferocity of Mahommedanism' (Bayly 2015: 832). The points made in the previous two paragraphs reveal how the relations between developments in different historical periods and geographical areas led to broadening support for European global 'civilizing offensives'. The European standard of civilization was central to the overall momentum – to the globalization of the emic conception of the civilizing offensive over the traditional non-European etic forms in the period under discussion.

The classical standard of civilization

The investigation of the standard of civilization has been a substantial contribution to English School analyses of the development of colonial international society. The most influential studies have been historical or legal rather than sociological (Gong 1984; see also Anghie 2005: ch 2). Process sociology complements English School inquiry by explaining the larger civilizing process of which the standard of civilization was part and by showing how this standard emerged from and shaped core established–outsider figurations in the global order. The resources of process sociology have not been harnessed in English School explorations of the standard of civilization which have ignored its relationship with the processes in which Europeans came to see themselves as uniquely civilized. James Lorimer's assertion that all human societies can be allocated their place in a tripartite hierarchy of forms of social and political organization remains the most frequently cited formulation of that 19th-century international legal principle. It remains an obvious point of departure for any inquiry into the standard of civilization, whether the analysis proceeds from an historical, legal or sociological standpoint. 'In its present condition', Lorimer (1883: vol 1, 101) maintained, the species consists of 'three concentric zones or spheres – that of civilized humanity, that of barbarous humanity, and that of savage humanity'. Western state-organized peoples governed by the rule of law and committed to basic personal liberties belonged to the first category. 'Barbarous' or 'semi-civilized' societies – including Turkey, China and Japan, which were judged to have complex state structures but lacked Western civilized governance – were located in the second tier. The lowest division of human types, who had not progressed beyond the most elementary forms of tribal social organization and lacked any semblance of state structures or government, comprised the realm of savagery.

The following comments consider descriptions of savage groups in influential legal texts before turning to the archetypal depictions of barbarous peoples. The general consensus among international lawyers was that 'savage humanity' lacked statehood which referred to 'political units possessed of proprietary rights over definite portions of the earth's surface' (Lawrence 1895: 136). By that yardstick, 'wandering tribes' could not be 'sovereign'; they 'failed the territorial requirement' since 'they were not in sole occupation of a particular area of land' (Anghie 1999: 27). 'Even now', argued Lorimer (1883: 13), 'the same rights and duties do not belong to savages and civilized men'. The position was not set to change. Three decades later, a leading international lawyer observed that 'of uncivilized natives, international law takes no account' (Westlake 1914: 138, 145). The 'rules of the international society', the thesis was, existed for the sole 'purpose of regulating the mutual conduct of its members'; questions regarding the treatment of native peoples were not immaterial, but they could be left to the 'conscience of the state to which the sovereignty is awarded' (Westlake 1914: 138ff).

It was a short step to the justification of colonial annexation. Several legal authorities argued that 'the occupation by uncivilized tribes of a tract, of which according to our habits a small part ought to have sufficed for them' did not 'interpose a serious obstacle to the right of the first civilized occupant' (Westlake 1914: 139). Indigenous groups were required to make way for advancing colonialists who would harness their technological prowess to build civilization through the productive occupation and exploitation of vacant areas, or *terra nullius* as it was called in official justifications of the appropriation of native land in Australia (Keal 2003). Colonial discourse reworked a judgement which was prevalent during the Spanish conquest of the Americas, namely that one of the main defining features of savagery was the absence of a lasting human imprint on the natural world (Pagden 1982). Collective pride in the domination of nature informed emic conceptions of civilization. It was combined with civilizing offensives to improve savage peoples who were trapped in magical and mythical orientations to their environment (Adas 2006; Adas 2015: 210ff). From the standpoint of advocates of the standard of civilization, the political implications of that state of affairs were obvious. As Lorimer (1883: 227) argued, the 'moment that the power to help a retrograde race forward towards the goal of humane life consciously exists in a civilized nation', it is 'bound to exercise its power' and to 'assume an attitude of guardianship' even if that largely ignored 'the proximate will of the retrograde race'. For many proponents of the standard of civilization there were essential limits to the moral and political responsibilities of the 'white man's burden' or *mission civilisatrice*. It was vital that the colonial powers did not incur serious costs by undertaking civilizing offensives to elevate social inferiors who were thought to be incapable of undergoing anything other than a slow and arduous ascent to a modicum of self-government (Keene 2002; Hobson 2004: 219ff). The prevalent notions of racial supremacy suffused those assumptions about the restricted possibilities of savage societies and about the necessity for prolonged paternalistic colonial tutelage (Vincent 1984; see also Koskenniemmi 2016 on Lorimer's racism).

Rather different rules pertained to 'barbarous' and 'semi-barbarous' societies which were not formal colonies and which were presumed to be capable of making substantial social and political advancement if they dutifully followed the example of the civilized imperial powers. The standard of civilization consisted of five interlocking elements of 'a universally applicable test' for assessing the progress of societies that belonged in the middle tier of human arrangements (Gong 1984: 14ff; see also Schwarzenberger 1962). To demonstrate progress in complying with the principles of 'liberal European civilization', 'semi-civilized' governments had first to offer proof that they could guarantee the rights and ensure the security of European nationals; a second requirement was the introduction of 'institutional capacities that included a functioning governing bureaucracy'; a third demand was that 'semi-barbarous' regimes had to adhere to European principles of international law; the fourth created the obligation to honour the responsibilities of membership of the society of states, not least by conforming with the principles of European diplomacy; the fifth measure was success in eliminating traditional practices such as slavery, piracy, polygamy and infanticide which contravened the principles of international society and blocked the path to admission to that union of civilized peoples (Gong 1984: 14ff).

European portrayals of India elaborated the key issues. Europeans recognized that all 'the major communities in India as well as elsewhere in the East Indies were politically organized; they were governed by their Sovereigns, they had their legal systems and lived according to centuries-old cultural traditions' (Alexandrowicz 1967: 14). They possessed some of the hallmarks of Western civilized states but they could not enforce the law within clearly defined, national borders; their authority petered out along imprecise frontiers in remote regions where lawlessness often prevailed (Horowitz 2004). As stated earlier, their semi-barbarous condition was presumed to lie in the inability to grant Europeans the levels of security to which they were accustomed in their respective state-organized, law-governed, metropolitan societies (Thomas 2018: 130ff). An additional factor was the failure to observe basic elements of the civilized laws of war such as the distinctions between armed forces and non-combatants or between belligerents and neutrals that helped to restrain the use of force. As noted in Chapter 2, colonial images of social practices such as *sati* underpinned binary divisions between the 'group charisma' of the civilized establishment and the 'group disgrace' of semi-civilized outsiders.

To comply with the standard of civilization, non-European governments were expected to fall into line with the European certainty that the modern state was the foundation stone and guarantor of 'civilized' interaction.[4] Two features of the civilizing process provided the context for those demands – progress in reducing the overall levels of intra-state violence, and advances in converting private monopolies of power into public authorities that upheld the impartial rule of law in accordance with liberal conceptions of the equal rights of citizens (Elias 2012 [1939]: 310). The standard of civilization channelled feelings of superiority over non-European societies into 'unequal treaties' and the principle of 'extraterritoriality'. Capitulations to the Western powers under those international treaties were demanded in order to exempt 'Western nationals from the criminal and civil jurisdiction' of semi-civilized societies (Lorimer 1883: 239). Under the rules of extraterritoriality, the consular office of the relevant Western state was granted jurisdiction over disputes involving conationals to guarantee they would be treated correctly (Fidler 2001; Keal 2003: 103ff; see also Roberson 2009 on the 'mixed courts' established in Egypt in the 1870s). Several European jurists devised new legal codes drawn from 'materials from all parts of the civilized world' with the aim of introducing civil order in subject territories (Gong 1984:182). One of the aims of extraterritorial arrangements was to devise the legal principles and procedures that would eventually be incorporated within non-Western judicial systems. Such civilizing offensives were undertaken to export the Westphalian state form. They were key steps in the globalization of the European civilizing process, as were related endeavours to secure compliance with the associated diplomatic protocols which will be reviewed in Chapter 5 (see Kayaoğlu 2010).

Europeans took pride in living in societies that had eliminated many cruel forms of punishment, and it is scarcely surprising that non-European barbaric punitive practices were singled out for special condemnation. Chinese punitive measures such as decapitation, strangling and torture were regarded as peculiarly savage by the European governments that imposed the rules of extraterritoriality at the end of the Opium Wars.[5] European elites were repelled by a presumed ethic of group responsibility for criminal acts in which a surrogate could be punished if it proved impossible to identify and detain the real offenders.[6] Such collectivist codes clashed with the regard for individual rights that reflected the evolving balance of power between the antithetical elements of nation-state moral codes (Benton 2002: 248–9). Early in the 20th century, international lawyers such as Georg Jellinek made a direct link with China's disregard of the civilized laws of war. Jellinek argued:

> International law in war owes its greatest development to ... substantial progress in the consciousness of right of the most civilized nations. China surely has not taken part in this progress. This progress is intimately related

to the growing valuation of the life and property of each individual. ... A government which causes its high officials to be beheaded without any legal proceeding, and which can order successfully the massacre of innumerable subjects, is not able to inculcate into its troops respect for the life and property of its enemy. Those that have been used to massacre their own countrymen can hardly understand that they should spare prisoners of war. (Jellinek 1901: 60–1)

This was the case, he continued, not just because of the need to honour treaty obligations but, more fundamentally, because 'civilized' standards demanded high levels of self-restraint. Allegations that Chinese forces had continued to wage war, ignoring the white flag of enemies, were drawn up to support European claims that the failure to respect individual rights was typical of semi-civilized humanity (Gong 1984: 156).

As part of the domestic legal reforms of 1905 the Chinese government abolished such practices as the dismemberment and desecration of the bodies of those who had been subjected to the death penalty. Whether those steps were merely an exercise in satisfying the European standard of civilization is contested. Domestic political campaigns to promote what many participants regarded as overdue social reforms that were entirely in keeping with ancient traditions certainly existed and may have been strengthened by European pressures. The European condemnation of Chinese cruelties may have had rather more to do with stirring up feelings of civilized superiority than with accurately describing local realities (Bourgon 2003). Highlighting cruel practices was also an integral part of the judgement that China lacked the level of civilization that was necessary to merit consideration for membership of the society of states.[7]

Condescending attitudes were already transparent in Lord Macartney's reports on the British mission to China in 1793–4. In a fascinating passage he claimed that one of the great merits of the British embassy was:

the opportunity it afforded of showing the Chinese to what a high degree of perfection the English nation had carried all the arts and accomplishment of civilized life; that their manners were calculated for the improvement of social intercourse and liberal commerce; that though great and

> powerful they were generous and humane, not fierce and
> impetuous like the Russians, but entitled to the respect
> and preference of the Chinese above the other European
> nations, whom they have knowledge of. (Macartney
> 2004: 181)

The embassy was a monument to what the international lawyers would call the standard of civilization; it was a symbol of the contrast between the 'civilized life' and a 'semi-barbarous' people who had been in steady decline since the conquest of the Manchu Tatars, as Macartney (2004: 176) stated in his private notebooks. Intriguingly, Macartney quoted Louis XIV's assertion that 'there is no point of honour with the Turks' in defence of the judgement that China could not be regarded as an equal of the 'civilized European nations' (cited in Marshall 1993: 22–3). But integral to the idea of the standard of civilization was the belief that the gulf between civilized and the semi-civilized societies was not forever unbridgeable. The stigmatization of Chinese practices was often counterbalanced by a disposition to play down cultural differences and, with respect to Japan, to see merit in the more refined practices of semi-civilized peoples.[8] Here it is useful to recall Elias's statement that the idea of civilization, in contrast with the notion of *Kultur*, played down 'national differences' and emphasized 'what is common to all human beings – or in the view of its bearers – should be' (see p. 59).

The ideas of progress and civilization were central to the belief that major differences between European and non-European state-organized societies could be bridged. The twinned concepts reflected a decisive shift away from static conceptions of social and political order – the movement towards more processual ways of thinking about societies and their prospects for improvement which the standard of civilization represented (Pagden 1988). During the first waves of overseas expansion, the European powers believed that an immutable natural law governed the relations between Christian and non-Christian peoples. According to one historian of international law, the standing of 'non-European State entities' under the 'universal law of nations' was diminished as the European powers replaced the idea of natural law obligations with the legal positivist thesis that binding international duties required the consent of sovereign governments. Semi-civilized state entities were nevertheless considered to be potential 'candidates for admission to ... the European community of States' (Alexandrowicz 1967: 10). From the standpoint of many non-European ruling elites, the discourse of civilized international society was not as exclusionary as Christian international society had been. Membership of the society of states on equal terms with the Western powers appeared to be achievable at some future point, albeit on the condition that the relevant governments succeeded with mimetic civilizing offensives to restructure state institutions in accordance with European standards. In that environment, the translation of the European idea of civilization into non-European languages (discussed in the Introduction) symbolized the great transformation that was under way. Such conceptual innovations were integral to the process in which reformist regimes modified the traditional means of orientation – in which, as outsiders, they imitated core aspects of the modes of government of the global establishment with its professed monopoly of truth about the foundations and constituent elements of civilized coexistence. Revealingly, as part of that realignment, some 'modernizing' elites incorporated Lorimer's tripartite classification of human groups into their own national discourses of self-elevation and self-improvement (Park 2015: 272).

For the most part in the period under discussion, the European ruling classes did not question the legitimacy of empire which was, in their minds, a force for good, but they did debate the rights and wrongs of using force in non-European regions. Support grew during the 19th century for a 'much more empathic internationalised form of imperialism', albeit 'premised on the same principle of the old national form of civilizing mission' (Hobson 2012: 173). The emergence of the 'humanitarian sensibility', which was one manifestation of the increased power of bourgeois forces, gave rise to the 'benign civilizing mission' in the shape of paternalistic government to root out barbaric practices such as infanticide, foot-binding and breast-binding in China as well as the Hindu custom of *sati* or widow burning (Messner 2015: 232; Hobson 2012: 25). Repugnance towards such non-European practices echoed evolving European attitudes to cruelty to women in civilized societies. As part of the bourgeois–liberal revolution, the eradication of violence to women became one of the principal litmus tests of the civilized condition and of progress towards civilization.

Support for duties of care for the spiritual and material well-being of colonial subjects had been a prominent theme in imperial narratives from the period of the Spanish conquest of the Americas. What altered during the 19th century was the balance of power between interventions based on Christian charity and interventions that drew on the discourse of human rights. In the new moral and political environment in which the standard of civilization was explicitly formulated, rather less was heard about extirpating conduct that was 'contrary to nature' and rather more about the moral imperative of eliminating the cruelties of empire and launching civilizing missions or offensives to improve the welfare of colonized peoples. One step towards a 'more empathetic internationalised' form of colonial rule was the 1815 *Declaration of the Eight Powers* at Berlin in which the signatories declared that 'the public voice, in all civilized countries, calls aloud for [the] prompt suppression' of the slave trade, a practice that was 'repugnant to the principles of humanity and universal morality' (Clark 2007: 55). More radically, the imperial powers pledged at the 1885 Berlin Conference on Africa to 'bind themselves to watch over the preservation of the native tribes', to care for 'the improvement of the conditions of their moral and material well-being', and to honour the responsibility for 'instructing the natives and bringing home to them the blessings of civilization' (cited in Paris 2002: 651). Moreover, in Article 22 of the Covenant of the League of Nations regarding the 'mandates system', the colonial governments committed themselves to the principle that the 'well-being and development of (the colonial) peoples form a sacred trust of civilization' which should suffuse the imperial administration of those who are 'not yet able to stand by themselves' (cited in Bain 2003: 101; Pedersen 2015).

Pledges to govern benevolently codified the belief that the colonial powers had to observe higher levels of self-restraint and accountability to other members of the civilized world than in the past (Alexandrowicz 1971). Condemnation of forms of colonial administration that relied on harsh labour exploitation and on maximizing riches without any regard for the welfare of subject peoples became louder and more prominent, not least because of the abuses that had occurred in the Belgian Congo under the reign of Leopold II who treated the colony as his personal fiefdom (Bain 2003: 68ff). Support for benign civilizing missions was therefore linked with measures to enlarge the earlier process of taming the warriors by pacifying the imperialists – with projects to ensure that they civilized themselves and each other. That did not end debates about the place of military force in the exportation of civilization. In Britain in the 1850s, the broad agreement was 'that Britain was civilized, that Asians were not yet civilized, and that the former had a moral duty to nudge the latter along the path from barbarism to civilization'; 'the scope for disagreement' arose over 'the question of how legitimate – if at all – the use of force might be in assisting Asia's progress towards civilization' (see Phillips 2011: 13 who discusses how the First Opium Wars [1839–42] 'starkly divided liberal opinion' on that point). In that period, many European governments believed that it was 'both just and prudent' to use the instruments of violence to crush rebellious elements and to destroy resistance to the colonial project of extending 'the frontiers of liberal civilization to the presumed benefit of civilizer and barbarian alike' (Phillips 2011: 13, 18). They subscribed to the variant on the split within civilization that was discussed in Chapter 3 – to what has been described as 'a discriminatory double standard within international society' in which civilized people claimed a license to use forms of violence in relations with barbarian outsiders, not least when suppressing insurrections, that were officially proscribed in their dealings with one another (Phillips 2011: 18; see also Keene 2002; Suzuki 2009).

At particular historical moments, the use of force was justified as the only means of assisting the victims of what have come to be known as serious human rights abuses. An episode in French policy in the Middle East in 1860 illustrates the point. In August of that year, the French General, Charles de Beaufort d'Hautpoul, commander of the French military expedition to protect Christian victims of the Syrian civil conflict, defended the right to violate the principle of non-intervention by declaring that 'the Emperor has decided that, in the name of civilized Europe, you will go to Syria to help the Sultan's troops avenge humanity disgracefully vilified' (Bass 2008: 194ff; Fawaz 1994: ch 5). But it was increasingly the case that those who believed that force was legitimate in relations with semi-civilized powers did not endorse the tenet that everything was permitted and nothing was forbidden in such conflicts. From that standpoint, it was essential that the Europeans promoted their civilizing offensives in more peaceful ways (Phillips 2011). Changing attitudes to the imperialist variant on the split within civilization were evident in the growing regard for the ethical stance that the European powers had to observe constraints on force in colonized regions that were consistent with the restraints that shaped their relations with each other. In the eyes of the self-defining progressive forces, that combination of restraints marked them out as the most civilized of peoples.

A final comment is that Europeans were convinced that many decades would have to pass before the most advanced non-Western state-organized societies could progress towards the higher levels of social and political development as defined by the standard of civilization – and, in all probability, many centuries would have to elapse in the case of stateless groups that comprised savage humanity. The consensus was that, in the foreseeable future, international society would remain an exclusive club of civilized states which alone would decide when their trustees had made sufficient progress to warrant consideration for inclusion as equally sovereign entities. Those assumptions about the standard of civilization, civilizing offensives, race and colonial international society were stamped on the global order in that era. Contrary to the dominant European beliefs about the strength and durability of the colonial systems, the legitimacy of monopolies of power in non-European regions eroded rapidly, especially in the post-Second World War period. As part of that process, the concept of imperialism lost its status as a 'praise word' that was integral to the 'group charisma' of the global colonial establishment and was used as a 'blame word' or weapon of 'group abuse' by traditional outsiders in the growing struggle against alien rule. The European concept of the standard of civilization was opposed and largely overturned as the global political order was reconfigured, ending a crucial phase in which many non-Western elites implemented their own mimetic civilizing offensives in an attempt to satisfy the standard of civilization and to convince the global establishment of their right of admission into international society. No doubt such practices reinforced the latter's belief that the globalization of constituent elements of the civilizing process was guaranteed and that the future world order would remain European or Western at its core – an assurance that would be overturned by 'Third World' anti-colonial, nationalist movements.

Conclusion

The Eliasian explanation of the civilizing process stated that the idea of civilization was central to the self-consciousness of colonizing peoples and to the narratives that legitimated overseas expansion, but there was little discussion of the part that colonialism had played in the emergence of civilized self-images. The brief analysis of narratives of conquest and discovery in this chapter has explored how representations of non-European peoples influenced later European conceptions of civilizational superiority. The discussion outlined ways in which Elias's approach can be taken further and how his analysis of the role of the manners books in the definition of civilized behaviour codes can be complemented by analyzing genres that may have been more influential in constructing the related sense of superiority over barbarians. The idea of civilizing offensives was employed to relate those comments to the 'standard of civilization'. The latter indicates how the civilizing process was expressed in the constitutive principles of colonial international society. It also reveals how Elias's explanation of the link between state-building and the civilizing process has to be broadened to take account of two interrelated phenomena from which it was inseparable – colonial expansion and the development of

European international society, keystones of the global order until the anticolonial revolution fundamentally altered the principal established–outsider formations in world politics.

This chapter has drawn on the working principles of the Eliasian method to advance a sociological explanation of the standard of civilization which complements the historical emphasis of English School investigations. The standard was a central instrument through which established groups sought to monopolize the means of orientation and to encourage outsiders to absorb feelings of backwardness. Unequal power relations were made concrete in an international legal principle that legitimated the exclusion of outsiders from the society of states and that codified the great powers' racialized assumptions that they had the right to stand in judgement of other cultures, to remake them in their image, and to specify the social and political reforms that had to take place before the colonized peoples could be considered eligible for membership of international society. Those presumptions were indicators of the course of the civilizing process, specifically the broad shift towards more benign forms of colonial administration which appeared alongside the rise of liberal conceptions of progress. The interrelations between 'top-down' initiatives to persuade non-European governments to conform with the standard of civilization and 'bottom–up' imitative strategies to comply with its tenets promoted the internationalization of the European civilizing process from the second half of the 19th century. The impact of those figurations on the modern global political order is the subject of the next chapter.

5

Civilization, Diplomacy and the Enlargement of International Society

This chapter builds on Elias's comment in the late 1930s that the increased acceptance of Western ideas of civilization in the non-Western world is the most recent phase of the civilizing process that can be observed (Elias 2012 [1939]: 426). Part of the explanation for that overall trend was the role of non-Western 'civilizing offensives' to create modern state structures and to alter prevailing orientations to the world order in the attempt to comply with diplomatic practice in the European society of states. The general movement suggested an increasing convergence of European and non-European ruling elites. To return to the seventh theme that was discussed in the Introduction, the whole process was driven by the unequal power relations between established and outsider groups that suppressed but did not remove underlying political tensions. These tensions intensified when global power distributions became more even and as anticolonial forces launched effective challenges to colonial domination and demanded admission into international society on equal terms with the founding European members. The 'revolt against the West' (which will be discussed in Chapter 6) led to the globalization of international society, initially reinforcing the belief, at least in the more optimistic liberal circles, that the whole of humanity might one day become united in the first worldwide civilization.

Explaining the social directions that Elias observed requires an extension of the discussion of civilizing offensives that was advanced in Chapter 4. That inquiry focused on how such an exploration could overcome Elias's failure to consider how European states had used their monopolies of power to control non-European regions.

The investigation can be taken further by considering how non-Western governing elites used their power monopolies to promote complementary civilizing projects. Their top-down civilizing offensives were instrumental in the globalization of the civilizing process which included the transition from a European to a universal society of states. The following comments may seem to echo Elias's comments in the late 1930s on tangible global trends in the first part of the century. He maintained that, with the 'spread of civilization', there was a 'reduction in the differences both of social power and of conduct between colonist and colonised' (Elias 2012 [1939]: 423–5). The former had become more dependent on the latter as a result of increasing global interconnectedness. The upshot was that colonists' 'civilized' standards percolated downwards to non-European upper class groups (Elias 2012 [1939]: 424–5). Although there were influences in both directions and 'new varieties of civilized conduct', the main trend was towards a 'reduction in contrasts', or towards 'diminishing contrasts' and 'increasing varieties' (Elias 2012 [1939]: 422ff). Through those established–outsider figurations, principal features of the European civilizing process became apparent in the relations between imperial powers and subordinated peoples (Elias 2012 [1939]: 425–7). The argument may seem vulnerable to the criticism that it replicated Eurocentric classical sociology by assuming that European ideas spread outwards and downwards to acquiescent, compliant peoples. A more nuanced standpoint can be found in an addendum to the observation about social strata that 'absorb the code of the established groups and thus undergo a process of assimilation', namely that 'people in that situation attempt, with varying degrees of success, to reconcile and fuse that pattern, the pattern of occidentally civilized societies, with the habits and traditions of their own society' (Elias 2012 [1939]: 474–5).[1]

Responding to that discussion, the following analysis does not advance a diffusionist model of change in which docile or supine non-European governments are presumed to have resigned to a global fate and passively replicated the institutions and belief systems of the imperial establishment. Such an image of change has been criticized by International Relations scholars who have argued that classical accounts of the globalization of international society largely ignored the role of non-Western agency in shaping the global order (Dunne and Reus-Smit 2017). Reflections on the globalization of the civilizing process in this chapter seek to avoid perpetuating the Eurocentric error of underestimating levels of non-European political agency (Lawson 2017). The argument begins by describing powerful external pressures on non-European governments to comply with civilized standards and it notes how uneven global relations placed very severe constraints on non-European initiatives (see Hobson 2017; Linklater 2017). They had restricted opportunities to do much more than contribute to the internationalization of specific features of the European civilizing process. However, many regimes emulated the European state model with the explicit short-term aim of preserving as much autonomy as possible and with the longer-term aspiration of maximizing their political capacities. High levels of resignation to global pressures existed but this discussion will stress how non-Western political agency was exercised, for example, by promoting novel alliances of nation and civilization. The globalization of the civilizing process was a powerful trend that was expressed in diverse nation-state formations in the non-European world. The foundations for subsequent challenges to Western power and principles that would transform the society of states were laid in the process. They did not at the time dent the Europeans' confidence in the global triumph of 'civilized' arrangements. Only a few decades later they would undermine any lingering belief in the imminent development of a world civilization.

Viewed in long-term perspective, European overseas expansion brought different standards of civilization – more accurately, from a process-sociological perspective, different civilizing processes in the etic sense – into contact and collision (Gong 1984: 3). As discussed in Chapter 4, the powerful civilizing offensive that evolved out of one dominant process of civilization was the primary determinant of global change. Relations between court societies revealed how diverse conceptions of civilized arrangements could clash. Lord Macartney's refusal to perform the traditional 'kowtow' in the presence of the Emperor during the diplomatic mission to China is the most famous example. The encounter lends support to Elias's conjecture that the close relationship between court society and civilizing processes was not confined to Europe but existed in many non-European regions and eras (Elias 2006: ch 1). The question raised was whether further research would reveal that many court figurations had been at the hub of processes of civilization in which the ruling elites displayed their superiority over the lower strata by constructing esoteric rituals and refined codes of conduct (see Spawforth 2007 on early civilizations).

The episode regarding the kowtow indicates how diplomatic protocols and etiquette were intertwined with formalized distinctions between the civilized and the barbarian, and between the established and the outsiders, in Chinese court conceptions of world order. The event was an example of tensions between court figurations with different standards of civilization and criteria for judging the relative standing or status of other courts – for defining the entitlements and obligations of the established in relations with outsiders, and for prescribing how inferiors should behave in the presence of overlords. That illustration of how different standards of civilization came into contact as a result of European outward expansion has been a core symbol in the West of actual and emerging shifts in global power balances that created immense pressures on traditional governing elites to submit to an alien conception of world order. The civilizing offensives that were spearheaded by non-Western court societies were decisive interventions to transform traditional means of orientation to the social world in the wake of their rapid incorporation within a Western-dominated global network of established–outsider relations that brought new anxieties, insecurities and dangers.

The remainder of this chapter provides brief overviews of major features of European diplomatic relations with court societies in China, Japan and Siam, and with Tsarist Russia and the Ottoman Empire that were instrumental in the dissemination of regulative principles that revealed the interdependencies between the European civilizing process and colonial international society. The five sections discuss external pressures on non-European court societies to abandon what Westerners regarded as engrained barbaric conceptions of political order which posited their intrinsic superiority over other peoples. They consider the relationship between European stigmatizing strategies and non-European elite concessions of backwardness and inferiority. The chapter shows how global civilizing offensives were refracted in the mimetic efforts by non-European court societies to reform governing structures and to master the rules of European diplomatic practice. What has been described as 'borrowed colonialism' was an additional part of those late-19th century non-European civilizing offensives (Deringil 2003). In the case of Russia, the Ottomans and Japan, imitative imperial ventures to promote civilization in their respective regions were designed to advertise the strength of the commitment to sharing the global burden of exporting civilization. In conjunction, those three state policies (state reform, adaptation to European diplomatic codes of behaviour, and colonial ventures) contributed to the internationalization of core dimensions of the European civilizing process.

China

The transformative effects of changing established–outsider relations in an emergent global political order were nowhere more evident than in the evolution of relations between the European great powers and

China between the 16th and 19th centuries. When Portuguese and Dutch traders first explored the prospects for commercial relations in China, they assumed the role of supplicants who sought to ingratiate themselves in the ruling circles. They had no choice but to hope to insert themselves into an existing East Asian trading system that was largely controlled by China and which required compliance with imperial standards of civilization (Zhang 2017: 213–4). Traders were accustomed to non-European practices of granting protection within designated areas, and they were the beneficiaries of established conventions as long as they did not exploit the good will of their hosts. But, as power balances shifted, Europeans began to insist on the right to impose their legal codes on disputes involving their own citizens (Benton and Clulow 2015). In the case of China, Europeans continued to display respectful attitudes as power relations became more even. Late 18th-century portrayals of China often commented favourably on the combination of civility and refinement, political order and enduring stability, with the aim of defending enlightened absolutist rule in Europe (Israel 2006: ch 25). But high regard for China gave way to contempt in radical Enlightenment circles with the intensification of power struggles between the traditional autocracy and a reforming bourgeoisie. Bourgeois strata increasingly contrasted the fast-changing European economic, cultural and political landscape with the frozen condition of 'oriental despotism' (Zhang 2017: 211–12). Stigmatizing representations of a dull and stagnant China were later embellished with the racial dichotomies through which Europeans imputed their superiority to natural qualities (Zhang 2017: 219).

The fate of the kowtow has long been regarded as a classic symbol of those evolving changing power relations. According to the traditional Chinese world order, inferiors were obliged to kowtow before the Emperor (a ritual in which kneeling three times and knocking the head on the ground nine times signified submission). Those who declined to follow the practice were firmly rebuffed. The Chinese court assumed that the first European traders and travellers would observe the social norms that governed relations with barbarians. Dutch merchants certainly did so towards the end of the 17th century in the knowledge that compliance with court ceremony in Peking was necessary in order to undertake commercial relations. A Russian envoy who had refused a few years earlier to comply with the rituals surrounding the kowtow, on the grounds that they were demeaning and appropriate only before God, offended Chinese court society with damaging results for Russia's trading objectives (Keene 1969: 4). The 1645 Chinese Rites Controversy, which stemmed from the issue of whether Chinese

Christians were obliged to follow the practice of kowtowing to the Emperor, was revealing in that context. The Jesuits argued that Chinese converts should perform the traditional rituals, a position rejected by the Dominicans and Franciscans but endorsed by the Pope in 1645. The outcome was that the Emperor ordered the expulsion of all non-Jesuit missionaries from China (Gong 1984: 133ff). The vexed issue of whether Lord Macartney, as representative of King George III, should act in accordance with imperial court practice inevitably arose during the official visit of 1793. Macartney refused to display voluntary submission by kowtowing in an audience with the Qing Emperor. He was permitted – apparently after complex diplomatic negotiations resulting in unusual Chinese concessions – to convey respect for the Emperor by bowing on only one knee (Gong 1984: 132ff; Tseng-Tsai 1993; see Macartney 2004 for his own account).

The episode can be interpreted as a meeting between court societies with different conceptions of the correct rituals for displaying respect for monarchs. How far there was compromise on the Chinese side – indeed on both sides – is a matter for specialists (see Hevia 2009 for a re-evaluation of traditional accounts of Macartney's rejection of Chinese protocols and a reassessment of Chinese standpoints). Crucial for the development of European self-images was the manner in which the diplomatic encounter was represented in Britain as the honourable refusal by a representative of the monarch of a civilized nation to participate in a humiliating ritual of slavish obeisance that an arrogant and ignorant China imposed on alleged barbarians. No less significant was the belief that non-compliance was the pre-eminent symbol of the inexorable decline of an outmoded world order in which human societies were organized hierarchically under the Son of Heaven, the Emperor of the Middle Kingdom. Objectionable from European standpoints was the Chinese supposition that the Emperor, 'far from being the ruler of one state among many' was 'the mediator between heaven and earth … the apex of civilization, unique in the universe' (Mancall 1968: 63). According to the neo-Confucian world view, East Asian societies were bound together in relations of civility in which China acted benevolently towards inferiors who were expected to act respectfully, showing due gratitude in return (Park 2015). Certainly, at different intervals in their history, ruling elites in Korea, Assam, Burma and Siam performed the rituals of deference that China expected of those who sought formal recognition as tributary states or vassals. The Chinese preference was that societies that failed to acknowledge its superiority should be kept at a safe distance, whether through the erection of physical barriers such as the Great Wall or through confinement to specialist commercial enclaves as in the case of European traders whose activities were restricted in the mid-18th century to Macao and Canton (see Hobson 2020: ch 2 for a more comprehensive analysis). Engaging with China on equal terms was emphatically ruled out (Zhang and Buzan 2012).

Collisions between standards of civilization highlight what the Chinese and the Europeans had in common. Each behaved as an establishment that stigmatized outsider groups. However, the idea of the sovereign equality of states was plainly anathema to Chinese court society which understandably regarded European assessments of China as an inferior civilization as deeply insulting. For their part, the diplomatic representatives of European court societies were offended by the Chinese practice of treating them as inferiors. Their sequestration in Canton and exposure to arbitrary customs duties were sources of resentment that were regarded as 'scarcely compatible with the regulations of Civilized Society' (Zhang 2017: 214). The Chinese imperial court resisted efforts to make it comply with the trading conventions which the Europeans regarded as quintessential features of a civilized international order but which, from certain Confucian ethical standpoints, privileged the accumulation of material wealth over higher human virtues (see Hobson 2020: ch 2, for a critique of traditional assumptions about neo-Confucian attitudes to free trade and commerce). Prior to the 'Arrow' affair (the *casus belli* for the Second Opium War when, in October 1856, Chinese officials had seized the Chinese crew of the 'Arrow', a vessel displaying the British flag and executed a French missionary), Europeans were forced to deal with the Emperor through intermediaries in the Canton 'viceroy system' (Gong 1984:149). After the 'Arrow' affair, Western diplomats were granted rights of residence in Peking but were still refused direct access to the imperial court.

The Chinese governing elite were compelled to give up their hegemonic conception of world order, their standard of civilization, and long-established diplomatic practices as the balance of power tilted towards Europe which was quick to impose its image of civilized inter-state conduct. To comply with European norms, at the end of the Second Opium War China acceded to the presence of foreign diplomatic representation in Peking (by accepting the terms of the 1858 Treaty of Tientsin which the Emperor ratified in the 1860 Convention of Peking). As part of the project of reforming state structures, it established the first centralized institution to manage China's external relations – *Zongli Yamen* (Zhang 1991). Chinese diplomatic missions to Western capitals were despatched between 1868 and 1870. It is revealing that the first overseas mission – the Burlingame mission which visited Europe and the United States – was led by the former American minister plenipotentiary to Peking, Anson Burlingame, but the first permanent mission in London was not established until 1877 (Zhang 1991). Several reports from officials who had been appointed to the Chinese Foreign Office in the mid-19th century described the shame and disgrace of having to undertake demeaning diplomatic responsibilities which symbolized the ascendancy of foreigners or 'red-haired devils' (Frodsham 1974: xxvi).

A detailed understanding of Western international law through the mastery of key legal treatises was a major element in the process of re-orientation and readjustment to the realities of China's rapid and traumatic entanglement in the long webs of interconnectedness that extended outwards from the West (Gong 1984: 151). As discussed earlier, international law was regarded in the West as 'the body of rules which the civilized states consider legally binding in their intercourse' with each other (Oppenheim 1955: 117). In 1864, the American missionary, W.A.P. Martin, who alleged that he had 'witnessed numerous Chinese blunders in diplomatic transactions', completed the Chinese translation of Wheaton's *Elements of International Law*; this was presented to the Emperor in January 1865 (Wright 1957: 237; see Gong 1984: 153 who adds that a Japanese edition was published in 1865). Significantly, Martin became chief instructor in the section of the Chinese Foreign Office (*Zongli Yamen*) with responsibility for the translation of Western international legal texts. The upshot was that, by the late 1860s, many other studies of international law were available in elite circles.

Such works were equivalent to the etiquette books that were centre stage in Elias's explanation of the civilizing process. What might be called 'manners books for aspiring civilized states' were the diplomatic equivalent of the guides to everyday conduct that Europeans had consulted in the zealous attempt to comply with the behaviour codes that emerged with increasing social interdependencies in state-organized societies. They were counterparts to the 'mirrors for princes' – the advice books for sovereign rulers which proliferated in court societies from the Renaissance – and they were not unlike the treatises on the ideal virtues of courtiers and ambassadors which had circulated in the European supranational court society (Linklater 2016: 154ff, 176ff). Those discourses on the state and diplomacy were the bridge between intra- and inter-societal civilizing processes that were moving outwards from Europe. Engaging with Chinese translations of Western legal texts was one of the means by which court officials became familiar with the protocols and rituals of European diplomacy and largely internalized the relevant standards of restraint – one of the ways then in which they adapted to unconventional 'meeting regimes' and alien 'meeting behaviour'. Core features of the civilizing process were internationalized in that way.

Lorimer (1883: 239) described the operative power relations when he argued that the 'semi-civilized' societies had a dual status in international society by belonging 'partly to the category of recognised and partly to the category of protected states'; accordingly, the global norms governing 'ambassadors whom states in the same civilization interchange' did not apply to relations with the 'semi-barbarous'; the representatives of 'civilized societies' had 'greater rights and responsibilities' than ambassadors sent in return. Concerned about possible future alterations in power balances, some European diplomats feared that Chinese translations of international legal texts would equip the governing Chinese elite with the capacity (which indeed is what it hoped to acquire) to mount a powerful attack on both the principle of extraterritoriality, which had been imposed by the 1842 Treaty of Nanking, and the unequal treaties that had been ratified at the end of the Second Opium War. Those challenges lay ahead. The main consequence of the global distribution of power around 1880 was that 'the traditional Chinese world order characterized by a tribute system' had almost been replaced by a treaty system' that clearly worked to the advantage of Western political and economic interests. China was reduced to a 'semi-colony' with 'nominal independence but incomplete sovereignty' (Zhang 1991: 5). Power shifts were not only evident in the rules governing civilized elite diplomatic interaction. Symptomatic of the radical realignment of established–outsider relations – and openly displaying contempt for social inferiors – were official signs posted outside parks in Shanghai stating that 'no Dogs or Chinese' were allowed entry (Gong 1984: 161).

A brief summary in process-sociological terms of the overall course of change in the period under discussion can therefore begin with the era in which power distributions tilted in favour of Western states which used their monopoly powers to launch civilizing offensives to promote China's conformity with Western notions of civilized statehood and diplomatic practice. Mimetic domestic offensives were undertaken in that phase in the attempt to elevate China's standing in the global order. New categories such as *wenming* (see the Introduction) were invented in the endeavour to move traditional means of orientation closer to Western ideas of civilization and progress. In the language of process sociology, uneven power balances forced outsiders to resign to external forces, but they did not eliminate underlying tensions, feelings of resentment or the pain of humiliation. Examples included hostility to European demands for the right to trade freely and for permanent diplomatic representation in Peking. The treaty ports that lay outside Chinese jurisdiction as part of the terms of unequal treaties and the principle of extraterritoriality were symbols of subjugation. Domestic struggles and conflicts pitched self-defining progressive forces against a backward-looking establishment that was accused of blocking the path to civilization. Those responses illustrate a recurrent feature in social groups which Elias (2007a: 9–10) described as the loss of collective 'self-love' and the traumatic experience of losing 'value as human beings' as a result of major shifts in power relations. Resentment and hostility fuelled open conflict during the Opium Wars and in the 1899–1901 Boxer Rebellion which was the high point of organized violent reaction against Western political and economic dominance and pressures to submit to civilization. Such resistance was ruthlessly suppressed.

In such conditions – in the context of highly asymmetrical power relations – governing elites may decide that the most prudent strategy is resignation, expressed in public declarations of voluntary compliance with the unwelcome demands of established groups. Just over ten years after the suppression of the Boxer Rebellion – on 1 January, 1912 when the Republic of China was founded – the first President, Sun Yat-sen, announced the intention to discharge the duties and acquire the rights of civilized peoples (Wang 1993). It would be unwise to regard such statements as evidence of the grateful incorporation of Western principles as opposed to the pragmatic acceptance of the realities of altered power relations. An insightful English School observation about the public discourse of 'Third World' movements in the immediate aftermath of national independence is worth keeping in mind. In that period, the argument was, the leaders 'spoke as supplicants in a world in which the Western powers were still in a dominant position'; appeals to and claims against them had to be justified in a language that was the creation of the Western powers; they 'had to be cast in terms that would have most resonance in Western societies' (Bull 1984a: 213). Those words hint at underlying patterns of reluctance on the part of the governments involved. This can be usefully complemented by the process-sociological point that only when power balances become 'more equal' can the forces of 'rebellion, resistance [and] emancipation' erupt and organize with increased prospects of success (see pp. 20–1). The era in which particular groups in societies such as China appeared to freely appropriate and embrace the European discourse of civilization should be seen in that light.

Japan

Parallels to the anxieties, tensions and conflicts which emerged in China as a result of the encroachment of the Western powers took place in Japan, as exemplified by the 1863 decree by the Emperor Komei to 'Revere the Emperor, Expel the Barbarians'. The slogan was steadily replaced in the period between 1873 and 1877 by the discourse of 'civilization and enlightenment'; this did not, however, connote the passive acceptance of a superior Western culture. Support for a synthesis of 'Eastern morality' and 'Western technology' was strong among members of the dominant strata in that era. Various groups defended traditional attitudes and behaviour by emphasizing the greater spirituality of Japanese culture compared to the crass materialism of the West (Miyoshi 1979: 121–2; Benesch 2015). Even so, specialist institutes to promote 'Western learning' and 'the study of barbarian books' were established in the 1850s in the attempt to 'modernize' Japan, not least by importing Western military technology and organization (Beasley 1995: 45ff; Miyoshi 1979: prologue, 169ff). The outward cultural turn represented a weakening of deep-seated hostility towards foreigners exemplified by the 'Tokugawa seclusion edicts' which had been introduced in the 1630s with the intention of insulating Japan from corrupting barbaric influences. Also significant was the move away from conventional attitudes regarding castaways in the 1830s and 1840s. Early 19th-century official positions rejected the idea of a moral duty to rescue 'ships in distress' as part of the 1825 doctrine of 'unconditional repulsion', a proclamation of Japanese cultural superiority that was, from Western standpoints, a brutal reminder that the Japanese were unashamedly 'barbaric in their treatment of foreigners' (Suganami 1984: 189). Such established orientations to outsiders, which typified the Japanese civilizing process in the etic meaning of the term (see Ohira 2014), became unsustainable as a result of Western encroachments into East Asia. These were most clearly symbolized by Commodore Perry's arrival in Japan in 1853 and by subsequent pressures on the Japanese government to accede to the establishment of the first United States consulate.

From 1868 onwards, the Meiji leadership was acutely aware that the European-dominated global order was sharply bifurcated between a civilized core and a barbaric periphery destined for colonial subjugation (Suzuki 2009: 56ff). To avoid imperial subordination, the ruling elite embarked on transforming governing institutions that were relatively weak by European standards into a civilized modern state (Smith 2018: ch 8). Participating in European wars (such as the conflict to suppress the Boxer Rebellion in China) was one of the means by which Japanese court society tried to earn 'a reputation among the Western Powers as a civilized nation' (Suzuki 2009, 2012). Japan's respect for Western legal restraints on the use of force in the 1905 war with Russia led several European observers to assert that Japan had made tangible progress in meeting the standards of civilized nations.

More than any other episode, the conflict with Russia led several Western governments to conclude that Japan was by far the more civilized of the two powers, and also much more advanced than barbaric China (Howland 2007). Japan was deemed to be more Anglo-Saxon than Slav because of its alliance with the Western powers in resisting Russian territorial expansion (Henning 2000: ch 6). A regime that had been widely condemned for the November 1894 'Port Arthur massacre' (in which Japanese armed forces killed Chinese military personnel and civilians allegedly in response to the mutilation of Japanese bodies) was elevated in some quarters to the exalted position of the 'Britain of the East' (Mégret 2006; see Howland 2007: 196 on Western legal opinion that the 'Port Arthur massacre' was a 'momentary but excusable lapse' from general compliance with international law which had been provoked by Chinese atrocities). Success in winning Western approval did not go unnoticed farther afield. In the Ottoman Empire, Japan's military achievements were greeted by 'modernizers' as proof that non-Western powers were not incapable by virtue of intrinsic deficiencies from undertaking a progressive journey from barbarism to civilization (Worringer 2014).

The encounter of Japanese elites with the dualistic nature of the European global order led to the internalization of the belief that civilized great powers had the moral entitlement to bring the achievements of civilization to uncivilized peoples. Ruling groups came to think that colonial civilizing offensives were crucial for forging national identity in an aspirant civilized state – the nation-based empire modelled on the European state form which Japan was the first non-Western society to emulate and which was widely admired internationally (Lam 2010; Suzuki 2012).

To analyze Japan's re-orientation towards the West, it is valuable to consider the role of the court official, Fukuzawa Yukichi, who studied the English language at one of the specialist institutes mentioned earlier and who was, in addition, a member of the 1872 Iwakura mission to Europe (and of the delegations that had visited the United States and

Europe in the 1860s). As one of the most influential 'modernizers', Fukuzawa Yukichi endeavoured to explain the principal features of Western civilization to a Japanese readership in his 1875 work, *Outline of a Theory of Civilization* (Fukuzawa 2008 [1875]). Striking evidence of the break with the classical Japanese position in which China was the celebrated, standard-setting society was the contention that:

> we cannot wait for our neighbour countries to become so civilized that all may combine together to make Asian progress. We must rather break out of formation and behave in the same way as the civilized countries of the West are doing. ... We would do better to treat China and Korea in the same way as do the Western nations. (cited in Miyoshi 1979: 53)

This standpoint was further developed in the startling comment that military conflict between Japan and China would be a war between the only 'civilized' society in the region and a 'barbarian' adversary (cited in Miyoshi 1979: 53; 167ff; Benesch 2014: 56ff). What Fukuzawa described elsewhere as 'escaping' from Asia (Eskildsen 2002) was central to the larger project of national re-orientation in which the Japanese brought an end to traditional cultural deference to the Middle Kingdom.

The rapid emergence of a positive image of Western societies was far from uncritical. Several thousand years from now, Fukuzawa (2008 [1875]: 33) argued, Western civilization might well be judged to have been 'pitifully primitive' but, in the perilous circumstances of the late 19th century, Japan had no alternative but to regard the West as the yardstick with which to assess its social and political progress. A major development given the vulnerabilities caused by fast-changing power relations was the realization that Japanese society lacked the social cohesion and organized political power that Western societies possessed as a result of the binding force of nationalism (Fukuzawa 2008 [1875]: ch 10). Only by fostering close emotional identification between citizens – rather than reinforcing their status as subjects of the Emperor – could Japan hope to preserve its political independence in the short term and to compete with vastly more powerful societies in future decades. The humiliating treatment of China and the violence of Western colonial expansion were warnings of Japan's probable fate if it did not succeed in emulating Western social, political and military developments. British and French shelling of the cities of Kagoshima and Shimonoseki in 1863 and 1864 was proof of the futility of military resistance and the impossibility of escaping punitive unequal treaties (Benesch 2015: 253).

Japan was at the forefront of the trend in which non-European societies attuned themselves to the traumatic effects of seismic shifts in global power balances by endeavouring to comply with an alien standard of civilization governing diverse phenomena such as state structures and the rules of diplomatic exchange. A relatively detached understanding of the place of 'civilization' in Western orientations to the social world was deemed critical for national success. References to fusing 'Eastern morality' with 'Western technology' in Japanese writings – and Fukuzawa's comment about how future generations might judge Western civilization – indicate that there was more to Japan's position than the slavish imitation of alien ways. The nuances were captured in the writings of Kume Kunitake – official chronicler of the Iwakura mission and Prince Iwakura's personal secretary – who understood the nature of the 'split within civilization'. It was apparent to him that 'civilized' peoples followed different codes of behaviour in relations with each other and in dealings with those who were portrayed as barbaric or semi-civilized. But it was vital to understand – and here Kume Kunitake regarded Bismarck as the authoritative guide to the fundamentals of Western international relations – that civilized 'siblings' which were bound together by a unique diplomatic code were often embroiled in violent struggles for security and in elimination contests to attain hegemony (Kunitake 2009: 53ff, 98). From that standpoint, the process of re-orientation to the realities of Western political and military engagement in East Asia demanded the detached analysis of how those interlocking aspects of the 'split within civilization' had transformed Japan's political and military environment. Vital was deciding how to adapt to the European states-system which had incorporated East Asian societies in its endemic tensions and struggles as a result of unprecedented global reach.

The anatomy of barbarous foreign practices resulted in efforts to emulate the Western state model and the parallel process of civilized colonial expansion. Japanese imperial ambitions in the Meiji period were partly motivated by the determination to show that the governing elite was committed to following the lead of the global establishment. They were evidence of the resolve 'to satisfy Western standards of civilization in external affairs' (Gong 1984: ch 7; Suganami 1984: 198). A central part of the project was the establishment of a Colonization Office, tellingly named the Bureau of Savage Affairs. As for Japan's practical ambitions, a major example was the 1874 proposed colonization of, and civilizing offensive in, Taiwan (aborted shortly after the invasion given the fear that colonization could lead to war with China). The strategy was initiated at a time when Japan was anxious to refute Western perceptions of its semi-civilized condition and keen to advertise its progress in creating a modern national political consciousness. One of the most influential prints of the period celebrating the invasion portrayed the samurai not in customary attire but in Western-style military uniforms (Eskildsen 2002). Such adaptations to Western dress codes appeared shortly after the decision that was made following the Ikawura diplomatic mission to the West to embrace the discourse of 'civilization and enlightenment' (*bunmei-kaika*) as part of the initiative to 'catch up' with the West (Gong 1984: 180).

Protestations by the Meiji leadership that it had the right to 'lead the natives gradually to civilization' appear to have been influenced not only by witnessing the practical consequences of how state, civilization and empire were conjoined in the Western political imagination but also by the active encouragement of US consular officials in Japan (Eskildsen 2002: 394ff). The Japanese author, Takekoshi Yosaburō later captured the relationship between imported notions of European civilization and Japanese colonialism when he wrote (in 1907) that the:

> Western nations have long believed that on their shoulders alone rested the responsibility of colonizing the yet unopened portions of the globe, and extending to the inhabitants the benefits of civilization; but now we Japanese, rising from the ocean in the extreme Orient, wish as a nation to take part in this great and glorious work. (cited in Suzuki 2012)

Domestic political programmes also contributed to external impressions that Japan was playing a valuable role in promoting civilization. Some US observers pointed to a direct parallel between Japan's relations with the indigenous Ainu people and America's 'civilizing mission' in relations with 'savage Indian tribes' (Henning 2000: ch 6). Such favourable comparisons mattered. They encouraged the view among the Japanese ruling elite that their society was on course to formal admission into the society of states as an equal sovereign member.

Fukuzawa Yukichi's contention that Japan 'would do better to treat China and Korea in the same way as do the Western nations' – and the general strategy of re-orientation towards the West – showed that the colonial project attached little value to emotional identification with 'fellow Asians' (Suzuki 2012). Japan strained to flourish its credentials as a civilized power by combining civilizing offensives with a 'Japanese-style Orientalism' (see Suzuki 2012) which was largely untouched by support for the universal and egalitarian principles that were part of the duality of Western nation-state normative codes (see the discussion on pp. 97ff). The overriding ambition of winning the respect of the European powers was pursued through nationalist policies of 'self-improvement' which were meant to show that Japan was considerably more advanced than other Asian societies. Its regional prestige rose quickly in a period in which many Asian governments regarded Japan as standard-setting as far as their own Western-style, civilizing initiatives were concerned. The Chinese government, for example, was keen to learn from Japanese initiatives in various spheres such as policing which had been central to the state's civilizing role in Western Europe in the late 18th century (Neocleous 2011). Success in that domain was imperative to convince Western governments that modernized state structures could provide levels of protection for their citizens as required by the 'standard of civilization'. Again, those political initiatives which were undertaken with the aim of bolstering the case for the abolition of the principle of extraterritoriality helped to globalize core features of the European civilizing process (Lam 2010).

Japan's standard-setting role also increased in a period in which 'modernizers' in Asian societies were shocked by the impotence of local state structures in the face of external pressures and highly critical of traditional cultural orientations to the world that underpinned the continuing dominance of traditional elites. An example was the early 20th-century Vietnamese Reform Movement which drew on Japanese as well as Chinese influences in the attempt to harness the 'emancipatory potential' of 'civilizational thinking' (Bradley 2004). The 1904 tract, *The Civilization of New Learning*, expressed growing demands for breaking the grip of a static Confucian moral code which was believed to obstruct the political and economic reforms that explained the global reach of the Western powers. But, for some societies, Japan, the most successful East Asian imitator of the West, was not a benign example of how modernization could equip Asian societies with ways of adapting to, as well as containing, Western encroachment but the source of new assaults on political autonomy. Those fears had been aroused and confirmed by an official memorandum to the Korean government in 1875 in which the Japanese government departed from diplomatic convention by threatening to use force to undermine its independence (Park 2015: 270–1).

Japan's hopes that it would win recognition as a civilized society by imitating the behaviour of the Western imperial great powers would meet with disappointment. Several Japanese intellectuals proclaimed its success in the 1905 Russian-Japanese war as incontrovertible evidence that Japan had become a 'civilized' nation – *bunmei kaika* – with the right to stand shoulder to shoulder with the Western great powers (Shimazu 1998: ch 4). Indicative of increased elite confidence was the sardonic comment by the Japanese scholar, Okakura Tenshin, that in the era 'when Japan was engaging in peaceful acts, the West used to think of it as an uncivilized country'; but ever since 'Japan started massacring thousands of people' (for example, in the 'battlefields of Manchuria') the Western powers had praised it as a 'civilized country' (cited in Suzuki 2005: 137). It was certainly the case that Japan's unexpected defeat of Russia had enormous global symbolic ramifications, raising its standing which had already been enhanced by its respect for international law in the conflict with China. Successful imitation of Western state institutions and related practices led the traditional colonial powers to acknowledge its right to be admitted into the society of states. Shuzo Aoki, the Japanese ambassador to Britain and Germany, declared that Japan joined the ranks of 'civilized' societies in 1899, the year in which the principle of extraterritoriality was officially lifted.

But formal admission into the society of states did not translate into equal respect and social status. Elias's observation about a recurrent tendency in the relations between established and outsiders groups, one that was evident in the changing relations between the traditional aristocratic establishment and the emergent bourgeoisie in absolutist court society, is relevant here. The former had long ensured that 'everything reminiscent of lower classes, everything vulgar, was kept at a distance', and not least because of 'constant pressure from below' to gain access to court circles (Elias 2012 [1939]: 464ff). Faced with such demands, and fearing the erosion of power and privileges, the upper strata continuously 'polished everything that distinguished them from people of lower rank: not only the external signs of status, but also their speech, their gestures, their social amusements and manners' (Elias 2012 [1939]: 467). They were adept at creating new forms of social distinction – new walls or barriers – to protect their specialness or 'group charisma'.

Elias (2012 [1939]: 425) identified similar processes in what he described as the 'double tendency' that was inherent in the 'expansion of Western civilization'. On the one hand, members of the imperial establishment inevitably transported elements of 'their own style of conduct and institutions' to subordinated regions. One of the driving forces behind that development – and 'one of the most remarkable characteristics of this civilizing process' within Europe and beyond – was the attraction of elite attitudes and behaviour to the members of rising or aspirant social groups (Elias 2012 [1939]: 473). The actions of the imperial powers 'together with the structure of the general movement which is carrying them along, force[d] them in the long run more and more to reduce these differences in standards of behaviour' (Elias 2012 [1939]: 425). The point can be extended to show how a combination of colonial civilizing offensives and mimetic initiatives in non-Western societies resulted in a partial reduction of cultural differences between at least the governing elites in the period under discussion. The other side of the 'double tendency' was the reality that the 'Western nations as a whole have an upper-class function' and are 'driven to maintain at all costs their special conduct and drive-control as marks of distinction' (Elias 2012 [1939]: 425). They continued to search for novel ways of 'building a wall between themselves and the groups that they are colonizing and whom – by the "right of the stronger" – they consider their inferiors' (Elias 2012 [1939]: 425).

The Western powers' rejection of the Japanese proposal in April 1919 that the principle of racial equality should be enshrined in the Covenant of the League of Nations was a dramatic example of how established groups can applaud a modernizing elite on its progress toward civilization while erecting new barriers (or, in this case, falling back on earlier ones) as markers of distinction and superiority (Shimazu 1998; Hobson 2012: 167ff). The establishment of great powers cemented the link between race and civilization to deny that Japan was their equal in international society. The refusal to make concessions to Japan had profound consequences for the globalization of civilized norms and practices. In response to perceived humiliations, increasingly nationalist and militarist reactions against the West accentuated the uniqueness of Japanese civilization and the necessity of pursuing a distinctive national destiny (Benesch 2015). The universalistic and egalitarian elements of nation-state normative codes – which were, in any case, in retreat in Europe in the final part of the 19th century – had little impact on Japan's foreign policy orientations. That was hardly surprising given that US President Wilson's faith in liberal-democratic precepts was suffused with racism and that other great powers such as Britain made the link between race and civilization central to their image of global order – hence their united opposition to Japan's advocacy of the principle of racial equality (Ambrosius 2007). There were unmistakable parallels between German claims that the discourse of humanity and civilization was no more than 'hypocrisy' or 'deception', and a cover for Britain's pursuit of naked self-interest, and Japanese nationalist protests against the Western international order (and here it is useful to recall that Kunitake had taken special note of Bismarck's claim that civilized 'siblings' were bound together by the same diplomatic code and by recurrent and frequently violent struggles for hegemony).

The first part of the 'double tendency', as described by Elias, was the process in which non-Western elites were drawn towards the ideas of civilization that had been promoted by the imperial powers; the second part was the counter-offensive in which the global establishment attempted to entrench and reinforce the symbols of social superiority. But there was a third tendency in which non-Western social and political forces organized to protect and restore an endangered traditional way of life. There were similarities between that development and German support for the 'praise word' *Kultur* over civilization – and not only in Japan. Several Ottoman intellectuals contended that German victory in the Franco-German war in 1871 was evidence of the superiority of *Kultur* (Wigen 2015). In the case of Japan, the influence of nationalist-Machiavellian principles of foreign policy greatly exceeded the emotive power of universal-egalitarian norms which lacked the support of powerful social groups. A particular combination of the imported ideas of nationalism and civilization weakened the position of any political movement that wished to undertake the civilizational 'critique of the nation'. The ensuing balance of power between competing elements of European nation-state moral codes did not augur well for those who believed that the Western powers had prepared the way for the first global civilization.

Siam

Linguistic innovations that have been noted with respect to the Chinese notion of *wenming* and the Japanese concept of *bunmei* (see Introduction) also occurred in the neighbouring kingdom of Siam. The concepts, *siwilai* (civilization) and *charoen* (material progress and technological advance), were introduced into the Siamese language as part of the same urgent quest to understand and assimilate European standards of civilization in the context of foreseeable foreign domination or annexation (Winichakul 2000). It is useful to consider those developments in longer-term perspective, beginning with the fact that up to the 19th century, Siam followed the rules and rituals of the Chinese imperial system, but exercised hegemonic power over Cambodia, Laos, and the Shan States (Englehart 2010: 435, note 4). As far back as 1684 and 1685, missions from the Siamese court had visited Versailles, and the reigning monarch, King Narai, had engaged a pro-French Greek adventurer, Constantine Phaulkon, to petition Louis XIV to send French troops to protect Siamese forts.

The ensuing French military presence fuelled 'anti-foreign sentiment' which resulted in the government's decision to expel the French and later to banish all Westerners from the country (Gong 1984: 203–4). The Siamese ruling elite set out in the mid- to late-19th century to discover first hand from courts in St Petersburg, London and Berlin how to secure European recognition as a 'civilized monarchy' while at the same time learning from Japan's pioneering efforts (Gong 1984: ch 7). The role of King Chulalongkorn was crucial here; he forged a close relationship with the Russian Tsar who, indicating the expansion of the traditional 'supranational' court society, wrote letters of introduction to the kings of Sweden and Denmark and Queen Victoria (Englehart 2010: 430). Building on such initiatives, the Siamese government sent representatives of the very 'highest social rank' to Britain to receive specialist training in 'proper decorum and European languages' which was virtually unobtainable in peripheral regions (Englehart 2010: 423). Success in understanding and observing 'court etiquette' led the *London Gazette* to applaud the Siamese delegation in the condescending tone of the period 'for setting an example of deference and good taste which it would be well for the Orientals frequenting our Court to be made to follow' (Englehart 2010: 425).

Specialist studies of Siam's incorporation into the European society of states have analyzed its adaptation to alien practices in intricate detail. In an attempt to secure recognition of Siam's civilized status, King Chulalongkorn made concessions to European standards with respect to everyday manners and diplomatic protocol. In two separate visits to Europe to meet heads of state – in 1897 and 1907 – he assiduously observed European diplomatic conventions and was especially enthusiastic to follow the behaviour codes that distinguished 'the most exclusive circles'; in short, he recognized that evidence of Siam's transition to civilization was heavily dependent on, and most effectively symbolized by, 'the deportment of its monarch' (Englehart 2010: 433). One ambition was to convince Europeans of the authenticity of Siam's commitment to observe the rules and rituals of elite conduct and to assuage any doubts that 'lower-class natives' were merely 'aping' refined customs (Englehart 2010: 424).

It is worth pausing to note that contempt for what would later be described as the 'mimic man' was integral to the 'double tendency' of European expansion that was discussed earlier. In perceptive comments about established–outsider relations in that era, Elias (2012 [1939]: 473) observed that the 'immense effort' that outsiders made to reconfigure themselves in the light of the codes of conduct of the dominant groups often resulted in 'specific deformations of consciousness and attitude' that exposed them to the 'constant threat' of 'crossfire' from 'below as from above'. Only rarely, he added, did 'total assimilation to a higher established group' occur within the span of a single generation (Elias 2012 [1939]: 473).[2] With respect to Siam, its decision to educate young princes at English public schools exhibited an awareness of the need to persuade the British establishment of the authenticity of its commitment to civilization and to avoid the suspicion or accusation of shallow or strategic mimicry (Englehart 2010: 430–1). A degree of success was highlighted in a British newspaper report which praised members of the elite because 'they live precisely after the English fashion, and drink wines and eat of the same food as ourselves, although they never saw an English table before their arrival in this country' (cited in Englehart 2010: 425). Clearly, the place of refined manners in assessments of gradations of civility and civilization was not a thing of the past. The value that was allocated to such patterns of behaviour revealed the power of 'aristocratic internationalism' – the union of ruling elites in observing a class-based behaviour code; this was skilfully exploited by King Chulalongkorn who emphasized racial distinctions between the Siamese and colonized outsiders in British India and Burma in his quest for acceptance by the civilized white establishment (Englehart 2010: 428ff).

The Siamese government was astute in placing princes at the head of diplomatic missions including the 1880 delegation which led to the establishment of a permanent Siamese representation in London (Englehart 2010: 425). European acceptance of high-status Siamese individuals as civilized persons directly implied the recognition that the kingdom was a potential member of civilized international society (Englehart 2010: 424). The contrast with a painful episode in an earlier phase of the process of re-orientation is striking. In 1857, during King Mongkut's reign, an unwitting violation of British court protocol led the Siamese mission to apologize for its ignorance and to seek to repair damage to its reputation. During an audience with Queen Victoria, members of the Siamese delegation who were wearing traditional attire astonished their hosts 'by crawling on all fours from the entrance of the hall of audience to the throne' (Gong 1984: 226). A subsequent eight-page letter to the Earl of Clarendon combined a plea for forgiveness with a formal request for instruction in court formalities. It seems plausible to suppose that the episode produced emotional responses that were not dissimilar to those that many Europeans had undergone as they faced pressures to exercise greater self-regulation and self-restraint in the emergent phase of the civilizing process. The chief aim was to avoid offending others, however unintentionally, to ensure protection against ridicule, and to avert the shame and embarrassment of transgressions of norms that were ascribed to social inferiority.

The encounter, in which the Siamese delegates became involved in a status degrading ceremony (as opposed to a 'status degradation ceremony' orchestrated by established groups – see p. 72), indicates how global reconfigurations were reflected in the changing ways in which people were bound together in particular figurations or micro-structures. The incident and the subsequent anxious correspondence shed light on the role of the symbolism surrounding ceremonial propriety for the politics of 'group charisma' and 'group disgrace' in established–outsider relations. Three underlying social forces of the period were on display: the process of 'attraction' in which outsiders sought to imitate and to be accepted by an established group; the cultural accommodation of the sense of inferiority as encouraged by a social elite with monopoly powers over the conferral of status and prestige; and the forms of self-monitoring and self-control that subordinate groups felt they had to display to win the approval of those who would decide their suitability for admission into the international society of civilized states (see also Zarakol 2014: 319ff).

Various internal political reforms were promoted under King Chulalongkorn's reign in order to show that Siam was indeed on course to satisfy the Western 'standard of civilization' with respect to modern forms of government. In 1873 he abolished the ancient custom of prostration and introduced new 'court formalities' which 'helped separate the political legitimacy of the regime from his person'; from then on, royal counsellors swore 'allegiance not to the king, but to the state' (Gong 1984: 220). In the attempt to establish a European-style constitutional monarchy, the Siamese court began to separate the royal household from public institutions. It promoted a parallel to the earlier transition in Western Europe in which private power monopolies were turned into public monopolies. Compliance with European diplomatic practice contributed to the Siamese endeavour to show that it was a civilized state. It was also necessary to prove that it was a modern, European-style regime which could impose its sovereign will across its whole territory – thereby ensuring that the enforcement of the rule of law within clearly demarcated borders replaced lawlessness along ungoverned frontiers (Englehart 2010: 429). In other initiatives, Chulalongkorn encouraged the ruling elite to abandon traditional attire and to dress in a 'civilized manner'. He abolished slavery (the relevant law was promulgated in 1905) and launched a civilized offensive to eliminate polygamy in the knowledge that both institutions were markers of barbarism in the eyes of Europeans (Gong 1984: 228). When

Chulalongkorn led members of the military on a mission to colonies in South East Asia, he demanded that they dress '*à l'européen*' and refrain from 'betel-nut chewing', a practice that disgusted Europeans whose sensibilities clashed with the indigenous aesthetic which valued black-stained teeth (Gong 1984: 221; Winichakul 2000).

Those efforts to conform to external definitions of civilized conduct were the means by which a small South East Asian power responded to great power encroachment. Compared to Japan, which had also acceded to European expectations of diplomatic practice as well as establishing European-style state institutions but which chose the path of realpolitik, Siam's political and military aspirations were strictly limited (Englehart 2010: 433). Preserving the autonomy of the ruling elite and avoiding colonial subjection were priorities. Attaining sovereign equality was the longer-term objective. A turning point was the 1907 diplomatic mission to ratify the treaty that brought an end to French extraterritorial rights in Siam. Siam achieved its goal of membership of the society of states in 1939. The specific case illustrates how the relationship between the European civilizing process, international established–outsider figurations, and local civilizing offensives configured the Western-dominated global order.

Tsarist Russia

Rather like Japan, Tsarist Russia endeavoured to gain international recognition by advertising its credentials as a civilized power and exemplary civilizing colonizer. Following an official visit to Western Europe in 1697–8, Peter the Great decreed that it was essential to abandon traditional dress codes and for subjects to shave off their beards; they should dispense with the kowtow which was a symbol of barbaric servility in Western Europe; and it was imperative to promote the emancipation of women (Gong 1984: 103–4; Watson 1984: 69). Related ambitions included breaking the 'power of the anti-Western Church and of the traditionalists among the aristocracy' (Watson 1984: 69). Conscious of the utility of political symbolism, and following a visit to Versailles in 1717, Peter modelled buildings and gardens in St Petersburg on the court of Louis XIV. He emulated French court practice by employing classical allegories to legitimate absolute power. Examples were the 'worship of idealised feminine forms': images of Hercules, Perseus and Mars, which expressed military strength and conquest, were combined with representations of Venus and Minerva, which conveyed the image of the beneficent conqueror who brought 'tranquillity, cultivation, and grace' to the realm (Wortman 2006: 29).

References to the classical world were no less esteemed in the court of Catherine the Great where, as at Versailles, they were used to draw parallels between Tsarist Russia and the grandeur of ancient Rome. Her monument to Peter the Great (which symbolized his powers over nature, exemplified by a horse trampling a snake) was known as the 'Marcus Aurelius' (Wortman 2006: 65–6; see also Burke 1992: 194, on the extent to which the statue of Marcus Aurelius in the Roman capital provided the model for later equestrian statues). Such exercises in self-elevation had limited success. In 1784, Count Louis-Philippe de Ségur, the French minister plenipotentiary and envoy extraordinaire of Louis XVI to Catherine's court, described St Petersburg as uniting 'the age of barbarism and that of civilization, the tenth and eighteenth centuries, the manners of Asia and those of Europe, coarse Scythians and polished Europeans, a brilliant, proud nobility, and a people plunged in servitude' (cited in Wolff 1994: 22).[3]

Pertinent to that comment on manners (which were so central to Elias's investigation of the civilizing process) is the fact that Peter the Great ordered the compilation of extracts from European manners books to ensure that Russian diplomats fully understood the necessary protocols. The resulting work, *The Honourable Mirror of Youth*, which was published in 1717, was designed to instruct diplomats who were to be despatched to 'Western court society' in 'how to eat and speak properly' and how to behave in the 'polished' ways that distinguished them from mere 'peasants' (Wortman 2006: 54). To ensure the requisite training and education, over one hundred members of the aristocratic elite were sent to the School for Diplomats in Strasbourg where they were educated in the 'ceremonial forms and gestures' of the 'aristocratic-courtly and cosmopolitan' diplomatic culture which Russian ambassadors would be required to observe (Scott 2007; Mastenbroek 1999).

As for Russia's role as a civilized colonial power, from the end of the 18th century its policy in Central Asia was closely modelled on British imperial role in India. From the perspective of several European observers such as Lord Curzon (1967 [1889]: 383ff), Russia had brought 'pacification' to lawless Central Asian regions; however, its expansion was an example not of 'Civilized Europe march[ing] forth to vanquish barbarian Asia' but of 'the conquest by Orientals by Orientals'. Russia was effectively 'civilizing' an earlier version of itself by reclaiming 'its own kith and kin' after the educative effects of its 'sojourn in civilized Europe' (Curzon 1967 [1889]: 392). Curzon (1967 [1889]: 401ff) drew the distinction between 'government' and 'civilization' to underline Russia's limited progress – when compared to the British Empire – in the elevation of peoples from 'the sloth of centuries'. Laudatory, however, was the relative ease with which the Russian elite had promoted the 'assimilation' of conquered groups within its empire, a practice that was described as relatively uncomplicated, however, given that 'no impassable chasm of intellect or character intervenes' (Curzon 1967 [1889]: 392).

Such comments depicted Russia as a society that was undergoing a process of liberating itself from behaviour patterns that disclosed its 'Asiatic heritage' and which led unsurprisingly to Russian resentment of European stigmatizing representations of the 'barbarian at the gate' (Neumann 1999: ch 3; Neumann and Welsh 1991). But the Russian elite was anxious to prove that 'in Asia, we too are Europeans' (Kaczmarska 2016). The treatment of the rebel Chechen leader, Shamil, captured in August 1859, revealed how the Russian imperial civilizing mission or offensive tried to eradicate Western European perceptions of its inferiority. Tsar Alexander II used Shamil's presence at official parades and ceremonies as a symbol of Russian success in subjugating elite warriors from 'a less civilized society' and in ensuring their successful integration into refined society (Wortman 2006: 203–4). The treatment of a barbaric conquered leader who enjoyed celebrity status in various parts of Europe, and who was idealized as a noble savage by nostalgic sections of Russian society, was intended to show that Russia had reached the level of civilization where it was possible to launch 'an Asian mission, to carry Enlightenment eastward, and to mediate between Europe and the Orient' (Barrett 1994: 363ff; see also Layton 1991). Merciful conduct towards a savage enemy who would have been treated harshly in the past was also designed to publicize Russia's marked progress towards civilization or *tsivilizatsia* (Barrett 1994). It was also meant to advertise its superiority over European societies where, according to Russian observers, the belief in racial supremacy precluded such cultural assimilation and stalled the rise of a shared national identity of the kind that would unite diverse peoples in imperial Russia (Becker 1991).

In November 1864, Russia's Foreign Minister, Gorchakov, celebrated Russia's territorial expansion as evidence of its membership of the exalted civilization of the imperial powers. The advance to the East had followed the example of 'all civilized states which are brought into contact with half savage nomad populations possessing no fixed social organisation'; security interests had necessitated the subjugation of 'Asiatics' who respected 'nothing but visible and palpable force'; 'civilizing' the eastern neighbours was a 'special mission' and a significant contribution to the larger march of progress that the US,

French, Dutch and British empires had achieved in their imperial zones (Wortman 2006: 203–4). Expansion into the Amur region of South Eastern Siberia from the 1840s onwards was undertaken in the spirit of the 'white man's burden' but with an interesting twist (Bassin 1999: 10ff). Territorial expansion was undertaken to impress Europeans of Russia's similarly 'civilized' trajectory but, for many sections of the Russian ruling elite, it had a fundamental nationalist dimension which was partly a reaction to the menace of Western incursions into China (Bassin 1999: ch 2, 112ff). The distinctive fusion of nationalist aims and civilizing offensives in the region was designed to satisfy and comply with European understandings of what it meant to be civilized but also to create a unique Russian cultural identity that was linked with the supposedly greater beneficence of its colonial rule (Bassin 1999: 182ff). Expansion into Siberian regions was undertaken to establish Russia's civilized credentials and to construct a national identity which was presumed to be superior in many respects to European social models (Bassin 1999: 199ff). Through such 'schizophrenic' responses to European civilization, Russia became entangled in intra- and inter-societal power struggles which survive on some accounts to this day (Bassin 1999: 199ff).

Several European reactions to Russia's civilizing offensive endorsed its self-image as an enlightened great power. Russian success in supporting the 'civilization' of peoples to the East impressed British liberals such as Richard Cobden; he criticized Britain's decision to declare war against Russia over Crimea on the grounds that a 'relatively civilized Russia' which was clearly progressing ought to have been allowed to colonise Turkey and to bring the 'blessings of civilization' to that 'backward, barbaric Eastern country' (Hobson 2012: 36). Certainly, cultural differentiation from such barbarous peoples was at the heart of Russian attempts to display its achievements in becoming a European, or significantly Europeanized, state that had earned the right to be recognized as an equal member of the great power imperial establishment.

As with many other Westernizing societies, internal debates and power struggles emerged around the question of how to position the state in response to European military and political dominance. The reforms that had been initiated by Peter the Great provoked the opposition of the nobility and the clergy who 'wanted to turn their backs on the West' and to 'revert' to endangered traditional 'manners and customs' (Watson 1984: 69). Government policies to achieve progress towards civilization were fiercely resisted by internal Russophiles who feared that Russian political and cultural distinctiveness would be lost in the programme of Europeanization that was advocated by disloyal 'Voltairians' (Gong 1984: 105–6). Efforts to re-orientate and reconstitute the Russian state and society by implementing an outward-looking, modernizing discourse that associated Europeanization with civilization clashed with traditional social forces that fought to protect what they saw as Russia's superior Eurasian identity (Tsygankov 2008). Domestic political fault lines that opened up around opposition to open acceptance of a position of inferiority in relation to the European powers were reminiscent of the tensions between *Kultur* and civilization discussed in Chapter 2. Such conflicts have been a recurring feature of traumatic encounters with European or Western societies, of rapid, unexpected and involuntary entanglement in the global chains of interconnectedness that extend outwards from the dominant civilization, and of the unrelenting pressures to submit to its superior practices and principles (see Abu-Lughod 2011; Mishra 2012 for further discussion). They persist in the current era. The rivalries can be intensified in periods of upheaval, as occurred following the collapse of the Soviet Union when rival groups clashed over whether Russia should embark on 'returning to civilization' or proudly recover its 'pre-Soviet' cultural heritage and collective identity (Neumann 1999: ch 6). At issue, once again, was the ideal relationship between 'nation' and 'civilization'.[4]

But in the 19th century European elites did not unanimously endorse 'progressive' Russian self-images; rather they portrayed their eastern neighbour as a 'less civilized civilizer' that was little more than 'semi-Asiatic' given its autocratic form of government that closely resembled 'Oriental Despotism' (Buranelli 2014).[5] One illustration was the condemnation of Russia's failure to prevent lawlessness and to improve conditions along the Danube (deemed to be the 'conduit of civilization' from the West to the East) – a rebuke of its breach of the 'standard of civilization' that led in 1856 to the establishment of the Danube River Commission (Yao 2019: 347–8). Such criticisms were used by sections of the Russian intelligentsia in the 19th century in their struggle against archaic power structures (Becker 1991). In turn, many European observers seized on the resulting internal clashes between 'traditionalists' and 'modernizers' – especially when the former seemed to have the upper hand – to support the contention that Russia was no more than a 'semi-civilized' polity. Russian attempts to win the respect of the great power establishment created a variant on the larger tapestry of established–outsider distinctions in the global order. Parallels between Russia's endeavour to proclaim its achievements as an imperial power and 'Japanese-style Orientalism' or Siam's racialized attitudes to the Indian and Burmese subjects of the British empire have been noted in this chapter. Similar developments in the Ottoman Empire and in the early phases of the Turkish Republic will be discussed in the next section. Some of those phenomena were interwoven, as is clear from Ottoman assertions that its alliance with the European powers against Russia in the Crimean War was proof of its acceptance by the more 'civilized' governments (Aydin 2007: introduction, ch 1). What may have been the first official proclamation to use the concept of civilization, the so-called Reform Rescript, declared, as the conflict drew to an end in 1856, that the Ottoman Empire intended to 'take its rightful and exalted place among the civilized nations' through its association with the Concert of Europe (Wigen 2015: 108). By such means, a complex web of interwoven domestic and international stigmatizing and counter-stigmatizing manoeuvres globalized European conceptions of a civilized world order but with marked national variants which were evidence of latent centrifugal forces that would strengthen in the coming decades.

The Ottoman Empire

Standard interpretations of the relations between Europe and the Ottoman Empire have stressed the similarities with interaction with China where a similarly hegemonial conception of world order had no place for the idea of the sovereign equality of territorial states. In its diplomatic relations with France in the first part of the 16th century, the Ottoman court was firmly opposed to establishing a permanent embassy in Paris, convinced that such an innovation would have conveyed a belief in social equality. On the other hand, the French decision to establish an embassy in Constantinople was welcomed precisely because it was thought to denote subservience and inequality (Jensen 1985). Of major significance was the traditional Ottoman standard of civilization which was predicated on unequal relations between true believers and infidels. As in the case of the Chinese imperial court, and as a result of similar changes in power distributions, external pressures mounted to create new state structures that included specialist institutions with responsibility for conducting external affairs in accordance with the civilized principles of European international society. Traditional established–outsider relations in the Ottoman Empire were transformed in the process.

Deserving comment in this context are the diplomatic encounters between the representatives of the Ottoman and Persian courts and the French government in the early 18th century. The French experience with Muslim ambassadors had not exactly been straightforward.

The Persian ambassador, Mehmed Riza Bey, who visited Paris in 1706, was described as 'cruel, eccentric, fierce and rude, unstable in his resolutions, and never willing to listen either to good reason or good sense' (Göçek 1987: 30). The visit of the Ottoman ambassador, Mehmed Efendi to the court of Louis XV in 1720–1, was a more civil affair. Nevertheless, Mehmed Efendi expressed surprise or shock when court aristocrats, with their pride in their own 'superior' manners, inquired as to whether they could observe Ottoman dining practice. The belief that the request was intrusive and that acceptance could well result in embarrassment suggested certain elite anxieties about how external perceptions of customs governing the consumption of food might influence the relative standing of court societies (Göçek 1987: 37ff). Suffice it to add that Ottoman endeavours to imitate European court behaviour increased in the aftermath of the diplomatic mission (Göçek 1987: chs 4–5). Unsurprising was the subsequent invitation of representatives of European court societies to Istanbul to provide what was seen as much-needed instruction in civilized diplomatic protocols (Naff 1984).

The gradual incorporation of the Ottoman Empire into European international society occurred through several phases that had close parallels in other regions. They included the destabilization of a traditional 'egocentric' world view, the rise of European-orientated elites that decided in the Tulip Period (1703–30) to import the scientific and technological know-how that underpinned European military and political prowess, and the accompanying internal social tensions about whether or how far such importations could be integrated into Ottoman social structures without undermining the authority of established groups and jeopardizing cherished traditional religious doctrines and customs (Abu-Lughod 2011: ch 7; Behnam 2002). The task was to determine the respects in which European societies had advanced beyond the Muslim world and to make the requisite changes to compete effectively in the economic, political and military spheres. Japan's success in importing Western accomplishments without sacrificing confidence in its achievements in the spiritual sphere explained the interest among members of the Ottoman elite in what it might learn from Japan's self-elevating national strategies. Greatly admired was the Japanese strategy of 'differential usage' in which the unmistakable achievements of Western 'technical-material civilization' were to be united with the greater 'spiritual civilization' of the East (Maruyama 1963: 140ff). Of particular interest are the official missions that were despatched to Europe to discover more about European civilization and which returned with self-confident proclamations about Europe's earlier indebtedness to the Islamic world, not least with respect to the natural sciences and mathematics (Said 1993: 317; Abu-Lughod 2011). Those expressions of 'group pride' could not alter the reality that the most powerful and threatening state-organized societies with unmatched 'group charisma' were located in Western Europe. However, they indicate the need to further modify the idea of the 'double tendency' of European expansion to emphasize how non-European societies endeavoured to maintain the sense of collective self-worth. What was in dispute was the extent to which it was possible to maintain 'group pride' while succumbing to the influence of European civilized tenets.

The Ottoman ruling elite deliberated, then, about what to borrow from Europe while refusing to capitulate to external pressures to internalize feelings of inferiority; however, many Ottoman groups including sections of an increasingly assertive bourgeoisie – were attracted by European notions of a 'civilizational hierarchy' of human groups (Worringer 2014: introduction). As in many other societies where internal power balances shifted alongside changing global power relations, the idea of civilization became central to debates and struggles over the traditional means of orientation, and particularly because of the initiatives of diplomats who visited the major European capital cities in the 1830s (Palayibik 2010: ch 7). *A Treatise on the Circumstances of Europe*, published in 1858 by the Ottoman reformist bureaucratic, Sadik Rifat Pasa, invoked the idea of civilization to explain 'European power and superiority', just as Fukuzawa Yukichi would do in his *Outline of a Theory of Civilization* almost two decades later (Aydin 2009: 125ff). In a notable difference, Pasa used the untranslated, French term (*civilisation*) which he linked with the governing structures and forms of statecraft that underpinned the post-Napoleonic international political order with which the Ottomans hoped to become aligned (see Wigen 2015: 110ff). Significantly, Pasa did not articulate that aspiration from the lowly standpoint of the outsider but proclaimed that basic commonalities between the Ottoman and European worlds were the products of a shared 'Hellenic legacy' (Aydin 2009).[6] Influential was the belief among leading intellectuals that the idea of European civilization possessed an inclusiveness that Christendom had lacked. They did not think that the long history of anti-Muslim sentiment and the racial dimensions of European civilized self-images were insurmountable barriers to the Empire's eventual admission into the international society of states.

However, the Ottoman social and political elite nevertheless appear to have felt trapped between the civilized Europeans they sought to emulate and the barbarous Oriental 'Other' from which they distinguished themselves. Once again, colonial 'civilizing offensives' proved to be a bridge to international recognition. As with Tsarist Russian and Japanese perspectives, 'Ottoman Orientalism' created a binary division between the civilized and civilizing, modernizers and the backward warring tribes that roamed the untamed peripheries of the empire (Becker 1991; Makdisi 2002). The so-called Reform Brigade encouraged the civilization of wild, lawless peoples through enforced resettlement on the supposition that it was plainly impossible to be both nomadic and civilized (Wigen 2015: 111; Deringil 2003). Official commitments to an Ottoman *mission civilisatrice* that betrayed the influence of Enlightenment ideas about temporality and progress led to the establishment in October 1892 of the Tribal School (closed in 1907 in large part because of student riots). The express purpose was to bring 'the light of civilization' to Arab tribes and to promote their loyalty to the Ottoman state – in short, to construct, in a parallel with Tsarist Russia, a 'civilized Ottoman Empire' to which all conationals, 'irrespective of religion or ethnicity', could belong (Deringil 1998: ch 4).

A decisive moment in the longer process of re-orientation was the 1839 Gülhane Imperial Edict (later known as the Tanzimat Proclamation) which identified the need for political reform that would find expression in the 1876 constitutional changes that were undertaken to modernize state structures and to strengthen the case for membership of European international society. Two members of the committee that drafted the Proclamation and who had experience as ambassadors in European capitals consulted Metternich (Chancellor of the Austrian Empire) and British Prime Minister Palmerston about the proposed changes, notwithstanding the latter's association of the Ottomans with the 'savage races' (Wigen 2015: 113). The edict was read by the Grand Vizier to an audience that included European diplomats. The Ottomans were well aware of the symbolism of such gatherings and they understood that there was much more to observing the 'polite necessities' of diplomacy than mere decorum. Nothing less than international recognition depended on it.[7] A case in point, the meeting addressed by the Grand Vizier provided an opportunity for the outsider to gain status in the eyes of established groups in direct contrast with the 'degradation ceremony' which was discussed earlier (see p. 72). The ritual or performance was one of the means by which a self-elevating regime could advertise its transition to civilized monarchy (Deringil 1998: chs 6–8). Moreover, as previously mentioned, participation alongside the French and British in the Crimean War was thought to indicate just far how European impressions of the Ottoman Empire had altered since the early part of the 19th century when support for the Greek struggle for national independence was bound up with anti-Ottoman sentiment.

Reformist governments that were following the curve of Western civilization were eager to learn from one another. All faced a similar problem of how to combine efforts to modernize state structures with attempts to bind diverse ethnic groups together in a new collective identity that was inspired by European ideas of 'the nation' (Deringil 1998: 108ff). The Ottomans admired Japan's modernizing project – influenced perhaps by the delegation that Prince Iwakura sent to Istanbul one year before high-level missions visited the United States and Europe. Japan served as a model of how to preserve national self-respect and promote patriotic feeling by blending tradition with selective borrowing from Western civilization which was conveyed by the Turkish term, *medeniyet* (Worringer 2004, 2014).[8] Japan's success in the 1905 war against Russia was regarded as proof of how a reforming nation-state could prevail over a backward multi-national empire in global power struggles while at the same time minimizing uncongenial external cultural influences. Japan did not repay the praise that was directed towards it by supporting the conclusion of treaties between equals. Rather like the Western powers in their relations with Japan, they demanded unequal obligations which expressed the conviction that the Ottoman Empire was an inferior civilization (Wigen 2015: 114).

For Ottoman rulers up to the beginning of the First World War there was no basic contradiction between modernising state structures and remaining devoutly Muslim. They did not think it was necessary – and it was impossible in any case – to create an exact copy of the European nation-state on Ottoman territories. In the final years of the 19th century, and in the period leading up to the First World War, the Ottoman Empire was a core symbol of 'aspirations for dignity and justice' across the Islamic world. Even the abolition of the Caliphate in 1924 could not dampen pan-Islamic enthusiasm for 'a transnational Muslim order' that would end the sense of humiliation that followed the European powers' decision at the end of the First World War to dismember the empire and distribute the parts between themselves (Aydin 2007, 2009). But the First World War had made it clear that sprawling imperial court societies could not survive violent struggles with highly organized nation-states. Under the rule of Kemal Atatürk the succeeding Turkish republic set out to replace the failed Ottoman modernizing experiment with robust civilizing offensives to anchor modern state structures in a secularized national identity. Contending that Europe was an 'example' rather than a 'goal', modernizers insisted that religious belief should be a private matter just as it had become in the civilized secular West; the broader contention was that long-overdue social and political reforms had been blocked by the stultifying role of Islam (Behnam 2002: 183).

Atatürk dramatized the radical break with the past in a speech in August 1925 in which he declared that the 'Turkish Republic cannot be a country of sheiks, dervishes, devotees and lunatics ... we derive our strength from civilization and science' (cited in Sakallioglu 1996: 236). Official government policy was to sweep aside outmoded Ottoman political structures and to establish modern public institutions which would, in Atatürk's words, permit Turkey to 'live as an advanced and civilized nation in the midst of contemporary civilization' (cited in Ahmad 1993: 53).[9] The Republic abolished the Caliphate in November 1924; the second article of the 1924 Constitution, which designated Islam as the state religion, was removed in April 1928; and the commitment to secular rule was enshrined in the Constitution in 1937. The traditional Muslim weekly prayer day was annulled with the adoption of the Gregorian calendar. In parallel civilizing offensives, the religious schools (madrassa) and the sharia courts were abolished, the latter replaced by judicial principles and procedures that were drawn from Swiss civil law and the Italian penal code. In November 1928, in an explicit attempt to align Turkey with Europe and to loosen the ties with Islamic societies to the east, the government announced that the Latin-based alphabet would replace the traditional Arabic equivalent; the upshot was that Turks would no longer automatically learn the alphabet of the Koran (Ahmad 1993: 81–2). A significant movement which had gathered pace in the later phase of the Ottoman Empire betrayed the influence of the Enlightenment contention that levels of civilizational attainment could be measured by assessing the position of women in male-dominated societies. Ending the custom of wearing the veil reflected the aspiration to create more even (but far from equal) relations between men and women (Göle 1996: chs. 2–3); this was a major element of an externally influenced, top–down 'civilizing thrust' to build a Western-style, Turkish nation in which all citizens would be bound together by a joint commitment to social and political progress (Sakallioglu1996: 233–4; Cagaptay 2006: ch 2).

The ambition to follow 'civilized' standards regarding the relations between men and women was one example of the value that social reformers allocated to changes in everyday life as well as in public institutions. Influential treatises on etiquette and decorum and on the instruction of children mirrored the role that manners books had played in the formation of European civilized self-images (Findley 1998). Transforming dress codes was also integral to civilizing offensives in which outsiders emulated established groups. In 1925, Kemal Atatürk condemned the fez (Ottoman-Muslim head gear for men which had replaced the turban around a century earlier) as a 'symbol of ignorance, negligence, fanaticism and the hatred of progress and civilization' (Cuno 2008: 72). Wearing the fez was subsequently outlawed. New legislation made it obligatory for men to wear Western-style hats, emblems of civilization and modernization (Cagaptay 2006: ch 2; Zarakol 2011: ch 3). The larger ensemble of civilizing initiatives included shaving, wearing ties, shaking hands, writing from left to right and, crucially in the light of European manners, eating with forks (Dösemeci 2013: 30). In a development that was strangely reminiscent of ancient Greek attitudes to what they saw as effeminate Persian bodies that lacked the discipline of the gymnasium, Kemalist civilizing offensives stressed the need to remake 'ill-shaped Turkish bodies' in accordance with idealized images of the Western male physique (see Alemdaroglu 2005 who stresses the influence of supposedly civilized Western eugenics programmes on Turkish nation-building projects). Musical aesthetics were also affected. The state banned traditional monophonic music in its attempt to promote the appreciation and enjoyment of Western polyphonic modalities (Alemdaroglu 2005).

All of those reforms were designed to complement the reconstitution of public institutions by recasting everyday behaviour in accordance with new social standards. The deeper aim was to alter the means of orientation and to instil new forms of self-restraint in an obvious parallel with the psychogenetic changes that developed alongside sociogenetic counterparts in the standard-setting European civilizing process (Alemdaroglu 2005). They were among the realignments that were deemed necessary to prepare Turkey for recognition as a civilized sovereign member of the international order.

Conclusion

This chapter has extended Elias's comment in the late 1930s that the increasing acceptance of Western ideas of civilization was the most recent observable phase of the continuously evolving civilizing process. The analysis has shifted attention from what European states did with their monopoly powers by initiating civilizing missions to how specific non-European ruling elites used their political agency in the form of civilizing offensives that had three objectives – to create modern state institutions, to understand and adapt to Western conceptions of international society, and – in three of the cases discussed above – to engage in mimetic imperialism. The combined developments led to the extraordinary global dominance of the civilizing process. Expressed differently, the diffusion of Western state institutions, diplomatic practices and forms of imperial domination defined the global political order that was emerging in the second half of the 19th century.

As analysts of that period have argued, European overseas expansion brought different standards of civilization – or different civilizing processes anchored in diverse court societies – into contact and collision. Each court possessed its image of international order. Each had its criteria for judging the relative standing or status of other peoples, its assumptions about the entitlements and obligations of superiors in dealings with subordinates, and its understandings about the rules of propriety and forms of deference that those of lesser standing should observe in the company of overlords. Those traditional established–outsider relations were undermined as a result of Western military, political and commercial expansion. Established groups that governed court societies were converted into outsiders involuntarily incorporated into a Western-dominated international order. Domestic civilizing offensives that were initiated in the context of asymmetrical power relations led to degrees of convergence of elite orientations to the global order, although tensions remained, not least in struggles between traditional social strata and modernizing forces in the societies involved. Unsurprisingly, many Western elites believed that they were incorporating other peoples within the first universal civilization, often underestimating in the process the significance of the nationalist dimensions of non-Western mimetic civilizing projects to gain recognition as equal members of the society of states. In Eliasian terms, they lived at a time when one civilizing process in its emic sense had clear dominance over non-European etic civilizing processes. To many observers, a continuing process of Westernization must have seemed inevitable, notwithstanding non-European efforts to preserve elements of tradition, to maintain group pride, and to link nation and civilization in new constellations that revealed resentment at the ways in which modern states had used and abused their monopolies of power.

In the first half of the 20th century, mimetic strategies and struggles against the great power establishment led to the renunciation of the extraterritorial privileges that had been imposed through unequal treaties. What followed was recognition of the sovereign equality of societies such as Japan which was admitted into the society of states in 1899/1900, Turkey which joined in 1923, Siam which followed in

1939, and China which was granted full membership in 1943. Those changes were extended as anticolonial political organizations across the 'Third World' succeeded in breaking the opposition of the colonial powers to their admission into international society.

The traditional European standard of civilization fell into disrepute with resulting shifts in global power relations. The transformation reflected the movement from the condition in which the dominant groups held power advantages that resulted in attempts to monopolize the meaning of civilized interaction to one in which 'rebellion, resistance, emancipation among the outsiders' steadily gained momentum (see pp. 20–1). With the globalization of nationalist ideology, traditional Western efforts to enforce the answerability of others to superior civilized norms were resented and rejected in equal measure, but variants on the standard of civilization and the binaries between the established and the outsiders did not exactly vanish from the scene, as the following chapter indicates.

6

Standards of Civilization in the Post-European Global Order

Commenting in the late 1930s on the emerging global order, Elias (2012 [1939]: 426) stated that the 'incipient transformation of Oriental or African people in the direction of Western standards represents the more recent wave of the continuing civilizing movement that we are able to observe'. The attitudes and behaviour of the ruling groups in non-Western societies had come to resemble the outlook and conduct of the global establishment that had brought non-European peoples into 'line with their own standards' (Elias (2012 [1939]: 425). Any countervailing tendencies resulted from the possibility that British colonial rule in India might suffer the fate of all past political systems that overextended their power (Elias (2012 [1939]: 300). Such propensities that Elias noted in passing accelerated in largely unexpected ways in the aftermath of the Second World War as nationalist organizations in non-Western countries struggled for sovereign independence, often contesting Western values and restoring 'traditional' ethics in the process. As part of that resetting of the relations between the Western global establishment and non-Western outsiders, nationalist leaders opposed one of the main symbols of colonial domination – the standard of civilization.[1]

The changing mood was reflected in the writings of Western international lawyers who condemned the standard as anachronistic and 'insulting' to the rising number of non-Western states (Gong 1984: 84). Some directed their aim at earlier jurists such as James Lorimer with his 'picturesque descriptions' of advanced peoples who complied with global principles of reciprocity and of backward groups who could not be trusted to observe international law (Lauterpacht 1947: 31–2). They contended that 'modern international law knows of no distinction, for the purposes of recognition, between civilized and uncivilized States or between States within and outside the international community of civilized States' (Lauterpacht 1947: 31–2). That development was evidence of what Elias described in other contexts as the process in which the 'group charismatic belief of established groups and its imposition on outsider groups gradually loses its power and conviction and finally disappears' – or as the process in which the 'collective self-praise' of some groups and the concurrent 'collective abuse' of others become more muted as power relations shift (Elias 2009: 75). The upshot was at least a partial reversal of an earlier phase in which established groups transformed a 'relatively moderate and controlled' denigration of other societies into more 'virulent and militant' forms (Elias 2009: 75). References to the 'insulting' nature of the standard of civilization also echoed broader changes within civilized societies in which established groups were required to refrain from engaging in, and deriving pleasure from, the contemptuous treatment and public humiliation of supposed inferiors (Wouters 1998). They were expected to become more restrained as conceptions of civilized behaviour altered with more equal or less uneven power balances.

In a close parallel in the post-Second World War global order, the classical discourse of civilization and barbarism that reflected the power disparities between older established and outsider groups came to be regarded as taboo. What had once been a 'praise word' in the language of supposedly superior peoples came to be seen as a term of abuse that displayed a lack of respect for other peoples. In a new phase of the civilizing process in which a more egalitarian ethic began to suffuse global political discourse, the classical standard of civilization lost the support of many groups in the West and was quietly dropped from official statements and legal proclamations. As discussed in Chapter 1, where the narrative of civilization has survived or resurfaced – for example, in government justifications of the use of force against outcasts or 'outlaws' in world politics (Simpson 2004) – it has been deployed to argue that national objectives are entirely compatible with principles that are shared by all civilizations. The balance of power has shifted between European claims to enjoy a monopoly of truth with regard to the nature of civilized relations and the contention in 'progressive' circles that multiple civilizations exist on a more or less equal plane, none higher than the rest, and none endowed with the right to shape the social and political future of the others in the light of its presumed superior way of life.[2]

That is not to suggest that the contemporary global order rests on impartial conceptions of civility that successfully bridge civilizational differences (see, however, Jackson 2000: 11–13, 408) nor that it has been remade by a neutral process of socialization in which the newly independent states have willingly embraced its organizing principles. Postcolonial critics have argued that such discourses fail to recognize the perpetuation of Western hegemony (Seth 2011) or the extent to which the primary 'socializers' are the powerful Western states that purport to be sole custodians of universally valid moral and political principles (Suzuki 2011). From those viewpoints, unequal power relations underpin contemporary 'civilizing offensives' that have direct links with related colonial missions in the imperial era (Bowden 2009: ch 7). These power imbalances are the foundation of the 'dynamic of difference' in which there is an 'endless process of creating a gap between two cultures, demarcating one as "universal" and civilized and the other as "particular" and uncivilized', while assiduously 'seeking to bridge the gap by developing techniques to normalize the aberrant society' (Anghie 2005: 4). There is a similarity here with Elias's analysis of a general trend in the interactions between the established and the outsiders which was evidenced by the most recent phase of the relations between European empires and non-European colonies. As shown above, Elias (2012 [1939]: 425) argued that European societies behaved like a troubled 'upper class' that constantly reinvented means of distinguishing themselves from peoples who were complying with their standards. The idea of the 'dynamic of difference' adds a dimension that Elias overlooked, namely the continuation of planned civilizing offensives to improve 'aberrant' societies. The consequence is that the contemporary global order may have outgrown Europe but it has not exactly outgrown its civilizing process. Although the Western powers have dispensed with the notion that the standard of civilization should underpin global governance, they have not cast aside aims and practices that hark back to the colonial era. Recent variations on the standard continue to demarcate the more or less civilized peoples and to legitimate normalizing, civilizing offensives against others.

To consider those issues in more detail, this chapter begins by discussing 'the cultural revolt against the West' and the rejection of the classical European standard of civilization during the transition from the colonial to the postcolonial or post-European society of states. It then turns to what are widely regarded as the main pillars of revamped standards of civilization – the universal human rights culture, exercises in democracy promotion, and initiatives with regard to the global expansion of market relations. Western humanitarian interventions in war-torn societies can be added to the list. The discussion concludes with brief observations about non-Western critiques of Western civilizing offensives that draw on Elias's discussion of how the balance between 'attraction' to, and 'revulsion' against, established groups tends to shift as outsiders increase their power capabilities and acquire or enhance collective pride and self-esteem. Considered in those terms, the tensions between revamped standards of civilization and the cultural revolt against the West raise large questions about principal global directions – in short, whether the era in which an establishment imposed its will on other societies in the quest to create a universal civilization is drawing to an end. Further reflections on contemporary global civilizing and decivilizing crosscurrents will be set out in the concluding chapter.

The 'cultural revolt against the West'

Reference was made earlier to Article 22 of the Covenant of the League of Nations which placed the 'sacred trust of civilization' at the heart of the newly established 'mandate system'. As with the later United Nations 'trusteeship system', the great powers proclaimed that imperial authorities had the legal and moral responsibility to prepare the colonies for membership of the society of states. The supposition was that 'full and equal membership' was possible for 'non-European, non-Christian, and even non-white states' as long as they were prepared to 'comply with relatively clear behavioural standards codified in positive international law' (Donnelly 1998: 8). Largely unquestioned by members of the global establishment was the supposition that they alone had the right to decide when colonized peoples had made sufficient progress under their tutelage to merit consideration for sovereign statehood. That assumption was contested by the 'revolt against the West' which included: the legal revolt in which societies such as China and Japan that had not been formal colonies of the Western powers launched the 'struggle for equal sovereignty'; the political revolt in which peoples who had been subject to imperial rule fought for national independence; the racial revolt in which Japan, for example, argued for embedding the principle of racial equality in the League of Nations Covenant;[3] the economic revolt which gained prominence in the early 1970s with the global movement for 'economic justice'; and the cultural revolt in which what were then called 'Third World' societies sought 'cultural liberation' from Western hegemony. The pioneering analysis of that process added that the first four dimensions of the struggle were conducted in the political language of the West and drew on Western values. The cultural revolt stood apart because its proponents either questioned or rejected core Western moral principles, including the idea of natural human rights

(Bull 1984a). The contention was that most 'Third World' governments had accepted the basic institutions of international society, such as the idea of territorial sovereignty and the principle of non-intervention, but many rejected the civilizational ethos that had underpinned the Western international system with as yet unknown ramifications for future levels of order and stability (Linklater 2010; Hall 2017).

Interpreted from the vantage point of process sociology, the cultural revolt signified the transition from a period of 'colonisation or assimilation' in which an outsider group emulates 'superiors' which, 'intentionally or unintentionally, permeates it with its own pattern of conduct', to a phase of 'repulsion, differentiation and emancipation' where a 'rising group' which has enjoyed 'gains ... in social power and self-confidence' launches its assault on the establishment (Elias 2012 [1939]: 472–3). In the case of the cultural revolt against the West, outsiders sought to free themselves from the standards of civilization that had underpinned the colonial powers' assumed right to determine their course of development. To developing world critics, the behaviour of the European powers in the two world wars had been proof of the folly of claims to global moral authority that were based on a supposed monopoly of truth about civilized existence. In India, revulsion took the form of condemnations of the mentality of 'winning at any cost' that led to the 'barbaric excesses of trench warfare' during the First World War where enemies 'lost all sense of [the] restraint (or self-control)' that was the alleged hallmark of civilization (Adas 2004: 52, referring to the writings of the Bengali 'sage-philosopher', Rabindranath Tagore).[4] Furthermore, 'the total abrogation of the laws of war' by the 'advanced' powers during the Second World War broadened the assault on the old international legal distinction between civilized and semi-civilized or savage peoples (Bowden 2005: 21). What stands out in those narratives is the supposition that the lack of civilized restraint that had been a feature of imperial expansion had infiltrated the West with clear consequences for the supposed moral entitlement to take its progressive 'civilizing mission ideology' to all parts of the world (Schwarzenberger 1962: 77; see also Mishra 2012: 209ff). For thinkers such as Tagore, the forces of revulsion and differentiation were crisply articulated in the contention that the destructiveness of the First World War was evidence of a 'civilization [that] was not fit to govern and decide the future of most of the rest of humanity; the colonized peoples [had to] draw on their own cultural resources and take charge of their own destinies' (Adas 2004: 51). Striking in this context was the contrast in Tagore's writings between 'the arrogance and chauvinism of European nationalism' and the standing of 'cosmopolitanism' and 'restraint' in Indian civilization from which Europe could surely learn (Adas 2004: 53).

The rejection of claims to cultural superiority dealt a fatal blow to the Western paternalistic view that the civilized powers alone could judge when colonial subjects were fit to govern themselves and able to cope with the trials of sovereign independence. If any single event symbolized the magnitude of the change that was under way, it was the United Nations General Assembly Resolution 1514, passed on 14 December 1960, which rejected the orthodox view that evidence of the capacity for good government had to exist prior to the conferral of self-government. After the Second World War, emancipation in the form of decolonization occurred at a pace that astonished most Western populations. The cultural revolt against the hegemony of Western civilized values intensified as a result of rising groups with greater power and self-confidence. Fanon's sardonic observation that 'there are civilizations without neckties, civilizations with loin-cloths, and others without hats' is perhaps the finest illustration of the moving balance of power between 'colonisation or assimilation' and 'repulsion, differentiation and emancipation' (Fanon 1970: 21).

Fanon's remark is a reminder of the civilizational dimensions of the revolt against the West which are often overlooked in discussions of the place of modernity in such struggles. From a process-sociological perspective, the idea of 'modernity' is problematic since it is a process-reducing concept. The most obvious alternative – 'modernization' – has the advantage of connoting societies in motion. The disadvantage is that it is associated with the notion of linear, progressive shifts from pre-modern to modern societies. Analysts of 'multiple modernities' have questioned that distinction. It has been argued that what are often regarded as anti-modern fundamentalist movements are 'distinctively modern' in one respect – in being as committed as many radical secular groups organizations to a 'project of modernity' in which political action is the means of realizing utopian visions (Eisenstadt 2000: 23; Göle 2000: 96ff).

Missing from that analysis is the focus on the civilizational dimensions of 'anti-modern' groups which was stressed by Huntington in the 'clash of civilizations' thesis (Huntington 1996). Its limitations will be discussed later. Suffice it to add that a civilizational focus recognizes the part that anti-Western sentiments have played in, for example, radical Islamist groups. Such hostility to Western ways of life was expressed in the influential concept of *gharbzedegi* which was introduced by the Islamist writer, Jalal Al-e-Ahmad, in the 1960s to condemn the Western 'cultural disease' which included the tolerance of sexual conduct that was deemed to transgress Islamic principles (Behnam 2002: 189; Dunning 2019). The critique of a corrupt and corrupting West is inseparable from the belief that the greater civilization is under attack from infidels. Islamist groups such as 'IS' initiated civilizing missions or recivilizing offensives in the etic sense to realize a utopian vision of the Caliphate in a past golden age. As documented in Chapter 1, for many observers, radical Islamist groups constitute the greatest threat to a global order based on civilized principles. As part of the continuing cultural (and religious) revolt against the West, radical Islamist movements have railed against the hegemony of despised Western standards of civilization. They have had the effect of reinforcing commitments to 'civilized values' among Western governments and peoples. The analysis of multiple modernities has lacked the relevant civilizational analytic that sheds light on those processes.

Good governance

Such revised standards of civilization have suffused the discourses of good governance which appeared in the 1990s in response to mounting opposition to the structural adjustment policies that the neoliberal global establishment had imposed on 'Third World' governments (Anghie 2005: 247ff). Critics stressed the part such policies played in widening social inequalities and fuelling political unrest and instability with the consequence that international organizations such as the United Nations turned to reforming state structures with a view to lending economic liberalization a 'human face' (Weiss 2000; Manji and O'Coill 2002). The resulting civilizing offensives, which included human rights initiatives, have been integral to a global order that is hallmarked by the growing 'complementarity' of international society and world society (Clark 2007). One of its manifestations is closer collaboration between national governments and non-governmental organizations in the joint enterprise of setting global standards and creating robust forms of transnational accountability (Peters et al 2009). Marked shifts with respect to standards of civilization occurred in this period. For the most part, 19th-century colonial civilizing offensives concentrated on the metamorphosis of non-Western state institutions and on the selective eradication of barbaric practices rather than on promoting the general adoption of 'a European cultural orientation' and way of life (Zhang 2014: 682). Their aspirations were necessarily limited given the restricted capability of influencing routine social interaction across vast expanses of space – given that 'intensive power' (the capacity 'to organize tightly and command a high level of mobilization or commitment' from subordinates) could not keep pace with increased 'extensive power' (the ability to project power over 'far-flung territories' (Mann 1986: 7ff). The greater intensive power of the dominant powers in the contemporary era has been apparent in ambitious programmes to promote deeper patterns of social and economic change in other societies such as increased respect for human rights and attendant changes in personality traits that accord with Western conceptions of civilized forms of life.

Human rights

What Elias described as major changes in the 'we/I balance' in the course of the civilizing process deserve pride of place in the analysis of the liberal project to locate individual human rights at the heart of the global political order. The expression was used to describe the profound changes in the relationship between the individual and society that accelerated from the time of the Renaissance. Some examples were given in Chapter 2. They included the erection of new 'walls' that separated people from each other to new degrees (Elias 2012 [1939]: 522ff). Three illustrations are worth recalling. They are the rise of the humble fork, the concealment of bodily functions behind the scenes in accordance with changing sources of shame and embarrassment, and, much later, the provision of private space in the form of separate bedrooms for children in bourgeois families (Elias 2008g). Elias maintained that small changes in everyday life might seem to have no intrinsic merit for analysts of large-scale changes in the organization of society such as the emergence of states with monopolies of control of violence and taxation. He added that such dichotomies are misleading. Seemingly trivial shifts in daily behaviour can provide insights into fundamental structural changes in the ways in which people are bound together. The examples given above were illustrations of an overall movement towards greater 'individuation' or 'individualization' that set the European civilizing process apart from non-European equivalents. They signified the momentum towards a new 'we/I balance', to new relations between the individual and society in which people came to cherish and expect a range of personal liberties such as the right to privacy, to bodily integrity, to freedom from violence, to free expression, and to take part in democratic forms of government as equal citizens.

Such entitlements found unique expression in the language of human rights. For Elias, the recent development of the rights of the child was one manifestation of the overall direction of travel in civilized societies.

Rights to be free from violence, from labour exploitation, and from other forms of harm were linked with moral concern for the welfare of children. In an essay on the 'civilizing of parents', Elias (2008g) cited the 1979 International Year of the Child (to which the 1990 United Nations *Convention on the Rights of the Child* must be added) as an expression of changing social standards of restraint in the recent period. International conventions regarding the rights of the child had to be understood in long-term perspective and to be seen as part of larger shifts in the 'we/I balance' in European societies. The relevant treaties were indicators of how emotional identification between people had changed in the most recent phase of the civilizing process.

The analysis of the changing 'we/I balance' is a reminder that human rights are far from natural but are 'the by-product of a particular kind of society' which is unusually 'civilized and secure' (Brown 1999: 120). The idea of 'natural rights' may have been a powerful weapon in the struggle to secure basic freedoms, but it is a process-reducing concept that comes with the implicit denial of any need for a sociological explanation of how societies with high levels of civilization and security developed in the first place. It is also important to understand the connections between old struggles between liberal and conservative forces over the ideal 'we/I balance' and the emergence of the discourse of universal human rights. By way of example, French conservatives in the late 18th century opposed the relatively new concept of *individualisme* which they saw as a threat to the preservation of 'society' (Lukes 1973: ch 1). An 'abrupt change in the evaluative significance of the term' became evident in the United States in the 1830s when individualism was linked with 'national values and ideals' that were draped in the language of civilization (Lukes 1973: chs 6–7). In that era, national pride in the defence of individual rights was anchored in visions of redirecting the 'course of civilization' (Lukes 1973: chs 6–7; see also Williams 1976: 133ff). The analysis invites recognition of the point that the discourse of human rights evolved within particular power relations; its rise was contested from the outset and remains disputed within liberal-democratic societies and within the world at large to this day. The implication is that established human rights could be reversed if significant power shifts occurred within liberal-democratic societies and if favourable global power distributions should come to an end.

Regarding global power relations and civilizing offensives, it was noted in Chapter 4 that the connection between individual rights and civilization in the 19th century was part of a colonial project to ensure the security of Western traders and travellers in non-Western societies. The emphasis changed in a later stage of the civilizing process in which liberal states and non-governmental actors used universal-egalitarian principles to affirm the inalienable individual rights of all people in pre-eminent legal conventions such as the 1976 *International Covenant on Civil and Political Rights.* From some perspectives, the human rights culture is to be applauded as 'inclusive and universal' – as embodying genuine 'commonalities' in line with the 'positive demands of civilization', and as expressing widely shared convictions that 'common humanity' dictates that egregious abuses of human rights are the 'legitimate concern' of international society as a whole (Donnelly 1998: 11ff). From other standpoints, the contemporary standard of civilization regarding human rights has not escaped the 'fatal tainting' of its connection with the colonial era (Donnelly 1998: 16).

The universal human rights discourse may seem to be 'relatively unproblematic' insofar as the purpose is to protect all individuals from cruelty and gratuitous violence (Donnelly 1998: 21). It is uncontroversial for groups in civilized societies that support collective measures to 'protect beleaguered populations' or to assist the victims of a 'dire humanitarian crisis' (Teitt 2017: 344). But, for many critics, the international legal obligations of sovereign governments to treat their respective populations humanely are rather more complicated. A recurrent contention – captured by the idea of 'human rights imperialism' – is that pressures to answer to the self-appointed Western custodians of civilized principles recreate colonial power relations. Earlier protests against the 'hypocrisy' of civilized powers are replayed in claims about the 'double standards' of liberal-democratic governments. Such concerns cannot be separated from criticisms of the relationship between the human rights culture and dichotomies between the civilized members of the global establishment and less civilized outsiders. From those vantage points, to relinquish sovereign control in the sphere of human rights to Western states and Western-dominated international organizations is to accept fundamental status divisions in the contemporary global order that hark back to the age of imperialism. A revamped standard of civilization reconstructs established–outsider hierarchies and conjoined forms of stigmatization as well as the possibility of external interference in the sovereign domain including intervention by great powers.

Liberal offensives to promote standards of civilization with respect to gross violations of human rights have been limited not just by fears about their significance for the global distribution of power and prestige but also by genuine clashes over ethical standpoints that reflect different 'we/I balances' in diverse civilizing processes. For example, social and political groups in, but not only in, several non-Western societies have opposed liberal efforts to strengthen international support for the firmly held belief that capital punishment has no place in a civilized society. Such resistance often reflects divergent views about the rights of the individual and the rights of society, and about appropriate systems of punishment, that have some similarities with earlier debates between French conservatives and liberals (Schabas 1997; Manners 2002). No one can be surprised that certain core elements of the human rights culture are rejected by groups in societies that have undergone civilizing processes in which there is no counterpart to the liberal notion of the ontological primacy of the individual. It is instructive to note the difficulties that the first Japanese translators of John Stuart Mill's *On Liberty* had in finding an appropriate indigenous term to capture the full meaning of the idea of personal rights to freedom of expression – a difficulty that reflected the very different 'we/I balance' in the Japanese civilizing process (Beasley 1995: 213; Howland 2001). The idea that individuals have inalienable rights has been mystifying to societies where the dominant 'we/I balance' has attached greatest value to honouring customary responsibilities that are integral to traditional family and to other social roles and which assigned little, if any, value to natural rights against the larger collectivity.

Different conceptions of the we/I balance clearly raise doubts about how far global agreements on human rights can go beyond condemnations of egregious abuses such as genocide and torture that never quite escape concerns about 'double standards'. The contact and collision between different standards of civilization regarding the place of women in society shed further light on the cultural revolt against Western moral principles, on shifting power balances, and on the international politics of attraction and repulsion. The idea that the litmus test of civilization is the extent to which men and women have equal rights to freedom from violence was affirmed by several leading Enlightenment thinkers (Towns 2009; Towns 2010: chs 4–5). As discussed earlier, related colonial standards of civilization condemned the barbarism of non-European practices such as *sati*, or widow-burning, in parts of India. Regarding that custom, a statement by the British government on 10 November 1828 proclaimed that 'every rational and civilized being must feel anxious for the termination of a practice so abhorrent from humanity', and added that the 'justification' of 'the continuance of the British rule' would be 'incomplete' if it did not secure the 'future happiness and improvement of the numerous population of this eastern world' that endured such subjection (cited in Yang 1999: 9; see Towns 2017 on how colonial measures to impose standards of civilization often reduced the power of women in several non-Western societies). Such revulsion at 'barbaric' practices led the British authorities to outlaw *sati* in 1829 and to legalize the rights of Hindu widows to remarry as of 1856. The heirs to such civilizing offensives in the postcolonial era include governmental and non-governmental organizations that work to eliminate female genital mutilation and, in many societies, to prosecute those who are found guilty of breaching legal standards of civilization with respect to the rights of women and children.

Such images of civilized existence have been enlarged to include the right of women to participate in the public sphere on equal terms with men and to enjoy personal liberties with respect to sexuality or the right to abortion. Those entitlements often clash with traditional constructions of the we/I balance in societies where men have been accustomed to exercising considerable control over women's life-choices in line with the relevant etic civilizing process. For many groups in Western societies, the 'Muslim veil' has been highlighted as an example of the senseless curtailment of freedom. 'No other symbol', it has been argued, has signified 'with such force the "otherness" of Islam to the West' (Göle 1996: 1). From 'enlightened' standpoints, the veil is one of the pre-eminent expressions of male domination – of the enforced 'separation of women' from the world of 'civilized human beings' (Göle 1996: 13). But, as is well known, such interpretations are complicated by the fact that many Muslim women regard the veil or the burqa as a freely chosen expression of religious identity and/or as a declaration of virtuous self-restraint when compared to the licentiousness of the West (Göle 1996: 93). Whether such positions ultimately reflect traditional patriarchal power relations is a matter for specialists. Suffice it to add that, especially since the 1979 Iranian revolution, 'fundamentalist' Islamic forces have condemned the polluting effects of Western cultural influences that celebrate individualism in the form of freedom to choose life styles that permit 'illicit' sexual behaviour (Mozaffari 2002: 208). Related Islamist civilizing offensives to preserve or promote a specific conception of the we/I balance have been a striking feature of the most recent phase of the cultural revolt against the West. They have been a reminder of the deficiencies of the 'secularization thesis' which many in the West largely took for granted, a thesis which underpinned now outmoded assumptions that all societies are converging towards similar civilized orientations towards the social and political world including shared commitments to the primacy of individual human rights.[5]

To conclude this section, a new standard of civilization with respect to universal human rights internationalized core features of the civilizing process that resulted from particular domestic power relations in a period of Western global dominance. Drawn to the Western liberal we/ I balance, many non-Western groups supported bourgeois universal-egalitarian principles in various struggles to end colonial domination and to promote domestic emancipation. But the radical Islamist aspect of the revolt against the West has demonstrated the weakness of certain liberal assumptions that a universal civilization based on respect for such egalitarian principles is imminent. In different societies and regions, competitions for power between political groupings that are either attracted to or repelled by Western values look certain to continue to shape the global order. It may be useful to recall at this juncture the process-sociological analysis of how the 'we identity' of established groups was defined in the aftermath of 9/11 by claims that the 'global war on terror' was undertaken to defeat the 'enemies of civilization' (see p. 33ff; see also Dunning 2016). Subsequent cycles of stigmatization and counter-stigmatization, related 'decivilizing' or 'brutalisation processes', and resulting entrapment in 'double bind processes' have been noted (see p. 41–2). Western standards of liberal-democratic civilization were reinforced in this context, arguably in more defensive ways than in the past because of new global power distributions and declining confidence in the prospects for success. But the belief in the self-evident nature of the universal human rights discourse has been weakened. Traditional liberal optimism about its central role in an emergent world civilization or in a more civilized global political order has been dashed. More critical reflections on its origins in a specific civilizing process, its interdependence with specific domestic power balances, and its relationship with inter-state rivalries for power and prestige have eroded its position within the liberal societies that so confidently affirmed its role as a global standard of civilization. Some implications of those changes will be considered in more detail in Chapter 7. But it is useful to end this part of the discussion by recalling that many in the West continue to regard the human rights culture as a monument to the 'special character' of their civilization (see p. 60).

Liberal democracy

The other side of a revitalized liberal standard of civilization regarding human rights is the belief that the legitimacy of states depends on the commitment to democratic governance (Hobson 2012: 261). At its core lies the 'Wilsonian' thesis that the internal constitution of states is a major determinant of foreign policy behaviour. Embellished by the 'democratic peace' thesis that was the subject of much academic and public discussion in the immediate aftermath of the bipolar era, leading advocates have drawn on a fund of empirical evidence to show that stable liberal-democratic societies do not go to war with one another (Doyle 1983). In process-sociological terms, liberal governments exercise high levels of civilized self-restraint in relations with other like-minded societies, but are disposed to relax the constraints on force in conflicts with illiberal regimes which are deemed to lack full legitimacy. In Eliasian terms, core elements of the age-old 'split within civilization' have been overcome – at least within the liberal world – through changing power balances between the Machiavellian and universal-egalitarian dimensions of 'nation-state normative codes'. Implicit within the more optimistic liberal standpoints was the more radical prediction that a world order that consists entirely of stable liberal-democratic states will be uniquely pacified. Related civilizing offensives took the form of robust democracy-promotion measures (Stivachtis 2006, 2008).

Western endeavours to promote democratic forms of government have sought to globalize central features of the civilizing process; this has included the conversion of private monopolies of power into public monopolies that are obliged to comply with the rule of law and to rule in accordance with universal-egalitarian ethical standards. From the standpoint of process sociology, civilizational factors in the etic sense of the term were as critical as organizational ingenuity and institutional innovation. The chief manifestation was the overall shift in the relative power of internal and external constraints on undemocratic behaviour (Visoka 2017: 163). The civilizational element of the democratic habitus is a matter to come back to later. The comment on the indispensability of considerable self-restraint resonates with Elias's observation that too many have assumed that the obstacles to democratization (which can be defined as a power shift between traditional establishments and outsiders and the greater accountability of the former to the latter) are cognitive – in short, that 'the transformation of an absolutist or dictatorial regime into a parliamentary regime' is principally 'a result of an intellectual decision in favour of a freer and more rational form of social life within a state' (Elias 2013 [1989]: 404 note 56). By failing to understand that democratization is a process that is disputed, uneven, partial and reversible, and by 'ignoring the related civilizing problem', it has been 'easy to lose sight of the difficulties' faced by societies that are trying to make the transition from 'a long-established dictatorial one-party regime to a multi-party regime' (Elias

2013: 404fn 56). It has been all too easy to succumb to the erroneous view that 'all manner of societies ... can easily adopt and maintain democracy in the sense of a multiparty regime, whatever the level of tensions within them or the capacity of their members to bear tensions' (Elias and Dunning 2008: 11).

One further observation about democratization warrants attention. It is that liberal democracies' confidence in the right and in the ability to transform autocratic societies has often displayed elements of the collective pride in the 'special character' of civilized societies that underpinned 'civilizing' missions (Elias 2012 [1939]: 15–17). Recent examples are not hard to find. They include the speech on 8 September 2003 in which President Bush defended military intervention to promote regime change in Iraq by celebrating the United States' earlier role in 'lift[ing] up the defeated nations of Germany and Japan' and standing 'by them while they built representative governments' in the post-war era (see also Hobson 2012: 306–7 on the neo-conservative vision of a 'Concert of Democracies' that would similarly elevate other societies and 'extend the civilized democratic zone of peace').[6] Emboldened perhaps by successful civilizing or 'recivilizing' offensives to achieve the 'demilitarisation and democratisation' of Germany and the 'detoxification' of 'pre-modern' Japan, the United States and its European allies made the offer of membership of the North Atlantic Treaty Organization and the European Union to the former members of the Soviet bloc from the early 1990s on the express condition that they accepted the need for democratic political organization (see van Benthem van den Bergh 2001 for a discussion of recivilizing processes; see also Dower 1999: 79ff; Jackson 2006; Jarausch 2006 on democracy promotion in Germany and Japan). The civilizational dimension of European Union membership conditionality has had certain continuities with the civilizing offensives of the colonial era (Stivachtis 2008). The implicit assumption in many circles that 'the Western democratic state' is the highest stage of 'civilized' statehood reworked earlier binary divisions between the established and the outsiders that was fundamental to the 19th-century standard of civilization (Stivachtis 2006).

Elias (2013a: 405) maintained that the 'idealisation of the multi-party parliamentary system' has often hindered 'public discussion' of basic 'structural problems' in Western societies with consequent 'difficulties'. Blindness to their own difficulties has been combined at times with false optimism about the possibility of democratic transformation in non-Western societies. The relevant transitions have been especially hard to achieve in postcolonial societies where diverse groups with distinctive belief systems had been forced together by imperial authorities and subjected to the colonial politics of 'divide and rule' (see Broadhurst et al 2015: 246ff, 316ff on the difficulties faced by international institutions that promoted a civilizing process in Cambodia). Democratization has often stalled or been reversed whenever groups have feared that they will be permanently weakened and even destroyed if their political opponents gain control of the state's monopoly of the instruments of violence (Wydra 1999; Visoka 2017: 166, 173). Returning to the case of Iraq, the scale of those difficulties was overlooked given fantasy-laden assumptions that all along the majority of people were silently craving the transition to democratic rule and would welcome external military intervention – the necessary catalyst of change for people who had been waiting for a latter-day variant on the 'Napoleonic moment' (see p. 65). Low levels of detachment were intrinsic to the failure to recognize that subsequent shifts in internal power relations could embroil the society in double-bind spirals that resulted in ferocious civil war.

Process sociologists have analyzed myths surrounding externally promoted democratization that are germane to an assessment of its role as a global standard of civilization. Elias argued that a more detached understanding of the difficulties involved in undergoing the transition to a parliamentary system required careful attention to the 'related civilizing problem' and specifically to the patterns of self-restraint that are essential if that form of government is to take root and survive. The main thesis was that 'a multi-party parliamentary regime requires a higher degree of self-constraint than an autocratic–monarchical or dictatorial regime, and in this sense represents a higher level of civilization', which was not to imply that democratic methods of resolving major social conflicts and tensions are the 'final and ideal form' of rule, 'as it is often made out to be' (Elias 2013: 404–5). The requisite patterns of self-restraint included not only abstaining from using the state's monopolies of power to settle old differences with adversaries (as noted previously) but also freely relinquishing public office when defeated in electoral contests (Elias and Dunning 2008: 11). Elias and Dunning (2008: 17) focused on England – the exception rather than the rule in the 18th century – to show how commitments to the 'verbal skills of debate, of rhetoric, and persuasion, all of which required greater restraint all round', enabled rival parties to achieve the non-violent resolution of major disputes and tensions in a 'civilizing spurt'. Using those vital parliamentary techniques, evenly balanced competing groups avoided double-bind processes in which struggles for supremacy could have become impossible to control. Furthermore, the emergence and refinement of the civilizational aspects of parliamentary government were the outcome of adventitious power balances between the aristocracy and the bourgeoisie rather than the result of changing 'intellectual' preferences for a new form of rule (see also Vertigans 2017 on the relationship between such balances of power and processes of democratization in Africa). Relatively equal power resources pushed adversaries towards the sober realization that outright victory through violent means was improbable and that fundamental interests were best satisfied through unreserved commitments to negotiated compromise (Elias 2013: 406). Rivals found common ground in concluding that observing stricter levels of self-restraint was essential to maintain political order, but steady movement in that direction was not pre-ordained (Elias 2012 [1939]: 352–3). In the more typical cases, many decades had to pass before higher levels of self-restraint overtook the role of external compulsions in ensuring compliance with 'parliamentary manners' and democratized 'meeting regimes' (van Vree 1999: 230ff; Elias and Dunning 2008: 11).

Supplementing Elias's standpoint, recent process-sociological inquiry has argued that the advocates of democratic restructuring have often paid insufficient attention to the 'habitual' as opposed to the 'institutional' features of parliamentary government (Alikhani, 2014, 2017). The analysis of the 'habitually democratic personality' has further explored the psychogenetic dimensions of multi-party systems (Alikhani 2014, 2017). The inquiry expands the list of personality dispositions that have already been described, specifically high degrees of individual self-control and unwavering commitments to the peaceful resolution of conflicts. Additional traits include: competence in making autonomous judgements as against relying on, and deferring to, external authorities; the aptitude for taking the long-term perspective, especially under crisis conditions when temporal horizons can shorten in struggles for immediate gain; the facility for rising above dualistic (black and white) orientations to the social world and for respecting difference; and finally, respect for the human rights of traditional outsiders (especially women, minority ethnic groups and so forth) in the spirit of inclusiveness (see also Vertigans 2017 on the need in several African societies for shifts towards democratic 'we identifications' that transcend 'tribal' or 'ethnic' solidarities).

The upshot is that secure democratic transitions require an intricate combination of institutional innovation and the cultivation of the democratic habitus that can be immensely difficult to achieve. A related theme is that the sponsors of democracy promotion can be blind to the danger that external pressures to reform political structures can unleash 'harmful competition' that weakens rather than strengthens 'civility', and not least when there is a presumption that social and political developments that took place over many centuries in Europe can be compressed into shorter timespans in other regions (Behnam 2002: 191; Paris 2004: 170; Berman 2013; Visoka 2017a). In short, democracy promoters must themselves possess and display essential psychological traits such as the capacity for foresight in order to anticipate and avert dangerous outcomes. Considered in the light of the comments on the method of process sociology in the Introduction to this work, the related skill of greater detachment is essential to reduce the dangers that accompany highly involved perspectives, namely the greater risk of failed social interventions that sentence people to the misery of prolonged subjection to unanticipated conflicts.

Elias (2013a: 404–5) contended that the emergence of 'multi-party parliamentary states' was 'a milestone in the state-formation and civilizing processes' because it involved a 'reduction of the power difference between the rulers and ruled' as well as a concomitant 'increase in the civilizing self-controls of both groups' which was facilitated by significant levels of support for universal and egalitarian principles. Collective pride in democratization was unsurprising in Western societies. But, for many observers in the West and elsewhere, 'group charisma' anchored in democratic accomplishments has often been attended by self-satisfaction and high-mindedness towards supposedly backward groups. There is a close parallel with the early shift in using the idea of civilization to refer not to a long process that was incomplete and could be reversed but to a settled condition that was testament to the special attributes of self-satisfied elites (see p. 16). For colonialists who understood civilization in process-reducing ways, the fundamental question was how to bring its benefits to the less enlightened.

Similar dangers have been inherent in the civilizing offensive of democracy promotion. Critics of the presumed link between the strategy and the advancement of civilization have called attention to the 'darker side' of 'exclusion, hierarchy and violence' in attitudes to and relations with undemocratic societies (Hobson 2008). They have interpreted democracy promotion as an instrument for 'exploiting and perpetuating the imbalance of power that the end of the Cold War had inaugurated' – alternatively, as a means of increasing 'Western state power' which, in process-sociological terms, was wrapped in a discourse of humanitarianism that echoed the earlier standard of civilization (Clark 2009). Those who take a more positive view cannot deny that democracy promotion, rather like the human rights culture with which it is connected, has an effective role in constructing a we-identity of established strata which is coupled with the stigmatization of alleged social inferiors. That is most transparent when Western groups have demonized societies that are deemed to be impossible to reform given irrational, atavistic resistance to external attempts to promote modes of coexistence based on voluntary submission to civilized restraints.

In those circumstances, a standard of civilization that is based on democracy promotion replicates certain features of colonial mentalities. That observation resonates with process-sociological reflections on the myths that may underlie and emerge from endeavours to improve human conditions but lack the requisite reality-congruent knowledge. The focus has been on limited understandings of the complex civilizational preconditions of successful transitions from autocratic to democratic governance. It can be enhanced by noting how failed interventions in that area can lead to exercises in the 'attribution of blame' (see pp. 40–1) – in regarding the ingrained shortcomings of outsiders as primarily responsible for the lack of success (see Vertigans 2017). On that account, the contributory role of incomplete knowledge of democratic transitions among established groups is not confronted. Failed interventions may entrench imbalances between involvement (moral judgements about other forms of life from established perspectives) and greater detachment about the complexities of democratic transitions. Advocates of the liberal-democratic standard of civilization have often been accused of privileging social ideals over the quest for reality-congruent knowledge about the social conditions of outsiders, and challenged because of a lack of self-criticism with respect to their working assumptions about the preconditions of democratic government. Taking sides in resulting disputes is not the strategy that is adopted here. This section has tried to detail what process sociology brings to an inquiry into the civilizational prerequisites of effective interventions to improve social and political conditions.

Intervention and civilization

In recent decades, Western responses to intra-state violence in several societies have provided further evidence that the standard of civilization endures in the modern world in the shape of the traditional presumption that the modern sovereign state remains the keystone of civilized conditions. By 'promoting the Westphalian model', it has been argued, peace-builders have attempted 'to prevent a reversal in the historic expansion of the modern state from Europe to the rest of the world'; the relevant 'civilizing missions' have been designed to ensure 'the ongoing reproduction of the Westphalian state model' that Europeans exported to 'semi-civilized' regions in the 19th century (Paris 2002; Horowitz 2004; Visoka 2017a; Waters 2016). In particular, civilized peoples have debated the moral and legal rights and wrongs of resorting to humanitarian intervention – and the pros and cons of embedding the principle in international society – in response to the failed 'modernization' of former colonies and the unanticipated collapse of the former Yugoslavia (Paris 2002; Andrieu 2010).

Some of the resulting problems are the product of dashed optimism regarding the prospects for successful state-formation and national integration in the former colonies and for concomitant advances in healing 'tribal' divisions and in facilitating the civilized resolution of disputes (Mandelbaum 2013; Pedersen 2015: 70ff). Political turmoil on the borderlands of many states has prompted the question of whether the long-term trend of globalizing state formation is nearing its end (Idler 2019). A few decades ago, European patterns of development appeared to be taking root in non-Western regions, but the reality was that a 'serious mismatch' between state institutions and traditional forms of collective identification generated rivalries and tensions that often led to political suppression and violent conflict (Zhang 2015: 365). In East Asia, for instance, major conflicts arose between 'traditional local norms and institutions' and the principal properties of the modern state such as 'exclusive jurisdiction' and 'direct and absolute authority' over a 'legally defined' territory which is grounded in 'the monopoly of the use of force' (Zhang 2015: 365).

It has been maintained from a postcolonial perspective that 'the political decolonization of Asia and Africa in the twentieth century or in other parts of the world was a monumental disappointment' (Go 2013: 30). Clearly, 'it did not bring equality between metropolitan and ex-colonial countries; nor did it bring 'a decolonization of consciousness or culture' (Go 2013: 30). For many new states in the post-Second World War era, it did not bring the promised or expected levels of public order and stability. Process sociologists have not ignored those developments. Regarding postcolonial societies in Africa, Elias (2008h: 135–6) observed that 'state formation' is 'hardly ever accepted without resistance'. The attempted 'higher level integration' of social groups produced a resented 'reduction or loss of relative autonomy … at many lower level positions – for example, the positions of chiefs and elders or of kings and their courts'. With 'great regularity', he added, groups can feel endangered by a sudden increase in 'dependence on former outsiders' and by the ensuing 'loss of identity, pride and meaning' that leads to 'specific tensions' or 'integration conflicts' (Elias 2008h: 135–6).

In the light of those complexities, process-sociological lines of investigation have stressed the imperative for a 'genuinely global process' in which international non-state actors enter into partnerships with domestic political groups to promote a taming or 'socialization' of state structures which is compatible with internal 'civilizing processes' (Bogner and Neubert 2016; see also Neubert 2009). Or, as argued in a related inquiry into the 'globalisation of civilizing standards', they have emphasized that it is vital to build 'closer interconnections between civilizing processes' at 'the global/interstate and the intrastate levels' (van Benthem van den Bergh 2001: 3). Those approaches dovetail with the argument that elite efforts to impose (as in Afghanistan and Iraq) the 'Westphalian-Weberian ideal of statehood' with its 'monopoly on the legitimate use of violence' have neglected the 'governance functions' of 'non-state' structures that attempt to resolve group tensions through exercises in transitional justice and inclusive political dialogue (Andrieu 2010; Baumann 2009; Paris 2015; see also Kühn 2016).

Western measures to promote internal pacification and to protect human rights through such global/local political alliances can be relatively uncontroversial, although analysts of the persistence of 'cultures of imperialism' advise caution (Go 2013: 30). Far from uncontroversial was the liberal case for humanitarian intervention that was made in response to genocidal killing in Rwanda in the mid-1990s, to the Yugoslav wars and, more recently, to the crises in Libya and Syria (see Steele 2019: ch 5 on the emphasis on restraint in US policy on Syria under the Obama administration). Resulting debates further illustrated the peculiar contortions and entanglements of civilized peoples. Participants included those who declare that societies cannot claim to be civilized if they fail to use force to prevent or end serious human rights abuses where ruling elites use the monopoly control of the instruments of violence to eliminate political opponents or where rivals commit atrocities in struggles to gain such powers. Opposing views include the contention that it is morally irresponsible to place military personnel in harm's way to protect people who may be judged incapable of restraining tribal violent impulses or an atavistic thirst for murderous revenge (Hansen 2000; Jacoby 2011; see also Berman 2013 on Western myths about African civil conflicts that highlight the absence of 'civilization' and ignore the extent to which global forces have weakened state power and fostered resource struggles between different ethnic groups). But respect for the belief that civilized societies cannot just ignore humanitarian emergencies, even though they decide against using force, constitutes a notable but contingent shift in the relative power of the universal-egalitarian and nationalist elements of nation-state normative codes. The not uncommon belief that it is 'almost a duty to do something about the misery of other human groups' – to cite Elias's observation about changing public orientations to global poverty – is present in such responses to human rights abuses (Elias 2013: 29). However, the high point of public approval of humanitarian intervention has passed (at least for now) and has been overtaken by the nationalist-populist political parties which insist that various globalist projects went too far and must be rolled back.

Turning finally to any new patterns of change in the global order, most states have adamantly opposed any movement towards incorporating a principle of humanitarian intervention in international society, and not least because of suspicions that Western governments will exploit the relevant conventions to justify self-interested violations of territorial sovereignty (Collet 2009; Reinold 2013: 99ff; Zeigler 2016). The idea of humanitarian intervention is not poised to become part of an agreed global standard of civilization, but there has been widespread support for the doctrine of the 'responsibility to protect' as defended in the 2001 report of the *International Commission on Intervention and State Sovereignty* which obligates national governments to comply with international legal prohibitions of war crimes and crimes against humanity (including ethnic cleansing and genocide) and to assist regimes that are unable to protect citizens from such atrocities.[7] Some analysts have added that the 'responsibility to protect' should not be summarily dismissed as just another 'Western idea' or as an expression of contested Western standards of civilization, but regarded instead as reflecting principles of benevolent or humane government that can be found in many non-Western societies or civilizations (O'Hagan 2015). Agreements in that sphere, however qualified, suggest the possibility of global standards of civilization that are no longer linked exclusively with Western moral principles and modes of social and political organization or tarnished by the colonial era (Zaum 2007: 231; see also Odgaard 2020). As for Western populations, they may well find that they are repeatedly involved in entanglements and contortions with respect to the rights and wrongs of humanitarian intervention.

Global market civilization

Contemporary 'standards of civilization in international relations', it has been argued, have been crafted to establish 'an international society of reasonably uniform states based on a largely Western ideal-type of liberal-democracy coupled to a market economy that prefer to trade peacefully among themselves as opposed to posturing and preparing for war' (Bowden 2014: 616). Proposed future directions for 'less developed' peoples were evidence of the impact of bourgeois civilized norms on the current global order (Blomert 2002). Marx and Engels (1977 [1848]: 224–5) were clear about the link between capitalism and the civilization of non-European peoples when they referred to the bourgeois project to introduce 'what it calls civilization into their midst'. From the standpoint of process sociology, Marxist analysis of the bourgeois era made significant progress in emphasizing the role of conflict in social groups and in highlighting the struggles that led to capitalist monopolies. But, as discussed previously, the perspective was mistaken in large part because of high involvement in political outcomes and insufficiently detached modes of inquiry. Capitalist modes of production and new class structures had been abstracted from larger patterns of change – from the process of state-formation and internal pacification that created the conditions in which capitalist industrialization became possible (Elias 2012a). In particular, the state's increased fiscal demands and growing dependence on successful commercial strata led to unplanned shifts in the power resources and capabilities of aristocratic and bourgeois groups. The growing power and prestige of the latter strata were manifested by their claim that commercial pursuits should enjoy the social esteem that had long been conferred on aristocratic warlike pursuits (Elias 2012 [1939]: 467). As just noted, Marx and Engels emphasized the civilizational dimension of the rise of the capitalist bourgeoisie but they were unable to explain it. A similar point which has been made in the critique of world systems theory but which also applies to neo-Marxist political economy in general emphasizes explanatory deficiencies that arise from the absence of the civilizational analytic which was developed in Elias's writings (Kilminster 2007: 158, note 6).

Elias's own analytic did not examine the relationship between the European civilizing process, global market civilization and associated civilizing offensives in non-European regions. Their interwoven nature was already apparent in the 19th-century 'standard of liberal globalized civilization' which demanded that non-Western governments throw open domestic markets to foreign competition (Fidler 2000). Unequal treaties and 'extra-territoriality' introduced commercial relations under Western rules; they expressed the demand that Chinese groups that traded with outsiders abide by alien legal conventions. Intertwined Western offensives and local responses (as in the case of Chinese commercial groups that lobbied the government to incorporate Western legal principles so that they could compete with outsiders on more equal terms) promoted the globalization of bourgeois features of the civilizing process (Fidler 2001). Explicit links between civilization and such pressures became central to 19th-century bourgeois progressive thought, building on antecedent standpoints (see Thomas 2018: 188ff, who draws attention, however, to early objections to the linkages between market relations and the weakening of 'ancient virtue').

In a representative exhortation of economic liberalism, Richard Cobden (1835: 36) argued that 'commerce is the grand panacea which, like a beneficent medical discovery, will serve to inoculate with … the taste of civilization all the nations of the world'. In 1875, Sir Louis Mallet, a leading figure in the Cobden Club, celebrated free trade because, in his view, it destroyed 'primitive barbarism' where 'every foreigner was an enemy' and where the presumed right 'to take every advantage of the adversary and injure him as much as possible entered into the spirit of all international dealings' (cited in Pigman 2006: 195). Exponents of 'Christian economics' announced that true commerce would not only abolish the last vestiges of the tyrannical slave trade but also replace habitual 'native indolence' with civilized self-discipline including precise time-management that was crucial for effective participation in the expanding world market (Grant 2005: 18–21; Adas 2015: 241ff). Liberals such as Cobden believed that the necessary reforms could be achieved by peaceful means. Others, including Palmerston's pro-war faction, argued that using force against China in the wake of the 1857 'Arrow' affair had been indispensable so that the 'beneficent influences' of the holy trinity of 'free trade, "responsible government" and Protestant Christianity' would liberate 'Asia's millions from the threefold scourges of monopoly, tyranny and idolatry' (Phillips 2011: 13). Such disputes over the best means of securing change assumed, however, that the expansion of capitalist markets was the key to a progressively civilized global order.

Turning to the contemporary period, Western governments that have spearheaded economic liberalization have typically described target societies as insufficiently globalized rather than less civilized, although the latter description has not entirely vanished from the language used by leading figures in such organizations as the International Monetary Fund (IMF) (Best 2006). That there are close connections between global market civilization and the European civilizing process is indisputable, but studies of economic globalization have often ignored the relevant civilizational elements. Recent investigations of the influence of a revamped standard of market civilization on the current global order restored the link. They focused on civilizing offensives in which 'all of the war-shattered states receiving aid from the IMF and World Bank [were] required to undertake market-oriented economic reforms including the privatisation of state-owned enterprises, the lowering of government subsidies, removal of wage and price controls, and the lifting of regulatory controls and barriers to foreign goods and investment' (Paris 2002: 644; Bowden and Seabrooke 2006). Impositions of market arrangements have been described as involving 'a kinder, gentler system of capitulations' than those that existed in the colonial era (Fidler 2000). A key element of recent variations on the classical liberal belief on the progressive nature of capitalist markets was the argument that the collapse of the Soviet Union had shown conclusively that command economies were so infested with structural inefficiencies that they could not keep pace with Western societies. A more gentle 'system of capitulations' was focused on the non-violent incorporation of developing societies within a demonstrably rational global market civilization, on promoting compliance with the relevant international legal conventions, and on establishing 'good governance' and the 'civilizing' rule of law in societies in transition (Kurki 2013: ch 10). One of many examples of efforts to promote the modern legal-rational, capitalist state was the creation of global anti-corruption norms that were designed to expose and prevent levels of 'collaboration between public officials and private actors for private financial gains' (Wang and Rosenau 2001: 26; Kim and Sharman 2014; see also Berman 2013 on how the erosion of state power and growing economic inequalities often had an entirely opposite effect of increasing levels of government corruption). Such campaigns drew on a central feature of the European civilizing process, namely the presumption that the modern law-governed state is the crucible of a civilized existence.

Three other aspects of bourgeois conceptions of the civilizing force of markets warrant consideration. The first is the conviction that market civilization imposes invaluable checks on state monopoly powers and is indispensable for safeguarding property rights and personal liberties. The second is that free market constraints on state capabilities have tamed the bellicose dispositions that dominated relations between states in the pre-capitalist era. The third is that global business civilization fosters a particular we/I balance in which individualism counteracts dangerous collectivist mentalities. Significant here are the psychological traits that Weber (1930: ch 2) regarded as fundamental to the 'social ethic of capitalist culture' or the 'spirit of capitalism'. They included self-reliance, emotional self-control and the related capacity to defer short-term gratification for longer-term rewards which provided immunity from the irrationalism of collectivist mentalities (Weber

1930: ch 2; see also Haskell 1985 and Gill 1995 on 'disciplinary neo-liberalism'). All three assumptions are integral to the assessment that market society is, in the terminology that has been used to describe how liberals regarded international law in the late 19th century, the 'gentle civilizer of nations' (Koskenniemi 2001). All three features remain pivotal to distinctions between progressive and backward conditions that are central to the 'we identity' of the established social strata in the contemporary global order.[8]

The contradictions between globalizing Western liberal-democracies and universalizing capitalist social relations have been stressed by radical critics of an expanding market civilization. In a parallel thesis to the argument that democratization can unleash 'harmful competition', they have insisted that reduced government subsidization and externally driven welfare cuts have frequently undercut one of the prerequisites of successful democratic transitions, namely trust in governing elites and public institutions (Robinson 2007: 10ff; Berman 2013). What process sociologists have added is an analysis of how greater inequalities between established and outsider groups in Western societies altered the overall pattern of development of the preceding decades. In those years, traditional outsiders succeeded in wrenching significant economic and political concessions from the dominant elites. Power balances had moved markedly in their favour; the established strata had become patently more dependent on them for attaining valued objectives. Mounting pressures on the ruling groups to agree to a more even distribution of resources resulted in the new social contracts of the period.

Hard-won gains have been eroded, however, with the increasing power inequalities that have resulted from neoliberal initiatives to construct a global market civilization. Dominant groups have been liberated from many of the earlier demands and incentives to make major economic and political concessions to less powerful social strata. With changing power relations they have less need to regard the latter as equal members of the same community who are entitled to basic economic and social rights; they have had less reason to think from the standpoint of the less powerful; they have become freer to behave as they please, often indifferent to how their actions and supporting institutions adversely affect the well-being of vulnerable groups (Newton 2003; Mennell 2007: ch 12). The scope of emotional identification has narrowed accordingly.

Other process-sociological reflections on global market civilization that focused on the 2008 global financial crisis have drawn attention to the role of 'guides to conduct' in the banking sectors that promised individual rewards for successful risk-taking in competitive struggles between financial institutions (Haro 2014). They have commented on the role of incentives to make short-term gains without regard for the risks not only for their commercial enterprises but also for the larger society and the global economic order (Blomert 2012; Mennell 2014 and van Benthem van den Bergh 2012). Inquiries into the political imperative 'of taming the financial aristocracies' have pointed to how a recurring feature of human societies – namely subjection to unforeseen and uncontrolled processes – has been evident in the contemporary era as a result of the orchestrated global relaxation of restraints on economic activity or neoliberal deregulation (Blomert 2012). The counter-reaction to the effects of global market civilization on the economic circumstances and cultural anxieties of vulnerable groups has been expressed in the largely unanticipated subsequent populist revolt against open markets and the free movement of labour. In what Elias described as the persistent 'drag effect of national loyalties' (discussed in Chapter 7), national-populist organizations have protested against globalism and globalization which are deemed to serve the interests of an establishment that has neglected the socioeconomic conditions of outsiders. As part of a larger assault on the standards of global market civilization, they have appealed to revitalized nation-states to provide security from poorly regulated or unregulated forces. Those developments mark a significant alternation of the course of the civilizing process.

The broader pattern of contestation includes reactions against the Western 'market state model' in which East Asian conceptions of the 'developmental state' necessitate strict controls on commercial activity (Stephen 2014; Zhang 2015). There is an unmistakable civilizational dimension, it has been argued, to those counter-images of the appropriate relationship between states and markets. Particular 'forces of civilization', the contention is, have shaped how capitalist social relations have been embedded in non-Western forms of life (Cox 2001: 114). The implicit supposition is that different civilizing processes underlie East Asian critiques of the 'market state model' for its failure to impose strict controls on capitalist relations.[9] Related themes are fundamental to the idea of an 'ecological civilization' (shengtai wenming) which has been a key part of Chinese official policy since the 2007 Seventeenth Congress of the Chinese Communist Party (see United Nations Environment Programme 2016). That image which is influenced by Western 'ecological Marxism' envisages interlocking increases in levels of national and global restraint that are necessary given how liberal notions of the civilizing role of capitalist markets have contributed to climate change (Zhihe et al 2014). It is not inconceivable that the vision of an 'ecological civilization' will become central to a future global standard of civilization as part of shifting balances of power between the advocates and the critics of free market liberalism. It is not impossible that the idea will become a valuable resource in global leadership claims with respect to promoting new levels of individual and collective restraint to deal effectively with the problem of environmental degradation. Were that to occur, new standards of civilization which are emancipated from the West (or that bridge the differences between Western and non-Western societies) could become a main pillar of the future global order.[10]

Those comments raise the question of whether the global order has entered a transitional phase which requires a deeper understanding of non-Western civilizations or, more accurately, of interrelated Western and non-Western civilizing processes. The issue is whether the classical project of creating a universal civilization anchored in the 'application of a standard of civilization based on Western values' has not only stalled but is being reversed (Mozaffari 2001). Analyses of China's rise to power have contended that as a result of changing global power balances, the epoch of deferral to a standard of civilization centred on Western liberal-democratic capitalist norms is giving way to an era of increasing tensions between rival 'civilizational' standards (Suzuki 2012). Specialists have described the ambivalence of Chinese elite attitudes to the West, noting how the desire to gain international recognition from sections of an 'idealized West' coexists with opposition to any effort to use liberal-democratic yardsticks in protests against its human rights record (Suzuki 2014; Buzan 2014). Painful memories of China's 'century of humiliation' in the colonial era find expression in a strong defence of territorial sovereignty and the principle of non-intervention (Suzuki 2009; see also Suzuki 2011 on China's ambivalent position on forms of international trusteeship).

Chinese pride and confidence in providing an alternative civilizational model for developing societies has led to the thesis that the global order has indeed entered a period of transition, particularly as a result of Chinese as well as Russian reactions against core Western liberal-democratic commitments. Immensely significant following high levels of economic growth and poverty reduction was the 'Beijing Consensus' which encapsulated the supposition that China's non-democratic model of economic development surpasses the Western 'market state model' as the appropriate ideal for many postcolonial societies (Luo and Zhang 2011: 1804–6). On some accounts, proclamations of 'exceptionalism' attempt to distinguish Chinese endeavours to forge alliances with former European colonies in common rejection of Western standards of civilization. There are, it has been maintained, significant connections between China's 'civilizing mission' with respect to development programmes in Africa and the history of 'civilizing offensives' towards minority ethnic groups such as the Tibetans who have been expected to assimilate into 'modern' Han civilization (Nyíri 2006; Suzuki 2012). Differentiation from African peoples, it is argued, has recognizable civilizational undertones which are reminiscent of European colonial conceptions of native indolence, notwithstanding the official Chinese egalitarian discourse of brotherhood (Nyíri 2006: 103; Cheng 2011; Luo and Zhang 2011: 10).

Such explorations of changing global power balances, competing standards of civilization, and protests against global market civilization underline the need for the comparative analysis of long-term, civilizing processes (see Hobson 2007). Process sociologists have argued that Elias's investigation of the European civilizing process provides a rough model for that larger-scale project. The thesis is that Eliasian sociology was 'Europe-centred', given that the objective was to explain how peoples in one region came to regard themselves as uniquely civilized, but it was not Eurocentric by presuming that the categories that underpinned that inquiry could be transferred directly – without modification – to inquiries into other civilizing processes. Preliminary investigations of Cambodian, Chinese and Japanese processes of civilization have explored key questions for an extended analysis of such patterns of development (Ikegami 1995, 2005; Mennell 1996, 2007; Ohira 2014; Stebbins 2009; Broadhurst et al 2015).

Further comparative analyses of civilizing processes can only enrich investigations of the changing global order. Essential is the adoption of a 'relational' approach which eschews 'civilizational isolationism' and takes a long-term perspective on how different civilizing processes have influenced one another across the centuries (Hobson 2007). At the heart of that argument is the observation that the global dominance of a seemingly separate European civilization occurred around the 'critical watershed' of 1800–40 (Hobson 2007: 425). As a result of changing power distributions, the world is now returning to the status quo ante in which other societies that have undergone distinctive civilizing processes can shape global political and economic relations on more even terms and may radically reform global market civilization (Hobson 2007). What may be a pivotal moment in the development of the modern global order requires long-term explorations of intra- and international interactions; process sociology is well placed to shape and inform this.

Conclusion

The classical standard of civilization lost its commanding place in a Western-dominated world order as a result of the revolt against the West and changes in the global power distributions, but traces of the doctrine survive in contested norms regarding human rights, democracy promotion, market relations, and state-building projects which many Western groups regard as testifying to the modern achievements of their civilization. Several studies have analyzed how far Western and non-Western societies are moving away from shared standards of civilized life; they have considered how that change may affect the future global order. In Eliasian terms, they have discussed the shifting relations between the forces of attraction and repulsion, and between the power of the traditional established and outsider groups. Those issues which have arisen as a result of opposition to the global dominance of Western civilized precepts will be considered in Chapter 7. The focus will be on the prospects for a global civilizing process or for what Elias called civilizing processes affecting humanity as a whole.

Process sociologists recognize that the terminology may cause confusion outside academic circles that are unfamiliar with the distinction between the emic and etic meanings of civilization. The argument of Chapter 7 is that the concept has advantages over alternatives which outweigh unquestionable difficulties. It can be used to extend the Eliasian perspective by analyzing social and political forces which have influenced the development of all societies. It can be employed in attempts to identify the main directions of global change – more specifically, whether there are clear trends with respect to the relative power of the forces of convergence and divergence or between integrative and disintegrative tendencies in world politics. Process sociology has been a neglected resource in investigations of such trends within the post-Western international order. The objective of the following chapter is to show that analyses of current tensions can profit from engaging with the concepts that Elias applied to his deliberations on civilizing processes that have shaped human societies over the millennia.

7

Civilizing Processes at the Level of Humanity as a Whole

The previous three chapters discussed the transition from the age in which the outlines of a world civilization based on European value-preferences seemed to be emerging to the current era in which support for a global order based on European or Western standards of civilized arrangements is in retreat. Elias's reflections on civilizing processes that affect humanity as whole have particular relevance for analyzing the relevant shifting power relations. His focus represented a widening of an inquiry into long-term patterns of change which had been initially confined to the European continent (Mennell 1998: ch 9). The driving force was a conception of sociology as a global social science that promoted 'education and knowledge-transfer' and that was not limited by the short-term preoccupations of particular societies but regarded 'humanity as its horizon' in the 'emerging world society' (Elias 2008d: 268).

The reality of lengthening and deepening webs of interconnectedness rather than any particular normative vision prompted the enlargement of the scope of process-sociological investigation. Elias observed that those who sought to understand those changes might hope to be comforted by reflections on the more 'pleasant and hopeful' features of 'humankind's development' but such partiality was the 'true meaning of the "*trahison des clercs*"'. Whether or not we 'welcome the increasing integration of humankind', Elias (2010c: 149) maintained, there is no doubt that greater global interconnectedness 'increases the impotence of the individual in relation to what is happening at the top level of humanity'. Those comments about the powerlessness of the individual in contemporary conditions highlighted the subjection of humans to forces they cannot control (an observation with clear contemporary relevance given the global COVID-19 crisis). They warned against assuming that future global integration will lead to higher levels of emotional identification between peoples. Indeed the opposite could turn out to be the case. Centrifugal national loyalties retained the capacity to constrain, if not reverse, international experiments in dealing with the consequences of rising global interconnections. The pertinence of that theme for understanding the rise of national-populist revolt against economic globalization will be considered later in this chapter.

Elias (2013b: 280ff) was adamant that there are no insuperable barriers – whether biological or cultural – to a condition in which people identify with global political institutions that supersede provincial 'survival units' and have responsibility for humanity at large. To develop a theme that was introduced earlier, he observed that it would be a 'very advanced form of human civilization' where people live together non-violently without the need for coercive mechanisms – in short, 'where people do not need external restraint in order to refrain from the use of violence in their relationships with others' but organize their relations instead around the compulsions of self-restraint or the inner conscience. That state of affairs might never be realized but, Elias (2007:140–1) suggested, it is well worth aiming for. One of the purposes of social-scientific inquiry was to achieve a deeper understanding of uncontrolled processes; it was to develop forms of knowledge and levels of awareness that would help people orientate themselves to many difficulties that stemmed from rising levels of unplanned global interconnections. No explicit normative claims were made about higher levels of integration (although the humanist foundations of the position that were discussed in the Introduction to this work should again be noted). The emphasis was on how the social sciences could provide a more detached understanding of social conflicts and divisions and a deeper awareness of the high-fantasy world views that have often developed alongside them. Societies would then be better equipped to reduce the tyranny of untamed processes.

The first part of this chapter considers Elias's long-term perspective on the monopolization of powers that have been central to civilizing processes which have affected most of humanity. It expands the focus by considering the part that inter-societal arrangements have played in the integration of human groups. Elias's observations about global civilizing trends in the recent period are discussed in that context. Part two discusses the criteria that can be used for assessing the relative impact of global civilizing and decivilizing processes on social and political directions that affect all of humanity. Two perspectives on the civilizational dimensions of the global order are reviewed from that standpoint – Huntington's notion of an emerging clash of civilization, which is considered in part three of the chapter, and English School writings on the problem of how to recreate world order in the absence of the shared civilizational norms that once underpinned the classical European international society, which is discussed in part four. The Huntington thesis which anticipated, in Eliasian terms, a major decivilizing trend in the global order is an example of how high fantasy-content perspectives often determine the course of events as established groups respond to changing power balances that threaten their influence and prestige. By contrast, English School writings contain more detached observations on the ramifications of the uncoupling of international society from the once hegemonic Western conceptions of civilized ways of life.

Assessed from the standpoint of process sociology, the two approaches shed light on very different and almost antithetical reactions to the 'integration conflicts' that can occur when human groups are forced together in longer webs of interconnectedness. Huntington's thesis emphasized the increased prospects for civilizational conflict. English School writings have concentrated on the potential for civilized commitments that bridge major divisions in the first universal society of states. Developing those themes, part five of this chapter considers the continuing influence of the 'drag effect of national loyalties' on endeavours to build international institutions that address the problems that arise with greater human interdependencies. The national-populist revolt provides a sharp reminder of the dominance of national symbolism and the relative weakness of global or cosmopolitan symbols that convey strong feelings of identification with humanity. That development has highlighted the enormity of the challenge in constructing a world order in which global civilizing processes substantially reduce the dangers that attend integration conflicts. The analysis of the idea of civilization in the making of the global order concludes with an argument for more detailed analyses of symbols and world politics. Of particular importance for the future of world order, it will be argued, is the power balance between symbols of national community and symbols of a global or human civilization. The relative appeal of those symbolic frameworks provides a window onto more general movements, and specifically on the evolving relations between civilizing and decivilizing processes that affect humanity as a whole through its incorporation in the first worldwide political order.

Global civilizing processes

Elias (2008: 4) referred, in what is now unfashionable language, to a long 'comprehensive, humanity-wide process of civilization'. The thesis was that there are 'weighty reasons' for 'treat[ing] the growth of humankind as the matrix of the growth of knowledge. In the long-run it is difficult and perhaps impossible for any particular sub-group of humankind to appropriate particular advances in knowledge'. Reflecting his recognition of the impact of international political rivalries on developments that have shaped most, if not all, human societies, he added that various steps in the acquisition and transmission of knowledge have been inextricably connected with the 'competitive struggles of human groups' (Elias 2011: 23–4). The overall processes included monopolizing thrusts and accompanying changes in patterns of individual and collective restraint within survival units that have transformed the planet. Two illustrations of the argument which exemplify Elias's long-term perspective on social and political life warrant consideration before expanding the discussion to include the study of international orders.

The first was the monopolization of the use of fire by early human groups and the spread of that technology to all societies (Elias 2010c: 125; and especially Goudsblom 1994a). Elias (2008: 4) maintained that a 'humanity-wide process of civilization' was apparent in the ways in which humans learned to conquer elementary fears of fire and acquired knowledge of how to turn fire technologies to their advantage in such activities as farming and warfare. Monopoly control of fire was the product of the cognitive breakthroughs that more detached orientations to the world made possible. Crucially for the following discussion, it was connected with some of the most complex features in the history of human societies – the formation of levels of individual and collective restraint and associated advancements in social planning that made the utilization of inherently dangerous forces possible (Elias 2010c: 125–6; Goudsblom 1994a). Here the idea of the triad of controls – controls over the self, the controls that people exercise over each other, and the controls they have over nature – is particularly relevant (see pp. 24–5). The monopolization of fire facilitated major increases in controlling natural processes, but that movement could not have occurred without levels of self-restraint and foresight that distinguished proto-human and human from non-human societies. The most detailed process-sociological investigation of those transformations maintains that such civilizing advances were fundamental in modifying the balance of power between humans and non-humans (Goudsblom 1994a). Along with the invention of complex tools and weapons (where equivalent species monopolies took place), social controls over fire enabled humans to begin to turn themselves from the hunted into the hunters – so starting the slow ascent to a position of astonishing dominance on the planet (Goudsblom 1994a; Mennell 1998: 207ff, 223). As a major process-sociological study has argued, the 'domestication of fire was the first great act of human interference with natural processes', the first step of the journey in which societies increased their powers over nature (Goudsblom 2002: 28). The emergence of collective restraints in that domain was a civilizing process that laid the foundations for later revolutionary epochs such as the rise of agrarian settlements and early state-organized societies (Goudsblom 2015: 193–4). Those developments marked the breakthrough to destructive capabilities (anchored in forms of individual and collective restraint intrinsic to the relevant civilizing processes) that have attended the course of human history ever since.

Those trends made possible a second web of civilizing processes which unfolded at the level of humanity, namely the formation of survival units of greater 'magnitude' as exemplified by radical transitions from 'village to town' and from 'tribe to state' (Elias 2008: 4). From the earliest small-scale 'kinship groups', the argument was, modern nation-states with tens of millions of citizens have emerged. Increases of scale conferred great advantages on survival units that were entangled in elimination struggles, and specifically on those that represented a 'breakthrough to a new *figuration* which was more or less pacified internally … a breakthrough to new patterns of reserve and detachment, [to] new patterns of civilization' (Elias 2008: 4, italics in original). The reference to civilization highlighted again how central the invention of new standards of restraint was for substantial increases in the magnitude of survival units. Shifts in the monopolization of power accompanied by the necessary emulation of the social, political and military capabilities of the most successful groups led to the marked pacification of the relations between people within larger territorial areas. A second 'comprehensive, humanity-wide process of civilization' took place through those transformations. Central to the transitions from 'village to town' and from 'tribe to state' was the emergence of more centralized political structures with increased controls over the instruments of violence. Inter-group struggles for security and survival led to the deepening diversification of human groups or to unmatched 'cultural divergence' (Goudsblom 2002: 39). Successful symbolic innovations bound groups together in the same survival unit by sharpening the distinctions between insiders and outsiders, or between friend and enemy. Symbolic inventiveness was a decisive part of civilizing processes at the level of societies of 'greater magnitude'. The capacity to withstand or prevail in elimination contests was highly dependent on the existence of effective social standards of restraint that were underpinned by symbolic codes that almost always demanded compliance with feared sacred or supernatural forces (Linklater 2019; Linklater in preparation).

Developments at the inter-state level provide a third example of civilizing processes that affected humanity as a whole. States, Elias (2007: 101) argued, 'form part of another less highly organized, less well-integrated' order which is centred on a 'balance of power system' in the modern world. Such arrangements stood at the summit of a 'hierarchy' of modes of social and political organization; they constituted the 'highest level of integration' of human groups or the highest level of 'organized power' with the 'capacity to regulate its own course' (Elias 2007: 101). The collective ability to exercise some level of control over relations between states reveals that patterns of civilization have existed in relations between, as well as in relations within, survival units that separately enjoy monopoly control of the instruments of violence. Moreover, as noted in the earlier discussion of societies of states, those processes of civilization have been connected with, and underpinned by, discourses of barbarism. Those dichotomies have been linked with a joint monopoly in which states exercise strict controls over the criteria for admission into such international figurations. The related established–outsider formations have been significant for such arrangements as the managed balance of power where states must place restraints through diplomatic interaction on their political ambitions; they must have the foresight to forego immediate strategic advantages and sufficient regard for collective restraints in order to preserve an equilibrium of forces that contributes to international order and stability. Such phenomena reflected a sharp change in the major threats that confronted human groups. In many regions, the dangers that societies posed to each other increased substantially relative to the threats posed by natural forces (Elias 2007: 76ff). To return to the triad of controls, increased powers over nature have not been accompanied by higher levels of self-restraint and collective restraint in the relations between societies of greater scale.

Nevertheless, balance of power systems exhibited the same tendency that has been especially pronounced within survival units: the growth of interdependence created pressures to exercise foresight and imperatives to exercise greater self-restraint especially in the context of relatively equal power ratios (Mennell 2012). Civilizing processes can therefore appear even in the relations between survival units that do not have to submit to global political institutions with monopoly control of the instruments of force. They have emerged in the recent period because the accumulation of increasingly destructive capabilities has been the other side of the trend towards larger survival units. They have evolved in response to a fundamental consequence of power monopolization: the state's capacity to harm more people in more destructive ways over greater distances – and in the case of 'annihilation units' to destroy millions of people and to lay waste to the human habitat (Elias 2010c: 186ff). The paradoxical nature of human development could not be clearer. The rise of 'new patterns of civilization' made increasingly devastating military capabilities and higher levels of control over nature possible, but parallel success with respect to agreed or enforceable international standards of restraint seriously lagged behind.

When considered in long-term perspective, Elias argued, the current era is little different from its predecessors. Human societies 'are still unable to understand and to control the social dynamics which (threaten) to drive rulers of different states towards settling their conflicts through the use of force' (Elias 2007a: 128). Even so, the present epoch might yet prove to be 'an early stage in the development of humanity' or part of 'humankind's prehistory' (Elias 2007a: 128). The species may already have entered an early stage of a global civilizing process in which societies become more restrained in their relations with one another and better attuned to each other's core interests. Certainly, pressures on nation-states to relinquish part of 'their function as guarantors of the physical security of their citizens, and thus as survival units, to supra-state units' had increased in the recent period (Elias 2010c: 195). There was some evidence that 'the function of the effective survival unit is now visibly shifting more and more from the level of the nation states to the post-national unions of states and, beyond them, to humanity' (Elias 2010c: 195ff). Indeed, a new historical era could be dawning in which 'it will no longer be individual states but unions of states which will serve humankind as the dominant social unit' (Elias 2010c: 147; see also 181).

The emphasis on post-national figurations that serve humankind reflected Elias's thesis that an overall increase in the level of restraints on physical violence is only one dimension of a civilizing process. As he explained in *The Germans*, 'the extent and depth of people's mutual identification with each other and, accordingly, the depth and extent of their ability to empathize and capacity to feel for and sympathize with other people in their relationships with them' are also 'central criteria of a civilizing process' (Elias 2013: 122; see also de Swaan 1995). Some small changes in the scope of emotional identification appeared to be taking place in an era in which social scientists could usefully employ the idea of humanity, which had been little more than 'a beautiful but unrealisable ideal' in earlier centuries, to examine the 'social reality' of 'the fast-growing interdependence of all hitherto independent subgroups of humankind' (Elias 2008a: 86–7). It was patently the case that some social strata 'are beginning to identify with something beyond state borders [and] that their we-group identity is moving towards the plane of humanity' (Elias 2010c: 207). The outlines of a global civilizing process could be discerned in humanitarian programmes to protect individuals from state violence and cruelty. Perhaps such endeavours to 'protect the individual against laws of his own state that they regard as inhumane' represented 'the early stage of a long process in the course of which humankind as the highest level of integration may gain equality' with sovereign associations (Elias 2011: 167).

Elias therefore singled out the human rights culture as embodied in 'private organisations, such as Amnesty International' as a key symbol of a notable 'widening of identification between person and person' – of the scaling up of a 'sense of responsibility among individuals for the fate of others far beyond the frontiers of their own country or continent' (Elias 2010c: 151). In association with current levels of global interconnectedness, more people than ever before were aware that:

> an enormously large part of humanity live their entire lives on the verge of starvation, that in fact there are always and in many places people [who] are dying of hunger. This is most certainly not a new problem. With few exceptions, famine is a constantly recurring feature of human societies. But it is a peculiarity of our times that poverty and high mortality rates are no longer taken for granted as a God-given condition of human life. (Elias 2013: 29)

Notwithstanding a growing sense of moral obligation, it had to be acknowledged that 'in actual fact relatively little is done' (Elias 2013: 29). Even so, 'conscience-formation has changed in the course of the twentieth century. The feeling of responsibility which people have for each other is certainly minimal, looked at in absolute terms, but compared with before it has increased' (Elias 2013: 29).

In summary, Elias maintained that human collectivities are involved, albeit unevenly and tentatively, in 'a great collective learning process' which includes higher levels of social organization to promote the 'pacification and organised unification of humankind' and to free people from needless pain and suffering (Elias 2008a: 92). The formulation identifies key criteria for determining whether social groups or the global order as a whole are undergoing a civilizing process – alternatively, for establishing whether substantial directional changes are under way as a consequence of shifts in the relations between civilizing and decivilizing forces. Those are matters to explore in the next section. Of more immediate importance are Elias's observations about the countervailing social and political forces that could reverse the advances noted. The observation that most people have little more than a 'minimal' sense of responsibility for the most vulnerable members of other societies highlights a central feature of the global order, which is that survival units continue to command very high levels of loyalty. Cross-border emotional ties may have strengthened among particular social strata but, in general, the argument was, such bonds still lag behind expanding human interdependencies. The most basic comprehension of the human past revealed that there is 'no basis for assuming' that the 'dominant' trend hitherto must survive in the coming decades and centuries (Elias 2008: 4). At least 'up to now – that is, from the Stone Age to our time', there had been an overall trend towards higher levels of human integration and associated patterns of civilization, but there had also been 'a continuous conflict with countervailing, decivilizing processes' that resulted in the collapse of many complex societies (Elias 2008: 4). Modern societies and the global order of which they were part could well succumb to a similar fate. The 'immense process of integration' in recent decades, which was accompanied by 'many subordinate disintegrations', could be replaced by a 'dominant disintegration process' in which a strong decivilizing counter-reaction against global interdependencies gains the upper hand (Elias 2010c: 148, also 202).

It was apparent that the long history of 'hegemonic wars' and 'elimination struggles' was reaching 'the end of the road' and that a major nuclear conflict could result in humanity's 'return to the caves' (see p. 96). However, the plain reality was that 'emotional bonds to state-societies – which nowadays are nation-states – take priority over bonds to other figurations' (Elias 2012b: 133ff; see also Kaspersen and Gabriel 2008). Throughout human history, political loyalties have usually been directed towards the pre-eminent 'survival unit' – towards the group that 'knits people together for common purposes – the common defence of their lives, the survival of their group in the face of attacks by other groups' and 'the use of physical force against others' (Elias 2012b: 134). Viable survival units have succeeded because of the strength of emotional as well as material ties between members – and by the power of 'common symbols' that have been 'objects of common identification' in their own right (Elias 2012b: 133). Profound issues regarding cultural identity were often at stake for those involved. Abundantly clear was the high regard for the 'passing down of legends, history, music and many other cultural values'; indeed, one of the principal 'survival functions' of such associations was their role in the 'continuity' of distinctive languages and cultural practices (Elias 2010c: 200). Individuals often found enormous personal satisfaction and great meaning in the fact that group membership created 'a chance of survival beyond actual physical existence', namely the knowledge of having contributed to an ongoing collective endeavour, and the possibility for the select few of surviving long in 'the memory of the chain of generations' (Elias 2010c: 200).

As this discussion has shown, Elias reflected on the complex relationship between increasing interdependencies between human societies and global civilizing processes that were products of the monopolization of fire and the development of societies of greater scale. His inquiry focused on the effects of global interconnections on the following three phenomena: on the dominant patterns of internal and external restraint in the relations between societies; on social attitudes to Bergson's question (see pp. 98–9) of how far the relevant community is limited to 'fellow citizens' who are 'members of the same state' or includes 'humanity as a whole'; and also on levels of support for post-national forms of social and political organization that deal with the problems of global integration. The inquiry emphasized the deep ambiguities of global interconnectedness (Linklater 2010a). On the one hand, as in the case of the early phases of the European civilizing process, the upshot was that 'more people are forced more often to pay more attention to more and more other people' (Goudsblom, cited in Liston and Mennell 2009: 60). With new entanglements came new compulsions to become more considerate of, and more responsive to, the interests of other peoples and, in addition, incentives to create political institutions that reflected changing circumstances. But integrative and disintegrative tendencies were often inextricably linked in the development of human societies, as evidenced by the recent phase of state-formation in Africa where traditional 'tribal units' had resisted what they regarded as a declining ability to shape crucial decisions made in remote political institutions and a potentially irretrievable loss of power, privilege and prestige (Elias 2008e: 136–7; Elias 2010c: 180ff; also pp. 206–7). Peaceful 'integration conflicts' had arisen in response to experiments in international institutional innovations that their architects believed were essential in order to secure joint responses to challenging lengthening webs of interconnectedness. But, for some groups, traditional national self-images are threatened by actual or proposed shifts in the balance of responsibilities between state institutions and distant continental and global meeting regimes (van Vree 1999: 332). Collective responses demonstrated the enormity of the task to construct a world order anchored in shared civilizational orientations – that is, in agreed standards of restraint expressed in, and underpinned by, emotionally powerful global symbols that represented a leap beyond narrow national identifications.

Finessing the inquiry, Elias observed that the 'habitus of individuals, their identification with limited sub-groups of humanity – particularly single states – lags' behind rising levels of global interconnections and impedes efforts to establish new forms of social and political coordination and planning (Elias 2010c: 206–7). As a result, many groups acknowledge the utility of regional organizations such as the European Union but do not find much emotional significance in them (Elias 2012 [1939]: 508, note 13; Elias 2010c: 195ff). National loyalties have stalled efforts to create higher-level associations (Elias 2010c: 188ff). In the context of intra- and inter-societal integration conflicts, such loyalties have been mobilized periodically to reverse 'post-national' institutional innovations that their advocates regard as increasingly mandatory (Elias 2010c: 180ff; Delmotte 2012). Elias's reflections on integration conflicts that are increasingly conducted on the international stage as well as within nation-states were prescient in the light of the current national-populist revolt against neoliberal economic globalization and the interrelated demand for restoring state powers which have been surrendered, the argument runs, to distant and unaccountable organizations such as the European Union (Alikhani 2017a; see also Alikhani 2017b on the connection between national-populism and the shifting relations between processes of 'democratization' and 'de-democratization' that are the consequence of the greater power and unaccountability of the established social strata). At the core of that protest lies collective resentment at involuntary incorporation within global chains of interdependence which outsider groups believe are detrimental to their interests and which they have been powerless (but now endeavour) to control (Elias 2007: 76–8). Emotional attachments to the nation-state have been intensified in power struggles to transform patterns of interconnectedness that outsiders regard as shackling them to a remote global establishment. As Elias observed, attempting to recreate earlier forms of political autonomy by breaking social webs that arouse anxiety or uncertainty can be highly attractive to groups who feel that their national identity is under threat and who feel deeply wounded by declining group pride and prestige (Dunning and Hughes 2020).

The national revolt against neoliberal economic globalization and the perception of entrapment in longer webs of interdependence have been expressed in levels of support for traditional loyalties and associated political symbols as shared objects of emotional identification that seemed to be losing some of their potency just three decades ago. The whole movement has shown that the dominant groups and their supporters within regional international institutions such as the European Union lack the symbolic power that nationalist parties can harness to their cause. Those groups have been unable to mobilize emotionally charged symbols that can compete with the myths and narratives of national belonging and sovereign statehood (Theiler 2005; Della Sala 2010; Manners 2011; Linklater 2019). There may be no biological and cultural obstacles to a global civilization, and there are no barriers to the requisite universal symbols. But what is unclear is how symbols denoting wider solidarities can develop and what form emotionally appealing post-national symbols might take. As a recent process-sociological analysis has emphasized, significant movement towards a post-national European civilizing process will not occur while large sections of the population believe that the leading institutions are heavily biased towards elite interests, preside over deepening social inequalities, and fail to meet expectations of democratic accountability (Alikhani 2017a).

There is little likelihood of change in the absence of a major redistribution of power resources between the established and the outsiders within the constituent societies. Nor are conditions likely to alter while many fear the loss of national pride as much as, if not more than, setbacks to economic interests. Integration conflicts within the member societies are central to Elias's claim that 'the integrating tendency' will remain interlinked with 'a disintegrating tendency' as 'long as humanity as a whole is not (the) effective frame of reference' (Elias 2013: 174). Those tensions within and between states provide a reminder that the idea of humanity 'as a frame of reference for we-identity' has little, if any, meaning for many people; it remains a 'blank space on the maps of their emotions' (Elias 2010c: 181). But future global civilizing processes cannot be ruled out, and not least because of concerns about global warming. It is necessary to have the sociological resources with which to detect significant changes of direction in balances of power between national and post-national emotional attachments, as expressed in collective symbols.

Analyzing global directions of change

The question arises of how to ascertain whether the general direction of global change indicates that civilizing processes have the upper hand or are less influential than decivilizing trends and tendencies. What are the yardsticks that analysts can employ to discern what may often be subtle shifts of direction? Eliasian sociology possesses precise criteria for undertaking that inquiry (see Fletcher 1997: 82ff). They were contained in Elias's analysis of the civilizing dimensions of monopolization processes that have affected humanity as a whole and in the earlier explanation of core elements of the European process of civilization. The previous section has shown that constraints on force were at the heart of the investigation of the overall historical trend towards ever larger territorial monopolies of power, as were psychological traits such as 'moderation' and 'reserve' for the emergence of more pacified social relations. Those psychogenetic developments complemented external pressures on people to control aggressive and violent impulses. As discussed in Chapter 2, the increasing influence of internal as opposed to external restraints on violence was a major theme in Elias's study of the European civilizing process, as was the growth of emotional identification between people who belonged to the same society or survival unit. Additionally, Elias's comments on the monopolization of fire, as well as Goudsblom's detailed study (1994a), emphasized the import of greater social coordination that involved new levels and forms of individual and collective self-restraint in transforming the power relations between human societies and non-human competitor species.

Those points can be organized more systematically in order to detect how far relations within and between groups are undergoing a process of civilization. Four criteria can be used in the attempt to ascertain the main directions of change in social figurations ranging from small kinship groups to large-scale state-organized societies and arrangements such as balance of power systems and international organizations that include the totality of human societies. They are: first, whether the practice of 'resolving conflicts on the basis of rules jointly acknowledged by social groups' is increasing or decreasing (Elias 2013a: 268); second, whether internal as opposed to external constraints on violence and on conduct more generally are gaining power or losing influence (Elias 2013: 35ff); third, whether there is or is not an overall widening of emotional identification between people as exemplified by the 'ability to empathize and capacity to feel for and sympathize with other people in their relationships with them' (Elias 2013: 122; see p. 223); and fourth, whether levels of social coordination and planning to protect people from harm are rising or falling.

All four yardsticks are evident in Elias's reflections on the global order which were summarised earlier in this chapter. First, increasingly destructive forms of modern warfare had created new external compulsions and pressures on states to tame violence and to moderate their behaviour. Second, societies were still far from the point where self-restraint took precedence over the constraints imposed by others in steering conduct. Third, concerns about poverty and famine revealed that emotional identification between certain groups had increased; however, national loyalties blocked commitments to humanity as a whole which could be expected to contract rapidly whenever people feared for their security. Fourth, although the sense of responsibility for the vulnerable had increased, the reality was that global coordination was extremely limited when compared to planning arrangements within modern sovereign states. Elias did not use those criteria in a systematic way to assess the dominant directions of global change, and they have yet to be used in process-sociological inquiry. Specific 'civilizing thrusts' in the global order were identified. But the greater emphasis was on the resident gulf between intra-societal civilizing processes in stable, pacified societies and recurrent double-bind figurations in relations between states.

To rephrase that last point, within European societies, state-formation and internal pacification prepared the way for additional trajectories. The development of 'larger and larger networks of interdependent people' made more people reliant on one other for the satisfaction of basic interests (Mennell 1994: 369, 374–5). Dominant groups came under pressure to show greater restraint in their dealing with traditional inferiors. Earlier habits of displaying open contempt for 'social inferiors' had to be muted or held back. Social subordinates had to be treated in more respectful and more considerate ways. With the equalization of power relations, there was a tendency 'for [more] people to identify more readily with other people as such, regardless of social origin' as part of the 'long-term civilizing trend towards more even and more thorough control over the emotions' (Elias 2012b: 150). The greater capacity of outsiders to alter the attitudes and behaviour of the dominant strata made achievements with respect to basic rights and entitlements possible. With changing 'power ratios', outsiders acquired new 'power chances' which were displayed by effective organization and mobilization that extracted concessions from the dominant groups. Broad commitments to social planning and organization that were designed to protect the vulnerable in society furthered earlier patterns of social and political change. They were integral to the conditions in which civilizing processes outweighed decivilizing processes in the relevant societies.

Those trajectories occurred in relatively peaceful societies that were governed by states with their monopolies of power. The precariousness of those developments in unstable state-organized societies was stressed repeatedly in Elias's writings. The analysis explained how the relative impact of civilizing and decivilizing processes could shift rapidly in those societies. The weakness of any global civilizing tendencies was necessarily more pronounced in the relations between states where no higher monopoly of force could regulate and control struggles for power and security. As discussed in Chapter 3, the danger of highly emotive orientations to the social world was high in that condition. Moreover, as already noted in this chapter, increased levels of human interconnectedness were evidence of major directions of change which were often attended by collective fears and anxieties that fuelled integration conflicts. The examination of such changes in the balances between intra- and inter-societal civilizing and decivilizing processes can be the starting point for future inquiries into global trajectories of development. Elias's investigation can inform those investigations in three ways: by providing a model of how to conduct such an exploration at the global level; by explaining how to assess perspectives that have explored the civilizational dimensions of relations between states; and, not least, by paving the way for the empirical examination of what the most powerful collective symbols in any period reveal about the leading global tendencies.

Civilizations in conflict

Huntington's polemic on the coming 'clash of civilizations' has been the most frequently discussed commentary on the civilizational dimensions of global order in the past 25 years. The central contention was that rising levels of civilizational identification in the recent period have increased the possibility of inter-state conflict. The sociological analysis of the Huntington thesis has not been explored at length in fields such as International Relations. The following discussion puts forward a process-sociological interpretation and critique of Huntington's analysis of global problems and the suggested policy prognosis. It maintains that the investigation was centred on the following three phenomena: the erosion of constraints on force, the contraction of mutual identification between peoples, and the weakening of coordinated responses to global challenges. It argues that Huntington's thesis shows how established groups can succumb to highly involved responses to the perceived dangers of changing power relations with traditional outsider societies. It is useful to begin however with a brief summary of his principal claims about the changing contours of world politics.

The defining trend of the era, according to Huntington (1996: 53), was the shift from the 'unidirectional impact of one civilization' on all others to 'multidirectional interactions among all civilizations'. The argument remonstrated against the liberal position that the collapse of the Soviet Union had removed the main barrier to a global civilization anchored in liberal-democratic principles. The prediction was that the global order 'will increasingly be de-Westernized' as 'non-Western civilizations' cease being the 'objects' of traditional great power machinations and become influential 'actors' in their own right (Huntington 1993: 48). More even distributions of power between Western and non-Western societies had facilitated the proud reassertion of 'indigenous, historically-rooted mores, languages, beliefs and institutions' (Huntington 1996: 91). Liberal images of a forthcoming 'universal civilization' had privileged Western political ideas that clashed with, among other things, the cultural 'particularism of most Asian societies' with their 'emphasis on what distinguishes one people from another' (Huntington 1993: 41). Opposition to 'human rights imperialism' indicated how tensions that were based on a stronger sense of 'civilization-consciousness' had risen with growing human interdependencies (Huntington 1993: 25, 40–1). It appeared that 'successful political, security and economic international institutions' would be 'more likely to develop within [rather] than across civilizations' (Huntington 1993: 48). The darker prospect was that 'conflicts between groups in different civilizations' would become 'more frequent, more sustained and more violent than conflicts between groups in the same civilization'; in so doing, they threatened to become 'the most likely and most dangerous source' of escalating conflicts that could result in 'global wars' (Huntington 1993: 48).

In Huntington's judgement, the liberal faith in an emergent universal civilization failed to appreciate that global civilizations are products of 'universal power', as the Roman Empire, the age of European colonial domination, and the more recent phase of US hegemony had proven. To return to an earlier part of this discussion, that assessment overlooked the extent to which accompanying images of civilizational superiority and efforts to encourage perceptions of social inferiority suppress social tensions that become pronounced as the relative power of the established and the outsiders shifts. The supposition was that the emergence of more even global power relations had released civilizational tensions that Western liberals had ignored, wrongly believing that such conflicts were the hallmarks of a dying era. In the Huntington thesis, there were echoes of late 19th-century Western fears that 'civilizing missions' to transform other societies had come up against the challenge of coping with the threats posed by outlying barbarous peoples (Hobson 2012: chs 5 and 11). A major claim was that new dangers existed along the 'perimeter of Islam' because of the 'Muslim propensity towards violent conflict' (Huntington 1996: 256ff). The prognosis was that the United States and its allies had to ensure that they had the 'economic and military power' to protect their interests in response to a 'world-wide' trend in which 'civilization' was 'yielding to barbarism' (Huntington 1996: 321). Its alarmist tenor was intended to promote a major reorientation of US elite perspectives and public attitudes to changing power structures and to the receding prospect of a world order which the United States had expected to control.

These citations show how a discourse of civilization and barbarism was used to overturn liberal triumphalist orientations to the global order that had the upper hand following the collapse of the Soviet Union. The discourse was used to affirm the classical realist thesis about the strategic necessity of acquiring sufficient political and military power to repulse external threats that seemed likely to result from growing civilizational identifications and evolving civilizational differences. Viewed in long-term perspective, and considering the late 19th-century shifts in orientation that have just been noted, the standpoint reflected the conviction that non-European peoples had failed to undergo the transformative experiences that various civilizing offensives were designed to bring about, namely greater convergence between different forms of life and closer emotional identification between, at least, elite groups in European and non-European societies. The upshot in the context of evolving power distributions was the resistance to Western claims to have a monopoly of truth with respect to the idea of civilized conditions. The Huntington thesis can be interpreted as an anxious reaction to the loss of that monopoly position.

The standard criticisms of the Huntington thesis need not detain us here since the focus of this work is on the process-sociological perspective but there are some shared objections. The contention that the idea of civilizational consciousness presumes that certain attitudes and beliefs are largely unchanging resonates with the Eliasian critique of recurrent tendencies to reduce the variable to the invariable or the mutable to the immutable. From that vantage point, the idea of civilization has limited social-scientific utility; it is a 'process-reducing' concept (see Bilgin 2012). The observation that emotional links with nations and states are far stronger than civilizational attachments is plainly correct (see Henderson and Tucker 2001) but was taken further in the Eliasian analysis of the connections between state-formation, civilizational orientations, the 'split within civilization', and the ambiguities of discourses of civilization that can be used either to justify or to condemn acts of violence. Relevant here – and particularly because of recent studies of how ruling groups in Russia and China have promoted the discourse of the 'civilizational state' – is Elias's discussion of how societies such as Great Britain combined nationalism and civilization in the 19th century (Coker 2019; see also pp. 100–1). Developments in Russia and China seem to testify to the influence of Huntington's thesis outside the liberal-democratic West. Its impact shows how 'integration conflicts' can find expression in the thwarting effect of national loyalties which are dressed up in the self-praising language of civilization.

Similar problems are evident, *mutatis mutandis*, in Huntington's discussion of the perils of rising levels of 'civilization consciousness'. As already noted, the 'clash of civilizations thesis' presumed that the United States' capacity to influence or shape global order was in decline as a result of changing power distributions. It claimed to identify a clear trend in which 'non-Western civilizations' (with the exception of Japan) sought to 'become modern without becoming Western', thereby replacing the earlier condition in which the West provided the social ideal to emulate (Huntington 1993: 49). From a process-sociological perspective, more general shifts in the power relations between the established and the outsiders explain key features of the Huntington thesis. Fundamental is the tendency for the 'symptoms of rebellion, resistance, emancipation' to erupt among outsiders as power balances become more even (see pp. 20–1). In those conditions, the balance of power often shifts between 'attraction' and 'repulsion' towards the previously admired ideas and practices of the establishment. The growing 'self-consciousness' of subordinate groups becomes forged through discourses that stress 'contrasts' and 'differences' from the dominant elites which may respond in kind in a spiral of reciprocal stigmatization (Elias 2012 [1939]: 472–3). Relations between the established and the outsiders are then shaped by mutually reinforcing, 'narcissistic' forms of 'self-representation' – by divisive orientations towards others which are one of the principal 'dangers which human groups constitute for each other' (see p. 95). As discussed earlier, in the related power struggles, the images that people have of themselves and others can become remarkably simplistic (see p. 94). Highly emotive standpoints lacking in significant detachment block levels of 'self-restraint' and 'patience' that facilitate the 'gradual toning down of mutual dislike, suspicion and hatred' (Elias 2007: 7). In short, the problems that people have in looking 'at themselves, at each other' and at the conditions in which they find themselves with a degree of detachment can result in a dangerous 'clash of involvements' (Bucholc 2015: 150ff). That analysis sheds light on the deficiencies of an image of an emergent global order that is supposedly shaped by growing civilizational tensions and rivalries.

Those considerations were not entirely missing from the Huntington thesis. The West could play a positive role, it was stated, by acquiring 'a more profound understanding of the basic religious and philosophical assumptions underlying other civilizations'; moreover, identifying 'elements of commonality between Western and other civilizations' could enable them to 'learn to coexist' amicably (Huntington 1993: 41, 49). In a concession to the critics, it was maintained that the Western powers had 'to accommodate … non-Western modern civilizations' with different 'values and interests' (Huntington 1996: 321). The supposition was that different societies were indeed capable of constructing and 'identifying with a distinct global culture that supplements or supplants civilizations' (Huntington 1996: 57). But the general tenor of the argument was that robust political or military responses to new security threats were imperative. In that context, a supposed 'Muslim propensity towards violent conflict' drew on classical 'Orientalist' myths about Islamic civilization which would in turn influence post 9/11 'neo-Orientalist' certainties that the more peaceful West was under attack from 'barbarous' forces driven by 'Muslim rage' (Bottici and Challand 2006; Linklater 2014).

The standpoint revealed how false diagnoses and flawed prognoses can intensify anxieties and fears. It explained how highly emotive responses to threats and the attendant demonization of opponents can overpower the quest for the more detached, longer-term perspective on the relations between adversaries that a commitment to exploring commonalties requires (see p. 41 on the 'blowback thesis' which argued for more detached reflections on the reasons for Islamist hostility to the United States). It showed how 'mythical' representations of threats as exemplified by Huntington's process-reducing claim that humanity consists of multiple civilizations – and the specific contention about the Muslim propensity for violence – can trap groups in double-bind processes with brutalizing effects.

Elias's conception of the sociologist as the 'destroyer of myths' was designed to subvert political orientations to changing interdependencies that promote integration conflicts that are in principle avoidable. From that position, the notion of a clash of civilizations is best understood as a symptom of highly emotive, parochial national reactions to global power transitions that stand in the way of more detached social-scientific investigation that has 'humanity at its horizon'. The fundamental task is to analyze how mythical orientations to the social world with potentially destructive consequences can influence public debate under conditions of insecurity. The aim is to expose the limitations of perspectives where ideological preferences which are best left on the 'back burner' infiltrate empirical analysis (see p. 25). Applied to the Huntington thesis, this mode of analysis reveals how an approach to the relationship between civilizational forces and world order reflected the fear that the dominant power in the global establishment was facing the prospect of opposition from outsider groups that could become impossible to control without the use of force. The contrast with English School reflections on changing global power relations is instructive. Classical analyses of the global effects of civilizational forces from the international society perspective were not only undertaken in a more detached way. They represented the shift toward a more humanity-centred perspective in which social-scientific investigation was freed to a degree from national standpoints.

The civilizational dimensions of international society

Core arguments within English School reflections on the reconfiguration of the modern society of states constitute a second approach to the civilizational dimensions of the global order, one which merits close attention. These arguments share with the 'Huntington thesis' the belief that shifts in the global distribution of power have eroded the hegemony of Western conceptions of civilization. English School writings have aimed to provide a relatively detached analysis of how the contestation of Western liberal-democratic conceptions of human rights deepened as a result of changing power balances. This was at the centre of Bull's reflections on the 'tensions' between 'different cultures or civilizations' that occurred in the transition from a European to a global society of states (Bull 2002 [1977]: 264). Many English School thinkers initially feared that the 'revolt against the West' – which opposed Western claims to have a monopoly of knowledge about the nature of civilized relations – would dissolve the civilizational bonds that had underpinned the European international order. They believed that the direction of change posed new diplomatic difficulties for the Western powers as traditional custodians of international society (Hall 2017). Especially from the late 1970s to the mid-1990s, innovative discussions focused on the ramifications of the dissolution of the civilizational foundations of the society of states that had emerged within, and had been confined to, Europe for approximately four centuries. These discussions reflected on the prospects of international society as a global civilizing force. The following comments provide a process-sociological interpretation of English School deliberations on patterns of change that remain highly relevant in the current era and which will repay study in future analyses of the post-Western international order.

The point has been made that English School writings investigated the relationship between the dilution of the civilizational foundations of the society of states and its potential as a civilizing force in world politics. As the following discussion will show, those were very much the terms in which leading members of the English School conducted their inquiry, although they did not draw on Elias's writings or distinguish even implicitly between the emic and etic meanings of civilization or cultural superiority which were considered in the Introduction to this volume. The *emic* sense was present in Wight's thesis that collective pride in belonging to societies that stood above barbarian peoples and practices was highly developed in the ancient Chinese and Greek societies as well as in the modern European society of states (Wight 1977, ch 1). In process-sociological language, 'group pride' (or 'group charisma') was one of the elements that bound the constituent political units together. Building on such themes, Bull 2002 [1977]: 15) observed that common to all 'historical international societies' were such 'elements' as a shared language, widely accepted religious and cosmological beliefs, similar artistic and aesthetic traditions, and a common currency of ethical convictions and standards of judgement. Significant commonalities encouraged diplomatic efforts to preserve order and stability and helped to 'validate or authenticate the rules of international society' (Bull 2002 [1977]: 62). They underpinned the 'common rules' and 'institutions' of international society as well as overlapping interests (Bull 2002 [1977]: 15). A collective consciousness of being part of a higher civilization was inseparable from 'cultural differentiation from what lay outside', and specifically from areas inhabited by 'lesser societies'; it was reinforced by the shared belief that the 'code of conduct' that governed relations between advanced peoples 'did not apply ... in their dealings' with inferiors (Bull 2002 [1977]: 32).

Those observations about the 'historical international societies' resonate with Elias's discussion of how 'new patterns of civilization' emerged in survival units of greater magnitude and in balance of power systems to some extent. They were underscored in a key reference point in English School inquiry, namely Heeren's claim that a states-system is a 'union of several contiguous states' that are bound together not only by the 'reciprocity of interests' but also by deeper societal forces including similar levels of 'social improvement' and shared beliefs with respect to 'religion' and to 'manners' – an interesting comment given the place of manners and manners books in the European civilizing process, in the diplomatic conventions of international society, and in the relations between the established and the outsiders, particularly in the colonial era (Heeren 1834: vii-viii). The civilizational dimensions of societies of states were also highlighted in Butterfield's reflections about the routines of behaviour that evolve as societies develop mutual sympathy along with the willingness to forego short-term advantages for the long-term benefits of orderly relations (Butterfield 1953, ch 7; Sharp 2003). The emphasis on emotional identification between regimes or peoples and on foresight and self-restraint underlines the role that societies of states have played in the long 'comprehensive, humanity-wide process of civilization' in its *etic* sense that was discussed earlier in this chapter. It demonstrates that the analysis of civilizing processes that have affected the whole of humanity should include the comparative analysis of societies of states and the standards of restraint that were built into international conventions.

Modern international society has a unique place in such an inquiry precisely because it has come to include all state-organized human groups. Reflecting on a major consequence of the transition from a European to the first universal international society, Bull (2002 [1977]: 304–5) described the slow uncoupling of the elite 'diplomatic culture' from the 'intellectual and moral culture' with which it had been linked in the European order. The 'common stock of ideas and values' that bound together the diplomatic 'representatives of states' had become detached from a deeper 'international political culture' that had united European peoples. That comment emphasized the changing balance between patterns of cultural convergence which prevailed when non-European regimes endeavoured to comply with the European standard of civilization and more recent patterns of cultural divergence, as exemplified by the rejection of European notions of civilized conditions including liberal ideas of human rights, democratic governance, state restructuring, and market civilization. It was clear that support for European principles such as the idea of sovereign equality and the duty of non-intervention had not melted away. Some of the most vigorous proponents were to be found among the governing elites of societies that had only recently achieved independence from European imperial rule. Recognition of the utility of basic institutions such as diplomacy and international law had not evaporated. Nevertheless, the revolt against the West had serious ramifications for the diplomatic culture. To return to an earlier point about the civilizational foundations of the 'historical international societies', there had been a weakening of shared beliefs that had supported the institutions and rules that facilitated the peaceful resolution of disputes. The upshot of Bull's analysis of global directions was that the society of states could lose valuable unifying forces, that it might come to rest on no more than Heeren's 'reciprocity of interests', and that significant political differences would become harder to resolve through the medium of diplomacy (see p. 238). Bull's approach recognized the increasing impact of centrifugal forces on the post-European international order but, in contrast with the 'Huntington thesis', focused on the practical ideal of amicable coexistence between highly unequal, culturally diverse societies.

Bull argued that the first universal society of states would be more stable if it was anchored in a counterpart to the civilizational bonds that had underpinned the diplomatic culture in the classical European order. Any equivalent to the European international political culture would have to be especially responsive to 'Third World' demands for global justice. Imaginative leadership by the great powers was imperative to secure essential reforms which, in a striking contrast with Huntington's thesis, required major transfers of power and wealth from 'North' to 'South' and the commitment 'to absorb non-Western elements' within a 'cosmopolitan culture' that commanded the consent not only of governments but of 'societies in general' (Bull 2002 [1977]: 303ff). With those modifications, the post-Western global order could acquire something of the 'underpinning' that had existed in 'the geographically smaller and culturally more homogeneous international societies of the past' (Bull 2002 [1977]: 303ff).

In Eliasian terms, Bull's relatively detached analysis of the directions of change was connected with the prognosis of promoting global justice that called for the metamorphosis of Western and non-Western modes of orientation to world politics. When compared to the Huntington thesis it was clearly closer to having 'humanity as its horizon'. The examination of evolving power relations between traditional established and outsider groups in international society was combined with an image of an etic global civilizing process that would widen the scope of emotional identification between peoples who lacked the common civilizational 'elements' in art, religion and ethics that had linked the constituent units of the classical European international society.

In short, the assumption was that – with great power vision and leadership – international society could have a civilizing role in bridging global inequalities of power and wealth as well as cultural differences in the modern era. With creative diplomacy, core arrangements might eventually promote levels of mutual sympathy and emotional identification between peoples that constituted a civilizing process in the emic sense. The implicit point was that a new we-identity could be grounded in an explicit sense of belonging to a universal civilization.

Bull's investigation of civilizational dimensions of global order was taken further in a renowned English School exploration of human rights and world politics (Vincent 1986). The main thesis was that major contests over universal rights involving the former imperial powers and the colonies as well as superpower rivalries could be overcome by the ethical judgement that 'the suffering of the starving and malnourished' is the 'worst offence' against human rights and also by collective planning to ensure that the necessary 'floor' was in place so that international society protected the vulnerable from avoidable suffering (Vincent 1986: 2, 126). There were echoes in Vincent's argument of Dr Johnson's contention, as reported by Boswell (1873 [1791]: 179), that 'a decent provision for the poor is the true test of civilization'. Johnson's standpoint reflected the radical Enlightenment phenomenon of 'compassionate cosmopolitanism' which embodied moral concerns about the harmful effects of global interdependencies on non-European peoples (most obviously slavery and the Atlantic slave trade) alongside increased awareness of distant suffering (Linklater 2016: ch 7). Greater emotional identification with the vulnerable was urged in line with the more radical interpretations of the constitution of a civilized society. A similar ethic informed Vincent's contention that enlightened Western powers could and should become the standard-bearers for the ethical principle that subsistence rights are 'the basis of civilized life' (Vincent 1986: 138). By assuming that role, they could communicate the sincerity of their commitment to 'civilized' standards (Linklater 2011b).

The differences between Huntington's use of 'civilization' in an alarmist response to new power distributions and anticipated power struggles and Vincent's invocation of the concept to defend global planning to promote humanitarian objectives will be obvious. The latter's argument exemplifies Elias's observation about how the idea has been used to encourage changes of behaviour – to promote 'the civilizing task' of altering attitudes and conduct (Elias 2008a: 89–90). Revealingly, in the light of Enlightenment condemnations of colonialism and slavery, Vincent (1986: 146ff) portrayed the struggle to abolish the Atlantic slave trade as a key symbol of how enlightened foreign policy can have a profound civilizing effect on global order. The campaign indicated how the diplomatic and international political cultures could be conjoined once again through a 'cosmopolitanisation' of ethical tenets that enjoyed 'mass' support across the society of states (Vincent 1980: 254).

The implication of Vincent's argument was that cosmopolitanism could not be summarily dismissed as a 'distinctively European concept' that will forever be associated with 'overseas empires' and colonial 'civilizing' missions (Pagden 2000: 3–4; Bowden 2009: 90ff). Promoting mutual identification between peoples through the protection of subsistence rights was one way in which Western civilized peoples could contribute to the establishment of a more just global order. The thesis was that very different societies could find common ground in supporting the rights in question – that they could appeal to peoples as well as governments. The belief that new levels of emotional identification could be built on a normative agreement on the fundamental role of subsistence rights therefore expressed confidence in the possibility of a global civilizing process in its etic sense. Fundamental was the observation that as a result of shifts in 'conscience-formation' many groups in 'richer countries' now believe that something has to be done 'about the misery of other human groups' (see p. 224).

In those ways, the English School has provided a distinctive approach to the civilizational dimensions of world politics that is vastly superior to the Huntington thesis for the following reasons. First, it has analyzed the process in which the European colonial establishment incorporated non-European regional international orders within a global system that was governed by its standard of civilization. Second, it has investigated how the revolt against the West was linked with new tensions between cultures and civilizations. Viewed from the vantage point of process-sociology, the inquiry traced long-term trends in global established–outsider relations. It considered the possible consequences of the contraction of the civilizational foundations of international society for future order and stability. It reflected on the potential for revised underpinnings of the 'civilized life' that restored the ties between the international political and diplomatic cultures. English School analyses of the tensions between patterns of cultural convergence and divergence recognize that the Western powers have a reduced capacity (or entitlement) to shape the course of international political change. Whereas the Huntington thesis was principally focused on altering national orientations to the wider world in the belief that the United States was ill prepared for emergent security threats, English School writings have concentrated on the need for fundamental revisions to Western orientations to the rest of the world in the post-European or post-Western era. Significant in this context is the investigation of the scope for agreements about global principles that are not tied to any single culture or civilization but represent forward steps in the quest for authentically universal rights and responsibilities (see Bucholc 2015: ch 5).

Three additional distinguishing features of the approach deserve consideration. First, influential English School writings have not lost faith in the possibility of the 'successful cosmopolitanisation' of moral ideals, as in the case of global support for subsistence rights. From an Eliasian perspective, they supported the universal-egalitarian dimensions of the 'duality of nation-state normative codes' in contrast with the emphasis on 'nationalist-Machiavellian' foreign policy principles in Huntington's expectation of growing civilizational fault lines and rivalries. Second, the writings under discussion displayed confidence in a future global civilizing process in which levels of emotional identification between peoples increase as a result of new forms of global organization to promote global justice and to protect the vulnerable. Third, English School perspectives implicitly recognized what Elias (2007a: 91) described as the danger that 'short-term feelings' which arise in the context of perceived threats and insecurities can thwart the 'longer-term diagnosis oriented towards facts, however unwelcome'. That reaction to power transitions characterized the notion of an impending clash of civilizations. By contrast, English School responses to changing established–outsider figurations and to the rising pressures to transform the global order in the light of the particular needs and interests of non-European peoples were geared towards restoring and recreating the civilizing role of international society.

Vincent's approach to human rights reflected what Elias (2013a: 29) called the 'factual observation' that changes in 'conscience-formation' can occur in conjunction with 'small shifts in power to the disadvantage of former established groups, and to the advantage of former outsider groups'. What was not considered at the time Vincent was writing (the early 1980s) was the possibility that power balances could alter again, with the consequence that support for protecting subsistence rights stalled or failed to have much practical effect. In the period since the case for those rights was made, global inequalities have widened. The most affluent strata have fewer incentives to think from the standpoint of vulnerable others, to emphasize or sympathize with them, or to reflect constructively on the long-term benefits of organizational innovations to alleviate their plight (Mennell 2007: ch 12). Moreover, Vincent's position which placed the West at the helm of global change is now largely out of step with strands of opinion which are suspicious of Western humanitarian missions – critical of the 'white saviour' mentality that informed 'benign' colonial government. Even so, other initiatives have developed in this period, for example in connection with global health programmes. They indicate that universal-egalitarian principles have a role in world politics that is unique in the history of the Western states-systems (Linklater 2016: 447ff). Other advances have occurred with respect to embedding the commitment to 'environmental stewardship' in the global order with the aim of protecting universal rights through safeguards for human health (Falkner and Buzan 2019). Moral support for global measures to protect human beings everywhere from senseless harm and unacceptable suffering is part of the outlook or habitus of many civilized groups. But the overall direction of global change with regard to levels of emotional identification between people has been profoundly affected by the recent national-populist revolt against globalism.

That movement has provided striking evidence of the continuing potency of national symbols and the relative paucity of internationalist or cosmopolitan equivalents. It invites academic discussion of the fact that strong support for any global order requires more than the 'reciprocity of interests' or the shared beliefs or principles that have been stressed by the English School, namely emotionally appealing global symbols which provide common objects of identification. Vincent's observation that the struggle to abolish the Atlantic slave trade was an inspiring symbol of what civilized peoples can accomplish in the humanitarian sphere recognized in passing the importance of the symbolic domain for new globalist initiatives. The Huntington thesis deployed opposing symbols, such as the clash of civilizations and the alleged Muslim propensity to violence, in defence of renewed national commitments to conventional strategic objectives. In his investigation of the Germans, Elias (2013a: 159ff) stressed the role of 'verbal symbols' in reinforcing national loyalties. He noted how 'symbols for a collectivity' can come to have a 'numinous existence' for people; the names for nation-states can acquire 'overtones of sanctity and awe'; collectivities can be endowed with special qualities not dissimilar to those imputed to 'superhuman beings'. Recent national-populist discourse such as the idea of 'Making America Great Again' confirms the point (see Dunning and Hughes 2020).

To build on those themes, this chapter concludes by pointing the way towards new analyses of the symbolic dimensions of civilizational forces in world politics. The argument is that the relative strength of national and post-national symbols in any era provides a litmus test of levels of support for a global civilizing process with the four characteristics that were described earlier. Their respective influence can illuminate the directions of global change and, more specifically, reveal how far constraints on violence are increasing, internal restraints are on the rise, the scope of emotional identification between people is on an upward trajectory, and support for global planning and organization to protect vulnerable groups is growing or in decline.

Collective symbols and global order

Future inquiries into the symbolic dimensions of civilizing processes can usefully begin by contemplating the themes that Elias highlighted in the discussion of the place of survival units of ever greater magnitude in 'a humanity-wide process of civilization'. The investigation focused on the rise of monopoly controls of the instruments of violence, of the methods of taxing or otherwise extracting wealth from society, and of the means of orientation. Elias (2009e: 135ff) stressed how ruling elites had used symbols to shape the ways in which their subjects orientated themselves to society and to the wider world. A valuable insight was that state power in the symbolic realm had been instrumental in maintaining controls in other domains. Consistent with this argument is the claim that successful symbolic innovations helped to shape the outcome of internal social and political struggles – to influence the distribution of power capabilities in society. Failures in the symbolic sphere, on the other hand, contributed to disintegrative tendencies (Linklater 2019).

It is unquestionably the case that, over millennia, ruling strata in state-organized societies have made major investments in the symbolic domain. They have recognized that political legitimacy depends in part on public symbols that have emotional resonance for subjects and citizens, at one and the same time binding them to one another and to governing groups. Collective symbols including rituals, ceremonies, festivals, historical myths, foundational narratives, and figureheads with heroic status have been central to survival units throughout human history. Symbol ingenuity tied people together in particular groups by marking them off from outsiders. By way of example, public monuments commemorating military victories over enemies have embodied the 'split within civilization' that has been a recurrent feature of social groups. Powerful national symbols have been the pre-eminent variation on those aspects of political organization in the modern period. Public commemorations of the ordeals and sacrifices of warfare illustrate how national symbols bind and separate, integrating people in a political community by memorializing differences from adversaries that were forged in defining conflicts. Although not uncontested, they have signified crucial collective achievements for large sections of the populations involved.

Shared symbols have existed at higher levels of integration. Several symbols of civilization or civilized restraint with global import have been identified in the previous chapters. They include the 'torture norm', as discussed in Chapter 1; codes of etiquette and diplomatic manners, which featured in Chapter 2; the humanitarian principles that were noted in Chapter 3; the idealized state-organized society, discussed in Chapter 4; the institutions of diplomacy, international law and borrowed colonialism, as described in Chapter 5; and, finally, liberal discourses of human rights, democracy, the modern state form, and market arrangements that were analyzed in Chapter 6. All of those symbols were considered alongside power structures and group struggles. Close links with state institutions and national pride were emphasized. Recurrent attempts to control the discourse of civilization for political ends were underlined, as were the transcendent qualities of civilization that underpin the 'critique of the nation' and hold out the promise of future civilizing processes at the level of the world order.

There is no escaping the reality that symbolic representations of civilized international orders have been less potent than intra-societal counterparts and prone to collapse in periods of escalating tensions. The balance of power between symbols that bind societies together in higher figurations and symbols that separate peoples from each other is hard to alter fundamentally. Even so, the influence of symbols of civilized humanity should not be underestimated. International non-governmental organizations and social movements have employed symbols such as the Red Cross or Red Crescent to encourage higher levels of emotional identification between different peoples which rest on common aversions to suffering. Global figureheads such as Gandhi or Mandela embody for many people cosmopolitan ideals of non-violent struggle and the peaceful resolution of differences. Other symbols warn of the moral depths to which societies can sink and which they must guard against (they include the Auschwitz death camp and various Holocaust memorials).

The question of whether such symbols are the harbingers of what is to come in the way of a global civilizing process or whether they will remain marginal to more fundamental inter-state power struggles is impossible to answer. There is merit in the argument that states have witnessed a reduction of their traditional powers in determining the core principles of international society. National governments are subject to stronger pressures to respect the normative claims advanced by international non-governmental organizations in world society (Clark 2007). However, the resurgence of national-populist political parties and ideologies has provided a sharp reminder of the ascendancy of national loyalties. A clear shift of direction in recent times has shown that traditional identities have not changed substantially in response to increasing global interconnections but have rather been revitalized and intensified by them. New integration conflicts have found expression in national-populist revolts in which self-proclaimed outsider groups have used national symbols in struggles with the dominant strata. Verbal symbols that reaffirm nationalism and reassert national power have acquired unexpected levels of political support that have set back regional and universal international governmental organizations. Opposition to globalism is evidence of a rejection of a civilizing process in which nation-states are committed to levels of international coordination that reflect the widening of emotional identification between people. Suffice it to add that the analysis of the power of national and post-national symbols is an underexplored way of identifying changes of direction within states that continue to have the greatest impact on the configuration of the global political order. Regarding the criteria for determining whether or not a global civilizing process is on the rise, the main contemporary shifts include the contraction of the scope of emotional identification and reduced support for global planning organizations but not the relaxation of the moral and legal constraints on inter-state force that developed in the post-Second World War era.

The divisive effects of national-populist forces and resulting political conflicts have particular relevance for understanding the shifting balances between the national-Machiavellian and universal-egalitarian elements of nation-state moral codes. It is useful to recall the earlier analysis of the 'torture debate' in the United States to emphasize the symbolic dimensions (see Chapter 1). Advocates of the relaxation of the prohibition of torture employed various verbal symbols including the argument that coercive interrogation techniques were vital in a war of 'necessity' against the 'enemies of civilization'. Opponents argued that torture was a symbol of barbarism and that the relevant global moral and legal constraints symbolized civilized existence. The torture debate highlighted tensions within liberal-democratic societies and between rival images of global order that have grown in recent years. On the one hand, recharged national symbols have been employed in reactions to globalism. On the other hand, global symbols have been used by opposing groups to defend threatened post-national collective identities and to protect 'civilized' domestic and international principles and practices that many regard as vulnerable.

The prospects for a major revival and extension of global symbols may seem slim not only because of the national-populist revolt but also because of political concerns that any such symbols will continue to reflect Western values and interests and therefore lack emotional power for non-Western peoples (Olesen 2015 and 2018). Discussions about the idea of the Anthropocene, which are central to some concluding reflections on global civilizing processes, are germane in this context. The concept represents a major reconfiguration of the symbolic order. It is a symbol that conveys scientific assessments that a new geological era is the result of the unforeseen human impact on the natural environment. That symbolic utility has become linked with its role as a political symbol in efforts to transform human self-images or the human means of orientation. Central are mounting concerns and increased resistance to the supposition that the domination of the natural world is a symbol of progress and civilization (Delanty 2017). The idea of the Anthropocene has been used to conjoin the discourse of 'climate emergency' with a chorus of appeals from environmental groups such as Extinction Rebellion for new levels of individual and collective self-restraint in order to bring an end to destructive unplanned processes. Such movements have deployed a symbolic repertoire that is designed to promote higher levels of global cooperation to solve problems that human societies have created.

For the critics, the allegedly neutral or technical nature of the Anthropocene ignores basic truths about climate change – most obviously, that it is not the case that humanity as a whole is responsible for environmental degradation and that all societies are equally culpable. Unequal power relations that are critical for deciding the fair distribution of responsibilities in future have been neglected (Harrington 2016). The critique further underlines the scale of the difficulty in creating global symbols that have emotional resonance for large sections of humanity. Nevertheless, the idea of the Anthropocene may come to be seen as a turning point in the relations between human groups, in the balance of power between national and global attachments or loyalties. It may come to be regarded as pivotal in the development of the realization that unrivalled levels of transnational as well as international cooperation are required to ensure that human societies and their individual members observe new social standards of restraint in relations with nature.

Whatever may become of the political symbolism of the Anthropocene, it is perfectly conceivable that contemporary social movements and non-governmental organizations that urge radical solutions to climate change may prove to be the principal architects of what recent process-sociological writings have described as a global 'ecological civilizing process' in which different societies and social strata agree on robust restraints on behaviour (Quilley 2009: 117; see also Rohloff 2018: chs 5–6, on the relationship between the new genre of 'green guides' and changing conceptions of civilized ecological conduct). Certainly, there have been advances in circulating patterns of orientation to the world that were once confined to activist groups and concerned citizens. Developments which indicate growing recognition of the need to recast the everyday behaviour of individuals for global ends include support for an 'ecological conscience' that is centred on collective demands for higher levels of individual and collective restraint and also for 'civilizing' feelings of shame or embarrassment when transgressions of highly valued or critical social standards take place (Quilley 2009: 117).

Intertwined with those phenomena is political action to establish a new 'socio-ecological regime' with responsibility for subordinating 'short-term goals to longer-term interests' and for monitoring behaviour in the context of greater awareness of the 'unintended and unforeseen' consequences of the human effect on the natural world (Goudsblom and de Vries 2002: 411ff). That development provides support for Elias's contention that some groups have moved from strong attachments to sovereign nation-states to the belief that a politically organised humanity must be the central survival unit given current fears that climate change could produce large-scale social and political upheaval. It represents a break with the traditional assumption that non-human nature can be endlessly manipulated and exploited to serve human purposes which was one of the unforeseeable consequences of very long-term civilizing processes at the level of humanity which were set in motion by the monopolization of fire as well as complex tools and weapons, the agrarian revolution and the formation of the first large 'survival units' such as cities and archaic states. It also marks a growing conviction that controls over powers over nature are imperative although, as Elias (2009g: 59) argued in brief reflections on those issues towards the end of his life, 'human beings have still not completely understood the responsibility that is inescapably bound up with this situation'. As one process-sociological study later observed, there is greater appreciation that through greater 'control over nature', societies hoped to make 'natural processes more predictable' but, paradoxically, 'the very processes over which they can exert most control may also be the most difficult to predict' (Goudsblom and de Vries 2002: 406). At least, Elias (2009h: 259) argued, it is increasingly the case that 'our wishes and hopes for what might be called utopias are being transferred to the inter-state level'. But an 'ethos of global solidarity' is held back by the fact that human loyalties remain 'restricted to local, national units of integration' even though 'real interdependences are already global' (Elias 2009c: 256). Calls for greater responsibility for nature required levels of 'self-mastery' that were 'still unattainable, still "utopian"' (Elias 2009c: 255).

It must be added that there is more to global ecological civilizing processes than campaigns to develop new technologies in the light of an unsustainable 'fossil-fuelled global society' – namely, the fear that many societies may collapse and that civilized ways of life may be destroyed by, among other things, increasingly violent struggles for scarce resources (Quilley 2011: 76ff). One can only speculate about the place of the discourse of civilization in future political projects which address problems that confront humanity as a whole (albeit unevenly) and which envisage a major restructuring of the global order. It is unclear whether 'civilization' will be regarded as the central problem (as no longer a 'praise word') or as a critical part of the solution. The social and political processes that Elias investigated resulted in global trends in the shape of state-formation, urbanization, industrialization and population increase due to improvements in health care and life expectancy that have led to unsustainable demands on the biosphere. In Elias's language, 'technicisation' – or the process in which people learn how to 'exploit lifeless materials' usually 'in the expectation of a better life' – has been central to processes of civilization (Elias 2008a: 57). It is hardly surprising that many ecological associations have been critical of 'civilization'. Although they might reject this interpretation, they can be described as architects of a global ecological civilizing process in which new standards of restraint and foresight, parallel levels of individual and collective self-monitoring, and new sources of shame and embarrassment may become deeply embedded in reconfigured forms of life.

It may seem something of a leap to turn from the idea of an ecological civilization to the possible ramifications of the COVID-19 health crisis for civilizing processes at the level of the global order. But not according to Elias (2011: 124), who maintained that 'humankind has gained the ascendancy over most of its potential rivals and enemies in the animal kingdom ... [Humans] have killed, imprisoned or confined to reserves other animal species, and are just beginning to notice that rule over others entails some responsibility for them'; but 'at the level of viruses and bacilli the struggle goes on'. That ongoing battle within the uneven development to which Elias referred has been resumed in unforeseen ways and with unknown consequences for human societies. Future global trajectories – and balances between civilizing and decivilizing processes – are impossible to predict but the Eliasian perspective provides criteria for tracking directions. The standpoint signals the way towards modes of inquiry which have 'humanity as [their] horizon' and which are animated by the goal of improving human, as opposed to national, means of orientation.

Six themes in the above analysis of civilizing processes that affect humanity as a whole have particular salience in the current COVID-19 crisis. First, the spread of the disease confirms Elias's point that humanity is no longer a 'beautiful' ideal but conveys the 'social reality' of 'the fast-growing interdependence of all hitherto independent subgroups of humankind' (Elias 2008a: 86–87), now more imprinted than ever on the consciousness of people everywhere. Second, that awareness exists alongside greatly increased dependency on state institutions. The state remains the primary survival unit to which most people turn for help under conditions of fear and insecurity. The importance of its traditional monopolies of power is manifest in its unrivalled capacity to break social webs through enforceable lockdown strategies and the closure of national borders. States, whether democratic or authoritarian, have greatly extended controls over their populations in the process of crisis response, something many will not relinquish.

Third, there has been an unexpected re-emergence in national–populist times of globalist narratives which call for higher levels of international cooperation and long-term planning to combat a danger to all humanity. But, fourth, national–populist ideologies remain strong in many societies. Humanity remains a 'blank space' on the emotional maps of large sections of the world population with clear ramifications for the prospects of closer international collaboration. Fifth, pressures may nevertheless mount to embed a new standard of civilization regarding the state's responsibility to others. Expectations may grow that states will report promptly and accurately to the world community about outbreaks of highly contagious diseases in their societies, coordinate their responses, and contribute to building more resilient healthcare systems in vulnerable societies. Sixth, as Elias repeatedly stressed, crises often engender highly involved, fear-driven reactions that generate 'double-bind processes' that make events even harder to control. The question for social-scientific investigation is how far greater detachment and the quest for 'reality-congruent knowledge' can gain the upper hand given the danger of the national-populist 'attribution of blame' to outsiders for causing what is portrayed as a national crisis. Of particular significance are levels of commitment to the scientific quest for reality-congruence that delivers medical treatments that benefit humanity as a single community.

One of Elias's main arguments was that little is known about how the balances of power between such phenomena fluctuate or about how broad directions of change are best tracked. Crucial is exploring future relations between high levels of emotional involvement in national dangers and more detached investigations of humanity-wide challenges. As this chapter has argued, the point of such an inquiry is to identify shifts in the scope of emotional identification between people, to assess levels of support for global steering mechanisms, and to ascertain the extent to which initiatives to create the requisite worldwide standards of self-restraint are balanced with the appropriate nation-centred strategies.

One of the aims of Elias's investigation was to explain long-term trends in the relative influence of inner controls and external compulsions in civilized European societies. An analysis of high levels of conformity with lockdown strategies in contemporary societies can usefully begin with his process-sociological investigation of the increasing power of self-restraint in the governance of behaviour (Goudsblom 1986, also p. 69). This inquiry has value for future examinations of how far government policies promote civilizing processes across world society (including high levels of national self-restraint exemplified by the voluntary observance of global norms and support for stronger international institutions). The approach invites close attention to the role of symbols in world politics. The following questions arise in the current context. Will the COVID-19 virus become a symbol of national fears and anxieties that result from the unpredictability of global interconnections? Will it come to symbolize threats to humanity that foster higher levels of transnational solidarity? What part will it play in future images of a global civilization? Process sociology suggests that political struggles over the symbolism of the COVID-19 virus may have a critical role in the coming period, and that attempts to control its meaning may have profound consequences for intra- and inter-societal civilizing processes.

It remains to be seen whether COVID-19 will be explicitly linked with ethical images of human civilization that run parallel with the visions of a global ecological civilization that were discussed earlier and with which this discussion must end. It has been stated that the discourse of civilization may enter a new phase in which highly interdependent peoples decide, in more planned ways than in the past, the standards that should govern their relations with nature. The part that the idea of civilization has played in shaping dominant understandings about permissible and forbidden conduct for more than two centuries may yet become central to deliberations about sustainable ways of life. Clearly articulated standards of civilization, modified in the light of current circumstances, may be embraced as a means of influencing dominant attitudes and behaviour in world politics. Whether or not movement in that direction is taking place can be ascertained by employing the yardsticks which have been considered in this chapter – whether or not there is success in controlling harm to the environment; whether there are discernible shifts in the relative power of internal and external restraints on behaviour; whether the scope of emotional identification between humans is widening; and, finally, whether or not there is a clear trend towards higher levels of planning in order to increase social controls on the exploitation of nature. Such investigations should not ignore power struggles in the symbolic sphere. Future rivalries over the relative worth of national and universal symbols will deserve the attention of students of the remarkable career of the idea of civilization, of its influence on the course of European history, and its enduring impact on the global political order.

Conclusion

This chapter began by summarizing Elias's reflections on civilizing processes that have affected humanity as a whole including the development of monopoly control over fire and the evolution of survival units of ever greater magnitude. That line of inquiry was augmented by highlighting the existence of global civilizing processes in formal and informal relations between survival units. Core features were identified: controls on force; the greater influence of internal as opposed to external restraints on violence; increasing emotional identification between peoples; and levels of cooperation to check violent and aggressive behaviour. Elias's analysis of those aspects of civilizing processes provides a novel way of identifying the main directions of global change in any era.

Political dynamics that influence the scope of emotional identification between peoples were central to two studies of the civilizational dimensions of the contemporary order which raise large questions about balances between cultural convergence and divergence given successful resistance to traditional Western monopoly claims about what it means to be civilized. They are Huntington's polemical deliberations on supposedly rising levels of civilizational consciousness and an imminent clash of civilizations, and English School reflections on the erosion of the civilizational underpinnings of an international society which is no longer confined to Europe. The second line of inquiry constitutes a significant step beyond Huntington's effort to influence national modes of orientation to evolving power relations and resistance to Western political and cultural hegemony. The focus on the potential for a global agreement on subsistence rights reflected the belief that sympathetic Western orientations to the cultural revolt against the West and demands for global justice could renew the civilizing properties of international society.

Humanitarian or cosmopolitan initiatives that signal an extension of emotional identification remain key elements of the contemporary global order. But optimism about future advancements that was prominent in the immediate aftermath of the bipolar era has stalled. A new phase of integration conflicts within Western societies, revolving around power struggles between established groups and outsiders, has shown how extensions of emotional identification between peoples are thwarted by national loyalties. The national-populist revolt provides a vivid reminder of how collective identities and shared symbols are inextricably linked. Analyses of global order have largely ignored the symbolic domain on the supposition that its foundations largely consist of some combination of the complementarity of interests and shared principles or norms. The continuing emotional potency of national symbolism requires new lines of investigation into the importance of global symbols as objects of emotional identification in future rivalries to shape world order.

The deeper integration of societies has often produced sharp divisions between groups with clear decivilizing consequences as well as pressures and incentives to create new patterns of civilization. Struggles between centrifugal and centripetal forces are at the heart of a global order which no longer has the civilizational foundations of the colonial era. The fate of the European standard of civilization is a reminder of how the link between civilization and global order has been weakened. Whether historical connections between civilization and world order have been sundered once and for all is a contentious issue. On some accounts, Western standards of civilization still shape global politics in sinister ways. From other vantage points, changing power relations have resulted in civilizational clashes and, more recently, in national-populist responses to the dominant global interconnections. From still other perspectives, there is an urgent task to create a more civilized and civilizing international society and, more specifically, to promote a global ecological civilizing process. The idea of civilization may be destined to lose its place in global political discourse because of its association with Western political, economic and cultural domination, but the idea of an ecological civilization suggests that it is not impossible that revised conceptions of civilized conduct will be pivotal to future discourses of global order. There is no obvious alternative to a concept which (in its most positive articulations) has long been associated with restraints on force, respect for and consideration of the interests of others, moderation in the pursuit of political goals, the resolve to contain short-term personal and national objectives for the longer-term benefits of amicable coexistence and, not least, with visions of transnational solidarities that bridge the divisions between peoples by stressing 'what is common to all human beings' (see p. 59).

Summary and Conclusions

This work has analyzed the impact of the idea of civilization on the global order since the concept came to prominence in French court circles in the late 18th century. Understanding the conditions under which civilized self-images emerged sheds light on their role in a critical period in recent world politics, namely the 'war on terror' and the 'torture debate', which was discussed in Chapter 1. The need for the long-term perspective on such narratives was a fundamental element in Elias's examination of the processes by which Europeans came to regard themselves as uniquely civilized. Chapter 2 discussed the Eliasian analysis of the interdependencies between state-formation, significant internal pacification and the general lowering of the threshold of repugnance towards violence. Elias was unconventional among sociologists of the time in rejecting the standard focus on 'society' that largely ignored the interwoven nature of domestic and international politics. As explained in Chapter 3, Elias stressed the recurrence of the 'split within civilization' – the firm judgement that the restraints on force in the relations between the members of the same 'survival unit' have to be relaxed in major struggles with adversaries. The discussion of the 'duality of nation–state normative codes' provided a more nuanced approach to relations between states by describing the tensions between nationalist-Machiavellian and universal-egalitarian principles in civilized societies – tensions that were abundantly clear in Western debates about the ethics of torture that have probably not yet run their course.

A core theme in the global 'war on terror' – namely that the constraints on force in the relations between civilized peoples cannot be observed in relations between the 'civilized' and the 'savage' – was a reminder that the 'split within civilization' runs deep in conflicts between 'advanced' and 'backward' societies. The former category belonged to a society of states with distinctive diplomatic rituals and protocols that were regarded as symbols of civility and refinement. As Elias argued, civilized self-images provided the rationale and justification for colonial domination, but he did not explore the relationship between the civilizing process and imperialism in detail. Missing from his analysis was an investigation of the conflict between the face of civilization that urged self-restraint with respect to using force against colonized and semi-colonized peoples and the face that legitimated suspending the customs of civilized warfare. Chapter 3 argued that an explanation of the civilizing process should focus on the interdependencies between state-formation, colonial expansion and the evolution of the society of states – three interwoven aspects of European conceptions of civilization. The broadened perspective advances Elias's sociological inquiry into the development of civilized self-images and their implications for inter-state relations. This revised standpoint places particular emphasis on the civilizational dimensions of the global order that was the product not only of European state-formation but also of overseas colonial expansion.

Basic working principles of process sociology, as set out in the Introduction, facilitate the explanation of the European standard of civilization which was one of the main junctions where state-formation, international society and imperialism met. Chapters 4, 5 and 6 drew on Eliasian analyses to explain the rise of formalized legal postulates that were central to European images of global order between the last quarter of the 19th century and the middle of the 20th century. Those chapters traced long-term patterns of change that began with the highly unequal power balances in which established groups were certain of their natural superiority over social inferiors who faced strong pressures to accept elite perceptions of their backwardness and to transform their governing structures until these complied with the European standard of civilization. Those that did so, as discussed in Chapter 5, deferred to European claims to possess a monopoly of truth about the nature of civilized forms of life that justified in European eyes a series of civilizing offensives to shape the global order. The translation of the concept of civilization and the related idea of progress into various non-European languages was one element of elite strategies to re-orientate their societies in a period of rapid Western outward expansion. Several non-European regimes that had been reduced to the position of outsiders in the emerging world order launched mimetic civilizing initiatives, including colonial projects, in the attempt to win the respect of the global establishment. Those measures contributed to the globalization of the European civilizing process. However, the image of the outward diffusion of European ideas and practices to the rest of the world in which non-European peoples followed the standard of civilization in every detail would be a distorted one. Political agency was exercised in creating new combinations of nation and civilization that developed as non-Western societies endeavoured to preserve certain traditional moral codes and to increase their power resources in colonial international society. They were among the antecedents of the 'revolt against the West' which reconfigured the global political order in the post-Second World War era.

Well into the 20th century, many observers of those established–outsider relations may have been convinced that a global order based on Western conceptions of civilization was under construction. But, with transformed power relations, attraction to the dominant notions of civilized existence was checked by 'Third World' affirmations of traditional or indigenous values in the 'cultural revolt against the West'. The rejection of the Western monopoly to decide when colonial societies were fit for national independence was a turning point in the collective refusal to answer to an alien standard of civilization. As discussed in Chapter 6, that aspect of traditional established–outsider forces has not exactly disappeared. Contemporary variations on the standard of civilization are manifested by the human rights discourse, democracy promotion and market arrangements as well as by narratives of state-reconstruction in war-torn societies. The related 'civilizing offensives' are deeply contested and can no longer provide the foundation for the global liberal civilization which many European observers had predicted only a few decades ago.

Process sociology provides a unique set of criteria for comprehending changing track lines or pathways in the future global order. Elias's examination of civilizing processes that have affected humanity as a whole is invaluable, not least by showing how new standards of restraint or 'patterns of civilization' appeared in different phases of the historical development of human societies. Analyses of world order can usefully foreground that theme for the purpose of understanding how societies respond to the tumultuous effects of lengthening and deepening global interconnections and, more specifically, how established groups react to shifting power relations that give traditional outsiders new opportunities to define the global order. Building on those ideas, Chapter 7 examined two approaches which have analyzed distinctive 'integration conflicts' in the first universal society of states where, in the language of the English School, the earlier civilizational foundations of the European society of states have been diluted and the old standard of civilization is no longer a fundamental part of the formal constitution of international society.

The discussion contrasted Huntington's forecast of increasing civilizational rivalries and the increasing possibility of reduced restraints on violence in the relations between the established and the outsiders with English School reflections on how imaginative diplomacy could rehabilitate the classical civilizing role of international society. Large-scale empirical analyses of the more recent national–populist revolt and the rise of environmental groupings can extend the Eliasian focus on 'integration conflicts' that give rise to tangible changes in social standards of restraint. Chapter 7 added that the rise of national-populism has underscored the importance of collective symbols for global trajectories. It stressed that the analysis of the changing fortunes of national and global symbols can shed light on the prospects for civilizing processes that affect humanity in its entirety. Meriting examination is the extent to which conceptions of global or human civilization will have a prominent role in concerted efforts to increase levels of support for universal standards of restraint in world politics.

The process-sociological conception of the main purpose of social-scientific explanation specifies what is at stake in such an inquiry. At its heart, is a profound recognition of the problems that arise when levels of understanding lag behind the closer interweaving of social groups and the ensuing antagonisms that arise because of fears about the loss of power and prestige and the reduced capacity to control events. That focus on human predicaments underpinned Elias's defence of social-scientific endeavours that forego the attraction of emotional satisfaction in taking sides in political struggles for the sake of greater detachment. It was pivotal to the argument for avoiding the 'retreat into the present' and for taking a long-term perspective with 'humanity as its horizon'. The central objective was to improve the human means of orientation to the social world through greater knowledge of interdependencies between social groups in different phases of human history. It is necessary to add that Elias believed that the social sciences had yet to make significant progress in understanding the struggles that were involved in shifting the balance of power between civilizing and decivilizing processes in different social figurations stretching from the local to the national and international or global levels. There was considerable work to do at the most basic level to create sophisticated social-scientific concepts with which to undertake investigations of social interdependencies. The commitment to more detached forms of sociological inquiry was animated by a deep humanism – by the conviction that greater knowledge of the social world could contribute to reducing failed interventions and, in the longer-run, to improving the prospects of limiting the damaging effects of unplanned and uncontrolled social processes.

Elias's conception of the sociological vocation shared some of the Enlightenment sensibilities that emerged in the court figurations and were central to the whole civilizing process. The idea of civilization itself was promoted by bourgeois elements in 18th-century French court society who thought that a deeper understanding of social processes would provide the foundations for more benevolent and effective government. Their orientation to the world was not confined to improving the nation, as is clear from how Enlightenment thinkers such as Holbach framed the problem of war. In 1774, Holbach argued that 'the continual wars into which thoughtless princes are drawn at every moment' blocked progressions in 'public happiness', the 'progress of human reason', and 'the entire civilization of men' (cited in Elias 2012 [1939]: 54–5). The *civilization of peoples*, he emphasized, is *not yet complete* (cited in Elias 2012 [1939]: 54–5, italics in original).

Elias cited Holbach's observation in the concluding section of the study of the civilizing process where he stated that only when the 'tensions between and within states have been mastered' will human beings earn the right to describe themselves as 'truly civilized' (Elias 2012 [1939]: 489). Until then, all they could reasonably maintain was that they were 'in the process of becoming civilized' (Elias 2012 [1939]: 490). There is no better summary of what is involved in understanding the role of civilization in the formation of the modern global order and no better statement about how human societies might best orientate themselves to the world in the current period and in future eras. The global imagination would be impoverished if the idea of civilization lost the place it has occupied in ethical visions of large-scale change and in associated projects of reform for over two hundred years. It would be impoverished further without a parallel understanding of how 'civilization' has been used as a praise word to elevate some groups and to devalue others with pernicious consequences. Elias's relatively detached investigation of the civilizing process remains the key starting point for those who wish to understand the nature and legacy of the peculiar civilized self-images that arose in the European region.

Notes

Introduction

[1]   The legacy of those transformations is evident to this day. For example, from 2002 the Congress of the Chinese Communist Party has used the term *jingshen wenming* to support its vision of a socialist 'spiritual civilization' and also to honour 'civilized households' and 'civilized work units'. The language reflects earlier changes in which traditional Confucian categories were reinterpreted and complemented by conceptual inventions in order to promote China's reorientation to the realities of rapidly changing global power balances (Nyíri 2006; Wang 1991). See also the discussion of Chinese depictions of an ecological civilization on pp. 213–14.

[2]   In the last years of his life, blindness and physical frailty meant that Elias dictated his final works to student assistants. For further details, see Richard Kilminster's introduction to Elias (2011).

[3]   Reference has been made to the decivilizing process that occurred under National Socialism. Elias used the term in its etic sense to refer to the erosion of constraints on violence and the reduction of levels of emotional identification between people. Of course, for many Germans the rise of National Socialism constituted a breakdown of civilization in the emic sense. It represented total moral collapse. Regarding the rise of parliamentary government, many participants believed that they were creating more civilized political arrangements. They were employing civilization in the emic sense whereas Elias' comments on its civilizing qualities relied on the etic meaning of the term.

[4]   The decision to emancipate the concept of civilization from its ideological connotations also reflected the influence of Freud's analysis of the connections between civilization and internal forms of repression that were the source of assorted psychological disorders (see Elias 2014 for a sympathetic but critical interpretation of Freud's writings). In the conclusion to the study of the civilizing process, Elias posed the question of whether people can construct ways of life in which the self-restraints that are essential for the functioning of every society are no longer as repressive and joyless as in the current era (Elias 2012 [1939]: 486ff). Far from embracing a progressivist analysis of civilized societies, Elias stressed the complex psychological demands, shackles, fears and anxieties that are linked with the compulsions of civilization.

[5]   For further discussion of the idea of figuration, see Elias 2009b. Elias developed the concept to break free from the traditional sociological focus on 'society'. The concept refers to any set of interdependencies between people extending from local to 'national' and international or transnational networks.

6   In an interview that was conducted in the late 1960s, Adorno (2002: 15) supported a position on social inquiry that seems very close to Elias's standpoint. He maintained that 'theory is much more capable of having practical consequences owing to the strength of its own objectivity than if it had subjected itself to practice from the start'. Elias used the language of greater detachment in the quest for reality-congruent knowledge rather the somewhat static concept of objectivity.

Chapter 1

1   See https://www.whitehouse.gov/administration/president-trump.

2   See www.reuters.com.

3   See www.wirenews.co.uk.

4   See whc.unesco.org.

5   See http://www.fmprc.gov.cn/mfa_z/engxxx_662805/t1317353/shtml.

6   See www.haaretz.com.

7   See https://www.whitehouse.gov/news/releases/2002/09/20020912–1.html.

8   See https://www.whitehouse.gov/news/releases/2001/11/20011110–3.html.

9   See https://www.theguardian.com > *World* > *Afghanistan*.

10   See https://www.whitehouse.gov/news/releases/2002/09/20020923–2.html.

11   See https://www.whitehouse.gov/news/releases/2001/11/20011108–13.html.

12   See https://www.whitehouse.gov/news/releases/2001/12/20011207.html.

13   See https://www.whitehouse.gov/news/releases/2001/09/20010920-8.html.

14   See https://www.theguardian.com › *World* › *Iraq*.

15   Elias frequently stressed the importance of the means of orientation for human groups but he did not define the term. The concept referred to 'the symbolic reference points ... people draw upon in order to navigate themselves successfully in the complex and shifting inter-group relations of society' (see Elias 2011: 120n8, editor's comment).

16   The relevant internal memoranda were leaked in 2004 resulting in heated national debates and robust international condemnation (Barnes 2016).

17   See http://treaties.un.org.

18   See http://www.supremecourt.gov/opinions/05pdf/05-184.pdf.

19   See http://www.supremecourt.gov/opinions/07pdf/07-290.pdf.

20   See https://www.justice.gov/sites/default/files/olc/opinions/2004/12/31/op-olc-v028-p0297_0.pdf (p 304).

21   See https://www.nytimes.com/2016/11/28/us/politics/trump-waterboarding-torture.html.

22   Recent discussions of US-initiated 'targeted killings' have analyzed official claims that such actions do not violate norms that prohibit assassination. They have noted efforts to stay within 'cosmopolitan norms' by preventing the death or injury of innocent civilians. There has been no parallel to the torture debate where the two sides of the national moral code came into conflict (Pratt 2019: 732, 740). Suffice it to add that the relationship between the defence of targeted killings and the civilizing process warrants further investigation.

Chapter 2

1   Elias (2013a:193) observed that one 'cannot fully understand the development of Germany' without considering its 'position in the inter-state framework and correspondingly in the power and status hierarchies of states. It is impossible here

to separate inter-state and intra-state lines of development; from a sociological standpoint, intra-state and inter-state structures are inseparable even though the sociological tradition up till now has involved a concentration mainly, and quite often exclusively, on the intra-state.'

2   I am grateful to Hidemi Suganami for many discussions on this point. This is not the place, however, to attempt to explain the differences between the causal analysis of law-like regularities and Elias's method which was predicated on the challenging supposition that 'processes can only be understood in terms of processes' (Elias 2007: 20).

3   It is important to add that, contrary to some interpretations (see Thomas 2018: 21), Elias did not argue that civilized peoples were uniformly more restrained than earlier peoples or 'so-called primitives'.

4   Not that Mill (2002 [1859]: 487) believed that the 'civilized' were entitled to treat 'barbarians' exactly as they pleased. 'The universal rules of morality between man and man', he argued, could not be casually brushed aside in the relations between 'a civilized and a barbarous government' (487).

5   The *Description de l'Egypte* was the result of the monumental analysis of Ancient Egypt which was undertaken by teams of specialists from various disciplines, including archaeology, geography and musicology, who travelled to Egypt with Napoleon's armed forces (Godlewska 1995).

6   As a measure of its importance in disseminating ideas about civil conduct, Erasmus's treatise, *On the Civility of Boys,* was translated into over 20 languages and appeared in several editions following its first publication in 1530. Elias selected the work to explain how civilized standards spread across the upper social strata and across state borders with the result that more and more literate people became bound together in the same expanding civilization.

7   Clear parallels exist with expansions of the 'danger zone' that reflected a growing awareness that 'intimate contact may be *physically* dangerous – dangerous not in the sense that others may suddenly draw a knife or a pistol, but that they may be the carriers of an infectious disease' (Goudsblom 1986: 164, italics in original). Goudsblom (1986: 166) also refers to the convention that, when in the company of healthy persons, lepers had to 'speak against the wind because of the foul air they exhumed, and they had to maintain a distance of six feet'. I am grateful to Alex Mack for drawing my attention to this article.

8   In a revealing contrast, US visitors to Japan in the late 19th-century admired the value attached to personal hygiene and to high levels of civility and politeness while condemning the 'barbarism' of concubinage and prostitution (Henning 2000: ch. 2).

9   Such admonitions are not merely of historical interest. Prior to the 2008 Beijing Olympics, the Chinese Civilization Committee urged people to refrain from behaving in ways that Western visitors would find offensive (Coonan, *The Independent*, 26 July 2008). 'Anti-spitting campaigns and manners classes' were at the heart of a state-driven 'civilizing mission' (Nyíri 2006: 90). The episode demonstrates the enduring global ramifications of European civilized standards regarding the management of bodily functions. Government efforts to advertise compliance with the requisite standards of self-restraint can be interpreted in different ways – as a genuine attempt to promote greater consideration for others and/or as a quest to win the recognition as a civilized people that was withheld in the 19th century when most Europeans looked down on Chinese 'barbaric' practices.

[10] Japanese unease at the greater occupational opportunities for women in the United States and their more prominent role in the public domain led to domestic legislation in 1890 that virtually banned women from participating in the political sphere (Benesch 2015: 255–6).

Chapter 3

[1] Elias argued that some of the problems in the relations between societies arise because of different conceptions of the standards of self-restraint that should be observed in the conduct of foreign policy. Greater dialogue, he added, was needed to explore the prospects for future inter-state agreements (Elias 2012 [1939]: 453, n19). Those insightful comments have important implications for the idea of a global civilizing process; this will be explored in Chapter 7. Steele (2019: introduction) emphasizes the extent to which relations between states often boil down to discussions and debates about necessary standards of restraint.

[2] A striking example of the change in orientations towards African peoples was Hegel's characterization of sub-Saharan Africa as a 'land of childhood ... enveloped in the dark mantle of Night' and populated by 'natural man in his completely wild and untamed state'. The 'want of self-control' which distinguished the 'character of the Negroes' was evident in cannibalism, enslavement and warfare; these displayed 'the most reckless inhumanity and disgusting barbarism' (Hegel 1956: 91ff). Steep power gradients that did not exist in the period when Europeans first encountered the empire in Mali underpinned the open stigmatization of peoples that were presumed to lack the Europeans' achievement of civilized self-restraint.

[3] Not that the two cases were identical. Following a court martial, Smith was formally retired from the army for issuing orders that (according to the official verdict) subordinates were not meant to take literally (see, however, Welch 1974).

[4] Condemning the 'disastrous effects of even slight loosening of the bonds of restraint' which occurred when the Allied troops entered Peking (Beijing) in 1900 in the search for 'souvenirs', one author attached less importance to the rights of the Chinese people to be spared suffering on account of the Europeans' 'innate sense of decency' than to the collapse of the military discipline that was expected of 'civilized' armies (Colby 1927: 286).

[5] Similar dichotomies can be found in later periods. For example, the classical Chinese tribute system consisted of an inner zone, in which China, Japan, Vietnam and Korea respected high levels of civility, and an outer zone, in which relations with the South East Asian polities generally complied with basis standards of self-restraint. Wars with nomadic 'savage' groups were commonplace prior to their incorporation in the Chinese empire. I am grateful to John Hobson for this point.

[6] The following discussion draws on Linklater (2016: 385, 393ff).

[7] From time to time, such sentiments find expression in official statements by Western leaders, an example being President Trump's speech in the aftermath of the 4 April 2017 air strike on Syrian military facilities in response to the Assad regime's alleged use of chemical weapons. The speech implored all 'civilized nations' to join the United States in ending 'barbaric' attacks such as the Syrian government's use of nerve gas against 'innocent civilians' which blatantly 'violated its obligations under the Chemical Weapons Convention' (see www. theguardian.com › Opinion › Syria).

[8] The words 'The Great War for Civilization, 1914–19' appeared on the reverse of the Inter-Allied Victory Medal, awarded to those who had served in the First World War (see http://www.forces-war-records.co.uk).

[9] See http://www.icj-cij.org/documents/?p1=4&p2=2.

[10] There have been interesting parallels in the recent period. Noteworthy were media representations of Lynndie England whose role in prisoner abuse at Abu Ghraib shocked large sections of the US public (Tucker and Triantafyllos 2008). Also significant for the present discussion, and specifically for the discourse of 'the minority of the best', was President Bush's statement at a news conference on 6 May 2004 that photographic images of prisoner abuse did not represent the 'true nature and heart of America' (http://www.presidency.ucsb.edu/ws/?pid=72619).

[11] Other cases include the trial of Captain Robert Semrau, who was dismissed from the Canadian army in October 2010 – but spared a prison sentence – following a guilty verdict for killing a wounded insurgent in Afghanistan two years earlier (see http://www.macleans/ca/news/canada-captain-robert-semrau). More recently, on 4 January 2017, a military court in Israel found Sergeant Azaria guilty of manslaughter for killing a wounded Palestinian assailant (see https://www. theguardian.com › World › Israel debate in Israel).

[12] See www.telegraph.co.uk /news/defence.10517321 for further details of the original legal case against 'Marine A'.

[13] Recent discussions in the United Kingdom about whether the government's decision to withdraw citizenship status from persons who left the country to join 'IS' should be condoned on national security grounds or criticized as a breach of international law is an additional example of how the tensions within a contradictory moral code arise unexpectedly.

Chapter 4

[1] An interesting point of comparison is the study of the French colonial state in Cambodia in Broadhurst et al 2015.

[2] Such feelings of revolution could be reciprocated. Greenblatt (1982: 62) refers to an Amerindian's disgust at the European practice of using handkerchiefs to collect and carry about mucus. 'If thou likest that filth', the person is quoted as saying, 'give me thy handkerchief and I will soon fill it'.

[3] Many contemporary travelogues, it has been argued, perpetuate dichotomies between former 'civilized' zones of safety which have been destroyed by political upheaval in 'barbarous' regions that had once been under colonial rule. They draw on earlier narratives about the linkages between imperialism, pacification and civilization (Lisle 2006: ch 4).

[4] Those tests of 'civilized' status are not simply of historical interest. They influenced, in modified form, official assessments by the US Bush administration of the legal standing of the Taliban government in the aftermath of 9/11. The 9 January 2002 memorandum on the *Application of Treaties and Laws to Al Qaeda and Taliban Detainees* prepared by the Office of the Deputy Assistant Attorney General for the General Counsel in the Department of Defense ruled that Afghanistan failed the test of statehood because it did not exercise administrative control of a 'clearly defined territory and population', was clearly incapable of 'acting effectively to conduct foreign policy and to fulfil international obligations', and lacked the requisite recognition of the 'international community'(Greenberg and Dratel 2005: 53ff). The point applies to all 'failed states' in the dominant contemporary Western narratives.

5 Britain's decision in late 1784 to permit the gunner of the British ship, the 'Lady Hughes', to be tried by the Chinese authorities would be a turning-point in Anglo-Chinese relations. Local officials demanded his trial for causing the death of two Chinese nationals in the course of firing an official salute. The verdict of punishment by strangling led the British to insist on the resented practice of extraterritoriality which was formalized by the August 1842 Treaty of Nanking (see Benton 2002: 247ff who stresses British opposition to a legal system which consisted entirely of criminal law and took no account of the intentions of the accused when determining the appropriate sentence). The 'Lady Hughes' incident has been described as critical in the formation of Western views of Chinese 'barbarism' and in the justification of a 'civilizing mission' to introduce 'the [British] 'rule of law' in the country (Chen 2009, especially p 44).

6 Chen (2009: 21ff) describes actual Chinese judicial procedures and refers to the fact that, in the late 18th and early 19th centuries, many Europeans commented positively on the Chinese legal system while condemning the severity and arbitrariness of the criminal justice system in many European societies. Judgements changed radically in a later phase of the civilizing process.

7 Brockman-Hawe, in an undated paper, argues that the great European powers did not shy away from resorting to punishment by beheading, as occurred in the case of Chinese officials who were held responsible for the massacre of Westers in Paoting-Fu during the Boxer Rebellion.

8 Macartney, whose comments on Chinese manners and customs were noted earlier, stressed the 'infernal distortion' of foot binding but he immediately stated his disinclination to 'despise and ridicule other nations' because of minor points of difference regarding 'manners and dress' given that 'we can very nearly match them with similar follies and absurdities of our own' (Macartney 2004: 187). Revealing was the response by Sir Ernest Satow (British Ambassador to Japan for over two decades from the early 1860s and again in the last few years of the 19th century) to comments that it was 'shameful' that he had witnessed such a 'disgusting exhibition' as the *hara-kiri*, a punishment that the Japanese authorities had imposed on a military commander who had ordered troops to open fire on foreigners. The punishment, Satow (1921: 346–7) observed, had been integral to a 'most decent and decorous ceremony' which was 'far more respectable than what our countrymen were in the habit of producing for the entertainment of the public in the front of Newgate prison'. I am grateful to Hidemi Suganami for drawing this work to my attention.

Chapter 5

1 In the 1968 postscript to his 1939 work, Elias (2012 [1939]: 475, note 6) commented on 'repeatedly' having 'to resist the temptation to change the original text in accordance with the present state of my knowledge' but did not elaborate.

2 Elias discussed those features of established–outsider relations with respect to 'Levantinism' which described the 'mimic man', the 'Orientalised European' or 'dragoman' of Syro-Lebanese descent (see Halim 2013: 200ff for further discussion). The key dynamics have been explored in more recent studies of the Indian concept of *babu*, which was used to mock those who behaved in the manner of the 'English gentleman', and also in analyses of the Turkish notion of *alafranga*, which ridiculed those who remade themselves in the image of 'French civility' (Wigen 2015: 116ff).

The idea of *shinjinrui* was used by Japanese nationalists in condemnation of fellow-citizens who were described as 'new editions of a human being recast according to Western specifications' (Coker 2019: 114). More detailed studies of the 'crossfire effect' are needed to build on Elias's observations about the relationship between the globalization of the civilizing process, the double tendency noted earlier, and attendant 'deformations' of character that exposed those involved to mockery and ridicule.

3   A recurring theme in that period was that Eastern Europe as a whole occupied 'the curious space between civilization and barbarism' (Wolff 1994: 23).

4   See Stivachtis (2015) for a discussion of President Yeltsin's speeches in February 1992 which announced the government's intention to transform Russia into a 'modern civilized state' that was restored to full membership of the international 'community of civilized nations'. As Stivachtis argues, the twin objectives of democratization and state-initiated transition to market arrangements signalled the desire to govern in compliance with modern liberal-democratic 'standards of civilization'. Linde (2016) discusses the prominence of the narrative of civilization or 'civilizational nationalism' in the period since Putin came to power, a standpoint that was partly influenced by Huntington's argument about the increased importance of civilizational identification in recent times. Coker (2019: 67ff, ch 7) discusses the robust anti-universalism that lies at the heart of Putin's image of Russia as a 'civilizational state', a concept that can be used to contain groups that are committed to the civilizational 'critique of the nation'. As noted earlier in connection with the US 'war on terror', the idea of civilization remains an important weapon in attempts to influence or control domestic 'power chances' (see the discussion on pp. 38–39).

5   Western assumptions that Russia remains incompletely 'European' or 'Western' – a form of 'oriental despotism' and therefore less than fully 'civilized' – have repeatedly clashed with more positive Western characterizations. Reflecting the former standpoint was the statement in the British House of Commons on 21 January 2016 by the then Home Secretary, Theresa May, following the official inquiry which concluded that the Russian state was probably involved in the killing of Alexander Litvinenko, a former member of the Russian secret service. The Commons' statement linked the condemnatory language of civilization with the older discourse of the legal responsibilities associated with membership of international society when it accused the Russian government of 'a blatant and unacceptable breach of the most fundamental tenets of international law and of civilized behaviour'. Employing similar themes, on 15 March 2018 the NATO Secretary General, Jens Stoltenberg, condemned Russia's alleged use of a nerve agent against Sergei Skripal and his daughter Yulia earlier that month as 'a breach of international norms and agreements' that had 'no place in a civilized world' (see https://www.nato.int/cps/en/natohq/opinions_152678.htm).

6   A similar strategy was adopted by Greek nationalists who advanced the case for liberation from alien Ottoman rule and for membership of the society of states by proclaiming that classical Greece was the birthplace of European civilization, an idea that flourished in the age of the Enlightenment (Herzfeld 1995; Stivachtis 1998: 106ff; Neumann and Welsh 1991; Ejdus 2014). The 1822 Greek provisional government promoted its claim for emancipation from Ottoman rule by contending that Greece was part of a superior Christian civilization (Stivachtis 1998: 155). Appeals to shared ancestry surfaced later in Turkey under Atatürk's rule when Turkish was described as the taproot of the Indo-European languages and contemporary Turks were portrayed as the descendants of ancient civilizations such as Sumer and Egypt and depicted as

a significant branch of the 'white race' (Cagaptay 2006: 48ff). They are examples of how outsiders tried to win European recognition through the rhetoric of ancient links and legacies, however real or imaginary.

[7] An interesting parallel as far as 'borrowed colonialism' is concerned was the invitation to British and French consuls to witness the 1869 project of pacifying the Bedouin in Jordan (Deringil 2003: 340). Bedouin submission had the desired effect of displaying the effectiveness of Ottoman state institutions to the foreign representatives of civilization.

[8] The Ottoman Empire was not the only state-organized society in the Middle East to look towards Japan for inspiration. Iran in the late 19th century also attempted to learn from Japan's success as a 'student of civilization' in its effort to catch up with European educational standards. The Society of Learning, established in Tehran in 1898, was designed to fund secular schools that would promote the new ideals of civilization which Persian intellectuals translated as *mada-niyyat* (Pistor-Hatam 1996).

[9] The idea of 'reaching the standards of contemporary civilization' became the 'unofficial mantra' of the Revolution (see Dösemeci 2013: 3 who adds that the ruling elite that initiated the application to join the European Economic Community as of 30 July 1959 argued that membership would represent the consummation of Atatürk's vision to 'raise Turkey to the level of contemporary civilization'). Opponents of the civilizational standpoint invoked a 'nationalist logic' that protested against the continuation of humiliating 'Ottoman capitulations' in the form of Turkey's quasi-colonial subordination to Western market relations. Their reaction to government policies that were deemed to perpetuate feelings of inferiority and to damage national pride stressed the existence of multiple civilizations, none of which had the right to measure others' achievements against supposedly universal criteria (Dösemeci 2013: 4ff, also chs 2–3). The European Union, on the other hand, consistently rejected Turkey's request for membership by arguing that it failed to meet the relevant 'standards of civilization' regarding human rights (Casanova 2006; Wigen 2014; Bilgic 2015).

Chapter 6

[1] In an important intellectual movement in France around the end of the First World War, scholars responded to increasingly nationalist, anti-Western sentiments with the call for a more detached understanding of other civilizations. The objective was to widen horizons before mounting resentment at colonial efforts 'to smother native life' with 'European civilizational imports' mutated into the politics of hatred (Said 2003: 248–9). The approach of Durkheim and Mauss (1971) [1913] was one illustration of a growing interest in the comparative analysis of civilizations (and an important step towards the investigation of different civilizing processes in the etic sense of the term).

[2] Those developments found expression in the notion of a 'dialogue between civilizations' which the Iranian President, Muhammad Khatami, advocated in the 1990s (Lynch 2000; Michael and Pettito 2009). The dialogic image embodied the 'progressive humanist' task of promoting mutual tolerance and respect through a greater understanding of different civilizations (Palumbo-Liu 2002). An important ethical ideal rested, however, on a process-reducing concept with limited explanatory value. Involvement in specific moral and political objectives obstructed the more detached inquiry that is the key to practical success (see p. 22).

[3] The racial revolt and the United Nations *International Convention on the Elimination of All Forms of Racial Discrimination* have been described as illustrations of how 'the Global South civilized the West' (Jensen 2016: 278–8). The case for a new standard of civilization in the UN General Assembly debates on the Convention included the claim by the Colombian and Senegalese delegates that 'the existence of racial barriers is repugnant to the ideals of any civilized society' and typical of the 'savage society' in which the principle that 'might is right' dominates (Jensen 2016: 119).

[4] Singh (2015: 200) observes that a series of 19th-century conflicts from the Crimean War through to the 1879 Anglo-Zulu colonial war led prominent Indian nationalists to ask if 'so much death and destruction and killing of innocent human beings was the basic meaning of [the] civilization' they were expected to admire and imitate.

[5] The question necessarily arises of whether Elias's analysis of the civilizing process was a variant on the secularization thesis that dominated the classical sociology tradition. On one interpretation, he advanced a nuanced version of the thesis, one that concentrated on changing fantasy-reality balances in civilized societies. There is no space to discuss this matter here. The issues are considered in more detail elsewhere (Linklater, in preparation).

[6] See www.news.bbc.co.uk/2/hi/Americas/3088936.stm. The larger historical context is worth noting, namely the revolutionary critique of parallels between the British colonial establishment and the corrupt practices of the Roman Empire which informed a three-tiered standard of civilization in which the United States was placed above the middle tier of European powers and the lowest rung of non-Western peoples (see Cha 2015 on Jeffersonian exceptionalism; also Mennell 2007: 25ff).

[7] See http//:www.responsibilitytoprotect.org/ICISS%20Report.pdf.

[8] By way of example, long-standing dichotomies between the admirably 'industrious' peoples of Northern Europe and the stigmatized 'undisciplined' and 'passionate' societies in the Southern or South Eastern regions surfaced in media representations of Greece in the aftermath of the 2008 global financial crisis (Bakic-Hayden and Hayden 1992). Central was the argument that ruling elites with the responsibility for managing a modern capitalist economy lacked the requisite 'civilized' levels of foresight, responsibility and self-restraint (Herzfeld 1995; also Haro 2014).

[9] Significantly, the Chinese government maintained at the World Economic Forum in Davos in January 2009 that the 2008 global financial crisis was the outcome of failures to regulate markets that flowed from the absence of the requisite 'self-discipline', an interesting formulation given the importance of self-constraint and control in Elias's analysis of the European civilizing process (see https://www.telegraph.co.uk/finance/financetopics/.../WEF;2009-Russia-and-China-blam).

[10] One can only speculate about whether the relevant doctrines will permit or preclude the civilizational 'critique of the nation' (see Coker 2019: 124ff). The issue will warrant close analysis, assuming that national loyalties are intertwined with claims to global leadership and associated affirmations of special responsibilities for protecting human civilization.

References

Abu-Lughod, I. (2011) *The Arab Rediscovery of Europe: A Study in Cultural Encounters*, Princeton: Princeton University Press.

Adas, M. (2004) 'Contested Hegemony: The Great War and the Afro-Asian Assault on the Civilizing Mission Ideology', *Journal of World History*, 15 (1), 31–63.

Adas, M. (2006) *Dominance by Design: Technological Imperatives and America's Civilizing Mission*, Cambridge, Massachusetts: Belknap Press/Harvard University Press.

Adas, M. (2015) *Machines as the Measure of Men: Science, Technology and Ideologies of Western Dominance*, Cornell: Cornell University Press.

Adler, E. and Barnett, M. (eds) (1998) *Security Communities*, Cambridge: Cambridge University Press.

Adler-Nissen, R. (2014) 'Stigma Management in International Relations: Transgressive Identities, Norms and Order in International Society', *International Organization*, 68 (1), 143–76.

Adorno, T. (2002) 'Whose Afraid of the Ivory Tower? A Conversation with Theodor W. Adorno', translated and edited by Gerhard Richter, *Monatschefte*, 94 (1), 10–23.

Ahmad, F. (1993) *The Making of Modern Turkey*, London: Routledge.

Aksu, E. (2009) 'Global Collective Memory: Conceptual Difficulties of an Appealing Idea', *Global Society*, 23 (3), 317–32.

Alemdaroglu, A. (2005) 'Politics of the Body and Eugenic Discourse in Early Republican Turkey', *Body and Society*, 11 (3), 61–76.

Alexandrowicz, C.H. (1967) *An Introduction to the History of the Law of Nations in the East Indies (16th, 17th and 18th Centuries)*, Oxford: Clarendon Press.

Alexandrowicz, C.H. (1971) 'The Juridical Expression of the Sacred Trust of Civilization', *American Journal of International Law*, 65 (1), 149–59.

Alikhani, B. (2014) 'Towards a Process-Oriented Model of Democratisation or De-Democratisation', *Human Figurations: Long-Term Perspectives on the Human Condition*, 3 (2). Available at http://hdl.handle.net/2027/spo.11217607.0003.202.

Alikhani, B. (2017) 'On the Habitual Dimension of Problems of Democratisation: Using the Example of Egypt after the Arab Spring', *Human Figurations: Long-Term Perspectives on the Human Condition*, 6 (1). Available at http://hdl.handle.net/2027/spo.11217607.0006.104.

Alikhani, B. (2017a) 'Difficulties of the EU as a Common Object for Identification', *Human Figurations: Long-Term Perspectives on the Human Condition*, 6 (2). Available at http://hdl.handle.net/2027/spo.11217607.0006.204.

Alikhani, B. (2017b) 'Post-Democracy or Processes of De-Democratization? United States Case Study', *Historical Social Research*, 42 (4), 189–206.

Ambrosius, L.E. (2007) 'Woodrow Wilson and the Birth of a Nation: American Democracy and International Relations', *Diplomacy and Statecraft*, 18 (4), 689–718.

Andrieu, K. (2010) 'Civilizing Peace-Building: Transitional Justice, Civil Society and the Liberal Paradigm', *Security Dialogue*, 41 (5), 537–58.

Anghie, A. (1999) 'Finding the Peripheries: Sovereignty and Colonialism in Nineteenth-Century International Law', *Harvard International Law Journal*, 40 (1), 1–80.

Anghie, A. (2000) 'Civilization and Commerce: The Concept of Governance in Historical Perspective', *Villanova Law Review*, 45 (5), 887–911.

Anghie, A. (2005) *Imperialism, Sovereignty, and the Making of International Law*, Cambridge: Cambridge University Press.

Arkush, R.D. and Lee, L.O. (eds) (1989) *Land without Ghosts: Chinese Impressions of America from the Mid-Nineteenth Century to the Present*, Berkeley: University of California Press.

Aydin, C. (2007) *The Politics of Anti-Westernism in Asia: Visions of World Order in Pan-Islamic and Pan-Asian Thought*, New York: Columbia University Press.

Aydin, C. (2009) 'The Ottoman Empire and the Global Muslim Identity', in M.S. Michael and F. Pettito (eds) *Civilizational Dialogue and World Order: The Other Politics of Cultures, Religions, and Civilizations in International Relations*, Basingstoke: Palgrave Macmillan.

Bain, W. (2003) *Between Anarchy and Society: Trusteeship and the Obligations of Power*, Oxford: Oxford University Press.

Bakic-Hayden, M. and Hayden, R.M. (1992) 'Orientalist Variations on the Theme, "Balkans": Symbolic Geography in Recent Yugoslav Cultural Politics', *Slavic Review*, 51 (1), 1–15.

Banner, S. (2002) *The Death Penalty: An American History*, Cambridge, Massachusetts: Harvard University Press.

Barnes, J. (2016) 'The "War on Terror" and the Battle for the Definition of Torture', *International Relations*, 30 (1), 102–24.

Barnes, J. (2016a) 'Black Sites, "Extraordinary Renditions" and the Legitimacy of the Torture Taboo', *International Politics*, 53 (2), 198–219.

Barrett, T.M. (1994) 'The Remaking of the Lion of Dagestan: Shamil in Captivity', *The Russian Review*, 53 (3), 353–66.

Bass, J.G. (2008) *Freedom's Battle: The Origins of Humanitarian Intervention*, New York: Knopf.

Bassin, M. (1999) *Imperial Visions: Nationalist Imagination and Geographical Expansion in the Russian Far East, 1840–1865*, Cambridge: Cambridge University Press.

Bauman, Z. (1989) *Modernity and the Holocaust*, Cambridge: Polity.

Baumann, M.M. (2009) 'Understanding the Other's "Understanding" of Violence: Legitimacy, Recognition and the Challenge of Dealing with the Past in Divided Societies', *International Journal of Conflict and Violence*, 3 (1), 107–23.

Bayly, M.J. (2015) 'Imperial Ontological (In)Security: "Buffer States", International Relations and the Case of Anglo-Afghan Relations, 1808–78', *European Journal of International Relations*, 21 (4), 816–40.

Beasley, W.G. (1995) *Japan Encounters the Barbarian: Japanese Travellers in America and Europe*, New Haven: Yale University Press.

Becker, S. (1991) 'Russia between East and West: The Intelligentsia, Russian National Identity and the Asian Borderlands', *Central Asian Survey*, 10 (4), 47–64.

Behnam, D. (2002) 'The Eastern Perception of the West', in M. Mozaffari (ed) *Globalization and Civilizations*, London: Routledge.

Bell, D.A. (2001) *The Cult of the Nation in France: Inventing Nationalism, 1680–1800*, Cambridge, Massachusetts: Harvard University Press.

Benesch, O. (2014) *Inventing the Way of the Samurai: Nationalism, Internationalism and Bushido in Modern Japan*, Oxford: Oxford University Press.

Benesch, O. (2015) 'Patriotism, Virtues and the Clash of Civilities in Japanese', in M. Pernau, H. Jordheim et al (eds) *Civilizing Emotions: Concepts in Nineteenth-Century Asia and Europe*, Oxford: Oxford University Press.

Benjamin, W. (1999) 'Theses on the Philosophy of History', in W. Benjamin, *Illuminations*, London: Pimlico.

Benton, L. (2002) *Law and Colonial Cultures: Legal Regimes in World History, 1400–1900*, Cambridge: Cambridge University Press.

Benton, L. and Clulow, A. (2015) 'Legal Encounters and the Origins of Global Law', in J.H. Bentley, S. Subrahmanyam and M.E. Wiesner-Hanks (eds) *The Cambridge World History, Volume 6, The Construction of a Global World, 1400–1800*, Cambridge: Cambridge University Press.

Bergh, G. van Benthem van den (1978) 'Attribution of Blame as the Past and Present Mode of Orientation: The Social Sciences as a Potential Improvement'. Available at http://www.norberteliasfoundation.nl/docs/pdf/BlameAttribution.pdf.

Bergh, G. van Benthem van den (1986) 'The Improvement of the Human Means of Orientation: Towards Synthesis in the Social Sciences'. Available at http://www.norberteliasfoundation.nl/network/essays.php.

Bergh, G. van Benthem van den (1992) *The Nuclear Revolution and the End of the Cold War: Forced Restraint*, Basingstoke: Macmillan.

Bergh, G. van Benthem van den (2001) 'Decivilizing Processes?', *Figurations: Newsletter of the Norbert Elias Foundation,* 16, 2–4.

Bergh, G. van Benthem van den (2012) 'Norbert Elias and the Human Condition', *Human Figurations: Long-Term Perspectives on the Human Condition* 1(2). Available at http.hdl.handle.net/2027/spo.11217607.0001.202.

Berman, B.J. (2013) 'Nationalism in Post-Colonial Africa', in J. Breuilly (ed) *The Oxford Handbook of the History of Nationalism*, Oxford: Oxford University Press.

Best, J. (2006) 'Civilizing through Transparency: The International Monetary Fund', in B. Bowden and L. Seabrooke (eds) *Global Standards of Market Civilization*, Abingdon: Routledge.

Bettiza, G. (2014) 'Civilizational Analysis in International Relations: Mapping the Field and Advancing a "Civilizational Politics" Line of Research', *International Studies Review*, 16, 1–28.

Bettiza, G. (2015) 'Constructing Civilizations: Embedding and Reproducing the "Muslim World" in American Foreign Policy Practices and Institutions since 9/11', *Review of International Studies,* 41 (4), 575–600.

Bhattacharya, S. (2011) *Talking Back: The Idea of Civilization in the Indian Nationalist Discourse*, Oxford: Oxford University Press.

Bilgic, A. (2015) '"We are not Barbarians": Gender Politics and Turkey's Quest for the West', *International Relations*, 29 (2), 198–218.

Bilgin, P. (2012) 'Civilization, Dialogue, Security: The Challenge of Post-Secularism and the Limits of Civilizational Dialogue', *Review of International Studies*, 38, 1099–115.

Billig, M. (2013) *Banal Nationalism*, London: Sage.

Birdsall, A. (2010) ' "A Monstrous Failure of Justice"? Guantanamo Bay and National Security Challenges to Fundamental Human Rights', *International Politics*, 47 (6), 680–97.

Blackman, A. (2019) *Marine A: The Truth about the Murder Conviction*, Mirror Books: London.

Bleiker, R. and Hutchison, E. (eds) (2014) 'Forum on Emotions and World Politics', *International Theory*, 6 (3).

Blomert, R. (2002) 'Re-Civilising Processes as Mission of the International Community? Problems of Economic Involvement and Military Overstretch', *Figurations: Newsletter of the Norbert Elias Foundation,* 17, 8–11. Available at www.norberteliasfoundation.

Blomert, R. (2012) 'The Taming of Economic Aristocracies', *Human Figurations: Long-Term Perspectives on the Human Condition,* 1 (2). Available at http.hdl.handle.net/2027/spo.11217607.0001.203.

Bogner, A. and Neubert, D. (2016) 'The Complexity of Actor-Figurations in "Conflict Transformation" and "Post-Conflict" Processes": Observations from Northern Ghana and Northern Sudan', in S. Tonah and A. S. Anamzoya (eds) *Managing Chieftaincy and Ethnic Conflicts in Ghana*, Accra: Woeli Publishing Services.

Bogucka, M. (1991) 'Gesture, Ritual and Social Order in Sixteenth- to Eighteenth-Century Poland', in J. Bremmer and H. Roodenburg (eds) *A Cultural History of Gesture*, Cambridge: Polity.

Bohnstedt, J.W. (1968) ' "The Infidel Scourge of God": The Turkish Menace as seen by German Pamphleteers of the Reformation Era', *Transactions of the American Philosophical Society*, 58 (9), 1–58.

Boister, N. and Cryer, R. (eds) (2008) *Documents on the Tokyo International Military Tribunal: Charter, Indictments and Judgments*, Oxford: Oxford University Press.

Boswell, J. (1873 [1791]) *The Life of Samuel Johnson*, Edinburgh: W. P. Nimmo.

Bottici, C. and Chaland, B. (2006) 'Rethinking Political Myth: The Clash of Civilizations as a Self-Fulfilling Prophecy', *European Journal of Social Theory*, 9 (3), 315–36.

Bourgon, J. (2003) 'Abolishing "Cruel Punishments": A Reappraisal of the Chinese Roots and Long-Term Efficiency of the Xinzheng Legal Reforms', *Modern Asian Studies*, 37 (4), 851–62.

Bowden, B. (2004) 'In the Name of Progress and Peace: The "Standard of Civilization" and the Universalizing Project', *Alternatives*, 29 (1), 43–68.

Bowden, B. (2005) 'The Colonial Origins of International Law: European Expansion and the Classical Standard of Civilization', *Journal of the History of International Law*, 7 (1), 1–23.

Bowden, B. (2007) 'The River of Inter-Civilizational Relations: The Ebb and Flow of Peoples, Ideas and Innovations', *Third World Quarterly*, 28 (7), 1359–74.

Bowden, B. (2009) *The Empire of Civilization: The Evolution of an Imperial Idea*, Chicago: University of Chicago Press.

Bowden, B. (2014) 'To Rethink Standards of Civilization, Start with the End', *Millennium*, 42 (3), 614–31.

Bowden, B. and Seabrooke, L. (eds) (2006) *Global Standards of Market Civilization*, Abingdon: Routledge.

Boxer, C.R. (1951) *The Christian Century in Japan: 1549–1650*, Berkeley: University of California Press.

Bradley, M.P. (2004) 'Becoming "Van Minh": Civilizational Discourse and Visions of the Self in Twentieth-Century Vietnam', *Journal of World History*, 15 (1), 65–83.

Braudel, F. (1993) *A History of Civilizations*, London: Penguin.

Brincat, S. (2013) 'The Harm Principle and Recognition Theory: On the Complementarity between Linklater, Honneth and the Project of Emancipation', *Critical Horizons*, 14 (2), 225–56.

British Manual of Military Law (1914), London: His Majesty's Stationery Office.

Broadhurst, R., Bouhours, T. and Bouhours, B. (2015) *Violence and the Civilizing Process in Cambodia*, Cambridge: Cambridge University Press.

Brockman-Hawe, B. (undated) 'Accountability for "Crimes against the Laws of Humanity" in Boxer China: An Experiment with International Justice at Paoting-Fu'. Available at https://works.bepress.com/benbh.

Brown, C. (1999) 'Universal Human Rights: A Critique', in T. Dunne and N.J. Wheeler (eds) *Human Rights in Global Politics*, Cambridge: Cambridge University Press.

Bucher, B. (1981) *Icon and Conquest: A Structural Analysis of the Illustrations of de Bry's Great Voyages*, Chicago: University of Chicago Press.

Bucholc, M. (2015) *A Global Community of Self-Defense: Norbert Elias on Normativity, Culture and Involvement*, Frankfurt am Main: Vittorio Klostermann.

Bull, H. (1966) 'The Grotian Conception of International Society', in H. Butterfield and M. Wight (eds) *Diplomatic Investigations: Essays in the Theory of International Politics*, London: Allen and Unwin.

Bull, H. (1984) 'European States and African Political Communities', in H. Bull and A. Watson (eds) *The Expansion of International Society*, Oxford: Clarendon Press.

Bull, H. (1984a) 'Justice in International Relations', *The Hagey Lectures*, Ottowa: University of Waterloo.

Bull, H. (2002) [1977] *The Anarchical Society: A Study of Order in World Politics*, London: Palgrave.

Bull, H. and Watson, A. (eds) (1984) *The Expansion of International Society*, Oxford: Clarendon Press.

Buranelli, F.C. (2014) 'Knocking on Heaven's Door: Russia, Central Asia and the Mediated Expansion of International Society', *Millennium*, 42 (3), 817–36.

Burke, E. (1889) [1790] *Reflections on the Revolution in France*, in *The Works of the Right Honourable Edmund Burke*, Volume 3, London: John C. Nimmo.

Burke, E. (1889) [1791] *Letter to a Member of the National Assembly*, in *The Works of the Right Honourable Edmund Burke*, Volume 4, London: John C. Nimmo.

Burke, E. (1999) [1795] *Letters on a Regicide Peace*, Indianapolis: Liberty Fund.

Burke, P. (1992) *The Fabrication of Louis XIV*, New Haven: Yale University Press.

Burkitt, I. (1996) 'Civilization and Ambivalence', *British Journal of Sociology*, 47 (1), 135–50.

Butterfield, H. (1953) *Christianity, War and Diplomacy*, London: Epworth Press.

Buzan, B. (2014) 'The Standard of Civilization as an English School Concept', *Millennium*, 42 (3), 576–94.

Buzan, B. and Little, R. (2000) *International Systems in World History: Remaking the Study of International Relations*, Oxford: Oxford University Press.

Cagaptay, S. (2006) *Islam, Secularism, and Nationalism in Modern Turkey: Who is a Turk?* Abingdon: Routledge.

Calaresu, M. (1999) 'Looking for Virgil's Tomb: The End of the Grand Tour and the Cosmopolitan Ideal in Europe', in Elsner and Rubiés 1999.

Callières, F. de (1983) [1716] *The Art of Diplomacy* (edited by H.M.A. Keens-Soper and K.W. Schweizer), Leicester: Leicester University Press.

Çapan, Z.G. (2017) 'Writing International Relations from the Other Side of the Abyssal Line', *Review of International Studies*, 43 (4), 602–11.

Carrier, J.G. (ed) (1995) *Occidentalism: Images of the West*, Oxford: Clarendon Press.

Carrillo, J. (1999) 'From Mt Ventoux to Mt Mayasa: The Rise and Fall of Subjectivity in Early Modern Travel Narrative', in Elsner and Rubiés 1999.

Casanova, J. (2006) 'The Long, Difficult, and Tortuous Journey of Turkey into Europe and the Dilemmas of European Civilization', *Constellations*, 13 (2), 234–47.

Cesari, J. (2019) 'Civilization as Disciplinization and the Consequences for Religion and World Politics', *The Review of Faith and International Affairs*, 17 (1), 24–33.

Cha, T. (2015) 'The Formation of American Exceptional Identities: A Three-Tier Model of the "Standard of Civilization" in US Foreign Policy', *European Journal of International Relations*, 21 (4), 743–67.

Chen, L. (2009) 'Law, Empire, and Historiography of Modern Sino-Western Relations: A Case Study of the *Lady Hughes* Controversy in 1784', *Law and History Review*, 27 (1), 1–54.

Cheng, Y. (2011) 'From Campus Racism to Cyber Racism: Discourse of Race and Chinese Nationalism', *The China Quarterly*, 207, 561–79.

Clark, I. (2007) *International Legitimacy and World Society*, Oxford: Oxford University Press.

Clark, I. (2009) 'Democracy in International Society: Promotion of Exclusion?', *Millennium*, 37 (3), 563–81.

Clark, I. (2013) *The Vulnerable and International Society*, Oxford: Oxford University Press.

Cobden, R. (1835) 'England, Ireland and America', in R. Cobden (1903) *Political Writings,* Volume 1 (with a preface by Lord Welby), London: Fisher Unwin.

Coker, C. (2019) *The Rise of the Civilizational State*, Cambridge: Polity Press.

Colby, E. (1927) 'How to Fight Savage Tribes', *American Journal of International Law*, 21 (2), 279–88.

Cole, R.G. (1972) 'Sixteenth-Century Travel Books as a Source of European Attitudes towards Non-White and Non-Western Culture', *Proceedings of the American Philosophical Society*, 116 (1), 59–67.

Collet, T. (2009) 'Civilization and Civilized in Post-9/11 US Presidential Speeches', *Discourse and Society*, 20 (4), 455–75.

Collins, R. (2001) 'Civilizations as Zones of Prestige and Social Contact', *International Sociology*, 16 (3), 421–37.

Conklin, A. (1997) *A Mission to Civilize: The Republican Idea of Empire in France and West Africa, 1895–1939*, Stanford: Stanford University Press.

Connolly, W.E. (1998) 'The New Cult of Civilizational Superiority, *Theory & Event*, 2 (4).

Cosgrove, D. (2001) *Apollo's Eye: A Cartographic Genealogy of the Earth in the Western Imagination*, Baltimore: The John Hopkins University.

Coughlin, C. (2003) 'How Soldiers Must Keep Emotions Under Control to Maintain the High Moral Ground', *Saturday Telegraph*, 8 November.

Cox, R. (2018) 'Historicizing Waterboarding as a Severe Torture Norm', *International Relations*, 32 (4), 488–512.

Cox, R.W. (2000) 'Thinking about Civilizations', *Review of International Studies*, 26 (5), 217–34.

Cox, R.W. (2001) 'Civilizations and the Twenty-First Century: Some Theoretical Considerations', *International Relations of the Asia-Pacific*, 1 (1), 105–30.

Crawford, N.C. (2002) *Argument and Change in World Politics: Ethics, Decolonization, and Humanitarian Intervention*, Cambridge: Cambridge University Press.

Cummings, B. (1999) 'Animal Passions and Human Sciences: Shame, Blushing and Nakedness in Early Modern Europe and the New World', in E. Fudge, R. Gilbert and S. Wiseman (eds) *At the Borders of the Human: Beasts, Bodies and Natural Philosophy in the Early Modern Period*, Basingstoke: Palgrave.

Cuno, J. (2008) *Who Owns Antiquity? Museums and the Battle over Our Ancient Heritage*, Princeton: Princeton University Press.

Curzon, G.N. (1967) [1889] *Russia in Central Asia in 1889 and the Anglo-Russian Problem*, London: Frank Cass.

Dalal, F. (2002) *Race, Colour and the Processes of Racialization: New Perspectives from Group Analysis, Psychoanalysis and Sociology*, Hove: Brunner-Routledge.

Delanty, G. (1995) *Inventing Europe: Idea, Identity, Reality*, Basingstoke: Macmillan.

Delanty, G. (ed) (2017) 'The Anthropocene and Social Theory: 20th Anniversary Special Issue', *European Journal of Social Theory*, 20 (1).

Della Sala, V. (2010) 'Political Myth, Mythology and the European Union', *Journal of Common Market Studies*, 48 (1), 1–19.

Delmotte, F. (2012) 'About Post-National Integration in Norbert Elias's Work: Towards a Socio-Historical Approach', *Human Figurations: Long-Term Perspectives on the Human Condition*, 2 (1). Available at http.hdl.handle.net/2027/spo.11217607.0001.209.

Dépeltau, F. (2013) 'Comparing Elias and Bourdieu as Relational Thinkers', in F. Dépeltau and T.S. Landini (eds) *Norbert Elias and Social Theory*, Palgrave Macmillan: London.

Deringil, S. (1998) *The Well-Protected Domains: Ideology and the Legitimation of Power in the Ottoman Empire, 1876–1909*, London: I.B. Tauris.

Deringil, S. (2003) '"They Live in a State of Nomadism and Savagery": The Late Ottoman Empire and the Post-Colonial Debate', *Comparative Studies in Society and History*, 45 (2), 311–42.

Dershowitz, A. (2004) 'Tortured Reasoning', in S. Levinson (ed) *Torture: A Collection*, Oxford: Oxford University Press.

Deutsch, K. (1970) *Political Community in the North Atlantic Area*, London: Archon Books.

de Vries, B. and Goudsblom, J. (eds) (2002) *Mappae Mundi: Humans and their Habitat in a Long-Term Socio-Ecological Perspective: Myths, Maps and Models*, Amsterdam: Amsterdam University Press.

Dew, N. (2009) *Orientalism in Louis XIV's France*, Oxford: Oxford University Press.

Donnelly, J. (1998) 'Human Rights: A New Standard of Civilization?', *International Affairs*, 74 (1), 1–24.

Dösemeci, M. (2013) *Debating Turkish Modernity: Civilization, Nationalism and the EEC*, Cambridge: Cambridge University Press.

Dower, J.W. (1999) *Embracing Defeat: Japan in the Wake of World War II*, New York: W.W. Norton.

Doyle, M. (1983) 'Kant, Liberal Legacies, and Foreign Affairs, Parts I and II', *Philosophy and Public Affairs*, 12 (3), 205–35 and 12 (4), 323–53.

Duara, P. (2001) 'The Discourse of Civilization and Pan-Asianism', *Journal of World History*, 12 (1), 99–130.

Duindam, J. (2003) *Vienna and Versailles: The Courts of Europe's Dynastic Rivals, 1550–1780*, Cambridge: Cambridge University Press.

Dunne, S. (2009) 'The Politics of Figurational Sociology', *The Sociological Review*, 57 (1), 28–57.

Dunne, T. (2003) 'Society and Hierarchy in International Relations', *International Relations*, 17 (3), 303–20.

Dunne, T. and Reus-Smit, C. (eds) (2017) *The Globalization of International Society*, Oxford: Oxford University Press.

Dunne, T. and Wheeler, N.J. (eds) (1999) *Human Rights in Global Politics*, Cambridge: Cambridge University Press.

Dunning, E. and Hughes, J. (2013) *Norbert Elias and Modern Sociology: Knowledge, Interdependence, Power, Process*, London: Bloomsbury.

Dunning, E. and Mennell S. (1998) 'Elias on Germany, Nazism and the Holocaust: On the Balance between "Civilizing" and "Decivilizing" Trends in the Social Development of Western Europe', *British Journal of Sociology*, 49 (3), 339–57.

Dunning, M. (2014) '"Terrorism" and "Civilization": Jihadism as a "Decivilizing Process"', *Erdélyi Társadalom Social Science Journal*, 12, 2.

Dunning, M. (2016) '"Established and Outsiders": Brutalisation Processes and the Development of "Jihadist Terrorists"', *Historical Social Research*, 41 (3), 31–53.

Dunning, M. (2016a) 'Terrorism and Civilization: The Case for a Relational Approach', *Belvedere Meridionale*, 28 (1), 5–26. Available at http://www.belvedere-meridionale.hu/wp-content/uploads/2016/01/03_Dunning_BelvedereMeridionale_vol28_2016_01.pdf.

Dunning, M. (2017) 'The Sociogenesis of "Terrorism" as Part of British-Irish Relations during the Nineteenth Century', *Human Figurations: Long-Term Perspectives on the Human Condition*, 6 (1). Available at http://hdl.handle.net/2027/spo.11217607.0006.103.

Dunning, M. (2019) 'Informalization and Brutalization: Jihadism as a Part-Process of Global Integration and Disintegration, in C. Wouters and M. Dunning (eds) *Civilization and Informalization: Connecting Long-Term Social and Psychic Processes*, Switzerland: Springer, Cham.

Dunning, M. and J. Hughes (2020) 'Power, Habitus and National Character: The Figurational Dynamics of Brexit', *Historical Social Research*, 45 (1).

Durkheim, E. (1973) [1925] *Moral Education: A Study in the Theory and Application of the Sociology of Education*, New York: The Free Press.

Durkheim, E. and Mauss, M. (1971) [1913] 'Note on the Notion of Civilization', *Social Research*, 38 (4), 808–13.

Eisenstadt, S.N. (2000) 'Multiple Modernities', *Daedalus*, 129 (1), 1–29.

Ejdus, F. (2014) 'Entry into International Society: Central and South East European Experiences', *International Relations*, 28(4), 446–9.

Elias, N. (2006) [1969] *The Court Society*, Dublin: University College Dublin Press.

Elias, N. (2006a) 'The Expulsion of the Huguenots', in Elias 2006b.

Elias, N. (2006b) *Early Writings*, Dublin: University College Dublin Press.

Elias, N. (2007) [1987] *Involvement and Detachment*, Dublin: University College Dublin Press.

Elias, N. (2007a) [1984] *An Essay on Time*, Dublin: University College Dublin Press.

Elias, N. (2008) 'Civilization', in Elias 2008i.

Elias, N. (2008a) 'Technization and Civilization', in Elias 2008i.

Elias, N. (2008b) 'What I Mean By Civilization: Reply to Hans Peter Duerr', in Elias 2008i.

Elias, N. (2008c) 'Towards a Theory of Established–Outsider Relations', in Elias and Scotson 2008.

Elias, N. (2008d) 'Has Hope a Future?', in Elias 2008i.

Elias, N. (2008e) 'The Genesis of a Sport as a Sociological Problem, Part I', in Elias and Dunning 2008.

Elias, N. (2008f) 'Power and Civilization', in Elias 2008i.

Elias, N. (2008g) 'The Civilizing of Parents', in Elias 2008i.

Elias, N. (2008h) 'Towards a Theory of Communities', in Elias 2008i.

Elias, N. (2008i) *On Civilizing Processes, State Formation and National Identity: Essays II*, Dublin: University College Dublin Press.

Elias, N. (2009) 'Group Charisma and Group Disgrace', in Elias 2009i.

Elias, N. (2009a) 'The Retreat of Sociologists into the Present', in Elias 2009i.

Elias, N. (2009b) 'Figuration', in Elias 2009i.

Elias, N. (2009c) 'Thomas More's Critique of the State', in Elias 2009j.

Elias, N. (2009d) 'Address on Adorno: Respect and Critique', in Elias 2009i.

Elias, N. (2009e) 'Scientific Establishments', in Elias 2009j.

Elias, N. (2009f) 'Theory of Science and History of Science: Comments on a Recent Discussion', in Elias 2009j.

Elias, N. (2009g) 'On Nature', in Elias 2009j.

Elias, N. (2009h) 'Thomas More and "Utopia"', in Elias 2009j.

Elias, N. (2009i) *On Sociology and the Humanities, Essays III*, Dublin: University College Dublin Press.

Elias, N. (2009j) *On the Sociology of Knowledge and the Sciences, Essays I*, Dublin: University College Dublin Press.

Elias, N. (2010) *The Loneliness of the Dying and Humana Conditio: Observations on the Development of Humanity on the Fortieth Anniversary of the End of a War (8 May 1985)*, Dublin: University College Dublin Press.

Elias, N. (2010a) 'The Fate of German Baroque Poetry: Between the Traditions of Court and Social Class', in Elias 2010b.

Elias, N. (2010b) *Mozart and Other Essays on Courtly Art*, Dublin: University College Dublin Press.

Elias, N. (2010c) [1987] *The Society of Individuals*, Dublin: University College Dublin Press.

Elias, N. (2011) [1987] *The Symbol Theory*, Dublin: University College Dublin Press.

Elias, N. (2012) [1939] *On the Process of Civilization: Sociogenetic and Psychogenetic Investigations*, Dublin: University College Dublin Press.

Elias, N. (2012a) 'Karl Marx as Sociologist and Political Ideologist', in Elias 2012b.

Elias, N. (2012b) [1970] *What is Sociology?*, Dublin: University College Dublin Press.

Elias, N. (2013) [1989] *The Germans: Power Struggles and the Development of Habitus in Nineteenth and Twentieth Centuries*, Dublin: University College Dublin Press.

Elias, N. (2013a) 'We Need More Empathy for the Human Difficulties of the Process of Civilization', in Elias 2013c.

Elias, N. (2013b) 'Perhaps I Have Had Something to Say that Will Have a Future', in Elias 2013c.

Elias, N. (2013c) *Interviews and Autobiographical Reflections*, Dublin: University College Dublin Press.

Elias, N. (2014) 'Freud's Concept of Society and Beyond It', in Elias 2014a.

Elias, N. (2014a) *Supplements and Index to the Collected Works*, Dublin: University College Dublin Press.

Elias, N. and Dunning, E. (2008) *The Quest for Excitement: Sport and Leisure in the Civilizing Process*, Dublin: University College Dublin Press.

Elias, N. and Scotson, J. (2008) *The Established and the Outsiders*, Dublin: University College Dublin Press.

Elsner, J. and Rubiés, J.P. (eds) (1999) *Voyages and Visions: Towards a Cultural History of Travel*, London: Reaktion.

Elshtain, J.B. (2004) 'Reflection on the Problem of "Dirty Hands"', in S. Levinson (ed) *Torture: A Collection*, Oxford: Oxford University Press.

Englehart, N.A. (2010) 'Representing Civilization: Solidarism, Ornamentalism, and Siam's Entry into International Society', *European Journal of International Relations*, 16 (3), 417–39.

Eskildsen, R. (2002) 'Of Civilization and Savages: The Mimetic Imperialism of Japan's 1874 Expedition to Taiwan', *American Historical Review*, 107 (2), 388–418.

Falkner, R. and Buzan, B. (2019) 'The Emergence of Environmental Stewardship as a Primary Institution of Global International Society', *European Journal of International Studies*, 25 (1), 131–55.

Fanon, F. (1970) 'Algeria Unveiled', in F. Fanon, *A Dying Colonialism*, Harmondsworth: Penguin.

Fawaz, L.T. (1994) *An Occasion for War: Civil Conflict in Lebanon and Damascus in 1860*, London: I.B. Tauris.

Febvre, L. (1973) '*Civilization*: Evolution of a Word and a Group of Ideas', in P. Burke (ed) *A New Kind of History from the Writings of Febvre*, London: Routledge and Kegan Paul.

Fidler, D.P. (2000) 'A Kinder, Gentler System of Capitulations? International Law, Structural Adjustment Policies, and the Standard of Liberal, Globalized Civilization', *Texas International Law Journal*, 35 (3), 387–414.

Fidler, D.P. (2001) 'The Return of the Standard of Civilization', *Chicago Journal of International Law*, 2 (1), 137–57.

Findley, C.V. (1998) 'An Ottoman Occidentalist in Europe: Ahmed Midhat Meets Madame Gülnar, 1889', *The American Historical Review*, 103 (1), 15–49.

Fitzpatrick, S. (ed) (2000) *Stalinism: New Directions*, London: Routledge.

Fletcher, J. (1997) *Violence and Civilization: An Introduction to the Work of Norbert Elias*, Cambridge: Polity Press.

Foot, R. (2006) 'Torture: The Struggle over a Peremptory Norm in a Counter-Terrorist Era', *International Relations*, 20 (2), 131–51.

Freedman, L. (2017) 'Force and the International Community: Blair's Chicago Speech and the Criteria for Intervention', *International Relations*, 31 (2), 107–24.

Freud, S. (1930) *Civilization and its Discontents*, London: The Hogarth Press.

Frey, L. and Frey, M. (1993) ' "The Reign of the Charlatans is Over": The French Revolutionary Attack on Diplomatic Practice', *The Journal of Modern History*, 65 (4), 706–44.

Frodsham, G.D. (1974) *The First Chinese Embassy to the West: The Journals of Kuo Sung-t'ao, Liu Hsi-hung and Chang Tê-yi*, Oxford: Clarendon Press.

Fukuzawa, Y. (2008) [1875] *An Outline of a Theory of Civilization*, New York: Columbia University Press.

Gallagher, P. (2015) 'How Britain's Treatment of the "Hooded Men" During the Troubles Became the Benchmark for US "Torture" in the Middle East', *The Independent*, 20 February.

Garfinkel, H. (1956) 'Conditions of Successful Degradation Ceremonies', *American Journal of Sociology*, 61 (5), 420–4.

Gatrell, V.A.C. (1994) *The Hanging Tree: Execution and the English People, 1770–1868*, Oxford: Oxford University Press.

Gill, S. (1995) 'Globalisation, Market Civilization and Disciplinary Neoliberalism', *Millennium*, 24 (3), 399–423.

Go, J. (2009) 'The "New" Sociology of Empire and Colonialism', *Sociology Compass*, 3/5: 775–88.

Go, J. (2013) 'For a Postcolonial Sociology', *Theory and Society: Renewal and Critique in Social Theory*', 42 (1), 25–55.

Go, J. (2013a) 'Introduction: Entangling Postcoloniality and Sociological Thought', in Go 2013b.

Go, J. (ed) (2013b) *Postcolonial Sociology: Political Power and Social Theory, Volume 24*, Emerald Group: Bingley.

Go, J. (2017) ' "Civilization" and its Subalterns', *Review of International Studies*, 43 (4), 612–20.

Göçek, F.M. (1987) *East Encounters West: France and the Ottoman Empire in the Eighteenth Century*, Oxford: Oxford University Press.

Godlewska, A. (1995) 'Map, Text and Image. The Mentality of Enlightened Conquerors: A New Look at the Description de l'Egypte', *Transactions of the Institute of British Geographers*, 20 (1), 5–28.

Göle, N. (1996) *The Forbidden Modern: Civilization and Veiling*, Ann Arbor: University of Michigan Press.

Göle, N. (2000) 'Snapshots of Islamic Modernities', *Daedalus*, 129 (1), 91–117.

Gong, G.W. (1984) *The Standard of 'Civilization' in International Society*, Oxford: Clarendon Press.

Gong, G.W. (2002) 'Standards of Civilization Today', in M. Mozaffari (ed) *Globalization and Civilizations*, London: Routledge.

Goody, J. (2010) *Renaissances: The One or the Many?* Cambridge: Cambridge University Press.

Górnicka, B. (2016) *Nakedness, Shame, and Embarrassment: A Long-Term Sociological Perspective*, Wiesbaden: Springer VS.

Goudsblom, J. (1986) 'Public Health and the Civilizing Process', *The Milbank Quarterly*, 64 (2), 161–88.

Goudsblom, J. (1994) 'The Theory of the Civilizing Process and Its Discontents'. Available at http://www.norberteliasfoundation.nl/network/essays.php.

Goudsblom, J. (1994a) *Fire and Civilization*, London: Penguin.

Goudsblom, J. (2002) 'Introductory Overview: The Expanding Anthroposphere', in de Vries and Goudsblom 2002.

Goudsblom, J. (2006) 'Civilization: The Career of a Controversial Concept', *History & Theory*, 45 (2), 288–97.

Goudsblom, J. (2015) 'Fire and Fuel in Human History', in D. Christian (ed) *Introducing World History to 10,000 BCE*, *The Cambridge World History*, *Volume 1*, Cambridge: Cambridge University Press.

Goudsblom, J. and de Vries, B. (2002) 'Conclusions: Retrospect and Prospects', in de Vries and Goudsblom 2002.

Goudsblom, J., Jones, E. and Mennell, S. (1996) *The Course of Human History: Economic Growth, Social Process and Civilization*, London: M.E. Sharpe.

Grant, K. (2005) *A Civilized Savagery: Britain and the New Slaveries in Africa, 1884–1926*, Abingdon: Routledge.

Green, J.M. (2000) 'Queen Elizabeth I's Latin Reply to the Polish Ambassador', *Sixteenth Century Journal*, 31 (4), 987–1008.

Greenberg, K.J. and Dratel, J.L. (eds) (2005) *The Torture Papers: The Road to Abu Ghraib*, Cambridge: Cambridge University Press.

Greenblatt, S. (1982) 'Filthy Rites', *Daedalus*, 111 (3), 1–16.

Gross, O. (2004) 'The Prohibition on Torture and the Limits of the Law', in Levinson 2004.

Guhin, J. and Wyrtzen, J. (2013) 'The Violence of Knowledge: Edward Said, Sociology and Post-Orientalist Reflexivity', in Go 2013b.

Guizot, F. (1899) [1829–32] *History of Civilization in Europe*, New York: The Colonial Press.

Halim, H. (2013) *Alexandrian Cosmopolitanism: An Archive*, New York: Fordham University Press.

Hall, C. (2002) *Civilizing Subjects: Metropole and Colony in the English Imagination: 1830–67*, Cambridge: Polity.

Hall, I. (2017) 'The "Revolt against the West" Revisited', in T. Dunne and C. Reus-Smit (eds) *The Globalisation of International Society*, Oxford: Oxford University Press.

Hall, W.E. (1880) *International Law*, Oxford: Clarendon Press.

Hall, M. and Jackson, P.T. (eds) (2007) *Civilizational Identity: The Production and Reproduction of 'Civilizations' in International Relations*, Basingstoke: Palgrave Macmillan.

Hansen, L. (2000) 'Past as Preface: Civilizational Politics and the "Third" Balkan War', *Journal of Peace Research*, 37 (3), 345–62.

Harbsmeier, M. (1985) 'Early Travels to Europe – Some Remarks on the Magic of Writing', *Europe and its Others*, 1, 72–88.

Haro, F.A. de (2014) 'The Decivilizing Effects of the Financial System', paper presented at the *Conference on Plunging into Turmoil: Social Science and the Crisis*, University of Lisbon, 16–17 October, 2014.

Harrington, C. (2016) 'The Ends of the World: International Relations and the Anthropocene', *Millennium*, 44 (3), 478–98.

Haskell, T.L. (1985) 'Capitalism and the Origins of the Humanitarian Sensibility', *American Historical Review*, 90 (2), 339–61; 90 (3), 547–66.

Heeren, A.H.L. (1834) *A Manual of the History of the Political System of Europe and its Colonies, Volume 1*, London: D.A. Talboys.

Hegel, G.W.F. (1956) *The Philosophy of History*, New York: Dover Publications.

Henderson, E.A. and Tucker, R. (2001) 'Clear and Present Strangers: The Clash of Civilizations and International Conflict', *International Studies Quarterly*, 45 (2), 317–38.

Henning, J.M. (2000) *Outposts of Civilization: Race, Religion and Formative Years of American-Japanese Relations*, New York: New York University Press.

Herzfeld, M. (1995) 'Hellenism and Occidentalism: The Permutations of Performance in Greek Bourgeois Identity', in Carrier 1995.

Hevia, J. (1990) 'Making China "Perfectly Equal"', *Journal of Historical Sociology*, 3 (4), 379–400.

Hevia, J.L. (2009) ' "The Ultimate Gesture of Deference and Debasement": Kowtowing in China', *Past and Present*, 4 (Supplement), 212–34.

Hirono, M. (2008) *Civilizing Missions: International Religious Agencies in China*, New York: Palgrave Macmillan.

Hobson, C. (2008) 'Democracy as Civilization', *Global Society*, 22 (1), 75–95.

Hobson, C. (2013) 'Democracy, Democratization and the Death Penalty', in M. Futamura and N. Bernaz (eds) *The Politics of the Death Penalty in Countries in Transition*, Abingdon: Routledge.

Hobson, J.M. (2004) *The Eastern Origins of Western Civilization*, Cambridge: Cambridge University Press.

Hobson, J.M. (2007) 'Reconstructing International Relations through World History: Oriental Globalization and the Global-Dialogic Conception of Inter-Civilizational Relations', *International Politics*, 44 (4): 414–30.

Hobson, J.M. (2012) *The Eurocentric Conception of World Politics: Western International Theory, 1760–2010*, Cambridge: Cambridge University Press.

Hobson, J.M. (2017) 'A Critical-Sympathetic Introduction to Linklater's Epic Odyssey: Building a Bridge over Troubled (Eurocentric?) Water', *Review of International Studies*, 43 (4), 581–601.

Hobson, J.M. (2020) *Multicultural Origins of the Global Economy: Beyond the Western-Centric Frontier*, Cambridge: Cambridge University Press.

Hodgen, M.T. (1964) *Early Anthropology in the Sixteenth and Seventeenth Centuries*, Philadelphia: University of Pennsylvania Press.

Horowitz, R.S. (2004) 'International Law and State Transformation in China, Siam, and the Ottoman Empire during the Nineteenth Century', *Journal of World History*, 15 (4), 445–86.

Howland, D. (2001) 'Translating Liberty in Nineteenth-Century Japan', *Journal of the History of Ideas*, 62 (1), 161–81.

Howland, D. (2007) 'Japan's "Civilized" War: International Law as Diplomacy in the Sino-Japanese War (1894–1895)', *Journal of the History of International Law*, 9, 179–201.

Hulton, P.H. (1984) *America, 1585: The Complete Drawings of John White*, London: University of North Carolina Press and British Museum Publications.

Hume, D. (1975) [1777] *An Enquiry Concerning the Principles of Morals*, Oxford: Clarendon Press.

Huntington, S.P. (1993) 'The Clash of Civilizations?', *Foreign Affairs*, 72 (3), 22–49.

Huntington, S.P. (1996) *The Clash of Civilizations and the Future of World Politics*, New York: Simon and Schuster.

Hurrell, A. (2002) '"There are no Rules"(George W. Bush): International Order after September 11', *International Relations*, 16 (2), 185–204.

Hutchison, E. (2016) *Affective Communities in World Politics: Collective Emotions after Trauma*, Cambridge: Cambridge University Press.

Idler, A. (2019) *Borderland Battles: Violence, Crime, and Governance at the Edges of Columbia's War*, Oxford: Oxford University Press.

Ikegami, E. (1995) *The Taming of the Samurai: Honorific Individualism and the Making of Modern Japan*, Cambridge, Massachusetts: Harvard University Press.

Ikegami, E. (2005) *Bonds of Civility: Aesthetic Networks and the Political Origins of Japanese Culture*, Cambridge: Cambridge University Press.

Inglis, D. (2010) 'Civilizations or Globalizations? Intellectual Rapprochements and Historical World-Visions', *European Journal of Social Theory*, 13 (1), 135–52.

Israel, J.I. (2006) *Enlightenment Contested: Philosophy, Modernity, and the Emancipation of Man 1670–1752*, Oxford: Oxford University Press.

Jackson, P.T. (2006) *Civilizing the Enemy: German Reconstruction and the Invention of the West*, Michigan: University of Michigan.

Jackson, R. (2000) *The Global Covenant: Human Conduct in a World of States*, Oxford: Oxford University Press.

Jackson, R. (2007) 'Language, Policy and the Construction of a Torture Culture in the War on Terror', *Review of International Studies*, 33 (3), 353–71.

Jacoby, T. (2011) 'Islam, Violence and the New Barbarism', in T. Crook, R. Gill, and B. Taithe (eds) *Evil, Barbarism and Empire: Britain and Abroad, c. 1830–2000*, Basingstoke: Palgrave.

Jahn, B. (2000) *The Cultural Construction of International Relations: The Invention of the State of Nature*, Basingstoke: Palgrave.

Jarausch, K.H. (2006) *After Hitler: Recivilizing Germans, 1945–95*, Oxford: Oxford University Press.

Jellinek, G. (1901) 'China and International Law', *International Law Review*, 35, 56–62.

Jensen, D.L. (1985) 'The Ottoman Turks in Sixteenth Century French Diplomacy', *The Sixteenth Century Journal*, 16 (4), 451–70.

Jensen, S.L.B. (2016) *The Making of International Human Rights: The 1960s, Decolonization and the Reconstruction of Global Values*, Cambridge: Cambridge University Press.

Johnson, C. (2000) *Blowback: The Costs and Consequences of American Empire*, London: Macmillan.

Johnson, C. (2001) 'Blowback', *The Nation*, 273 (11): 13–15.

Jordan, W.D. (1969) *White over Black: American Attitudes to the Negro, 1550–1812*, Baltimore: Penguin Books.

Kaczmarska, K. (2016) ' "But in Asia we too are Europeans": Russia's Multifaceted Engagement with the Standard of Civilization', *International Politics*, 30 (4), 432–55.

Kaspersen, L.B. and Gabriel, N. (2008) 'The Importance of Survival Units for Norbert Elias's Figurational Perspective', *The Sociological Review*, 56 (3), 370–87.

Katzenstein, P. (ed) (2009) *Civilizations and World Politics: Plural and Pluralistic Perspectives*, Abingdon: Routledge.

Kayaoğlu, T. (2010) *Legal Imperialism: Sovereignty and Extraterritoriality in Japan, the Ottoman Empire, and China*, Cambridge: Cambridge University Press.

Keal, P. (2003) *European Conquest and the Rights of Indigenous Peoples: The Moral Backwardness of International Society*, Cambridge: Cambridge University Press.

Keene, D. (1969) *The Japanese Discovery of Europe, 1720–1830*, Stanford: Stanford University Press.

Keene, E. (2002) *Beyond the Anarchical Society: Grotius, Colonialism and Order in World Politics*, Cambridge: Cambridge University Press.

Kilminster, R. (1987) 'Introduction to Elias', *Theory, Culture and Society*, 4, 213–22.

Kilminster, R. (2007) *Norbert Elias: Post-Philosophical Sociology*, Abingdon: Routledge.

Kilminster, R. (2011) 'Norbert Elias's Post-Philosophical Sociology: From "Critique" to Relative Detachment', in N. Gabriel and S. Mennell (eds) (2011) *Norbert Elias and Figurational Research: Processual Thinking in Sociology*, Oxford: Blackwell.

Kilminster, R. (2013) 'Norbert Elias and Karl Mannheim: Contrasting Perspectives on the Sociology of Knowledge', in F. Dépeltau, and T.S. Landini (eds) *Norbert Elias and Social Theory*, Basingstoke: Palgrave Macmillan.

Kilminster. R. (2014) 'The Dawn of Detachment: Norbert Elias and Sociology's Two Tracks', *History of the Human Sciences*, 27 (3), 96–115.

Kim, H.J. and Sharman, J.C. (2014) 'Accounts and Accountability: Corruption, Human Rights, and Individual Accountability Norms', *International Organization*, 68 (2), 417–48.

Koskenniemi, M. (2001) *The Gentle Civilizer of Nations: The Rise and Fall of International Law, 1870–1960*, Cambridge: Cambridge University Press.

Koskenniemi, M. (2016) 'Race, Hierarchy and International Law: Lorimer's Legal Science', *European Journal of International Law*, 27 (2), 415–29.

Kramer, A. (2007) *Dynamic of Destruction: Culture and Mass Killing in the First World War*, Oxford: Oxford University Press.

Krieken, R. van (1998) *Norbert Elias*, London: Routledge.

Krieken, R. van (1999) 'The Barbarism of Civilization: Cultural Genocide and the "Stolen Generations"', *British Journal of Sociology*, 50 (2), 297–315.

Krieken, R. van (2011) 'Three Faces of Civilization: "In the Beginning All the World was Ireland"', *The Sociological Review*, 59 (1), 24–47.

Kühn, F.P. (2016) 'Afghanistan and the "Graveyard of Empires": Blumenberg, Under-complex Analogy and Basic Myths in International Politics', in B. Bliesemann de Guevara (ed) *Myth and Narrative in International Politics: Interpretive Approaches to the Study of IR*, London: Palgrave Macmillan.

Kunitake, K. (2009) *Japan Rising: The Iwakura Embassy to the United States and Europe, 1871–73*, Cambridge: Cambridge University Press.

Kurki, M. (2013) *Democratic Futures: Revisioning Democracy Promotion*, Abingdon: Routledge.

Lacassagne, A. (2012) 'Cultures of Anarchy as Figurations: Reflections on Wendt, Elias and the English School', *Human Figurations: Long-Term Perspectives on the Human Condition*, 2 (1). Available at http://hdl.handle.net/2027/spo.11217607.0001.207.

Lam, T. (2010) 'Policing the Imperial Nation: Sovereignty, International Law, and the Civilizing Mission in Late Qing China', *Comparative Studies in Society and History*, 52 (4), 881–908.

Landini, T.S. (2013) 'Main Principles of Elias's Sociology', in F. Dépeltau and T.S. Landini (eds) *Norbert Elias and Social Theory*, Basingstoke: Palgrave Macmillan.

Larson, F. (2014) *Severed: A History of Heads Lost and Heads Found*, London: Granta.

Lauterpacht, H. (1947) *Recognition in International Law*, Cambridge: Cambridge University Press.

Lawrence, T.J. (1895) *Principles of International Law*, Boston: D.C. Heath and Co.

Lawson, G. (2017) 'The Untimely Historical Sociologist', *Review of International Studies*, 43 (4), 671–85.

Layton, S. (1991) 'Primitive Despot and Noble Savage: The Two Faces of Shamil in Russian Literature', *Central Asian Survey*, 10 (4), 31–45.

Leão, A.B. (2014) 'Elias and Literature: Psychogenesis of Brazil in French Books for Young People', in T.S. Landini and F. Dépeltau (eds) *Norbert Elias and Empirical Research*, Basingstoke: Palgrave Macmillan.

Lever, J. and Powell, R. (2017) '"Problems of Involvement and Detachment": Norbert Elias and the Investigation of Contemporary Social Processes', *Human Figurations: Long-Term Perspectives on the Human Condition*, 6(2). Available at http://hdl.handle.net/2027/spo.11217607.0006.209.

Levinson, S. (2004) 'Contemplating Torture: An Introduction', in S. Levinson (ed) *Torture: A Collection*, Oxford: Oxford University Press.

Linde, F. (2016) 'The Civilizational Turn in Russian Political Discourse: From Pan-Europeanism to Civilizational Distinctiveness', *The Russian Review*, 75 (October): 604–25.

Linklater, A. (1990) [1982] *Men and Citizens in the Theory of International Relations*, London: Macmillan.

Linklater, A. (2005) 'Discourse Ethics and the Civilizing Process', *Review of International Studies*, 31 (1), 141–54.

Linklater, A. (2007) 'Torture and Civilization', *International Relations*, 21 (1), 111–18.

Linklater, A. (2010) 'The English School Conception of International Society: Reflections on Western and Non-Western Perspectives', *Ritsumaiken Annual Review of International Studies*, (9), 1–13.

Linklater, A. (2010a) 'Global Civilizing Processes and the Ambiguities of Interconnectedness', *European Journal of International Relations*, 16 (2), 155–78.

Linklater, A. (2011) *The Problem of Harm in World Politics: Theoretical Investigations*, Cambridge: Cambridge University Press.

Linklater, A, (2011a) 'Long-Term Patterns of Change in Human Interconnectedness: A View from International Relations', *Human Figurations: Long-Term Perspective* 1 (1). Available at http://www.norberteliasfoundation.nl.

Linklater, A. (2011b) 'Prudence and Principle in International Society Politics: Reflections on Vincent's Perspective on Human Rights', *International Affairs*, 87 (5), 1179–91.

Linklater, A. (2014) 'Anger and World Politics: How Collective Emotions Change over Time', *International Theory*, 6 (3), 574–8.

Linklater, A. (2016) *Violence and Civilization in the Western States-Systems*, Cambridge: Cambridge University Press.

Linklater, A. (2017) 'Process Sociology, the English School and Post-Colonialism: Understanding Violence and Civilization: A Reply to the Critics', *Review of International Studies*, 43 (4), 700–19.

Linklater, A. (2019) 'Symbols and World Politics: Towards a Long-Term Perspective on Historical Term Trends and Contemporary Challenges', *European Journal of International Relations*, 25 (3), 931–54.

Linklater, A. (in preparation) 'Norbert Elias, Religion and Civilization: Fantasy-Reality Balances in Long-Term Perspective'.

Linklater, A. and Suganami, H. (2006) *The English School of International Relations: A Contemporary Reassessment*, Cambridge: Cambridge University Press.

Lisle, D. (2006) *The Global Politics of Contemporary Travel Writing*, Cambridge: Cambridge University Press.

Liston, K. and Mennell, S. (2009) 'Ill Met in Ghana: Jack Goody and Norbert Elias on Process and Progress in Africa', *Theory, Culture and Society*, 26 (7–8), 52–70.

Lorimer, J. (1883) *The Institutes of the Law of Nations*, Edinburgh and London: William Blackwood and Sons.

Loyal, S. and Quilley, S. (eds) (2004) *The Sociology of Norbert Elias*, Cambridge: Cambridge University Press.

Luban, D. (2005) 'Liberalism, Torture, and the Ticking Bomb', *Virginia Law Review*, 91, 1425–61.

Lukes, S. (1973) *Individualism*, Oxford: Basil Blackwell.

Luo, J. and Zhang, X. (2011) 'Multilateral Cooperation in Africa between China and Western Countries: From Differences to Consensus', *Review of International Studies*, 37 (4), 1793–813.

Lynch, M. (2000) 'The Dialogue of Civilizations and International Public Spheres', *Millennium*, 29 (2), 307–37.

McKeown, R. (2009) 'Norm Regress: US Revisionism and the Slow Death of the Torture Norm', *International Relations*, 23 (1), 5–25.

Macartney, Lord (2004) *An Embassy to China: Being the Journal Kept by Lord Macartney during his Embassy to the Emperor, Ch'ien-lung 1793–1794* (introduced by J. Spence and edited by J.L. Cranmer-Byng), London: The Folio Society.

Makdisi, U. (2002) 'Ottoman Orientalism', *American Historical Review*, 107 (3), 768–96.

Malerba, J. (2013) 'The New Style: Etiquette during the Exile of the Portuguese Court in Rio de Janeiro', in F. Dépeltau, and T.S. Landini (eds) *Norbert Elias and Social Theory*, Basingstoke: Palgrave Macmillan.

Mancall, M. (1968) 'The Ch'ing Tribute System: An Interpretive Essay', in J.K. Fairbank (ed) *The Chinese World Order: Traditional China's Foreign Relations*, Cambridge, Massachusetts: Harvard University Press.

Mandelbaum, M.M. (2013) 'One State-One Nation: The Naturalisation of Nation-State Congruency in IR Theory', *Journal of International Relations and Development*, 16, 514–38.

Manji, F. and O'Coill, C. (2002) 'The Missionary Position: NGOs and Development in Africa', *International Affairs*, 78 (3), 567–83.

Mann, M. (1986) *The Sources of Social Power: Volume One, A History of Power from the Beginning to 1760*, Cambridge: Cambridge University Press.

Manners, I. (2002) 'Normative Power Europe: A Contradiction in Terms?', *Journal of Common Market Studies*, 40 (2), 235–58.

Manners, I. (2011) 'Symbolism in European Integration', *Contemporary European Politics*, 9 (3), 243–68.

Mansfield, H.C. (1984) *Selected Letters of Edmund Burke*, Chicago: University of Chicago Press.

Marrus, M.R. (1997) *The Nuremberg War Crimes Trial, 1945–46: A Documentary History*, Boston: Bedford.

Marshall, P.J. (1993) 'Britain and China in the Late Eighteenth Century', in R.A. Bickers (ed) *Ritual and Diplomacy: The Macartney Mission to China 1792–1794*, London: The British Association for Chinese Studies in association with The Wellsweep Press.

Marshall, P.J. and Williams, G. (1982) *The Great Map of Mankind: British Perceptions of the World in the Age of Enlightenment*, London: J.M. Dent.

Martin, J.L. and Neal, A.D. (2002) *Defending Civilization: How Our Universities Are Failing America and What Can Be Done about It*, Washington: The American Council of Trustees and Alumni.

Martin, M. (2015) 'Mirror Reflections: Louis XIV, Phra Narai and the Material Culture of Kingship', *Art History*, 38 (5), 652–67.

Maruyama, M. (1963) *Thought and Behaviour in Japanese Politics*, London: Oxford University Press.

Marx, K. and Engels, F. (1977) [1848] 'The Communist Manifesto', in D. McLellan (ed) *Karl Marx: Selected Writings*, Oxford: Oxford University Press.

Mastenbroek, W. (1999) 'Negotiating as Emotion Management', *Theory, Culture and Society*, 16 (4), 49–73.

Mazlish, B. (2001) 'Civilization in a Historical and Global Perspective', *International Sociology*, 16 (3), 293–300.

Mazlish, B. (2004) *Civilization and its Contents*, Stanford: Stanford University Press.

Mégret, F. (2006) 'From "Savages" to "Unlawful Combatants": A Postcolonial Look at International Law's "Other"', in A. Orford (ed) *International Law and its Others*, Cambridge: Cambridge University Press.

Melko, M. and Scott, L.R. (eds) (1987) *The Boundaries of Civilizations in Space and Time*, Lanham: United Press of America.

Memorandum for Alberto R. Gonzales, Council to the President, 'Standards of Conduct for Interrogation under 18 U.S.C. 2340–2340A' (1 August 2002), in K.J. Greenberg and J.L. Dratel (eds) *The Torture Papers: The Road to Abu Ghraib*, Cambridge: Cambridge University Press.

Memorandum Opinion for the Deputy Attorney General, 'Definition of Torture under 118 U.S.C. 2340–2340a' (30 December 2004). Available at www.justice.gov/sites/default/files/olc/opinions/2004/12/31/op-olc-v028-p02970.pdf.

Mennell, S. (1990) 'Decivilizing Processes: Theoretical Significance and Some Lines of Research', *International Sociology*, 5 (2), 205–23.

Mennell, S. (1994) 'The Formation of We-Images: A Process Theory', in C. Calhoun (ed) *Social Theory and the Politics of Identity*, Oxford: Blackwell.

Mennell, S. (1996) 'Asia and Europe: Comparing Civilizing Processes', in J.E. Goudsblom, E. Jones and S. Mennell (1996) *The Course of Human History: Economic Growth, Social Process and Civilization*, London: M.E. Sharpe.

Mennell, S. (1998) *Norbert Elias: An Introduction*, Dublin: University College Dublin Press.

Mennell, S. (2006) 'Elias and the Counter Ego: Personal Recollections', *History of the Human Sciences*, 19 (2), 73–91.

Mennell, S. (2007) *The American Civilizing Process*, Cambridge: Polity Press.

Mennell, S. (2010) 'Reflections on American Religiosity from an Eliasian Point of View', *Historická Sociologie: Historical Sociology: A Journal of Historical Social Sciences*, Prague, 2: 9–29.

Mennell, S. (2012) '*Abschiedsvorlesung*: Realism and Reality Congruence: Sociology and International Relations', *Human Figurations: Long-Term Perspectives on the Human Condition*, 1 (2). Available at http://hdl.handle.net/2027/spo.11217607.0001.210.

Mennell, S. (2014) 'What Economists Forgot and What Wall Street (and the City Never Learned): A Sociological Perspective on the Crisis in Economics', *History of Human Sciences*, 27 (3), 20–37.

Mennell, S. (2015) 'Civilizing Offensives and Decivilizing Processes: Between the Emic and the Etic', *Human Figurations: Long-Term Perspectives on the Human Condition*, 4 (1). Available at http://hdl.handle.net/2027/spo.11217607.0004.109.

Mennell, S. (2017) '*Apologia Pro Vita Sociologica Sua*: Social Character and Historical Process, and Why I Became an Eliasian Sociologist', *Human Figurations: Long-Term Perspectives on the Human Condition*, 6 (1). Available at http://hdl.handle.net/2027/spo.11217607.0006.102.

Messner, A.C. (2015) 'Transforming Chinese Hearts, Minds and Bodies in the Name of Progress, Civility, and Civilization', in M. Pernau, H. Jordheim et al (eds) *Civilizing Emotions: Concepts in Nineteenth-Century Asia and Europe*, Oxford: Oxford University Press.

Mettraux, G. (2003) 'US Courts-Martial and the Armed Conflict in the Philippines (1899–1902): Their Contribution to National Case Law on War Crimes', *Journal of Criminal International Justice*, 1, 135–50.

Michael, M.S. and Pettito, F. (eds) (2009) *Civilizational Dialogue and World Order: The Other Politics of Cultures, Religions, and Civilizations in International Relations*, Basingstoke: Palgrave Macmillan.

Mill, J.S. (1977) [1836] 'Civilization', in *Collected Works of John Stuart Mill, Volume 18*, J.M. Robson (ed), Toronto: University of Toronto Press.

Mill, J.S. (2002) [1859] 'A Few Words on Non-Intervention', in C. Brown, T. Nardin and N. Rengger (eds) *International Relations in Political Thought: Texts from the Ancient Greeks to the First World War*, Cambridge: Cambridge University Press.

Mishra, P. (2012) *From the Ruins of the West: The Revolt against the West and the Remaking of Asia*, London: Allen Lane.

Miyoshi, M. (1979) *As We Saw Them: The First Japanese Embassy to the United States (1860)*, Berkeley: University of California Press.

Morgenthau, H.J. (1965) *Scientific Man versus Power Politics*, London: University of Chicago Press.

Moses, A.D. (2008) 'Empire, Colony, Genocide: Keywords and the Philosophy of History', in A.D. Moses (ed) *Empire, Colony, Genocide: Conquest, Occupation, and Subaltern Resistance in World History*, Oxford: Berghahn Books.

Moses, A.D. (2010) 'Colonialism', in P. Hayes and J.K. Roth (eds) *The Oxford Handbook of Holocaust Studies*, Oxford: Oxford University Press.

Mozaffari, M. (2001) 'The Transformationalist Perspective and the Rise of a Global Standard of Civilization', *International Relations of the Asia-Pacific*, 1(2), 247–64.

Mozaffari, M. (2002) 'Islamic Civilization between Medina and Athens', in M. Mozaffari (ed) *Globalization and Civilizations*, London: Routledge.

Myles, E. (2002) '"Humanity", "Civilization" and the "International Community" in the Late Imperial Russian Mirror: Three Ideas "Topical for Our Days"', *Journal of the History of International Law*, 4, 310–34.

Naff, T. (1984) 'The Ottoman Empire and the European States System', in H. Bull and A. Watson (eds) *The Expansion of International Society*, Oxford: Clarendon Press.

Nelson, B. (1973) 'Civilizational Analysis and Inter-Civilizational Relations', *Sociological Analysis*, 34 (2), 79–105.

Neocleous, M. (2011) 'The Police of Civilization: The War on Terror as Civilizing Offensive', *International Political Sociology*, 5, 144–59.

Neubert, D. (2009) 'Local and Regional Non-State Actors on the Margins of Public Policy in Ghana', in A. Peters, L. Koechlin, T. Förster and G.F. Zinkernagel (eds) (2009) *Non-State Actors as Standard Setters*, Cambridge: Cambridge University Press.

Neumann, I.B. (1999) *Uses of the Other: The 'East' in European Identity Formation*, Minneapolis: University of Minnesota Press.

Neumann, I.B. and Welsh, J.M. (1991) 'The Other in European Self-Definition: An Addendum to the Literature on International Society', *Review of International Studies*, 17 (4), 327–48.

Newton, T. (2003) 'Credit and Civilization', *British Journal of Sociology*, 54 (3), 347–71.

Nyíri, P. (2006) 'The Yellow Man's Burden: Chinese Migrants on a Civilizing Mission', *The China Journal*, 56 (July), 83–106.

O'Hagan, J. (2002) *Conceptualizing the West in International Relations: From Spengler to Said*, Basingstoke: Palgrave.

O'Hagan, C. (2015) 'The Responsibility to Protect: A Western Idea?', in R. Thakur and W. Maley (eds) *Theorising the Responsibility to Protect*, Cambridge: Cambridge University Press.

Odgaard, L. (2020) 'Responsibility to Protect Goes to China: An Interpretivist Analysis of how China's Co-existence Policy Made it a Responsibility to Protect Insider', *Journal of International Political Theory*, 16 (2), 231–48.

Ohira, A. (ed) (2014) 'On the Japanese Civilizing Process: The Antithesis Between *Zivilization* and *Kultur*', in A. Ohira (ed) *Norbert Elias as Social Theorist: Figurational Sociology and its Applications*, DTP Publishing: Tokyo.

Olesen, T. (2015) *Global Injustice Symbols and Social Movements*, Basingstoke: Palgrave Macmillan.

Olesen, T. (2018) 'Adaptation and Self-Celebration: The Formation of Injustice Icons in a North-South Perspective', *International Journal of Political Cultural Studies*, 31 (3), 313–28.

Oppenheim, L. (1914) *The Collected Papers of John Westlake on Public International Law*, Cambridge: Cambridge University Press.

Oppenheim, L. (1955) *International Law* (edited by H. Lauterpacht), London: Longmans and Green.

Pagden, A. (1982) *The Fall of Natural Man: The American Indian and the Origins of Comparative Ethnology*, Cambridge: Cambridge University Press.

Pagden, A. (1988) 'The "Defence of Civilization" in Eighteenth-Century Social Theory', *History of the Human Sciences*, 1(1), 33–45.

Pagden, A. (2000) 'Stoicism, Cosmopolitanism, and the Legacy of European Imperialism', *Constellations*, 7 (1), 3–22.

Palayibik, M.S. (2010) 'Travel, Civilization and the East: Ottoman Travellers' Perception of the "East" in the Late Ottoman Empire', PhD thesis, Middle East Technical University, Ankara. Available at www.etd.lib.metu.edu.tr/upload/3/12611743/index.pdf.

Palumbo-Liu, D. (2002) 'Multiculturalism Now: Civilization, National Identity, and Difference Before and After September 11', *Boundary*, 29 (2), 87–108.

Paris, R. (2002) 'International Peace-Building and the "Mission Civilisatrice"', *Review of International Studies*, 28 (4), 637–56.

Paris, R. (2004) *At War's End: Building Peace after Civil Conflict*, Cambridge: Cambridge University Press.

Paris, R. (2015) 'States of Mind: The Role of Governance Schemes in Foreign-Imposed Regime Change', *International Relations*, 29 (2), 139–76.

Park, M. (2015) 'From Shame to Sympathy: Civilization and Emotion in Korea, 1860–1920', in M. Pernau, H. Jordheim et al (eds) *Civilizing Emotions: Concepts in Nineteenth-Century Asia and Europe*, Oxford: Oxford University Press.

Patrick, R. and MacDonald, A. (2012) 'Symbolism and the City: From Towers of Power to "Ground Zero"': *Prairie Perspectives: Geographical Essays*, 15, 14–18. Available at www.pcag.uwinnipeg.ca.

Pedersen, S. (2015) *The Guardians: The League of Nations and the Crisis of Empire*, Oxford: Oxford University Press.

Pepperell, N. (2016) 'The Unease with Civilization: Norbert Elias and the Violence of the Civilizing Process', *Thesis Eleven*, 137 (1), 1–19.

Pernau, M. and Jordheim, H. (2015) 'Introduction', in M. Pernau, H. Jordheim et al (eds) *Civilizing Emotions: Concepts in Nineteenth-Century Asia and Europe*, Oxford: Oxford University Press.

Peters, A. et al (eds) (2009) *The Role of Non-State Actors as Standard Setters*, Cambridge: Cambridge University Press.

Phillips, A. (2011) 'Saving Civilization from Empire: Belligerency, Pacifism and the Two Faces of Civilization during the Second Opium War', *European Journal of International Relations*, 18 (1), 5–27.

Phillips, A. (2014) 'Civilizing Missions and the Rise of International Hierarchies in Early Modern Asia', *Millennium*, 42 (3), 697–717.

Pigman, G.A. (2006) 'Civilizing Global Trade: Alterglobalizers and the "Double Movement"', in B. Bowden and L. Seabrooke (eds) *Global Standards of Market Civilization*, Abingdon: Routledge.

Pinker, S. (2011) *The Better Angels of Our Nature: The Decline of Violence in History and its Causes*, London: Allen Lane.

Pistor-Hatam, A. (1996) 'Progress and Civilization in Nineteenth-Century Japan: The Far Eastern State as a Model for Modernization', *Iranian Studies*, 29 (1–2), 111–26.

Powell, R. (2013) 'The Theoretical Concept of the "Civilizing Offensive" (*Beschavingoffensief*): Notes on its Origins and Uses', *Human Figurations: Long-Term Perspectives on the Human Condition*, 2 (2). Available at http://quod.lib.umich.edu/h/humfig/11217607.0002.2.

Pratt, J. (2004) 'Elias and Modern Penal Development', in Loyal and Quilley 2004.

Pratt S.F. (2019) 'Norm Transformation and the Institutionalisation of Targeted Killings in the US', *European Journal of International Relations*, 25 (3), 723–47.

Price, R.M. (1997) *The Chemical Weapons Taboo*, Ithaca: Cornell University Press.

Quilley, S. (2009) 'The Land Ethics as an Ecological Civilizing Process: Aldo Leopold, Norbert Elias and Environmental Philosophy', *Environmental Ethics*, 31 (2), 115–34.

Quilley, S. (2011) 'Entropy, the Anthropocene and the Ecology of Civilization: An Essay on the Problem of "Liberalism in One Village" in the Long View', in N. Gabriel and S. Mennell (eds) (2011) *Norbert Elias and Figurational Research: Processual Thinking in Sociology*, Oxford: Wiley Blackwell.

Ranum, O. (1980) 'Courtesy, Absolutism and the Rise of the French State, 1630–60', *Journal of Modern History*, 52, (3), 426–51.

Reinold, T. (2013) *Sovereignty and the Responsibility to Protect: The Power of Norms and the Norms of the Powerful*, Abingdon: Routledge.

Report of the Senate Committee on Intelligence (2014). Available at S.Rept.113-288-congress.gov.

Ringmar, E. (2013) *Liberal Barbarism: The European Destruction of the Palace of the Emperor of China*, New York: Palgrave Macmillan.

Roberson, B.A. (2009) 'Law, Power and the Expansion of International Society', in C. Navari (ed) *Theorising International Society: English School Methods*, Basingstoke: Palgrave.

Roberts, A. and Guelff, R. (eds) (2001) *Documents on the Laws of War*, Oxford: Oxford University Press.

Roberts, M.J.D. (2004) *Making English Morals: Voluntary Association and Moral Reform in England, 1787–1886*, Cambridge: Cambridge University Press.

Robertson, L.R. (2003) *The Dream of Civilized Warfare: World War I Flying Aces and the American Imagination*, Minneapolis: Minnesota University Press.

Robinson, N. (2007) 'State-Building and International Politics: The Emergence of a "New" Problem and Agenda', in A. Hehir and N. Robinson (eds) *State-Building: Theory and Practice*, Abingdon: Routledge.

Rohloff, A. (2018) *Climate Change, Moral Panics and Civilization* (edited by A. Saramago), Abingdon: Routledge.

Sahlins, P. (2012) 'The Royal Menageries of Louis XIV and the Civilizing Process Revisited', *French Historical Studies*, 35 (2), 237–67.

Said, E.W. (1993) *Culture and Imperialism*, London: Chatto and Windus.

Said, E.W. (2003) *Orientalism*, London: Penguin Books.

Sakallioglu, U.C. (1996) 'Parameters and Strategies of Islam–State Interaction in Republican Turkey', *International Journal of Middle East Studies*, 28 (2), 231–51.

Salter, M.B. (2002) *Barbarians and Civilization in International Relations*, London: Pluto Press.

Saramago. A. (2015) 'Problems of Orientation and Control: Marx, Elias and the Involvement-Detachment Balance in Figurational Sociology', *Human Figurations: Long-Term Perspectives on the Human Condition*, 4 (2). Available at http://hdl.handle.net/2027/spo.11217607.0004.205.

Satow, Sir E. (1921) *A Diplomat in Japan*, London: Seeley, Service and Co.

Schabas, W.A. (1997) *The Abolition of the Death Penalty in International Law*, Cambridge: Cambridge University Press.

Schuster, L. (2003) *The Use and Abuse of Political Asylum in Britain and Germany*, London: Frank Cass.

Schwarzenberger, G. (1962) *The Frontiers of International Law*, London: Stevens and Sons.

Scott, H. (2007) 'Diplomatic Culture in Old Regime Europe', in H. Scott and B. Sims (eds) *Cultures of Power in Europe During the Long Eighteenth Century*, Cambridge: Cambridge University Press.

Seabrooke, L. (2006) 'Civilizing Global Capital Markets: Room to Groove?', in B. Bowden and L. Seabrooke (eds) *Global Standards of Market Civilization*, Abingdon: Routledge.

Seth, S. (2011) 'Postcolonial Theory and the Critique of International Relations', *Millennium*, 40 (1), 167–83.

Sharp, P. (2003) 'Herbert Butterfield, the English School and the Civilizing Virtues of Diplomacy', *International Affairs*, 79 (4), 855–78.

Sherratt, A. (1995) 'Reviving the Grand Narrative: Archaeology and Long-Term Change', *European Journal of Archaeology*, 3 (1), 1–32.

Shilliam, R. (2012) 'Civilization and the Poetics of Slavery', *Thesis Eleven*, 108 (1), 99–117.

Shimazu, N. (1998) *Japan, Race and Equality: The Racial Equality Proposal of 1919*, London: Routledge.

Simpson, G. (2004) *Great Powers and Outlaw States: Unequal Sovereigns in the International Legal Order*, Cambridge: Cambridge University Press.

Simpson, G. (2016) 'Lorimer's Institutes', *European Journal of International Law*, 27(2), 431–46.

Singh, M. (2015) 'Spectres of the West: Negotiating a Civilizational Figure in Hindi', in M. Pernau, H. Jordheim et al (eds) *Civilizing Emotions: Concepts in Nineteenth-Century Asia and Europe*, Oxford: Oxford University Press.

Smith, A.D. (2009) *Ethno-Symbolism and Nationalism: A Cultural Approach*, Routledge: Abingdon.

Smith, D. (2001) *Norbert Elias and Modern Social Theory*, Sage: London.

Smith, J. (2006) *Europe and the Americas: State-Formation, Capitalism and Civilizations in Atlantic Modernity*, Leiden: Brill.

Smith, J.C.A. (2018) *Debating Civilizations: Interrogating Civilizational Analysis in a Global Age*, Manchester: Manchester University Press.

Smith, K.E. (2010) *Genocide and the Europeans*, Oxford: Oxford University Press.

Sontag, S. (2003) *Regarding the Pain of Others*, Glasgow: Hamish Hamilton.

Spawforth, A.J.S. (ed) (2007) *The Court and Court Society in Ancient Monarchies*, Cambridge: Cambridge University Press.

Starobinski, J. (1993) 'The Word *Civilization*', in J. Starobinski, *Blessings in Disguise; or, the Morality of Evil*, Cambridge, Massachusetts: Harvard University Press.

Stebbins, A. (2009) *The Chinese Civilizing Process: Eliasian Thought as an Effective Analytical Tool for the Chinese Cultural Context*, PhD submitted to Murdoch University, Australia 2009. Available at www,trove.nla. gov.au/work/37010866?versionId=48065821+49713833.

Steele, B. (2019) *Restraint in International Relations*, Cambridge: Cambridge University Press.

Steiger, H. (2001) 'From the International Law of Christianity to the International Law of the World Citizen – Reflections on the Formation of the Epochs of International Law', *Journal of the History of International Law*, 3 (2), 180–93.

Stephen, M.D. (2014) 'Rising Powers, Global Capitalism and Liberal Global Governance: A Historical Materialist Account of the BRICs Challenge', *European Journal of International Relations*, 20 (4), 912–38.

Stivachtis, Y.A. (1998) *The Enlargement of International Society: Culture versus Anarchy and Greece's Entry into International Society*, Basingstoke: Macmillan.

Stivachtis, Y.A. (2006) 'Democracy: The Highest Stage of "Civilized" Statehood', *Global Dialogue*, 8 (3–4), 101–12.

Stivachtis, Y.A. (2008) 'Civilization and International Society: The Case of European Union Expansion', *Contemporary Politics*, 14 (1), 71–89.

Stivachtis, Y.A. (2015) 'Liberal Democracy, Market Economy and International Conduct as Standards of "Civilization" in Contemporary International Society: The Case of Russia's Entry into the "Community of Civilized States"', *Journal of Eurasian Studies*, 6 (2), 130–42.

Stone, D. (ed) (2008) *The Historiography of Genocide*, Basingstoke: Palgrave Macmillan.

Strasser, S. (ed) (2004) *The Abu Ghraib Investigations: The Official Reports of the Independent Panel and Pentagon on the Shocking Prisoner Abuse in Iraq*, New York: Public Affairs.

Suganami, H. (1984) 'Japan's Entry into International Society', in Bull and Watson 1984.

Suler, J. (2004) 'The Online Disinhibition Effect', *Cyberpsychology and Behaviour*, 7 (3), 321–6.

Sutton, P.W. and Vertigans, S. (2005) *Resurgent Islam: A Sociological Approach*, Cambridge: Polity.

Suzuki, S. (2005) 'Japan's Socialisation into Janus-Faced European International Society', *European Journal of International Relations*, 11 (1), 137–64.

Suzuki, S. (2009) *Civilization and Empire: China and Japan's Encounter with European International Society*, Abingdon: Routledge.

Suzuki, S. (2011) 'Paternal Authority, "Civilized" State: China's Evolving Attitudes towards International Trusteeships', in J. Mayall and R.S. de Oliveira (eds) *New Protectorates: International Tutelage and the Making of Liberal States*, London: Hurst.

Suzuki, S. (2012) 'Viewing the Development of Human Society from Asia', *Human Figurations: Long-Term Perspectives on the Human Condition*, 1 (2). Available at http.hdl.handle.net/2027/spo.11217607.0001.205.

Suzuki, S. (2014) 'Journey to the West: China Debates its "Great Power" Identity', *Millennium*, 42 (3), 632–50.

Swaan, A. de (1995) 'Widening Circles of Identification: Emotional Concerns in Sociogenetic Perspective', *Theory, Culture and Society*, 12 (2), 25–39.

Swaan, A. de (1997) 'Widening Circles of Disidentification: On the Psycho- and Sociogenesis of the Hatred of Distant Strangers – Reflections on Rwanda', *Theory, Culture and Society*, 41 (2), 105–22.

Swaan, A. de (2001) 'Dyscivilization, Mass Extermination and the State', *Theory, Culture and Society*, 18 (2–3), 265–76.

Swaan, A. de (2015) *The Killing Compartments: The Mentality of Mass Murder*, New Haven: Yale University Press.

Taïeb, E. (2014) 'The Civilization of Capital Punishment in France', in T.S. Landini and Dépeltau, F. (eds) *Norbert Elias and Empirical Research*, Basingstoke: Palgrave Macmillan.

Teitt, S. (2017) 'Sovereignty as Responsibility', in T. Dunne and C. Reus-Smit (eds) *The Globalization of International Society*, Oxford: Oxford University Press.

Theiler, T. (2005) *Political Symbolism and European Integration*, Manchester: Manchester University Press.

Thomas, K. (1984) *Man and the Natural World: Changing Attitudes in England, 1500–1800*, Harmondsworth: Penguin.

Thomas, K. (2018) *In Pursuit of Civility: Manners and Civilization in Early Modern England*, London: Yale University Press.

Tilly, C. (1992) *Coercion, Capital, and European States: AD 990–1992*, Oxford: Blackwell.

Towns, A. (2009) 'The Status of Women as a Standard of "Civilization"', *European Journal of International Relations*, 15 (4), 681–706.

Towns, A.E. (2010) *Women and States: Norms and Hierarchies in International Society*, Cambridge: Cambridge University Press.

Towns, A.E. (2017) 'Gender, Power and International Society', in T. Dunne and C. Reus-Smit (eds) *The Globalization of International Society*, Oxford: Oxford University Press.

Tschurenev, J. (2004) 'Between Non-Interference in Matters of Religion and the Civilizing Mission: The Prohibition of *Suttee* in 1829', in H. Fischer-Tiné and M. Mann (eds) *Colonialism as Civilizing Mission: Cultural Ideology in British India*, London: Wimbledon Publishing Company.

Tseng-Tsai, W. (1993) 'The Macartney Mission: A Bicentenial Review', in R.A. Bickers (ed) *Ritual and Diplomacy: The Macartney Mission to China 1792–1794*, London: The British Association for Chinese Studies in association with The Wellsweep Press.

Tsygankov, A.P. (2008) 'Self and Other in International Relations Theory: Learning from Russian Civilizational Debates', *International Studies Review*, 10 (4), 762–75.

Tucker B. and Triantafyllos, S. (2008) 'Lynndie England, Abu Ghraib, and the New Imperialism', *Canadian Review of American Studies*, 38 (1), 83–100.

Twells, A. (2009) *The Civilizing Mission and the English Middle Class, 1792–1857: The 'Heathen' at Home and Overseas*, Basingstoke: Palgrave Macmillan.

United Nations Environment Programme (2016) *Green is Gold: The Strategy and Actions of China's Ecological Civilization*. Available at www.unep.org.

van Vree, W (1999) *Meetings, Manners and Civilization: The Development of Modern Meeting Behaviour*, London: Leicester University Press.

Vertigans, S. (2010) 'British Muslims and the UK Government's "War on Terror" Within: Evidence of a Clash of Civilizations or Emergent De-Civilizing Processes?', *British Journal of Sociology*, 61 (1), 26–44.

Vertigans, S. (2017) 'Death by "African" Democracy: Killing Consequences of Western Political Prognosis', *Historical Social Research*, 42 (4), 169–88.

Vincent, R.J. (1980) 'The Factor of Culture in the Global International Order', *The Year Book of World Affairs*, 34: 252–64.

Vincent, R.J. (1984) 'Racial Inequality', in H. Bull and A. Watson (eds) *The Expansion of International Society*, Oxford: Clarendon Press.

Vincent, R.J. (1986) *Human Rights and International Relations*, Cambridge: Cambridge University Press.

Visoka, G. (2017) *Shaping Peace in Kosovo: The Politics of Peacebuilding and Statehood*, Basingstoke: Palgrave Macmillan.

Visoka, G. (2017a) 'Norbert Elias and State-Building after Violent Conflict', in T.S. Landini and F. Dépeltau (eds) *Norbert Elias and Violence*, New York: Palgrave Macmillan.

Volkov, V. (2000) 'The Concept of *Kul'turnost*: Notes on the Stalinist Civilizing Process', in Fitzpatrick 2000.

Waltz, K.N. (1979) *Theory of International Politics*, New York: Addison Wesley.

Wang, G. (1991) 'The Chinese Urge to Civilize: Reflections on Change', in G. Wang, *The Chineseness of China: Selected Essays*, Oxford: Oxford University Press.

Wang, G. (1993) 'To Reform a Revolution: Under the Righteous Mandate', *Daedalus*, 122 (2), 71–94.

Wang, H. and Rosenau J.N. (2001) 'Transparency International and Corruption as an Issue of Global Governance', *Global Governance*, 7 (1), 25–49.

Waters, T.W. (2016) 'The Spear Point and the Ground Beneath: Territorial Constraints on the Logic of Responsibility to Protect', *International Relations*, 30 (3), 314–27.

Watson, A. (1984) 'Russia and the European States-System', in H. Bull and A. Watson (eds) (1984) *The Expansion of International Society*, Oxford: Clarendon Press.

Weber, M. (1930) *The Protestant Ethic and the Spirit of Capitalism*, London: Unwin University Books.

Weiss, T.G. (2000) 'Governance, Good Governance and Global Governance: Conceptual and Actual Challenges', *Third World Quarterly*, 21 (5), 795–814.

Welch, R.E. (1974) 'American Atrocities in the Philippines: The Indictment and the Response', *Pacific Historical Review*, 43 (2), 233–53.

Westlake, J. (1914) *The Collected Papers of John Westlake on Public International Law* (edited by L. Oppenheim), Cambridge: Cambridge University Press.

Wheaton, H. (1936) [1866] *Elements of International Law*, Oxford: Clarendon Press.

Wheeler, N. (2000) *Saving Strangers: Humanitarian Intervention in International Society*, Oxford: Oxford University Press.

Wigen, E. (2014) 'Go West! Turkey's Entry into International Society', *International Relations*, 28 (4), 468–78.

Wigen, E. (2015) 'The Education of Ottoman Man and the Practice of Orderliness', in H. Pernau, H. Jordheim et al (eds) *Civilizing Emotions: Concepts in Nineteenth-Century Asia and Europe*, Oxford: Oxford University Press.

Wight, M. (1977) *Systems of States*, Leicester: Leicester University Press.

Wilcken, P. (2004) *Empire Adrift: The Portuguese Court in Rio de Janeiro, 1808–21*, London: Bloomsbury.

Williams, R. (1976) 'Individual', in R. Williams *Keywords: A Vocabulary of Culture and Society*, Glasgow: William Collins.

Winichakul, T. (2000) 'The Quest for "Siwilai"? A Geographical Discourse of Civilizational Thinking in the late Nineteenth and Early Twentieth-Century Siam', *The Journal of Asian Studies*, 59 (3), 528–49.

Wolfers, A. (1965) 'Statesmanship and Moral Choice', in A. Wolfers, *Discord and Collaboration: Essays on International Politics*, Baltimore: The John Hopkins Press.

Wolff, L. (1994) *Inventing Eastern Europe: The Map of Civilization on the Mind of the Enlightenment*, Stanford: Stanford University Press.

Worringer, R. (2004) '"Sick Man of Europe" or "Japan of the Near East"? Constructing Ottoman Modernity in the Hamidian and Young Turk Eras', *International Journal of Middle East Studies*, 36 (2), 207–30.

Worringer, R. (2014) *Ottomans Imagining Japan: East, Middle East, and Non-Western Modernity at the Turn of the Twentieth Century*, Basingstoke: Palgrave Macmillan.

Wortman, R.S. (2006) *Scenarios of Power: Myth and Ceremony in Russian Monarchy from Peter the Great to the Abdication of Nicholas II*, Princeton: Princeton University Press.

Wouters, C. (1998) 'How Strange to Ourselves are Our Feelings of Superiority and Inferiority? Notes on *Fremde* und *Zivilisierung* by Hans-Peter Waldhoff', *Theory, Culture and Society*, 15 (1), 131–50.

Wright. M.C. (1957) *The Last Stand of Chinese Conservatism: The T'ung Chih Restoration, 1862–1874*, Stanford: Stanford University Press.

Wydra, H. (1999) 'Democracy in Eastern Europe as a Civilizing Process', *The Sociological Review*, 48 (1), 288–310.

Yair, G. and Akbari, B. (2014) 'From Cultural Trauma to Nuclear War? Interpreting the Iranian-Israeli Conflict', *Human Figurations: Long-Term Perspectives on the Human Condition*, 3 (2). Available at http://hdl.handle.net/2027/spo.11217607.0003.204.

Yang, A.A. (1999) 'Whose *Sati*? Widow Burning in Early 19th Century India', *Journal of Women's History*, 1 (2), 8–33.

Yao, J. (2019) '"Conquest from Barbarism": The Danube Commission, International Order and the Control of Nature as a Standard of Civilization', *European Journal of International Relations*, 25 (2), 335–59.

Yurdusev, A.N. (2003) *International Relations and the Philosophy of History: A Civilizational Approach*, Basingstoke: Palgrave Macmillan.

Yurdusev, A.N. (2007) 'Re-Visiting the European Identity Formation: The Turkish Other', *Journal of South Asian and Middle Eastern Studies*, 30 (3), 62–73.

Zarakol, A. (2011) *After Defeat: How the East Learned to Live with the West*, Cambridge: Cambridge University Press.

Zarakol, A. (2014) 'What Made the Modern World Hang Together: Socialisation or Stigmatisation?', *International Theory*, 6 (2), 311–32.

Zaum, D. (2007) *The Sovereignty Paradox: The Norms and Politics of International State-Building*, Oxford: Oxford University Press.

Zeigler, C.E. (2016) 'Critical Perspectives on the Responsibility to Protect: BRICS and Beyond', *International Relations*, 30 (3), 262–77.

Zhang, Y. (1991) 'China's Entry into International Society: Beyond the Standard of "Civilization"', *Review of International Studies*, 17 (1), 3–16.

Zhang, Y. (2014) 'The Standard of "Civilization" Redux: Towards the Expansion of International Society 3.0?', *Millennium*, 42 (3), 674–96.

Zhang, Y. (2015) 'Regional International Society in East Asia? A Critical Investigation', *Global Discourse: An Interdisciplinary Journal of Current Affairs and Applied Contemporary Thought*, 5 (3), 360–73.

Zhang, Y. (2017) 'Worlding China, 1500–1800', in T. Dunne and C. Reus-Smit (eds) *The Globalization of International Society*, Oxford: Oxford University Press.

Zhang, Y. and Buzan, B. (2012) 'The Tributary System as International Society in Theory and Practice', *The Chinese Journal of International Politics*, 5 (1), 3–36.

Zhihe, W., Huili, H. and Meijun, F. (2014) 'The Role of Ecological Marxism and Constructive Postmodernism: Beyond the Predicament of Legislation', *Monthly Review*, 66 (6).

Index